AF528673

BUDDHIST ART IN INDIA

BUDDHIST ART IN INDIA

By

JAS BURGESS

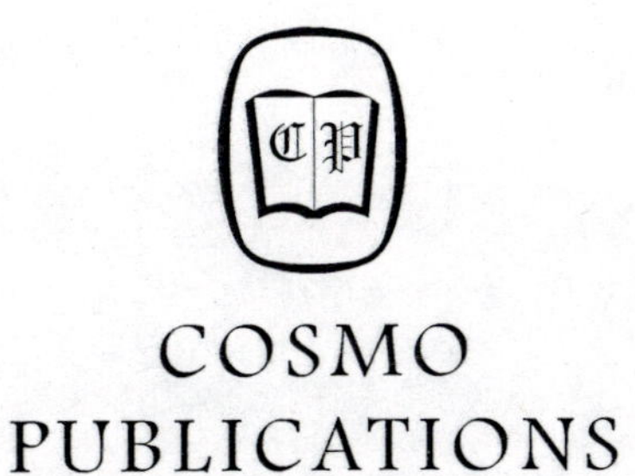

COSMO
PUBLICATIONS

BUDDHIST ART IN INDIA

ISBN-10 81-7020-097-0
Price: Rs. 1,100/-

This COSMO Edition 2000

Published by
COSMO PUBLICATIONS
24-B, Ansari Road, Darya Ganj,
New Delhi-110 002,
INDIA
TEL. +91-011-2328 0455 AND +91-011-2327 8779
FAX.: +91-011-2324 1200
EMAIL : genesis@ndb.vsnl.net.in

PRINTED AND BOUND IN INDIA

CONTENTS.

PREFACE

THE first edition of Professor Albert Grunwedel's handbook on *Buddhistische Kunst in Indien* appeared in 1893, and the hope was expressed in the *Journal* of the Royal Asiatic Society that the work might appear in English, as "it ought to be in the hands of all antiquarians in India." Believing that so important a publication might, by a few additions, form a useful general guide to the Buddhist sculptures in the museums alike of India and Europe, I have prepared the present edition. Miss A. C. Gibson very kindly translated for me the first edition; but by the time it was ready for the press, Prof. Grünwedel had begun his second edition containing extensive additions and alterations. This involved delay and a revision of the whole MS. Considerable additions have also been made to this translation, which have, partly at least, been indicated, and about fifty illustrations are added.

The difficulties in interpreting the Gândhâra Buddhist sculptures arise chiefly from their fragmentary and unconnected condition. This has been lamentably increased by the ignorance or disregard of scientific methods on the part of the excavators of these remains. Monasteries and stûpas were dug into and demolished without regard to what might be learnt in the process by modern methods; the more complete fragments only were saved, without note of their relative positions or any attempt to recover smaller portions and chips by which they might have been pieced together; and the spoils were sent to various museums, often without mention of the sites from which they emanated. They were often further scattered at the will of excavators among different museums and private collections, and we cannot now place together the whole of the find from a single site, so as to compare the style,—and still less the order of the reliefs;—while, of the more carefully surveyed, such plans and sections as were made are defective, and without explanatory descriptions. It is sincerely to be desired that, in future, the Government of India will prevent amateur excavations, and make sure that their excavators really know how such work ought to be executed.

To the "General-Verwaltung" of the Royal Museum, Berlin, I am very deeply indebted for the use of the whole of the illustrations in the second edition, and to Professor Grünwedel himself for others from *Globus* (3 Feb. 1900); he has also kindly looked over the proofs: and for these favours I would respectfully tender grateful acknowledgments.

To the Royal Institute of British Architects I am indebted for the use of illustrations 51, 55, 102, 103, and 104; and to Mr. W. Griggs for 35 blocks that had been prepared for papers on the Gândhâra sculptures in the *Journal of Indian Art and Industry* (Nos. 62, 63, and 69).

With this manual in his hand, it is hoped, the visitor to any collection of Buddhist sculptures will find it no difficult task to understand their character and meaning. Much still remains to be added to our information; but it is only when complete delineations of the sculptures in various museums and private collections, on the Barâhat fragments, and in the Kaṇheri, Elura, and other Bauddha caves are made available, that we shall be able to interpret more fully the iconography of Buddhism. Towards this object some real progress has recently been made by the Government of India having ordered the photographing in detail of the Sâñchî reliefs and of the small collections of Gândhâra sculptures in the Bombay and Madras museums.

JAS. BURGESS.

Edinburgh,

1st May, 1901.

CHAPTER IV.—REPRESENTATION OF BUDDHA AND BODHISATTVA. 158-214.

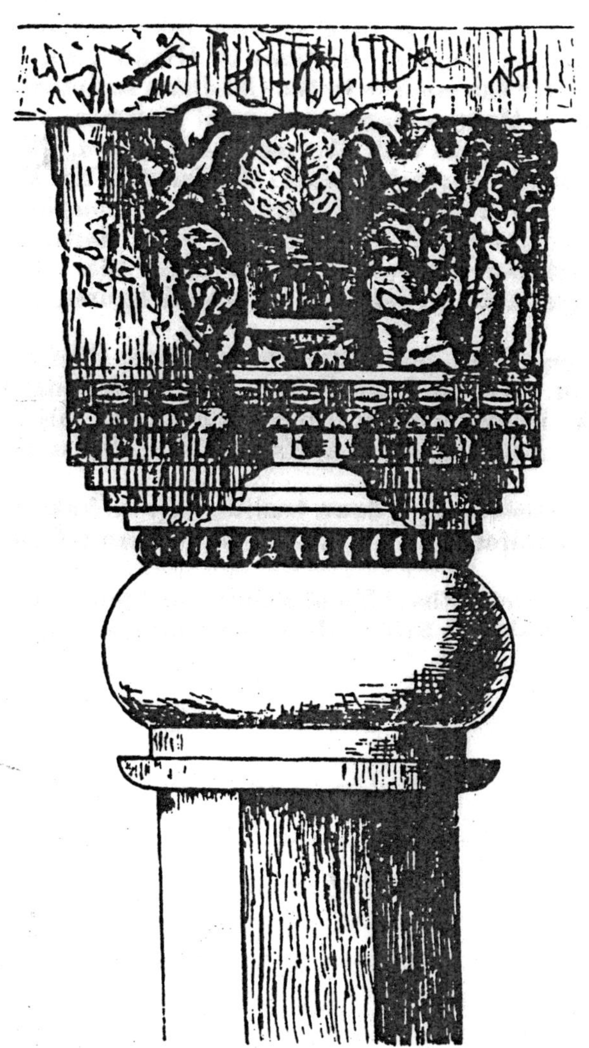

EARLY WORSHIP OF BUDDHA'S FOOTPRINTS
AND THE BODHI TREE.
Pillar capital from Kanheri Caves.

BUDDHIST ART IN INDIA.

CHAPTER I.

INTRODUCTION.

THE artistic efforts of ancient India, specially of the early Buddhist period, are only slightly connected with the general history of art. From the very first two separate schools are met with: one of them, the older—(when the political history of the far East under the Persians had come to an end)—borrows Persian forms, and, indirectly, some Greek ones; and confined as it is to India, subsequently becomes the basis of all that may be called Indian art—Buddhist as well as Brahmanical. The other, which originated in the extreme north-west of India, depends on the antique art which expired when the Roman empire had accomplished its development of the Mediterranean nations; later it formed a basis for the hierarchical art of Central and Eastern Asia. No other reaction to the art of the West has occurred: the types developed on Indian soil are permanently found in the civilized world of India and Eastern Asia.[1] The religious character, so deeply rooted in the national life of the Indian races, has also continued the guiding principle in their art. In a critical examination of the monuments of ancient India, therefore, it is the antiquarian interest, connected with the history of religion and civilization, that is the most prominent.

The art of ancient India has always been a purely religious one; its architecture as well as the sculpture, which has always been intimately connected therewith, was never and nowhere employed for secular purposes. It owed its origin to the growth of a religion which has been called in Europe Buddhism from the honorary title of its founder—"the Buddha"—'the Enlightened one.'

The sculpture of ancient India, originating as it did in religious tendencies and destined to serve religious purposes, could only

[1] Conf. especially *Kuki Ryûichi*, The source of Japanese art, Hansei Zasshi. xii. 1, 1897, 10-13. The figurative part of Brâhman art, so far as we are now acquainted with it, is based essentially upon Buddhist elements,—so much so indeed that the Saiva figures originated at the same time as the Northern Buddhist, appear to have fixed types, whilst the iconography of the Vishnu cult embraces chiefly Buddhist elements to which a different interpretation has been given. But still more dependent on Buddhism are the representations of Jaina art. How far this theory may be modified by the new excavations promised by Oldenburg (*Vostocnyja Zametki*, p. 359, and note 3) is for the future to decide.

follow its own immediate purpose in sacred representations: otherwise it was, and remained, simply decorative and always connected with architecture. In accordance with the Indian character, the sacred representations themselves were not so much the outset of the development as its end. According to the view of life prevailing among the Hindus, purely artistic execution never found scope in the existence of schools, but only in sporadic instances. The sacred figures themselves even came to be employed again decoratively.

Since the history of Indian civilization became better known in Europe, our previous ideas respecting the antiquity of Hindu art have been found to be very exaggerated. In fact, Indian art is the most modern of all Oriental artistic efforts. No important monument goes further back than the third century B.C. The period of its development comprises about a thousand years—from the third century B.C. to the sixth or seventh century A.D In Asiatic countries, outside India, which subsequently embraced the doctrines of Buddha, ecclesiastical art is developed on the basis of Indian types until the middle ages (13th to 14th century). Till then the sculptures are executed in stone and frequently on a large scale, but gradually the Buddhist sculpture becomes a miniature manufacture in different materials—wood and clay in place of stone, and later, in metal casts—carried on as a trade.

Indian art, as already mentioned, borrowed from two artistic schools, complete in themselves, but of very different characters—the ancient Oriental, introduced through the Achæmenides, and the Græco-Roman: and the elements thus acquired it utilized for national themes. In its relation on one hand to the vague hybrid style of the Achæmenides whose influence, in the more ancient monumental groups of India, led to the introduction of certain Greek elements, the native Indian style, with its animated and powerful conceptions of nature, succeeded in preserving its independence and in developing itself up to a certain point. The introduction of early ideal types and the antique style of composition, on the other hand, resulted in a rigid adherence to consecrated forms, that is, to a canon.

Above all, stress must be laid on the fact that in comparison with the vast extent of the country, the monuments are far from numerous, that great numbers of them have been destroyed through the indolence or by the sheer Vandalism of men of other faiths, so that considerable monumental groups in good preservation, remain only where the districts subsequently became deserted and the monuments were consequently forgotten and so saved from direct destruction at the hand of man; or where, as happened in Ceylon, the old religion remained and protected the monuments of olden times. It is therefore exceedingly difficult to represent a continuous development; the individual monuments appear as independent groups, the connexion of which can be sketched only in a general way. Add to this the difficulty of dating the separate monuments, dependent on chance discoveries of inscriptions dated in eras that are not always sufficiently defined, inferences from the form of alphabet used, etc. It is true that in this domain new and important materials may any day be discovered. As concerns further the development of the artistic canon of the modern schools of Buddhism—which, on account of their valuable tradition, afford (as we shall see) a valuable source of information for the analysis of the subjects represented—as yet critical works thereon hardly exist.

In India itself, Buddhism has been extinct for centuries. The remains of the first golden age, under king Asoka, have for the most part perished: single monumental groups—gigantic heaps of rubbish, still testify to the time when Central India was quite covered with Buddhist buildings. But in the traditional forms of the temples still in existence outside India, we find highly important materials for an explanation of the old representations. Buddhist archæology must therefore begin with the investigation of the modern pantheon, especially of the northern schools, *i.e.* of the religious forms of Tibet, China, and Japan, so as to recognise the different artistic types, and trying to identify them with the ancient Indian. Combined with researches into the history of the sects and, above all, of the hierarchy, there must be a separation of the different phases from one another, and the earliest forms must be looked for to a certain extent by eliminating later developments.

The solution of many difficulties will be reached when the history of the different types of Buddhas and Bodhisattvas, gods and demons, &c., is traced. Unfortunately, however, the raw material required for this task has not yet, to any extent, been made accessible But besides pictures and sculptures there is a class of literature, belonging especially to the northern school, that is of great importance to Bauddha archæology. The modern precepts for the manufacture of representations of Buddhas and Bodhisattvas —containing the dimensions and arrangement of the figure with the ceremonial rites to be performed, even to the animating of the figure by means of a relic, the opening of the eyes, and so on,— these, as well as the voluminous descriptions of the gods, found in the Tibetan Kanjur and especially in the Tan-jur,[1] with data as to

[1] Kanjur—written in Tibetan: *b*Ka-gyur, the "translated word of Buddha"—is the title of the canonical literature of Tibet. In the Royal Library at Berlin is a handsomely executed MS. copy in 108 folios. Its richly decorated covers exhibit representations of the gods executed in gold and gay colours; all are named. It would be a meritorious and, for the history of the sects, an important task to compare these pictures with the contents of the volumes. The comparison of the illustrations of the Tibetan gods (*Pantheon des Tschanangtscha Hutuku*, the five hundred gods of Narthang, &c.) with the *Buddha Pantheon of Nippon* published by Hoffmann, as well as with the Nepalese miniatures described by A. Foucher, would be another useful task. See Burgess, *Gandhâra Sculptures*, sep. repr., p. 18, or *Jour. Ind. Art*, vol. VIII, p. 40. The Tanjur, Tib. *bs*Tan-gyur, literally "The translated doctrine," forms to some extent the commentary to the Kanjur: the edition at Berlin is in 225 volumes (Nar-thang printing) and contains much material for the history of art. The Indian miniatures are of course more valuable than the Tibetan sources—and the Japanese tradition, which has in many cases retained the oldest forms, should not be overlooked

the proportions of the figures, aureoles, attributes, &c., are authorities on Buddhist iconography. To these, as yet, little attention has been paid, but their importance must not be underestimated. Just as little known are the manuals on sorcery—the *Sādhanamālā*: they are important inasmuch as they prescribe for the exorcist the dress and attributes by which, according to the conceptions of the degenerate northern school, the Bodhisattva to be conjured may be propitiated: but these attributes are always the same as those of the deity himself.

In the following investigation an attempt will be made to retrace this retrograde path and to determine some of the principal types, on the basis of the materials now accessible, and to analyse the component forms. For this reason—although the investigation only concerns ancient Indian art—we shall frequently have to go beyond India, especially with a view to determine the types; for Tibetan and Japanese forms present highly interesting developments of Indian models. As an aid to understanding the summary of the history of the Buddhist religion, the following chronological table[1] may be found useful.

CHRONOLOGICAL TABLE.

B.C. 558-529.	Cyrus or Kurush of the Achæmenian dynasty took Babylon and founded the Persian Empire.
557	Probable date of the birth of Siddhârtha, or Gautama *S*âkya Muni, the Buddha.
528	Siddhârtha became an ascetic; assumed Buddhahood.
500 BEFORE CHRIST.	
521-485	Dareios Hystaspes (Daryavush Vishtaspa) king of Persia.
514-486.	Bimbisâra or *S*re*n*ika, king of Magadha.
486-461.	Ajâta*s*atru or Kûnika, son of Bimbisâra, king of Magadha.
485-465.	Xerxes (Khshayârshâ), king of Persia; Thermopylæ, 480.
478	Virûdhaka of Kosala exterminated the *S*âkya clan.
477	Parinirvâ*n*a or death of *S*âkya Muni; and first Buddhist Council at Râjag*ri*ha.
400 BEFORE CHRIST.	
377	Second Buddhist Council (?), said to have been held at Vai*s*ali in the 10th year of Kala*s*oka.
326	Alexander of Macedon invaded India after conquering Persia and Sogdiana.
321-280.	Seleukos Nikator, in the partition of Alexander's empire, obtained Babylon, Syria, and Persia: Porus and Taxiles were allowed to hold the Panjâb.
315-291.	Chandragupta (Sandrakottos) founded the Maurya dynasty in India.
312	Era of the Seleukides, Oct. 1st.
305	Seleukos invaded Baktria and India; Megasthenes his ambassador.
300 BEFORE CHRIST.	
291-263.	Bindusâra successor of Chandragupta: Deimakhos ambassador from Seleukos.
263-221.	A*s*oka, installed 259, third king of the Maurya dynasty.
256	Baktria revolted from Antiokhos Theos under Diodotos or Theodotos who founded the Græco-Baktrian kingdom.
250 cir.	Arsakes founded the Parthian kingdom.
242	Third Buddhist Council held at Pâ*t*aliputra; and missionaries sent to Ceylon, Gandhâra, Kashmir, &c.

[1] This table is an extension of that given by Prof. Grunwedel in the *Handbüch*, pp. 165, 166.—J. B.

300 BEFORE CHRIST, continued.

220 Euthydêmos usurped Baktria and extended the Greek power in India and Tartary.

205 Antiokhos III, Magnus, formed a treaty with Sophagasenos, an Indian prince.

200 BEFORE CHRIST.

180 Eukratides extended his power in the Panjâb and Baktria.

178 The Suñga dynasty in India, founded by Pushyamitra.

178 cir. The Andhrabhritya dynasty founded in the Dekhan.

145 cir. Menander (or Milinda) of Sangala in the Panjâb.

140 cir. Probable date of Sâñchi gateways.

139 Mithridates of Parthia overthrew the Græco-Baktrian kingdom.

126 Baktria overrun by Skythians.

110-86 cir. Du*tth*a Gâma*n*i ruling in Ceylon.

100 BEFORE CHRIST.

65 Syria became a Roman province.

57 Samvat era of Malwa and Western India, Sept. 18th.

45 cir. The Bauddha doctrines first reduced to writing in Ceylon: the Dharmaruchika schism.

30 The Kusha*n*a tribe of the Yueh-ti under Kozulo Kadphises subjugates Kabul.

BIRTH OF CHRIST.

A.D. 30 cir. Gondophares or Gudaphara ruled west of the Indus or in Gandhâra and the Kâbul valley.

„ „ Gandhâra school of sculpture began.

67 Ming-ti, emperor of China, received Buddhist missionaries.

78 Kanishka the Kushan, king of North-Western India.

100 AFTER CHRIST.

100 cir. Buddhist Council at Jâlandhara, presided over by Vasumitra.

107 Indian embassy to Trajan.

130 cir. Nâsik Buddhist caves excavated.

138 Indian embassy to Antoninus Pius.

150-200 cir. Nâgârjuna, founder of the Madhyamika system, flourished.

170 cir. Amarâvati stûpa rail; earlier caves at Kasheri excavated.

200 AFTER CHRIST.

226 Ardeshir-Bâbegân of Parthia founded the Sâsânian dynasty of Persia.

260 Valerian defeated by Shapur the Sâsânian.

264 Odenathus of Palmyra repulsed Shapur; period of Palmyrene greatest prosperity.

270 Manes flourished; Manichæan heresy: he died 274.

273 Defeat of Zenobia and fall of Palmyra.

300 AFTER CHRIST.

319 Chandragupta I. of the Gupta dynasty crowned: Gupta epoch.

360 Repulse of the Romans by Shapur II. at Singara and Bezabda.

371 Shapur II. renewed the war against Rome and was defeated: died 379.

372 Buddhism introduced into Korea.

400 AFTER CHRIST.

399-414. Fah-hian, a Chinese Buddhist, travelled in India and Ceylon.

401-414. Chandragupta II, Gupta king; inscriptions at Sañchi and Udayagiri.

420 Buddhaghosa of Ceylon, translator of the *Atthakathâ* and author of the *Vasuddhi Magga*.

422 War between Baharâm or Varahrâm of Persia and the emperor Theodosius.

430 Kidâra Shahi established the kingdom of the little Kushans in Gandhâra, but they were expelled by the Ephthalites or White Huns, A.D. 470.

463 Dutasena, king of Ceylon erected an image of Maitreya.

472 Si*m*ha, the Buddhist patriarch, put to death by Mihirakula of Sâgala, who persecuted the Buddhists in Gandhâra.

500 AFTER CHRIST.

518 Sung-yun, Chinese pilgrim, resided in Gandhâra.

„ The Buddhist *Tripitaka*, first collected in Chinese by Wu-ti.

500 AFTER CHRIST, continued.

520 cir. Vasubandha and Arya Asanga, Buddhist teachers in Gandhâra.
552 Buddhism introduced into Japan from Korea.
578 Bâdâmi Brahmanical caves excavated.
591 Khusrû Parviz restored to the throne of Persia by the emperor Maurice.

600 AFTER CHRIST.

606 Harshavardhana of Thâneśvar: epoch of his era.
609 Khusrû overran Syria and took Damascus and Jerusalem, 614.
625 cir. Pulikesin II., the Chalukya king, received an embassy from Khusrû of Persia.
629-645. Hiuen Thsang, from China, travelled and studied in India.
632 Buddhism propagated in Tibet under king Srong-*b*tsan-*s*gam-po.
634 Council held at Kanyakubja under Harshavardhana.
632-651. Yazdijard, the last Sâsânian king, overthrown by the Musalmans, 651.
639 Buddhism introduced into Siam.
671-695. I-tsing from China travelled in India and the Malay archipelago.

We may now attempt a very brief sketch of ancient Indian history. The civilization of the country is ascribed to the Arya race, a branch of the so-called Indo-Germanic family, which immigrated into the peninsula from the north-west and, in part, at once overcame the peoples settled there, and, after two thousand years' labour, compelled them, partly, to adopt their system of civilization. The Indian peninsula forms a world by itself, whose inhabitants, originally totally different, thus amalgamated into one whole, whilst in detail they represent all grades of social life from barbarism of the rudest kind to the most refined hyperculture. Entirely cut off from the outer world, this mighty land seems intended by nature to provide for its inhabitants a peculiar development with a sufficiently independent movement. From north-west to north-east the peninsula is sharply separated from North Asia by a mountainous range of prodigious height in the snow peaks of the Himâlayas: only the Kâbul passes on the Kâbul river afford free communication with the north-west. This is the old high road by which the Aryans penetrated and which the conquerors of antiquity and of the Middle Ages also followed.

On the north-west frontier several large rivers come down from the western regions of the Himâlayas towards the south-west, and flow through a broad, hot, and storm-beaten plain. This is the land of the Five Rivers, the Panjâb,—the first land that the Aryans possessed themselves of, when they conquered and penetrated into India (cir. 2000 B.C.?), while the Irânians, a people closely akin to them, directed their course to the nearer East. Other mighty rivers of far greater volume than those of the Panjâb also flow from the Himâlayas, but towards the east. They traverse a vast, sandy, low-lying plain which owes to them its tropical vegetation. This plain is Hindustân proper—the cradle of ancient Indian civilization which, following thence the course of the rivers, advanced to their mouths. In the period which followed, the Aryans by degrees became acquainted with the coasts of the peninsula of the Dekhan (Sanskrit: Dakshinapatha—the path on the right), which lies to the south of Hindustân, and they also made their way gradually into its interior—a high plateau rising towards the south. Notwithstanding the enclosed position of the Peninsula, extraneous influences have not been wanting; indeed, they operated only the more decidedly and perceptibly, the rarer they were.

To these foreign elements, which penetrated from the north-west, Indian art belongs in a very marked degree. The most important basis for the development of an independent art among any people lies in its religion. The gods of the Indian Aryans, when the race was still in the Panjâb, were personified nature forces of an unusually vague form. The old "ritual-poems" of this people, the Ṛigveda, gives us sufficient information as to this. The ever-recurring myth of the theft of the fertilizing Rain by malicious demons, which are then killed by the gods (*devas*), whereon the Rain is again set at liberty, and brings food, riches, and happiness, is, for example, ascribed to almost all the principal deities. The stolen Rain appears as "treasures," as "cows," as "Wet:" Milk or Water. The place whence the demons get these treasures is sometimes a bank of clouds, sometimes a mountain: in the language of these old poems, the words for clouds and mountains are confounded. In short, the world of gods merges into nature, so that the Vedic mythology, in common with other nature religions (*e.g.* the German), has an elementary and quite unplastic character. The Vedic idea indeed goes further: each individual god, unrestricted by the control of another deity, appears when the sacrificer calls upon him; for the sacrificer each is the chief god, in full possession of all the divine attributes. Thus it is difficult to define the peculiarities of the separate divinities; a development into fixed characters does not belong to this early period. But it is important in the history of art that in the thunder-storm all the principal figures fight against the demons. One is specially prominent in the *Veda*; it is *Sakra* (Pâli, Sakka), the god of thunder, and in the oldest Buddhist *Sûtras* also, he is almost the only deity of clearly pronounced type. Artistic representations of the very hazy figures of Vedic mythology were clearly impossible. The precise reduction to rule of the qualities, spheres of influence, and attributes of the Hindu gods, belongs only to the post-Buddhist period when, by the sanction of numerous popular cults, till then disdained, more defined figures appeared.

In Vedic times sacred representations were not required. As the offering of sacrifice strengthened the god,—made him capable of granting the desires of the suppliant,—it was the principal thing. On the strength of this idea a laboriously developed sacrificial ritual arose, which, when properly performed, could compel the god to the service of men. Of course, we meet with specimens of primitively artistic character: altars in the form of a Garuḍa, &c., without being able to form a clear idea of the architecture and plastic art of that early period. For the rest, from the Vedic poems we learn little of pictorial art. Some passages certainly, in quite late poems may be regarded as speaking of idols, possibly belonging to domestic worship.

In the primitive period, the spoked-wheel is referred to as the grandest kind of work of the Vedic Aryans. And for primitive man, the construction of a spoked wheel does, indeed, betoken a vast stride forwards. In the *Rigveda* the wheel (with its spokes, of which "none is the last") and its form are favourite similes, and often executed representations. "The much-lauded Indra," (thus it says in the *Rigveda*, vii. 32, 20) "I incline by means of the song, as a cartwright bends the rim of a wheel made of good wood;" or (*S*akra) "the lightning in his hand, rules over all men, as the rim of a wheel embraces the spokes" (*Rigv.* i. 32, 35). It would carry us too far to follow out all the similes; the wheel remains in the Indian civilised world of antiquity, and even down to modern times, as the symbol of occult power, the theme for grand poetical similes. The Buddhists took the wheel, as we shall see below, as one of the distinctive emblems of their religion.

As for stone buildings at that early age, we may at least suppose strong walls for defence and rough conical stone constructions over the graves of kings, which latter custom has been inferred from a study of the stûpa architecture to be discussed below. All buildings for secular ends were in wood, as they are in Indo-China and the eastern archipelago to the present day.

It should be mentioned that, in the early period of Indian civilization, rich and really quite artistic gold ornamentation was everywhere known.

Over-population, and perhaps also the crowding-in of other Aryan races, forced a portion of the Aryans to leave the Panjâb and follow the course of the rivers flowing eastwards. The close of the Vedic period shows us confederations of peoples opposing each other and bands of Aryans pouring into the valley of the Ganges, in the tropical climate of which a civilization is developed altogether different from that of the Vedic age in the Panjâb. The races left behind in the Panjâb have no share in this new period of civilization; from this time forward they go their own way, are considered by the inhabitants of Hindustan as kingless and excluded (Arâ*sht*ra, the Adraistoi of the Greeks), but retain their full fighting powers.

The fifth century before Christ plays a decisive rôle in the history of the early peoples of the so-called Indo-Germanic race. The three nations that first left their impress on the history of mankind as civilizing powers of the noblest kind, were the Indian Aryans, the Irânians who hardly differed from them in dialect, and the Hellenes with their kindred races. We cannot here discuss the fundamentally different practical proofs of the national dispositions of these peoples; but it is important to mention that the essentially religiously and philosophically disposed character of the Indian Aryans is met with again in the course of history among the western peoples allied to them, and they derived from them faculties which the Indian soil could not have brought to maturity At the end of the sixth century the Persians and Medes had laid the foundations of the first veritable empire of the ancient Orient—the empire of the Achæmenides. Darius, the son of Hystaspes, succeeded in recovering the conquests of the great Cyrus, and organizing them into a powerful state under Medo-Persian supremacy. With this the ancient history of the East closes its first period; the Persians become the heirs of all the previous currents of civilization which, under their rule, merge into one. In the course of the fifth century Greek freedom is developed in the struggles with the kingdom of the Achæmenides, and at the same time Greek culture attains its apogee. Now about the time that Pythagoras taught in Italy and before Socrates and Plato, Gautama Siddhârtha the "Buddha," the sage of the *S*âkya race (*S*âkyamuni) was preaching deliverance from transmigration. The ethical precepts based on his teachings were the first among the religions of the world to spread beyond the bounds of the nation where they had birth. When the strict preservation of the national element among the peoples of antiquity is considered, this fact is of distinctive importance.

A glance at the map shows India as the heart of the old world; in fact, the ideas that emanated from India, the elements of culture matured there, had been derived from outside, had been recast and transformed over and over again by an indescribably fertile imagination, sometimes indeed worked up even to extravagance, and in all these stages given out again broadcast to the world. In the rise of Indian studies, India was looked on as "the cradle of mankind," the "seat of primæval wisdom:" this was a mistake. Still in one's zeal to reduce everything to proper proportions we must not go so far as either to ignore or to minimise the immense importance of Indian life in the history of human culture.

Afterwards, the civilization of Athens became the foundation of all western culture; the religion of Buddha is the first universal religion, at least, for all countries lying east and north of India,—from the steppes of the Mongols and the mountainous wildernesses of Tibet, through Japan and far into the Indian archipelago.[1] A century and a half after the Buddha's death the Macedonian empire combined the states of Greece into a universal monarchy, which became the heir of the Achæmenides. The Hellenes formed

[1] It may be worth referring to Lucian Schermann's critique of Oldenberg's *Buddha*, 3rd ed. 1897, in the *Deutschen Literatur-Zeitung*, Nr. 5, 1899, Ss. 177ff. It is noteworthy that, in contrast with the zeal shown in representing Buddha's system as a mere parrot-like imitation of the Brahmanical, it should not have occurred to anyone that all Brâhman philosophy works *pro domo*—for the Brâhman caste; and further that, amid the constant squabbles on purely religious questions, we forget the meaning of Buddhism in its bearing on the history of civilization. (Conf. Ehrenreich in *Zeitschr. f. Ethnologie*, 1897, V, 171). If Buddha were only an echo of the Brâhmans, whence his success? He seems, however, to have been an uncommon personality!

the western frontier of this powerful kingdom; while on the east it was defined by the countries of north-western India first opened by Alexander the Great.

It is important in the history of ancient Buddhist sculptures to remember the political relations which prevailed between the kingdom of the Achæmenides and N.W. India. Darius (old Persian Daryavaush),[1] son of Hystaspes, was the first king of the dynasty regarding whose territorial acquisitions and explorations in India we have trustworthy information. After this king, in great measure through struggles with cognate peoples, had restored the empire of his famous ancestors and had prepared the way at least for its powerful organization, he attempted, as Herodotus says, "to explore large parts of Asia." One of these undertakings was the search for the mouth of the Indus,[2] whither an expedition, under Skylax of Karyanda, was sent. In the later inscriptions[3] of this monarch, the Hindus (Hidhu) and the Gandhâras (Gadâra) are mentioned among the subject peoples. They are the tributary dwellers by the Indus (Sansk. Sindhu; Old Pers. Hindhu), and the Aryan inhabitants of Kâbûl and that district, known in India as Gandhâra, in Herodotus the Gandarioi. Under Xerxes, the son and successor of Darius, the Hindhu and Gandhâra peoples belonging to the Arakhosian satrapy, still owed allegiance to the Persian king; Indian troops went to Greece with the great army, wintered with Persians and Medes under Mardonios in Thessaly, and sustained with them the defeat of Platæa.[5] Later they seem to have regained some of their independence; still we know far too little about events in the east of the kingdom of the Achæmenides to be able to pronounce any judgment.

To return to India: in the fifth century B.C. we find the Indian Aryans, who had made their way from the Panjâb into the plain of the Ganges, divided into a number of kingdoms under Brâhman civilization. The most powerful of these states is the kingdom of Magadha; a rival state is that of Kosala, with its capital Sravasti (Pali: Sâvatthî) on the Râptî, in what is now the Nepâl Tarai. Fierce feuds raged between these States and the neighbouring principalities tributary to them; the struggles against the original inhabitants had ceased long before. The system of caste is fully established. Side by side with the richly developed court life of the numerous great and small principalities—large fortified places are described—a luxurious city-life appears; trade flourishes; in the towns a vigorous industrial activity prevails. Along with

[1] Rawlinson's *Herodotus*, vol. III., p. 544, and *Jour. R. As. Soc.*, vol. XI., p. 185.

[2] Herodotus, Bk. iv. c. 44.

[3] Behistun Inscrip. in Rawlinson's *Herodotus*, vol. II., p. 593, and *J. R. As. Soc.*, vol. X., p. 280; Nakhsh-i-Rustam inscr., *J. R. A. Soc.*, vol. X., p. 294; see also Lassen, *Indische Alterthums*, Bd. I., Ss. 503f.

[4] Herodotus, Bk. iii, c. 91; vii, c. 66.

[5] Herodotus, Bk. vii, c. 65; viii, 113; ix, 31.

this is a frugal peasant-class much left to itself—the real basis of Indian national life at all periods of Indian civilization. Religion is entirely in the hands of the Brâhmans; a laboriously constructed sacrificial ritual has sprung from the ancient Indian Nature-worship. The Brâhmans alone are in possession of this ritual, and through the sacred power of their sacrifices they can put a curb on the warrior nobles who are always at strife. The forms of worship of the other castes, especially of the common people, were quite left to themselves. In this way a popular worship which becomes gradually more refined in proportion as the caste is higher, is everywhere found side by side with the official religion of the "gods in human form," *i.e.* the Brâhmans. In the great sacrificial festivals of the princes the people participated at most as spectators; the domestic rites, the *Pûjá*, were a repetition on a smaller scale of the official ceremonies. Every village had its sacred fig-tree which was supposed to be the abode of a god, to whom gifts (food, flowers, etc.) were brought (*balikammam kar*). The whole structure of Indian life is permeated by a deep religious character, which, without being called forth by exterior pressure, is the result of their condition. Whilst in the luxury of the cities a tendency towards pessimism makes itself felt, the people do not feel so much the need of an organised Nature-religion. The want of national feeling, the enervating influence of the climate, the contrasts between rich and poor, the exclusiveness of the State-worship, may have been the basis of this religious impulse. The caste system, which had been built up to keep the Aryan blood pure and to prevent intermarriages, was inimical to all true national feeling; for the Indian, indeed, the caste system embraced the whole world. One who had no caste was of no account, and thus was no worthy adversary. The contrasts between poor and rich had a different effect in India from that produced elsewhere. In a land where Nature provides everything, and a handful of rice suffices to sustain life, the tendency is to shake off the worries of civilization and to return to Nature itself. But the degree of civilization to which the nation had attained even in the Panjâb had penetrated so deeply, at least among the upper castes, that a relapse into barbarism was in consequence impossible. This return to the simple life which the tropical wilderness afforded was prescribed for the Brâhmans. We see them in their retreats occupied in solving the enigma of life and, if the answers they found rightly seem pessimistic to the European, it cannot be denied that the intense moral earnestness of the whole movement, which proceeded from the wisest heads in the nation, effected a magnificent development of the theorems themselves. The interrogations astound by their boldness; the answers by their inexorable logic.

The doctrine of the transmigration of souls—really only a further development of the caste system—held out the possibility of winning a better reincarnation. But the chief aim was how to escape being reincarnated at all. Stated as briefly as possible, the concatenation of ideas was much as follows: The Nature-gods of ancient times could be forced by means of rightly performed sacrifice to grant what was asked. In this way the attempt to conceive of the origin of the world as independent of the gods (*i.e.* without a real creation) may be explained. The World-Soul, that is, the Brahma, is recognised as the fundamental substance from which all individual souls (*âtman*) emanate in order ultimately to return to it, after freeing themselves from any corporeal vestment. Now the union into which the individual soul, emanating from the Brahma, enters in its embodiment (the one being eternal like the other), brings it into bondage; for, through the embodiment, it becomes conscious of its own personal individuality and begins to act: but every action tends to good or evil, reward or punishment, joy or sorrow. According to what these actions are, the soul, after its separation from the body, passes through heaven and hell, and when reward and punishment are there exhausted, it returns once more to a bodily existence, and, according to the sum of its previous actions, is born again as Brâhman, god, human being of high or low caste, animal, plant, or mineral, to re-enter the cycle (*sânsara*) of transmigration. Now in the choice of the means of escaping from this cycle to freedom and re-union with the All-Soul the schools differ. But the fundamental idea remains in all the ancient Indian forms of religion, and down to modern times. Not only, however, do the Brâhmans give themselves up to these speculations in their schools; at kings' courts these matters are discussed; rich citizens take part in the movement, and, side by side with professional monks of the first rank, schools of monks and ascetics are developed, composed of members of the other castes. The Brâhmans themselves, quite in the middle of the movement, were far from being, on principle, opponents of new schools of philosophy. The opposition of these new sects to the official doctrines gradually became very marked and showed itself clearly in the fact that the heterodox disdained to quote examples and proofs for their theorems from the Vedic literature. In India, diametrically opposed religions have always treated each other with a tolerance which would be quite inconceivable in other lands.

It need scarcely be mentioned that the condition of things thus indicated was not calculated to promote the growth of a powerful national art. The efforts of ancient Indian civilization were confined to the domain of the intellectual; their fundamental character was speculative, although their expression might point to aims of a religious and mystical, or philosophical and scientific character. Though a religio-mystical element may serve as a scanty foil for fully perfected or decadent artistic efforts, the philosophical-scientific tendency, especially with the practical side which it had in ancient India, is an altogether barren soil for art.

Deliverance from reincarnation was sought for in different ways; different sects arose which did not, however, take up an attitude of conscious opposition to the Brâhman religion. The pressure from without, the heavy taxation, the bloody wars between the different states may have combined to attract proselytes to the religious sects. But the fact that the founder of Buddhism was himself a prince, refutes the idea that exterior pressure played the leading rôle. For even if the legends exaggerate, it cannot be doubted that Buddha came of a powerful and opulent family.[1]

At the foot of the Himâlayas to the north of Gorakhpur, on the river Rohi*n*î (*i.e.* Kohân) a tributary of the Râptî, was the town and domain of Kapilavastu (Pâli, Kapilavatthu)[2] which belonged to the *S*âkya family or clan. In the sixth century B.C. this principality belonged to *S*uddhodana, and was at constant feud with its next neighbours the Ko*d*ya (Pâli, Koliya) clan, dwelling on the east of the Rohi*n*î. To the chief of Kapilavastu, who had wedded two sisters—Mâyâ and Prajâpatî.—there was born a son who received the name of Gautama Siddhârtha (Pâli, Gotama Siddhattho).[3] The legends further relate how the child was recognised by the old Brâhman ascetic Asita as the coming Deliverer, and how the young prince surpassed all his companions of his own age in bodily strength and mental capacity. To terminate peacefully the old feuds with the Ko*l*iya, the young prince was betrothed to the Ko*l*iya princess Ya*s*odharâ, and maintained a brilliant court.

Once, as he drives out, a god appears to him four times—as an infirm old man, as a sick man, as a corpse in a state of decomposition, and as an ascetic (freed from human wants). This sight and the explanations which Gautama receives from his coachman, Chha*nd*aka, raise in him the first thoughts of determination to renounce the world. After a son, Râhula, has been born to him he carries out his resolve. He parts from his sleeping wife, and flees from the well-guarded palace.

A canonical text (*Avidûrenidâna*) describes[4] the flight from the palace thus: "Gautama lays himself down upon a magnificent couch. Immediately his women-servants, beautiful as goddesses, skilled in the dance, in song and in music, and decked with rich

[1] The earliest traditions represent *S*uddhodana as only one of the great and wealthy landowners of the *S*âkya race,—not as a king. Oldenberg's *Life*, Hoey's transl., pp. 99, 416; Rhys Davids, *Hibbert Lect.*, p. 126; Copleston, *Buddhism*, p. 20. Apart from this, little that is certain is known about Buddha's family circumstances; even the name of his wife Ya*s*odharâ, "Râhula's mother," is reconstructed; conf. Rhys Davids, *Buddhism*, p. 50.

[2] Buddha's birthplace has now been found; see Oldenberg, *Life of Buddha*, Hoey's transl., pp. 92, 105, 415; *Jour. R. As. Soc.*, 1898, p. 580; and the critique mentioned above note 1, p. 9; G. Bühler, *Anzeige Kk. Acad. Wiss. Wien*, 1897, Ss. 319ff; *Epig. Ind.*, vol. V, p. 1; and conf. *Or. Bibliog.*, Bd. XI, 1, 1898, S. 64. Nrs. 1257-8; 2, Ss. 218f., Nrs. 4129, 4149-52, &c.

[3] Siddhârtha of the Gautama *gotra* or priestly family. By caste he is described as a pure Kshattriya.

[4] Rhys Davids' *Buddhist Birth Stories*, pp. 80-82.

ornaments, ranged themselves in order and began to dance, sing, and play on their instruments to please him. But Gautama, whose mind was already turned away from the delights of the world, paid no heed to the dance and fell into a slumber. Then the women said: 'What shall we play, when he for whose pleasure we perform is gone to sleep?' Then they laid aside their instruments where they had taken them up, and lay down. Only the lamps, fed with fragrant oil, continued to burn. Then Gautama awoke, and leaning on his arm on the couch, he saw the women lying sleeping after they had flung aside their instruments. Spittle ran out of the mouths of some, others were grinding their teeth, others snoring, others again muttering in their sleep, or lying uncovered and with open mouths. This repulsive sight rendered him still more indifferent to the charms of sense. 'Oh, horrible! disgusting!' he cried, and thought seriously about adopting a life of solitude. Thereupon, with the words 'This is the day of separation from the world,' he rose from his couch and went to the door, calling his charioteer. Before fleeing with Chhanna, he thought, 'I will just look at my son,' and rising, he went towards the apartments occupied by Râhula's mother and entered her chamber. Râhula's mother lay sleeping on a couch decked with flowers; her right hand resting on the head of the child. Gautama remained standing on the threshold and looked at them; he thought if he removed his wife's hand he would wake her, and that thus his movements would be impeded; if he became Buddha he would come again and see his son; then he left the palace."

With Chhanna he fled in the night to the river Anomâ or Anavamâ; there he gave to the faithful coachman his weapons, his ornaments and his horse, exchanged clothes with a beggar, and, living on alms, hastened to Râjag*ri*ha, the capital of the kingdom of Magadha. In Râjag*ri*ha he studies Brâhman philosophy, but dissatisfied with this, he retires to the Uruvilvâ (Pâli, Uruvelâ) forest, where the temple of Buddha-Gayâ now stands. There he submits to the severest privations, till he sees the folly of attempting to obtain enlightenment by enfeebling the body. The legend proceeds to describe the mental struggles through which Gautama passed under the fig-tree at Gayâ as a victory over creatures of a diabolical nature, which Mâra, "the Evil One," the demon of passion, had sent against him. In a following chapter this struggle against Mâra's seductions will be more fully noticed.

From the place where he obtained enlightenment, on the diamond throne (*vajrâsana*), under the "tree of knowledge" (*bodhidruma*), he hastened back to the world to proclaim the way of salvation—victory over self and love towards all creatures. First of all, he converts some merchants; then Brâhmans and people of all ranks. From among those who were willing to follow him as disciples there arose by and by a body of monks (*bhikshûs*), clad in yellow and shaven, who became the foundation for the later monasticism. A Christian traveller of the 13th century, the Venetian Marco Polo, says of Buddha,[1] after narrating pretty correctly the story of his life: "If Buddha had been a Christian, he would have been a great saint of our Lord Jesus Christ, so good and pure was the life he led." This is a significant judgment at a time when religious tolerance was certainly not great.

During the forty-five years which Buddha journeyed about in Behâr, we see him vigorously supported by the royal courts; and his followers increasing; still Buddha's doctrines do not yet seem to have been received as a separate religion. In the year 477 B.C. (probably), in the grove of the Malla princes at Kusinara, he fell asleep, or as the ritual of his followers puts it, he entered *Nirvana*.

His funeral was solemnized with great pomp, and the relics were distributed among the princes and cities of the district. Over these eight Stupas were erected,—at Rajagriha, Vaisalî, Kapilavastu, Allakappa, Râmagrâma, Vethadîpa, Pava, and Kusinârâ, besides the shrines erected by Drona and the Mauryas.[2] But though the princes of Magadha and Kosala (Audh) may have taken a personal interest in the Buddha, they did not adopt his doctrines as their private religion in supercession of the Brâhman state-religion. It was only in later times that a closer organization appeared among the numerous followers of Buddha. After the death of the Master, a council was held in the Sataparna (Pali, Sattapanni) cave of the Vaibhâra hill at Râjagriha, which was prepared for the meeting by king Ajatasatru of Magadha. The task devolving upon this council was to fix authoritatively the words of the Master gone into Nirvâna. About a century later there is said to have been a second council, held at Vaisâlî to suppress the heresies that had appeared in the community; but the fact of such a council is doubtful.

In the hundred and thirty years between the second and third councils, there had been great political changes. Alexander the Great had invaded the Panjâb; the Magadha state (the Prachya, "Easterns," Greek, Prasioi) had attained a dominating position; the old dynasty had been overturned by an upstart, and Chandragupta (Gr. Sandrakottos or Sandrakyptos) had taken possession of the throne of Magadha.

Neither Chandragupta nor his successor Bindusâra adopted the Buddhist doctrines, the force and authority of which had already created for them an independent position. Asoka (B.C. 264-222) —in his inscriptions called Piyadasi,—the third king of the new dynasty known as the Maurya (Pali, Mora), was the first patron of the religion, which he publicly acknowledged. He was the founder of numerous monasteries (*vihâras*) and other ecclesiastical

[1] Yule's *Marco Polo*, vol. II, p. 300.

[2] Kern, *Manual of Buddhism*, p. 46; Rockhill, *Life of the Buddha*, pp. 145-147; Rhys Davids, *Buddhist Suttas*, S.B.E., vol. XI, pp. 131-132.

buildings; the sacred texts testify in extravagant terms to the king's zeal for the faith. He is said to have had 84,000 stûpas erected in different parts of his wide realm; and to have gifted his whole kingdom to Buddha's followers several times, receiving it from them again.

But the most striking witnesses to his zeal for Buddha's doctrines are his edicts. These documents, which are unique among the inscriptions of antiquity, relate that Piyadasi, the king "beloved of the gods," interested himself in the faith and its professors, that he endeavoured to establish the sacred tradition, that he had roads, wells, and hospitals made for the use of all living creatures. The only historical inscriptions of Western Asia which are akin to the Indian, both as regards the sense and the form, are those left by the Achæmenides, especially by Darius. The largest, and for our purpose the most valuable, is the inscription of Bagistan (Behistun). The simple language which expresses unreserved sincerity, the truly regal tone of the style, which avoids floridness, simply relates the facts, and does not pass over the names of the leaders who fought the battles,—are significant of the noble character of him who founded anew the Persian empire. The punishment to which he condemns the rebels "because they have lied," may be called humane compared with the barbarities of the Assyrians and other so-called civilized peoples. Now the inscriptions of Asoka may have some connexion with those of the Achæmenides.[1] This appears most strikingly in the form of the language itself. The idioms of the Persians and Indian Aryans were, even until the days of the Achæmenides, nearly allied dialectically: it cannot have been very difficult for these peoples, to some extent, to understand each other directly. The royal inscriptions of the Persians show us language still struggling for expression; everything is still fresh and new. But Asoka's inscriptions, though differing somewhat dialectically from one another, show everywhere the same courtly style (closely allied to the Persian) which is to be remarked especially in the formulating of the introductory sentences, the arrangement of the titles, and so on. It was necessary to mention this fact, for it has a decided connection with other things which intimately concern us.[2]

No important monument among those preserved in India is anterior to the time of king Asoka. All that have been preserved show undoubted Persian influence in their style. It has been declared, with reason, that stone-building on a large scale was first executed in India in Asoka's time: the criticisms of Indian

[1] Conf: Senart, *Jour. Asiat.*, 8me ser. t. V. (1885) pp. 269ff; or *Inscr. de Piyadasi*, t. II, pp. 219ff.

[2] The Asoka edicts are found on rocks at Girnâr in Gujarât, Shâhbâzgarhî in Yusufzai, at Mânsahri, at Kâlsî, at Dhauli in Orissa, Jaugada in Gânjâm, and in Maisur, —also on pillars at Dehli, Allahâbâd, Râdhia, Mâthia, and Râmpûrva. See *Epigraphia Indica*, vol. II, pp. 245ff; *Arch. Sur. S. Ind.: Amarâvati*, vol. I, pp. 114ff, &c.

patriotism can alter nothing as to this fact.[1] The Persian style, which the Achæmenides employed in their buildings at Susa and Persepolis, has inherited West Asian forms in its constructive as well as in its decorative features. This Persian style, which

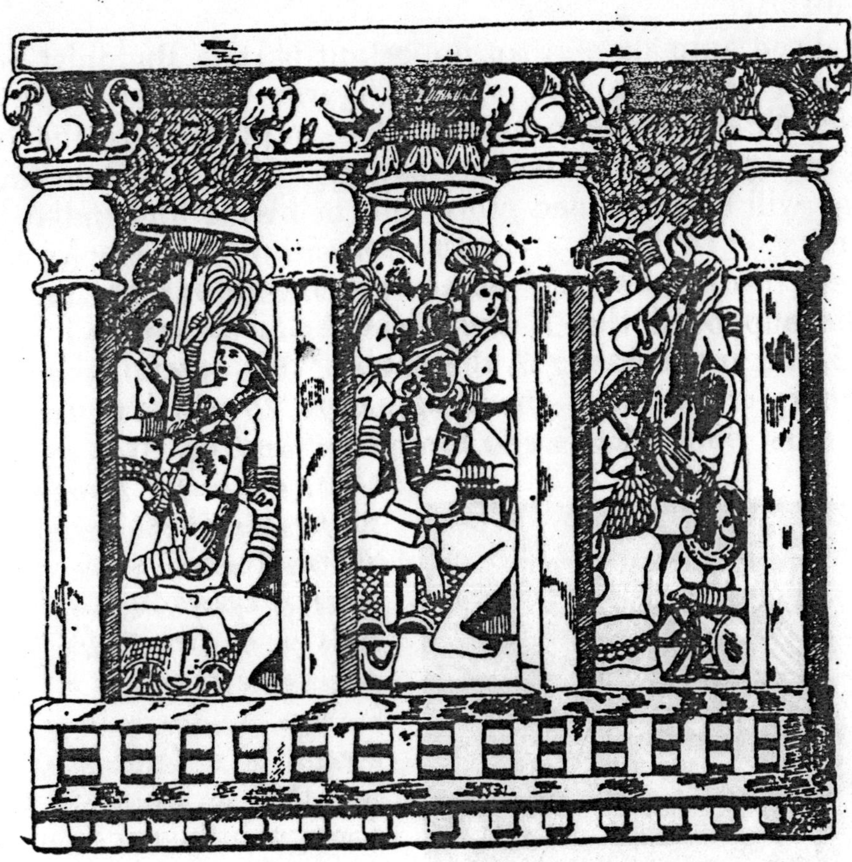

1. HALL WITH PERSO-INDIAN COLUMNS, REPRESENTING A FLOOR IN A GREAT PALACE: FROM THE RIGHT JAMB OF THE EAST GATEWAY AT SÂNCHÎ.

shows many peculiarities, is unfortunately represented only by a few monuments upon which it is almost impossible to pronounce judgment. But undoubtedly its elements may again be recognised in the buildings of Asoka's day and of the older Indian style, dependent on that of Asoka, as grafted upon the native wooden style.

As chief elements, so far as the Buddhist sculptures are concerned, the following forms may be indicated:—The Persian pillar with bell-shaped capital was adopted directly; it was set up by itself as an inscription-pillar; the famous iron pillar of Dehli is a later example. In sculptures it is seen not only in representations of palace-halls, but also decoratively,—often to divide spaces, and with many interesting variants. The bell-capital frequently serves as a basis for one or more lions or elephants, or for a religious symbol (*e.g.* the wheel) when the pillar is considered as standing alone. If the pillar is used as a support in a building, the bell-capital serves as base for an abacus on which, turned towards

[1] Fergusson, *Archæology in India*, pp. 9, 13, 16ff.; *Ind. and East. Archit.*, pp. 47–49.

the sides, winged figures of animals (winged horses, gazelles, goats, lions, or sitting elephants) are placed. This last form resembles the Persian "unicorn-pillar." The appearance of the whole pillar in India, however, is rough and clumsy compared with Persian forms.[1]

Orientalised animals play an important part in Buddhist art. All these hybrid creatures and winged figures—besides their purely decorative rôle—have been employed in representing the inferior mythical beings of the native mythology. Still it is uncommonly difficult, as will be explained more fully below, to find Indian names for these hybrid forms, in the formation and employment of which great inconstancy and some misconceptions are noticeable. It may be supposed that if the West Asian forms had not been preserved, this inconstancy in the shapes, this careful fashioning of extraordinary creatures of the imagination, to which names cannot be given, must point likewise to foreign influences. It is interesting that, even in Asoka's time, alongside these purely hither Asian forms, some also appeared sporadically which can only be of Greek origin.[2] The representation of divine beings under purely human forms is a feature of native art that is opposed to these foreign influences on ancient Buddhist art; and a marked contrast to the chimæras (Kinnaras) of West Asia is presented by the native animal world, which is not so frequently met with decoratively, but leaves this rôle to the foreign forms.

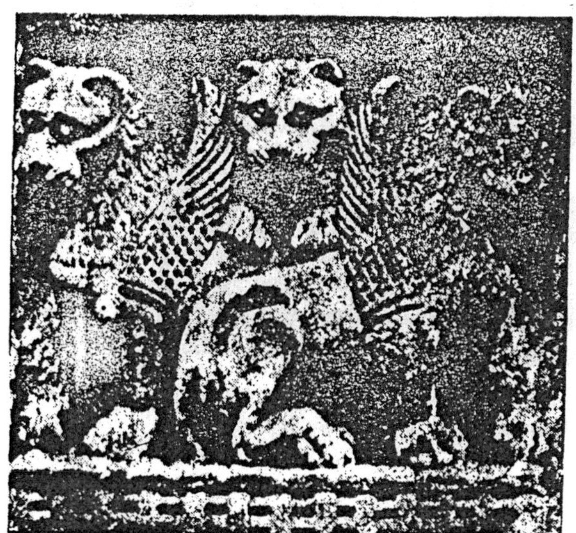

2. WINGED LIONS FROM THE SECOND CROSS-BEAM OF THE EAST GATEWAY AT SÂNCHÎ.

With exceptions we shall meet with in a later chapter, the wings of the Oriental animals are mostly at rest and devoid of signifi-

[1] Conf. Cunningham, *Arch. Sur. Ind. Rep.*, vol. V. pll. xlv, xlvi, pp. 187, 188; and interesting capitals with such creatures in Burgess, *Archæol. Sur. W. Ind.*, vol. IV, pp. 5, 12; and *Cave Temples*, pll. xvi, xxiii, xcvi.

[2] The reader is reminded of the centaurs at Gayâ; Râjendralâl Mitra's *Buddha-Gayâ*, pl. xlv, fig. 12. Centaurs are also found at a later date when the Gandhâra influence appears more distinctly, and it is then impossible to prove whence they arose; *Epig. Ind.*, vol. II, p. 314, pl. ii, fig. 6. The aprons that strike one are doubtless to be regarded as leaves, and have a noteworthy parallel in the relief in the British Museum, *Jour. Ind. Art and Industry*, vol. VIII (1898), pl. xvii, 1, or sep. ed., pl. xv, 1, and p. 16. The Jaina relief is also a companion piece to ill. 23. East Asian tradition, which represents the Tiryagyonis as centaurs, proves that the human-faced oxen on the Jaina relief indicate the centaurs as representations of the animal kingdom in the Sañsâra.

cance;[1] the most remarkable are those in the lion group of the applied plaques of the first and second architraves of the east gateway of the large stûpa at Sâñchî, as will be shewn at the end of the second chapter.

Along with representations of mythical plants, which may be traced to the Assyrian tree of life, and to which is attached a series of symbols difficult to explain, appears the native plant-world. A detailed description of the *dharma* symbols,[2] &c., which belong to the first type, would contribute little to the history of art; the second class is of more value. The Indian plant-world, notwithstanding simple and sometimes even rough modelling, is reproduced with astonishing fidelity to nature. A favourite subject is the lotus-flower (*Padma*, *Nelumbium speciosum*), which is employed decoratively and with great taste in the arrangement. Here and there West Asian (Egyptianised) lotus flowers and palms have crept into designs of this category, which are remarkable for the richness of their device (fig. 3). The broad disc of the full-blown flower is employed in all positions as a decoration and, owing to its resemblance to the wheel, is a favourite subject. In contrast with Assyrian art, which cuts the ornament through, like wall-paper, where the wall to be decorated ends, the flower lying under the capital in fig. 3 is turned upwards. In spite of the predominantly picturesque character of the pattern, this preference

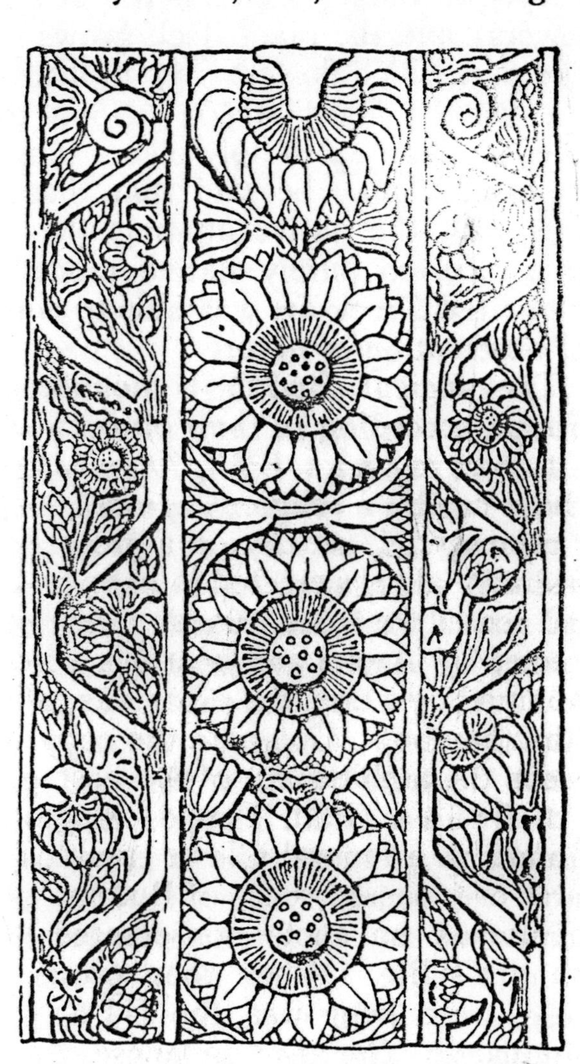

3. - LOTUS FLOWER DECORATION FROM THE OUTER SIDE OF THE PILLARS OF THE EAST GATEWAY OF THE GREAT STÛPA AT SÂNCHÎ.

[1] Originally the wings were only externally attached symbols of speed. Conf. on this point the notes in the *Festschrift für Prof. Veth*, Leiden, pp. 222 and 224, note 3. A group of these winged creatures (horned lions, the so-called *ki-lin*, &c.) have been faithfully preserved in the art of eastern Asia. The wings are, however, represented as flames.

[2] W. Simpson, *The Buddhist Praying-Wheel*, Lond. 1896, p. 15, note 2; Goblet d'Alviella, *Migration des Symboles*, 1891, pp. 294ff; conf. also G. Bühler, *Epig. Ind.*, vol. II, p. 312.

for accommodation to the ornamental design is noteworthy. The Hindu sculptor does not care for purely geometrical designs, and so we frequently find creepers with aquatic birds, &c., which, on a smaller scale, fill in the spaces, and are rich and animated with fine observation of nature. The two outer sides of the east gateway at Sâñchî are a good example of this. While on the left side the design is carried out as geometrically as is permitted in Indian art, the creeper on the right side is full of life. Birds flit about among the flowers; and the plant itself grows from the jaws of a sea-monster. The part which flowers play in later Buddhist art is an important one, yet the finest *motifs* belong to this older period; flowering creepers hung up in holy places may have provided the models. In the main it may be said that these plants, represented in simple lines, with the native animals that animate them—both of which have received purely native modelling—mostly surpass what the celebrated Greek art was able to command: they rest upon a faithful observation of nature.

The ancient Buddhist monuments may be divided into five groups, according to their object:—[1]

1. Stambhas (Pâli, *Thambhas*; Hindûstâni, *Lâts*), pillars on whose capital a religious symbol, as the Wheel or *dharma*-symbol, is represented, usually on a group of lions or elephants. They were probably always erected in connexion with Vihâras or Chaityas, and served for inscriptions. Some of the finest Buddhist Lâts were erected by Asoka and bear his edicts. When the capital was surmounted by a lion, the pillar was called a Si*m*hasta*m*bha (Pâli, Sihatthambo). Compare the copy on the small middle pillars (between the architraves) of the east gateway at Sâñchî (fig. 36).

2. Stûpa (Pâli, Thupo; Anglo-Indian "tope") applies to any mound, as a funeral pile or tumulus; and hence to domical structures over sacred relics of Buddha or other Sthavira or saint, or as memorials on spots consecrated by some remarkable event in Buddha's life. When they preserved relics, the shrine in which these were kept was the Dhâtugarbha (Pâli, *Dhâtugabbho*; Singhalese, *Dâgaba*; Japanese, *Tô*); and as most Stûpas were erected over relics (*dhâtu*), the whole structure came to be called a Dâgaba. A stûpa consists of a circular or square base supporting a dome (*garbha*), on which stands a square block or neck (*gala*) representing a box to hold a relic, crowned by a capital consisting of a number of flat tiles. Above this is the umbrella or spire (*chûdamanî*,—Burmese, *hti*)—single or with several roofs usually three, over one another.

3. Chaityas (Pâli, Chetiya). Like Stûpa, the word Chaitya[2] is applied to a monument or cenotaph, and in a secondary sense to a temple or shrine containing a *Chaitya* or *Dhâtugarbha*. Chaityas

[1] Conf. Fergusson, *Ind. and East. Architecture*, p. 50.

[2] In Nepâl and Tibet (chaitya=Tib. *m*Chod.rten, pronounced Chhor.ten) the word is used in the sense of stûpa (dhâtugarbha=Tib. *m*Dun.rten). Conf. Burgess, *Cave Temples*, p. 174.

or Dâgabas are an essential feature of temples or chapels constructed for purposes of worship, there being a passage round the Chaitya for circumambulation (*pradakshinaya*), and from these such temples have received their appellation. The name of Chaitya, however, applies not only to sanctuaries, but to sacred trees, holy spots, or other religious monuments.[1]

4. Vihâras were monasteries for the accommodation of monks living together in communities, and were mostly, if not always, connected with Chaityas.

5. Ornamental Rails (*suchaka*) were mostly employed as the enclosures of stûpas, or to surround a terrace on which stood a sacred tree, &c. The stone railings are among the most important monuments in the representation of Indian sculpture, as most of them are ornamented with reliefs on the upright shafts and transoms (*suchi*) or cross-bars. In some places great stone gates (tora*n*as) are connected with the railings. These gates—the best preserved are those at Sâñchî—are mostly richly adorned with sculptured scenes. They show the stereotyped wooden style not only in the decoration but also in the form of the building. They seem to have been introduced into farther Asia very early; at any rate the well-known Chinese *pai-lus* and the Japanese *tori-is* are to be connected with these ancient tora*n*as. Originally they were, no doubt, somewhat like our triumphal arches.[2]

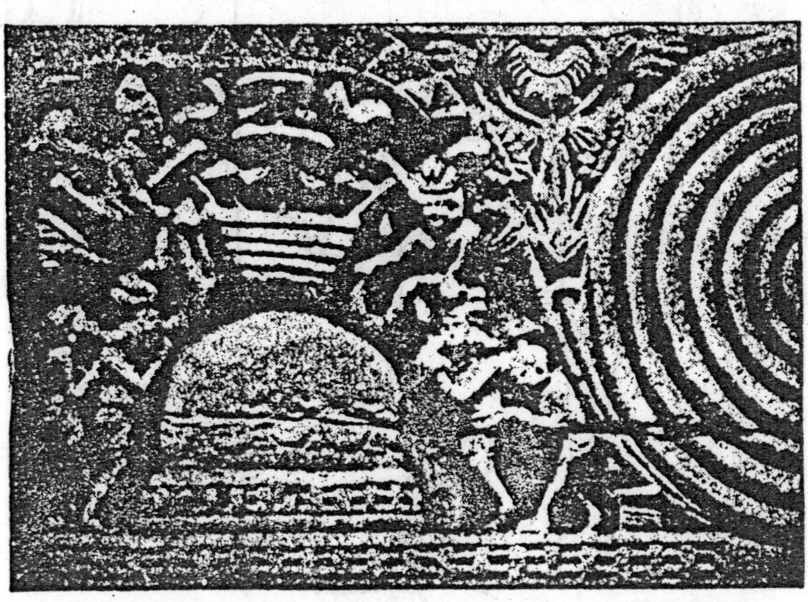

4. Representation of a Stûpa: gods and men before it. From the east gateway of the great stûpa at Sâñchî.

Now the monuments, the sculptures of which show the principal phases of ancient Indian art, are divided into two large groups. The older, and properly Indian group, in which Persian influence

[1] Conf. *Jour. As. Soc. Beng.* vol. VII, p. 1001.

[2] Fergusson and Burgess, *Cave Temples*, pp. 171-177; Goblet d'Alviella, *Ce que l'Inde doit à la Grèce*, pp. 44-48.

appears. begins in Asoka's time; to it belong the monuments in India proper; lâts at Dehli, Tirhut, Sankisa, Sâñchî, etc.; chaitya-caves and vihâras in Bihâr, at Nâsik, Ajantâ, Elura, Kârle, Kânhêri, Bhâjâ, Bêdsâ, Dhamnâr, at Udayagiri near Katak, Bâgh, etc.; stûpas of Mânikyâla, Sarnâth, Sâñchî, and Amarâvatî: stone railings with gates at Barâhat

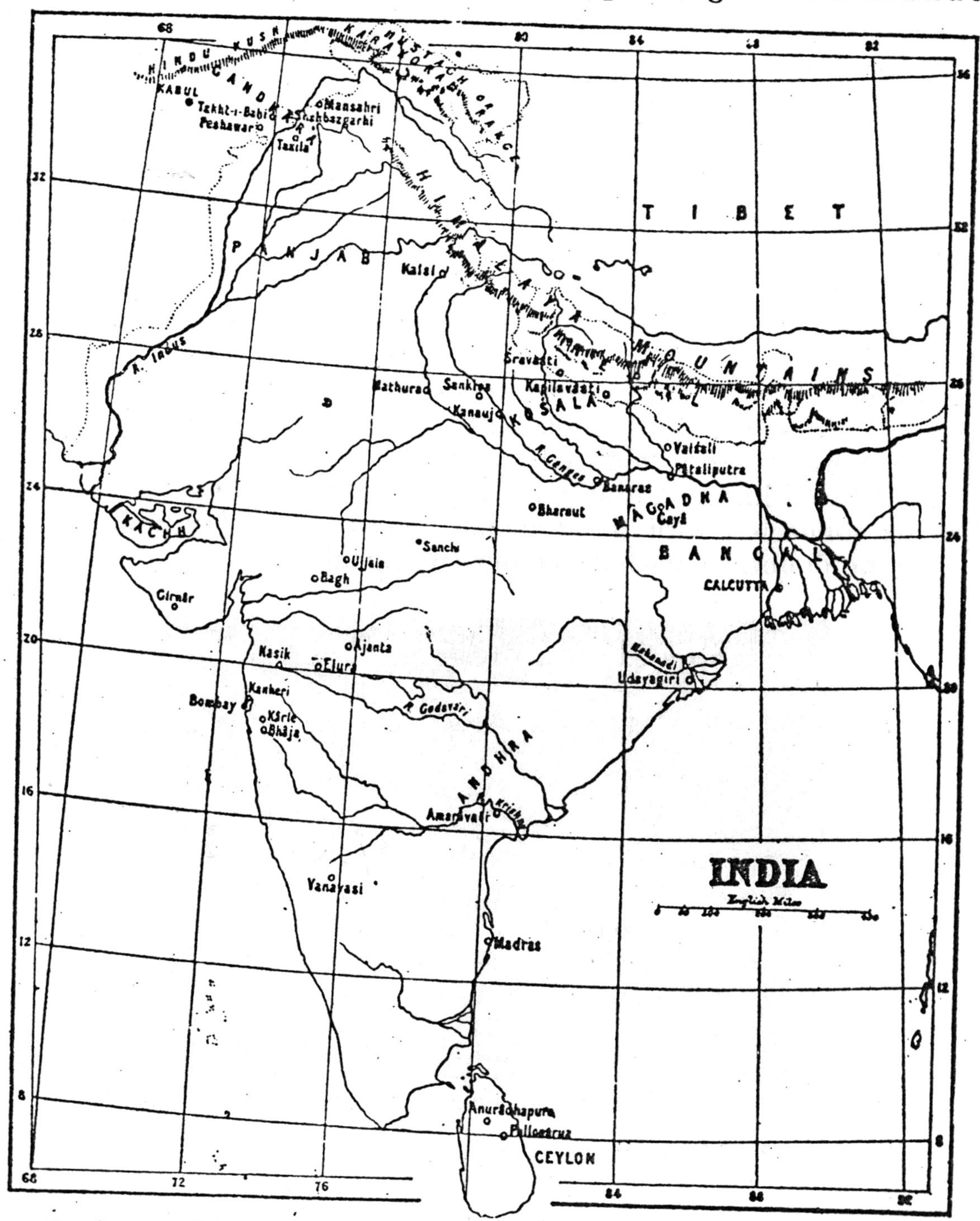

5. Sketch Map of India with the names of the principal sites of the Buddhist period.

(Bharhut or Bharaut), Mathura, Gayâ, Sâñchî, and Amarâvatî. The second group, the so-called Græco-Buddhist, or rather, as Fergusson first called it, that of the Gandhâra monasteries, embraces the numerous remains of the monasteries of Jamâlgarhî, Takht-i-Bâhi, Shâhdêhri, Sanghâo, Natthu in Yûsufzâi, and at Loriyân Tangai and other localities in the Swât territory. An older branch perhaps precedes it,—the Indo-Hellenic school, Smith styles it,—which is represented chiefly by sculptures from Mathurâ.

While in the older Indian group the native element forms the groundwork, and so is developed farther on the soil of India, the Gandhâra school presents strange antique forms. Later it influences Indian art, but, from geographical and other reasons which contributed also to the splitting of Buddhism into two schools, it remains isolated and is thenceforward most permanent in the ecclesiastical art of the northern or Mahâyâna school.

Among the oldest sculptures of India are perhaps those of the caves of Udayagiri in the Puri district of Orissa. The most interesting are in the two-storeyed Râj-Rânî or Rânî-ka Nûr caves. These remarkable reliefs show an uncommonly animated style, little influenced by foreign elements.[1] They form, so to speak, the primitive basis from which issued the purified and refined forms of later times.

In general, the ruins of the richly ornamented stone-railing and of the gates of the stûpa at Barâhat (Bharhut), which has now all but completely vanished from the spot, show on their reliefs the same style as the sculptures of the Sâñchî gates described below, though they are somewhat harsh in form; this is most apparent where women are represented. The distorted exaggerations of the female figures, and the fondness for the nude are seen on the Sâñchî reliefs; in Barâhat scarcely anything of this is to be remarked. The sculptures of Barâhat are of special value, inasmuch as all the representations are accompanied by inscriptions, and so can easily be explained. Most of the pillars from the south and east gateways and the connecting rail were removed to the India Museum in Calcutta, and only a few fragments left *in situ*. The ruins which, when found, had been terribly destroyed, date from about the first half of the second century B.C.[2]

The sculpture of the earlier stone-railing at Gayâ (Buddhagayâ) are somewhat later than those at Barâhat, and are no doubt to be traced back to Asoka. In ancient times it enclosed a terrace, on which the bodhi-tree—the fig-tree under which Gautama obtained enlightenment—stood, apparently in a sort of chapel. The temple at Gayâ is of much later date: it was built by Amaradeva in the fifth century A.D., restored by the Burmese

[1] Fergusson, *Archæology in India*, p. 42; *Cave Temples*, pp. 77-86, 94.

[2] Fergusson, *Ind. and East. Architecture*, pp. 85-91; Cunningham, *Bharhut Stûpa* (1879); Le Bon, *Monum. de l'Inde*, pp. 52-55. Bharhut lies to the S.S.W. of Allahâbâd, about 200 miles E.N.E. from Sâñchî, and 160 W.S.W. from Banâras, near to the railway. The remains of the stûpa there were reported to Gen. Cunningham by a native in 1873, and excavated by him in Feb. 1874.

in 1306-9, and again, it lately underwent a renovation at the hands of the Bengal Government, that must be regretted. Some fine panels from the old Asoka railing seem to have found their way to the Berlin Museum.

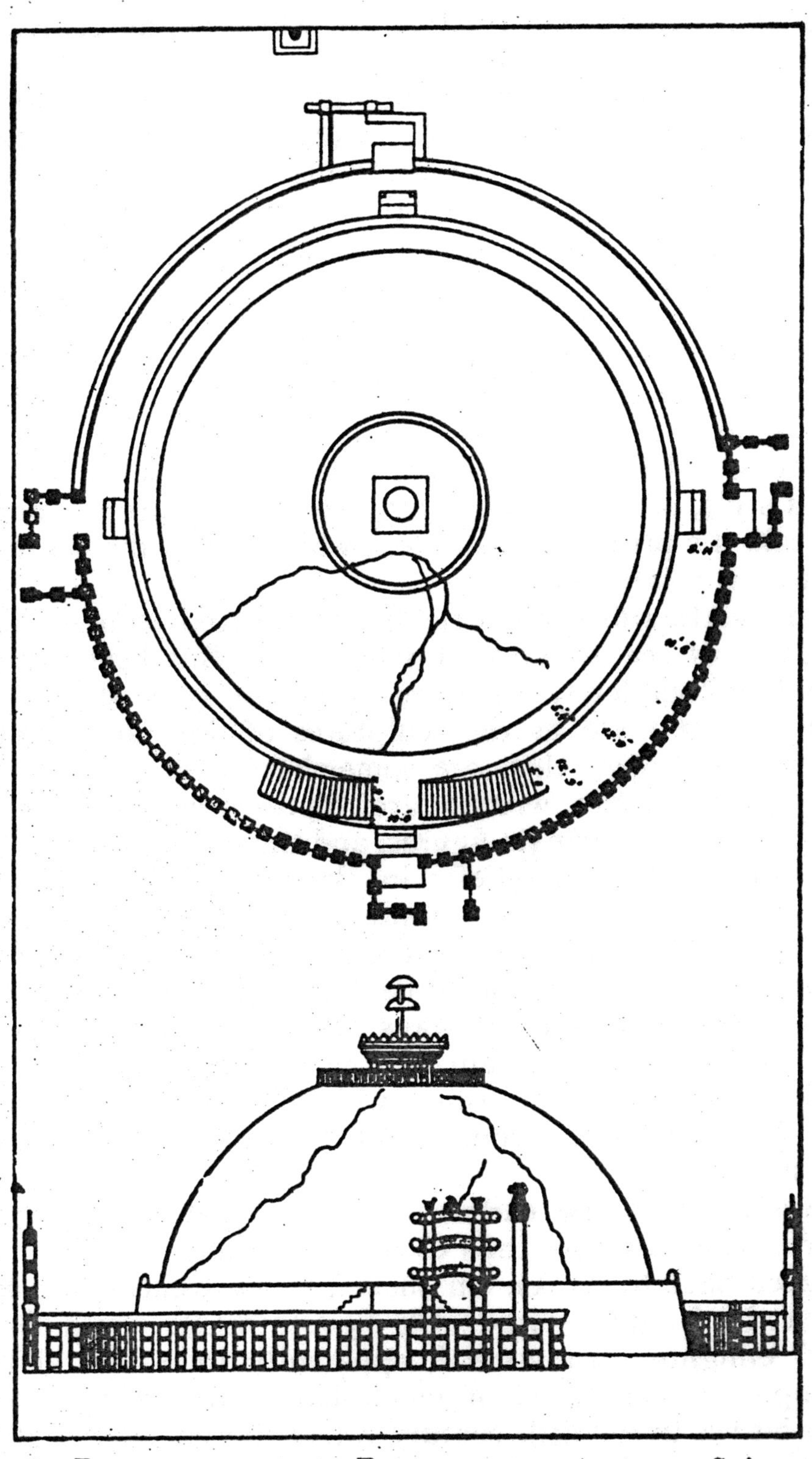

6. PLAN AND RESTORED ELEVATION OF THE GREAT STÛPA AT SÂNCHÎ.

At Sâñchî, or Sâñchî-Kânâkeda, about twenty miles N.E. of the capital of Bhopâl, and S.W. from Bhilsâ, the ancient Vidisa, there was a group of ancient stûpas and other religious buildings. Till about 1820 the largest and second stûpas, with a third, were still entire. The place was first seen by Colonel Taylor and then by Captain E. Fell and Dr. Yeld in 1818. Soon after, Mr. H. Maddock got permission from the native government to dig into the stûpas, and by December 1822, Captain Johnson, the Agent's assistant, had opened the largest to its foundations. This carelessly conducted search for supposed treasure did immense damage to the structure of three stûpas and hastened the dilapidation of their enclosures, while no discovery compensated in any way for the destruction. They were again further opened up by Major A. Cunningham and Capt. F. C. Maisey in 1851, when several relic caskets were found.[1]

The largest stûpa is surrounded by a massive stone railing; access to the space inside the railing is afforded by four lofty gateways of fine grained sandstone facing the four points of the compass. This stûpa is a massive, solid brick and stone building of 121 feet in diameter and about 53½ feet high; the dome rises from a plinth 14 feet high, standing out 5½ feet from its circumference. On the top of the building was a terrace 34 feet in diameter, enclosed by a stone-railing (cf. plan and sketch, fig. 6). The ascent to the ramp which surrounds the building was reached by a double stair on the south side. The whole structure is surrounded by a massive colonnade measuring 144 feet from west to east and 151 feet from north to south. In this way the space on the south side of the terrace, where the steps are, is broader. The encircling rail shows numerous inscriptions, but no sculpture on the frieze or coping. On the other hand, the figured work of the four great gateways is particularly rich.

At the instigation of Mr. Fergusson,[2] a cast of the eastern gateway was made in 1869 and copies of it are in the Museums of Science and Art at S. Kensington, Edinburgh and Dublin, in the Royal Museum at Berlin, at Paris, &c.

The inscriptions on the railings of both the two existing stûpas are short but very numerous. Unfortunately, they contain scarcely any indication by help of which a date might be inferred. But the great majority of them are in the form of alphabet which goes back to the time of Asoka (B.C. 250) and which had altered for some time before the Christian era.[3] It seems most probable then

[1] *Jour. A. S. Ben.*, vol. III, pp. 488-494; vol. IV, p. 712; also vol. VI, pp. 451ff; vol. XVI, pp. 744ff; Cunningham, *Bhilsa Topes*, pp. x, 183, 269f. 275, 285f.; Fergusson, *Tree and Serp. Wor.* p. 96; *Picturesque Illust. of Anc. Archit.* pp. 21, 22; *Ind. and East. Arch.* pp. 60-75, 92-99; and Maisey, *Sânchi and its Remains.*

[2] The first half of Fergusson's *Tree and Serpent Worship* (1868, 2d ed. 1873) was devoted to the illustration of the Sâñchî Topes or Stûpas, from the drawings of Colonel Maisey, and a few photographs. A complete photographic representation of all the sculptures is required adequately to illustrate the monument.

[3] *Epigraphia Indica*, vol. II, pp. 88, 89. An inscription on the representation of a stûpa on the south gateway, mentions that the block "was the gift of Ananda, the son of Vâsish*tha*, in the reign of *Srî Sâtakarni.*" Among the Andhra kings there were several bearing this name, one of whom seems to have ruled over the Dakhan about 150 B.C.

that the gateways were erected in the second century before the Christian era. Stress may also be laid on the fact that the south gate, to judge from the style, is apparently the oldest. For different reasons it is probable that it was Asoka who erected the stûpa. The Singhalese chronicle, the *Mahâvansa*, relates that Asoka, when he was sent by his father as regent to Ujjayinî (Ujjain), made a stay of some time at Chetiyagiri or Vessanagara (Besnagar near Bhilsâ) There he married the daughter of a prince, and had by her two sons, Ujjeniya and Mahinda, and afterwards a daughter, Sanghamittâ. The two last took orders, and at the behest of their royal father went to Ceylon at the invitation of King Tissa, to take thither a shoot of the sacred bodhi-tree and to spread Buddhism in the island. Before their departure for Ceylon they were received by the princess their mother, who visited them at Chetiyagiri, in a hall built by herself. Now before the south gate there stood a Lat (with lion capital), of which a fragment still remains, bearing part of an inscription—apparently of an edict of Asoka,[1]—from which it follows that the erection of the great stûpa belongs to Asoka's time, about 250 B.C.: the commencement of the rail followed very soon after; and the erection of the south gateway, about or before 150 B.C. According to their probable age, the gateways stand in the following order—the southern, the northern, the eastern, the western. As the reliefs of the gateways exhibit the most extensive monument of older Buddhist sculpture, and in general represent the Asoka style, the character of this style will be described in more detail in the following chapter. For the reliefs of the east gate see the end of Chapter II.

The great Stûpa of Amarâvatî, on the right or south bank of the lower Krishna river, about twenty miles above Bejwâdâ, was first heard of by Colonel Colin Mackenzie in 1797. It was then being removed by the local chief to be used for building purposes. Mackenzie paid a prolonged visit to it in 1816 and again in the end of 1819, and made many careful drawings from the slabs of the railing and of those that had been round the base of the stûpa. Many sculptures had then been destroyed, but a few were secured by Mackenzie and sent to Madras and Calcutta. Further excavations were made in 1845 by Sir W. Elliott, and the sculptures recovered are now in the British Museum. The Madras Government excavated the whole area in 1881, and a large number of the sculptures then recovered were sent to the Madras Museum.

The Amarâvatî stûpa appears to have been deserted in the seventh century, when Hiwen Tsiang visited the district. The short inscriptions found range over a considerable period, and there were evidently enlargements and reconstructions; but the discovery of an epigraph of Pulumâyi—an Andhra king of the second century A.D., and the reported association of Nâgârjuna's name

[1] *Epig. Ind.*, vol. II, p. 367.

with the creation of the rail, combined with other indications, point to the second century A.D. as the period when most of the sculptures were executed and the work completed. It is due to Fergusson's ingenuity that the railing, adorned with richly composed reliefs, of which the pieces were completely dissevered, has been so far reconstructed that we have a picture of the whole.[1]

The Amarâvatî railing thus belongs apparently to the second century A.D.; the stûpa itself was older. The style of the sculpture on the railings had its origin in that of the Asoka period, but it has an entirely new kind of formation. The types are all closely preserved; but in the representation of the single figures, as in the composition, other laws prevailed. It will suffice, however, to indicate below some striking points in which the style of this older period—as Fergusson was the first to show—exerted an influence upon the reliefs of Amarâvatî. As to the further development of the elements which Amarâvatî has in common with Sâñchî, and so on, it will suffice to notice that a certain coquettish elegance, an over-luxuriance of the compositions, is the characteristic feature. (cf. illus. 8, 20, &c.).

The paintings of the cave-temples of Ajantâ, N.N.W. of the town of the same name in the Indhyâdri Hills which form the boundary between the Dekhan and Khândesh, do not fall quite within the scope of this book, and the reader is referred therefore to the literary works indicated in the bibliography for what concerns the history of the discovery as well as the artistic character of these specimens of ancient Indian paintings, so important to Indian archæology. Fergusson conjectured that, besides the Gandhâra school of sculpture, an early school of painting existed in Gandhâra: how far what is established in the third chapter as to the survival of Gandhâra types in the ecclesiastical paintings of Tibet, China and Japan, is calculated to support this undoubtedly correct conjecture of Fergusson, will no doubt be seen when our knowledge of the latter has been assured. Now the frescoes of Ajantâ and Bâgh are also connected with these ancient ecclesiastical paintings animated by antique elements. It is only necessary to refer occasionally to an Ajantâ representation where it seems of value for the history of a type. The uncommon beauty and grace of these pictures,—the sad fate of which I need not dwell on here,—was made evident by the outline drawings which Dr. J. Burgess incorporated in his account of the pictures (Bombay, 1879). The recent splendid publication of the Ajantâ pictures by Mr. Griffiths has made them accessible in a worthy form.

[1] The materials acquired have been utilized in the second half of Fergusson's *Tree and Serpent Worship* and in the volume of the Archæological Survey of S. India on the *Amarâvatî and Jaggayyapeta Stûpas*.

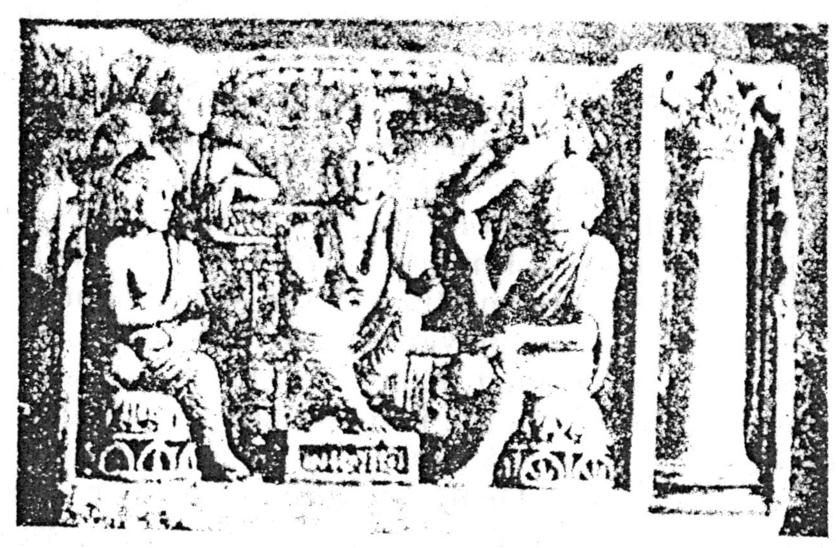

7. A Chief seated on a throne, talking with ascetics: from Swât.

CHAPTER II.

THE EARLY INDIAN STYLE.[1]

The form of art which was, and remained, national in India, and which constantly influenced the stone-architecture was wood-carving. The stone gates at Sâñchî, for example, are copied from wooden ones, which perhaps originally stood there; the general construction as well as the detail show this most clearly. The same stylistic features of the gates are met with, on a smaller scale, also in the throne-seats in reliefs of a still earlier period. Thus, among other things, some examples of thrones with backs are preserved on the reliefs of the stone railings of Amarâvatî, which represent the old Aryan native style in a quite distinctive manner. It is astonishing how intimately related these forms are to those of the Middle Ages, especially those of the north (conf. figs. 7, 8). The transoms of the broad low support are worked at the ends so as to project, and the ends themselves are ornamented with fantastic animals' heads (heads of dragons). On the relief from Amarâvatî (shown in fig. 31) the Toraṇa appears to be treated similarly—so far as the architrave is concerned—but the representations are not quite distinct enough. The interstices are adorned with reliefs and little round figures. The West Asian animal forms that are here introduced will be treated more in detail below (conf. figs. 28 and 29).

[1] As the examples of this style are all within the limits of India proper, I prefer this term to "Perso-Indian" employed by Prof. Grünwedel.—J.B.

At the present day wood-carving is still preserved in rustic forms—the characteristic feature of the national life of ancient India, as of the life of modern times, being the peasant class—although these purely archaic forms, reminding one of German compositions of the Middle Ages, have been lost. As in ancient Buddhist sculpture, the carved-wood style reappeared in India at a

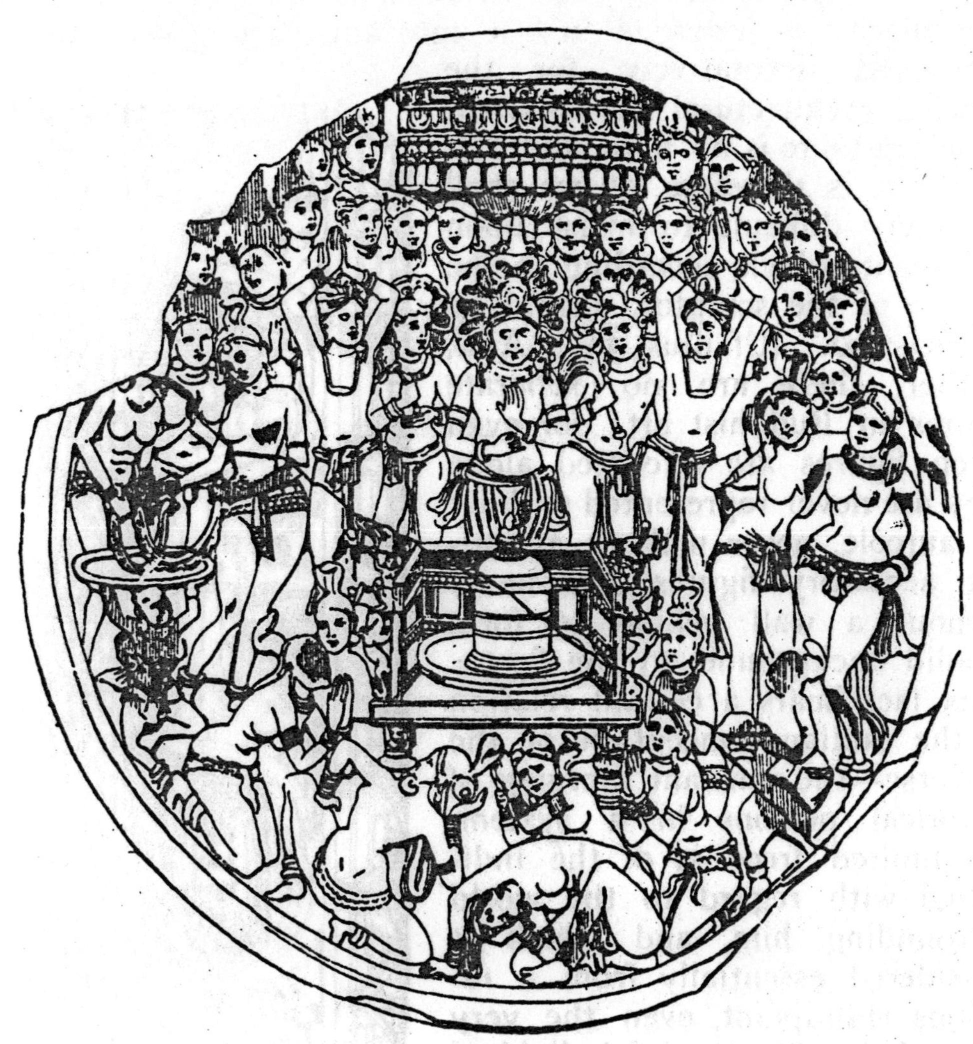

8. **Throne supporting a small Stûpa, worshipped by Nâgas.**
On a slab from Amarâvatî. Fergusson, *Tree and Serp. Wor.*, pl. lxii.

later period in the sacred buildings of the Jains under the Chalukya rulers of the Middle Ages. These buildings were executed in stone (white marble), and the fine lace-like interwoven work that forms the decoration of the buildings on Mount Abu and in other Jaina temples in Western India had then its origin. How these Jaina buildings, in turn,—with the omission of the figure elements—became the models for the trellis and stone filigree work of the Muhammadans in their buildings at Ahmadâbâd and elsewhere belongs to a different chapter of Indian art. We see then, that early Indian sculpture had an auxiliary in an ancient, indigenous, and deeply rooted branch of art: though it is true it was only in the hands of an artizan class. When working in stone began it was an aid in modelling, but an obstacle in the way of development. It is the wood-carving style, above all, which is to blame for the fact that Indian sculpture never became more than a *rilievo* serving for the decoration of large buildings,—so much so, indeed, that the buildings executed in stone appear overlaid with carved mouldings. The ornamental relief only seldom, and as if by chance, attains organic completeness; even in ancient Buddhist art a certain irregularity is indulged in—a constant varying of the panels employed decoratively, for the normal architectural development of which there is no hard and fast rule. It is therefore, as we shall see, very difficult to insist upon the points which, according to the design of the sculptor, should be emphasized. (Cf. illus. 36). And, further, there are no separate figures in Buddhist art: for even when figures are executed alone they are never represented without an aureole, never without attendant accessory figures, and never without a wall behind to form a solid background to the figure. This fact bears a certain relation to the Indian conception of the universe—the constant merging of historical persons in a system, the limited freedom of the individual with regard to the world surrounding him, and which is considered essentially from a religious standpoint, even the very idea of the identity of individual souls with the Universal Soul: it is to this that their incapacity is owing to attain a really artistic conception which could have developed the independent figure.

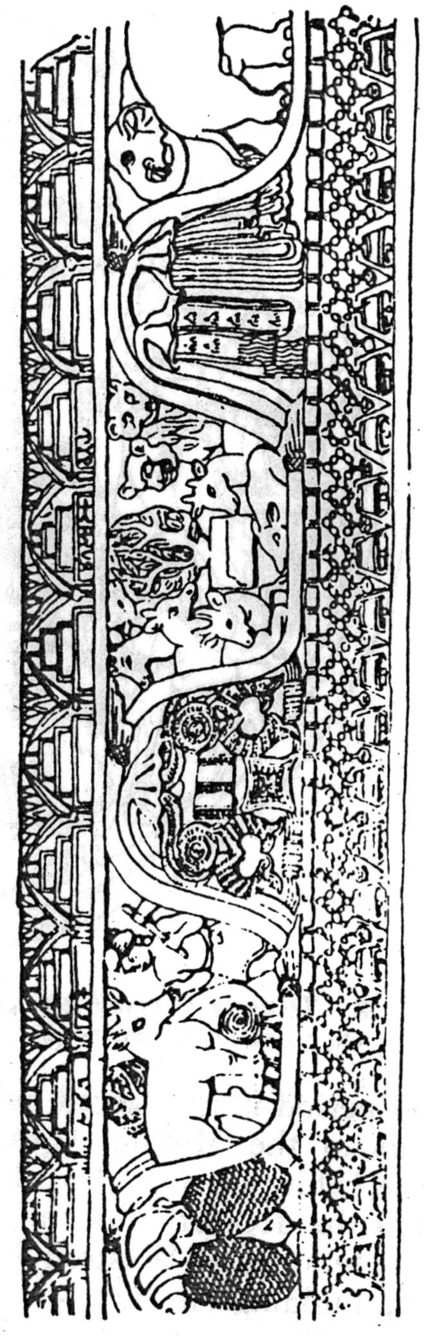

9. Relief with representation of the Isimiga Jātaka, Lions and Antelopes before the Sacred Tree, &c.[1]

A second branch of Indian art,—more delicate in form, and, by reason of the allusions to models in nature, apparently more productive,—was intimately connected, and that from very early times, with the popular ideas: this was the art of the goldsmith.

[1] So Cunningham, *Bharhut*, pl. xliii. The inscriptions designate the two representations as *Isimiga Jâtaka* and *Miga samadaka chetaya*,—"the rebirth as Rishi Antelope," and "the antelope enjoying chaitya." Conf. Hultzsch, 'Bharhut Inschriften' in *Zeit. d. Morg. Ges.*, Bd. XL., Ss. 58-76, Nrs. 10, 11.

Its influence is confirmed in two directions. The sculptures show how the decorative element in goldsmiths' work—often nearly resembling basket-work—everywhere aids in the devising of those chains and other ornaments, with flowers, leaves, rosettes, and finely linked bands, found along with panels which are adorned with figure compositions. The lower decorative lines on fig. 9 present patterns borrowed from ornaments; little bells and chains such as are worn by women for the feet.

For the separation of the different representations in the central belt the tendrils of plants are employed, from which ornaments grow out: the representation of the "Wishing tree" (*Kalpavriksha*), which at a later date becomes common, springs from this ornamental form.

But the goldsmith's art has had a fatal effect on the modelling of the human figure. The heroic form of Indian sculptured figures has been, and at all times remained the same,—they are decked as for gala occasions. This form has been preserved with unalterable tenacity through the whole history of Indian art, and even in neighbouring countries. The old, partly ancient Aryan, forms of festal ornaments passed, along with the Aryan colonists, beyond the limits of India, in manifold varieties in accordance with the peculiar style of the particular country; in Burma and Siam, Tibet and Mongolia, Java and Bali, the modified forms of ancient Indian gala ornaments are still to be found in the gala costume of the kings, or of brides and bridegrooms, or, finally, in the costumes of the theatres which everywhere represent subjects taken from the ancient Indian legends. It is a surprising fact that the non-Aryan districts of India, or the lower castes in the old civilised parts, like the above-named countries outside India, frequently now show more antique forms of articles of jewellery than the ancient civilised kingdoms of India itself, since in the course of time the latter adopted other fashions in costume and ornament. The whole question deserves special and detailed examination in which the monuments of antiquity should play a prominent part. At present I must content myself with suggestions.

The ornaments are uncommonly rich and tastefully arranged, whilst they also in themselves form an artistic motif. The ancient Buddhist plastic art never deteriorated into the rough, monotonous and mechanical sort of style in which the so-called Assyrian art covers its figures with ornaments and garments in rich patterns. But on the other hand the ornament, in the painfully careful execution it received, hindered very considerably the development of the human figure, since it always retained the conventional type for the forms. Here, too, it is to be observed, that tropical Nature has exercised its influence in India; for the very names of articles of jewellery in all Indian tongues clearly prove the most part of them to be imitations of the splendid blossoms and creepers which the flora of this lovely land holds out to man for his adornment on festive occasions. From ancient literature we clearly learn, for example, that the same flowers served directly for adorning the hair which, at the present day, have given their names to the corresponding metal ornaments. Thus we read in the *Ritusamhâra* ('Description of the seasons'), ii. 21: "Now (in the rainy season) the women wear on their heads garlands of Kadamba, Kesara, and Ketaki, and ear ornaments of Kakubha-umbels, which, being thrust into the earlap hang down over its edge."[1] These floral adornments varied according to the seasons. With regard to the names mentioned it may here be noted that even at the present day a broad ornamental plate in the shape of a pandanus-blossom is quite commonly worn as a head-ornament. It bears the same name: Hindî, *Ketakî*; Marâthî, *Keorá*; Malayâlam, *Keidappû*; &c. Even along with metal ornaments, flowers assert their rights: the Tamil women when in gala costume, along with metal ear-ornaments and ornamental plates on their heads, wear a cluster of single yellow or white flowers strung together by means of threads, and hung from their ears, &c., &c. Among the lower castes similar articles—perhaps imitations—woven of grass and straw, with festoons and chains made of nuts and bright coloured seeds, are still to be seen side by side with metal ornaments.

However pleasing and charming this joy in Nature may appear, the reproduction of these articles of adornment had an unfortunate artistic influence with respect to modelling. The shoulders loaded with broad chains, the arms and legs covered with metal rings, the bodies encircled with richly linked girdles, could never have attained an anatomically correct form. Everywhere the carrying out of a clear outline was interfered with by broad ornamental lines, rich and tasteful in themselves, disturbing the natural position of the muscles of the leg and arm, and, in consequence, the limbs have received at the best, an effeminate seemingly correct finish; but at the worst, they have been subjected to a complete distortion of the skeleton, whilst the muscles stand unduly out.

Connected with this overloading with ornament, certain physical peculiarities which accompany the wearing of heavy ornament are regarded as beauties and are still further exaggerated in the copies. This is especially due to the wearing of large and heavy ornaments. This, again, is in keeping with the fact that the types on the monuments, *e.g.* illust. 8, 14, 22, bear a greater resemblance to certain ornaments of the Aryan races than those worn by the women of the early civilized territory at the present day. The great metal, wood, or horn discs (Mal., *takka*; Tamil, *takkei*) of the Nâyarchchi of Malabar, the extended ear-lobes of the Maravatti, &c., are well known.[2]

[1] These in order are:—Nauclea kadamba, Mimusops elengi, Pandanus odoratissimus, Pentaptera arjuna.

[2] To indicate to the reader what stress is laid on this perception of beauty in the Indian mind, it may be noted that, among the beneficent acts (Tam. *aram*) enumerated by Tamil moralists, besides digging wells, building hospitals, feeding Brâhmans,

Out of this emphasizing of ornament came the treatment of the nude. The naked body, as such, was never an object of representation in Buddhist art.

Apart from the fact that nudity is repugnant to Buddha's doctrine, the peculiar ideas of the Hindus as to the purpose of the human body is to be taken into account; the human form is at best a part of Nature itself, the ephemeral garment of the soul, in which the latter lingers against its will. It is important to remember here what ideas were not accepted by the Hindus. Man never appears as the lord of Nature, which was there just to serve him: never is he regarded as the crown of creation. Re-incarnation into the world of human beings is only desirable inasmuch as that alone makes redemption—final escape—possible. With this may be connected the fact that no general interest is taken in the symmetrical training of the body. Physical exercise is not unknown in India, but its ends are professional, not æsthetic. Physical beauty appears as the result of good works in former births: not as that of individual energy and pleasure in life; it is a gift of Nature and transient as the tropical flowers. It is quite true that, in India, people wore, and still wear, as light clothing as was worn in ancient Greece, and bare limbs are common. Physically, too, the Hindu differs from the ancient Greek. With his delicate and supple-jointed limbs, miserable calves and feeble muscles, the Hindu was in early times, as the ancient Buddhist sculptures show, the very same lightly-built, slippery, eel-like creature that he is to-day. On the whole, it may be said that ancient Buddhist art has represented the Hindu excellently, with an agreeable childlike naturalism which, notwithstanding the graceful moulding, is far from idealising. As strict training was unknown, a refinement soon appears which is seen chiefly in the representations of women, and becomes by and by baroque or rococo in style. With this conception of the human form agrees the circumstance that even at an early date an interest in portraiture, at least in national portraits—if one may be allowed the expression—is evinced. The different peoples that lived side by side in India were distinguished from one another above all physically: contact with peoples of hither Asia, in the time of Asoka, revealed new types, and thus we undoubtedly see an attempt for instance to represent foreign nations in the equestrian groups that adorn the Sâñchî gateways.

On the eastern gateway, for example, besides mythical foreign peoples, two figures are represented riding on horned lions. One of the heads is clearly not of the Aryan type: the woolly negro-like hair and the thick coarse shape of the whole head surprises

"giving palmyra palm bands (*kâdôlei*) to women," is specified, that with these rolled spirally in discs they may enlarge the holes in their ears and so wear large and imposing ornaments (*tôdu*, Mal. *tôda*). Conf. Rottler, *Tamil-Eng. Dict.* s.v. *aram*. In this connexion see also E. Thurston, *Madras Govt. Mus. Bullet.* vol. II (1898), pll. xxii, xxv, pp. 123ff.

one; this same figure holds a bunch of grapes in his hand. In India wine is unknown. There appears to be no word in the early language for the vine or its cluster.[1] Even at the present day,

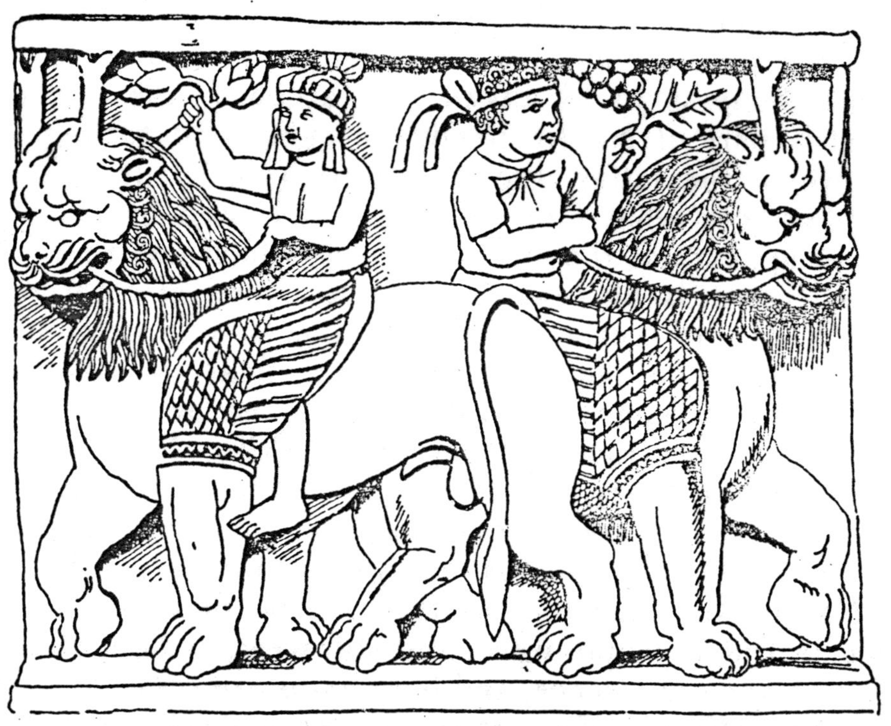

10. COMPARTMENT FROM THE THIRD ARCHWAY OF THE EAST GATEWAY AT SÂNCHÎ.

grapes are mostly brought from Kâbul, though they are now cultivated about Daulatâbâd. Thus the rider represents one who is not Indian, and has perhaps a remote connexion with the representations of Silenus that have been found at Mathura.[2] Although the framework of the figure is in the Perso-Indian style, at any rate this and the corresponding equestrian figures represent foreign nations, regarded as living far away in the North-west. The whole series of these figures—those mounted on goats, on dromedaries, on lions—present a distinct contrast to the Hindus riding on elephants. The mythical-geographical conceptions on which they are based remind one of those fabulous creatures of which Herodotus tells the Greeks,[3] from Persian traditions related by Aristeas of Prokonnêsos, and which, on the strength of Indian tales, Megasthenes described at a later date.

The great majority of the other reliefs at Sânchî present the Hindu type—a long head with full round face, large eyes, and thick lips. At Barâhat (Bharhut) the same type appears, but it is somewhat harsher. The greatly extending ear-lobes are never wanting; the way in which the head-dress is emphasized often

[1] Sanskrit drâkshâ is 'ρώξ; *mridvikâ*, *mridri*, is a new form. On the probable borrowing of *βότρυς* in Chinese, conf. Hirth, *Fremde Einflüsse in d. Chin. Kunst*, S. 15, 28, note 1.

[2] *Jour. A. S. Beng.* vol. V, pp. 517, 567; *Arch. Sur. Ind. Rep.*, vol. I, pp. 242-44; and Growse, *Mathura*, 2d. ed. p. 156.

[3] Herodotus, lib. iii, c. 116; lib. iv, c. 13.

causes the heads to appear disproportionately large, so that, in the case of accessory personages especially, the whole figure has something childish and dwarfish about it (conf. fig. 17, &c.). In this way real dwarfs appear, which are presumably connected with antique pigmy types (conf. fig. 11). This question, which demands much preliminary investigation, cannot here be discussed in detail. Still it may be said that they represent the basis of the thick-set, dwarfish type of demon that appears later and extends into Lamaist art. It seems not to be without purpose that the dwarf capital appears on the west gateway at Sâñchî, since the architrave represents the attack of the demons on the Bodhi-tree.[1]

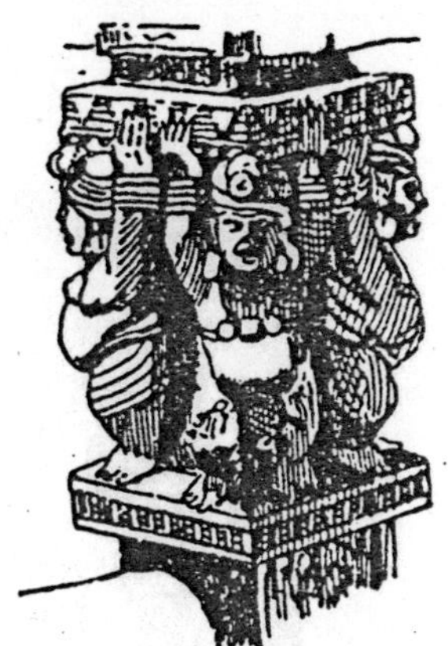

11. PILLAR CAPITAL WITH DWARF-LIKE DEMONS. From the west gateway at Sâñchi.

In the treatment of drapery, the earlier Buddhist art is very successful,—though unusual articles of clothing, such as the monk's cowl, present difficulties. The dress of the men consists, in the main, of the same articles as are generally worn at the present day,—a loin-cloth worn so as to resemble trowsers (Hind. *dhôti*, Tam. *mundu*) forms the garment proper. The upper part of the body is always bare; the modern jacket, for example (Hind. *angiyá*, Tam. *sokkag*), or other forms of this article of attire, nowhere appear. As covering for the upper part of the body a long shawl-like cloth is used, which is thrown about the shoulders in various ways—the modern *añgavastram*, and so on. In descriptions contained in the sacred texts of gala costumes and the like, the *chelukkhepa*, *i.e.* the waving with the dress, that is the upper garment, is always mentioned (fig. 37). This upper garment has ever remained the heroic costume, if one may be allowed the expression, and in the earlier and later representations of Buddhist gods, forms the folds that wave about the figure like an aureole. This arrangement is often completely misunderstood in badly executed pictures, though East Asian art knows how to employ tastefully this Indian dress. (Conf. illus. in Chapters III and IV). Japanese articles of export, nevertheless, when they represent Buddhist deities often manifest the rudest misconceptions.

The women on the sculptures of the older period are seen clothed in the loin-cloth only, but their ornaments and head-dresses are all the more rich. The long loin-cloth, reaching to the ankles, is sometimes treated as transparent, and is then—since the sculptor lacked the means of expressing his idea—indicated by representing the figure without covering, yet so that the edge of a garment is visible over the ankles and between the legs. The upper part of the body is always uncovered: this light kind of dress is still to be

[1] *Tree and Serp. Worsh.*, pl. xviii; *Pres. Nat. Monts. in India* (Lond. 1896), pl. xxvi, or Cole, *Sáñchi* (1885), pl. ix.

found in the south of modern India among the Nâyar-chchhîs of Malabar, whose large ear-ornaments have been already mentioned. On several reliefs the women appear without any garment but a narrow loin-cloth, the ornamented girdle, head, arm and leg ornaments being all the richer. Further details relating to these matters belong to the history of costume. It was important to notice here, that, from the nature of the garments, the hip, and not the breast and upper part of the body, becomes the fixed point starting from which the figure was composed. One has the feeling that the artist wished to provide against the loin-cloth slipping from the figure. This condition, imposed by the character of the vestments, explains much in the modern Hindu; but it also explains the strained attitude of the figures both in

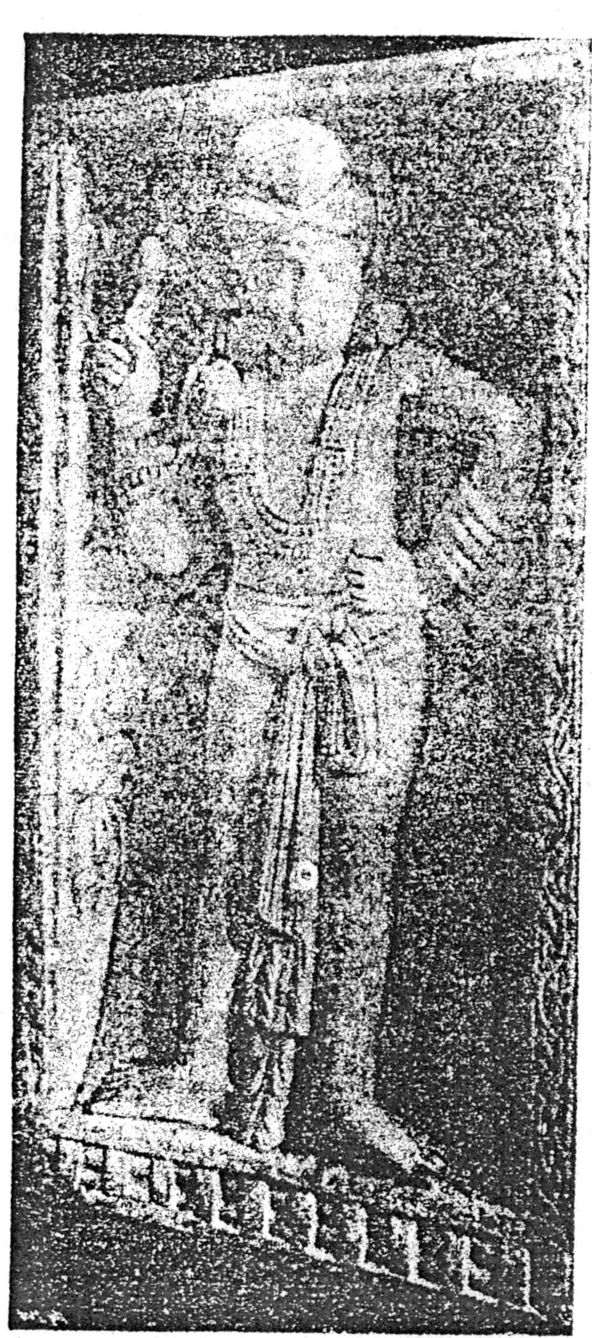

12. RELIEF ON THE INNER SIDE OF THE LEFT PILLAR OF THE EAST GATEWAY AT SÂNCHÎ; A YAKSHA.[1]

[1] This is possibly Dhṛitarâshṭa, the white Yaksha ruler of the East: conf. Rockhill, *Life of Buddha*, p. 48, note; Minayeff, *Recherches sur la Buddh.* (in *Ann. Mus. Guimet*), pp. 138f.; *Arch. Sur. W. Ind.*, vol. IV, p. 99. inscr. 3; and *Cave Temples*, pl. xxv.—J.B.

the older and later art of India. Modern proverbs are conversant with this.

An artistic feature which naturally originated from the sort of clothing described above,—the rich hip chains and girdle—is the prominence of one hip, the figure being represented with one foot firmly planted while the other, bent or in the act of stepping forward, is almost entirely relieved of the burden. This beauty device is of very ancient standing in Indian art; it is usually, if not exclusively, seen in female figures. Modern miniatures have faithfully preserved it and developed it to a certain coquettish elegance; conf. figs. 8 and 13.

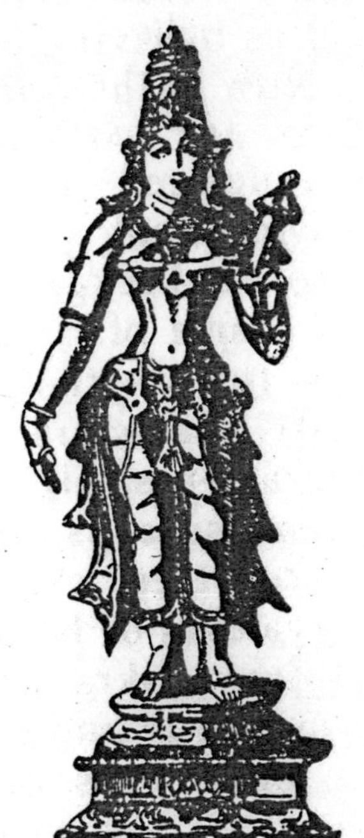

13. THE GODDESS KAMALÂ,[1] a form of SRÎ (Tirumagal). Modern S. Indian bronze.

The subjects that were represented were taken from the traditions of the life of the founder of the religion, and referred to local incidents. His life, until he attained Buddhattam—to use their own expression—seems to have been the chief subject for the earlier period. But besides these, there exist at least as many scenes representing solely the adoration and worship of religious symbols, processions to holy places, and so on. Besides there appear even on the monuments of the Asoka period a few representations which refer to the so-called *Jâtakas* or stories of Buddha's previous incarnations. The *Jâtakas* form a part of the canonical literature (of the *Sûtra* class); they are an inexhaustible storehouse of fables and legends, but are also of exceptional importance in the history of civilization in ancient India. The plan of the work is briefly as follows:—According to the tradition, Gautama had passed through five hundred and fifty existences in all created forms,—as god, as man, as animal,—till, in his last incarnation, as the son of Suddhodana, he appeared as the deliverer of mankind. Five hundred and fifty verses, or groups of verses, which contain sayings of the Master, form the themes for as many tales told in support of them from Buddha's last earthly life. Some event—an annoying incident with insubordinate monks, for example, or a contest with some adversary, a conversion, et cætera, is related in the attached commentary: Buddha adjusts matters, or delivers a discourse, which contains a parallel from one of his previous lives and concludes with the verse that forms the title as *fabula docet*.

Owing to the simplicity of the religious ideas of the people at the

[1] Or Bhûmidevî, the goddess of the earth, Vishnu's second wife, who is represented with two arms, holding a lotus flower in one while the other hangs down empty; she wears a crown, and her black hair hangs down to near her feet; she stands on a lotus. Tirumagal, 'the divine or illustrious daughter,' is a name of Lakshmî.—J.B.

time, the figures required by Buddhist art for the representation of the subjects referred to, are few in number, and represent divinities of a low order—demons and beings half divine,—for Buddhism had taken root chiefly among the masses and everywhere employed the speech of the people. According to their teaching all the abovementioned beings are mortal; even the gods owe their positions to their virtuous actions in previous existences, and appear throughout as believing promoters of the religion of the 'Vanquisher.'

Now in the *Sûtras*, especially in the *Jâtakas*, a god and a goddess are particularly prominent. In the Vedic pantheon, the thunder-god Indra or *S*akra (the mighty) had attained a predominant position, and had thrust the older class of gods into the background; even in the Pâli *Sûtras* he is familiar, under the name of Sakka, as the chief god. The Buddhists adopted into their mythology certain of the Brahmanical gods, but modified their characters and importance. To Sakka, Mahâbrahmâ and Mâra,—possibly influenced by the Persian conceptions of the Ameshaspends,—they assigned the rank of archangels, and represented them as ruling in great magnificence in their respective Devalokas or heavens, but often descending to interfere in human affairs. *S*akra, like Jupiter Fulgurator, is the Brâhma*n* god of the atmosphere and king of the minor gods; and with the Buddhists he even bears like names—as Vâsava, Vajrapâ*n*i, Devinda, Maghavâ, Sahassanetta (Sansk. Sahasranetra), &c., but they change Purindara ('destroyer of towns') into the Buddhistic epithet of Purindada ('bestower of towns'). He is inferior in majesty to the other two archangels, but rules over the five lowest of the six Kâmadevalokas and has his abode in the Tâvati*ms*a (S. Trayastri*ms*a) heavens. As in Brâhma*n* mythology, his consort is Sujâtâ or *S*achî, his palace or car is called Vejayanta, his elephant Erâva*n*a (S. Airâvata), and his charioteer Mâtali.[1] In Hindu iconography also he holds the Vajrâyudha, which he is represented as giving to those practising austerities to render them invincible. He appears in sculptures in the ornaments and costume of a king: indeed, he is not distinguishable from royal figures.

On the east gateway at Sâñchî (on the front of the right pillar) a large palace of the gods is represented, on the different terraces of which persons in regal costume are represented sitting and waited on by women who dance and play. They are certainly gods: in their left hands they hold a small bottle, in the right an object—not readily recognisable, but which resembles the later thunderbolts (conf. fig. 1), the well-known ritual sceptres (*vajra*: Tibetan, *rdo-rje*) of the priests of the northern school). It must be the thunderbolt, the attribute of divine power—an attribute corresponding well with the storm-myths of the Ri*gveda*.

[1] In Persian myth, Indra is the demon opposed to the Ameshaspend Asha-Vahista Darmsteter, *Zandavesta* (Sac. Bks. of the East, vol. IV), vol. II, p. lxxii, or in *Ann. Mus. Guim.*, tom. III, pp. xliv, xlv.—J.B.

Mahâbrahmâ, Brahmâ Sahampati or Pitâmahâ, is the greatest of all Devas. Though vastly inferior to Buddha, he rules the second of the Trailokya regions—the Brahmâ heaven, called Rûpâvachara, which is beyond the Kâmadevalokas. He has, as a symbol of sovereignty, a silver *chhattra* (Pâli, *chhatta*).[1]

Mârarâja, the third of these Devas, is variously named Vasavattimâra, Namuchi, Pâpîyân, Kâmadhâturâja, K*r*ish*n*a, Pi*s*una, &c. He is ruler of the highest of the six Kâmadevaloka heavens—the Paranimmita-vasavatti Devaloka (Sans. Paranirmita-va*s*avar*t*in) or Vasavattî,—where life lasts 32,000 years. He has a position analogous to that of Ahriman among the Zoroastrians; is the lord of pleasure, sin and death,—the tempter, the evil principle, the representative of inherent sin. He is represented as riding on an elephant, and attended by the Mârakâyikas. He has a hundred arms and assumes monstrous forms. He owes his exalted rank to his having in a previous birth exercised a high degree of charity. His realm (Mâradheyya) is that of re-birth as opposed to Nirvâ*n*a.[2]

The pantheon, however, is otherwise vague and accessory: in the legends a confused crowd of Devaputtas—'sons of the gods'—appear; names are mentioned even, such as Mâlâbhârî or Mâlâdharî—'garland bearer'; but these names are ephemeral for beings living a life of pleasure in their heavens—an idealized representation of Indian royal courts. Notwithstanding the magnificence of the representations set forth, the principal theme of the legends is the inculcation of the vanity of sensuous pleasure and the brevity of human life. It is very evident that this tendency of the texts—which are undoubtedly very old—was by no means calculated to develope plastic figures of individual gods.

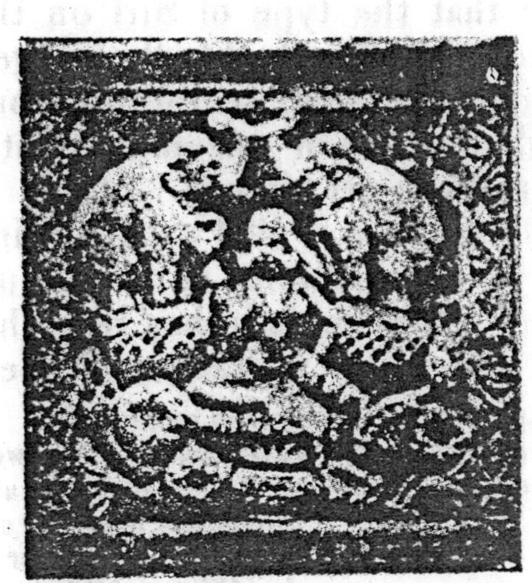

14. The goddess Sirî (*S*rî).
From the east gateway at Sâñchî, conf. ill. 39.

One divinity only appears as a fully developed type and is always reproduced with a certain evident pleasure; it is the ideal of the Indian woman, the goddess of beauty, of prosperity, of domestic blessing, of wealth: Pâli, Sirî; Sanskrit, *S*rî (Lakshmî). The worship of this popular goddess must have prevailed, in Buddhist times, throughout the whole of India. Strî and *S*rî,

[1] Conf. Burnouf, *Int. Bud: Ind.*, 2d. ed., pp. 116, 532f, 546f; Rhys Davids, *Buddhist Suttas* (Sac. Bks. of the East, vol. XI), pp. 162f.

[2] Conf. Burnouf, *Intr. Bud. Ind.*, 2d. ed. p. 68n.

"woman and goddess of fortune," says a still current proverb,[1]—which affords a valuable reminiscence from Indian antiquity, according to the conception of which woman was by birth the equal of man.[2] *Srî*, as Tyche or Fortuna, is frequently represented on gates, stone-railings, &c. Of special interest is the type at Udayagiri, where it is fully developed; it appears in the Barâhat (Bharhut) sculptures and is frequently repeated at Sâñchî.[3] Sirî is represented as a woman in the costume and ornaments of a Hindu, seated or standing on a lotus-flower; two of her hands (when she is represented with four) are empty, the other two are raised each holding a water-lily, while two white elephants, holding water-pots in their trunks, water the flowers in her hands. Even to this day this oldest type is firmly established in the Brâhman miniatures. The representation is of unusual interest because it forms the Indian analogy to the Greek Aphrodite Anadyomene. According to the legend in the *Râmâyana*, she sprang from the froth of the ocean when it was churned by the gods. This is not the place to enter on the mythological accounts of the goddess: it is enough to indicate that the type of Sirî on the early Buddhist monuments is an ancient and undoubtedly indigenous one.

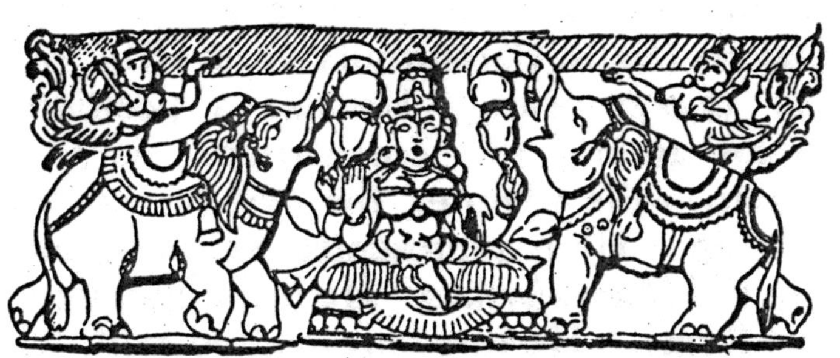

15. THE GODDESS TÎRUMAGAL (*Srî*).
Wood carving from a side chapel of the temple of Mînâkshî at Madurâ, S. India.

Among the pillar sculptures from Barâhat,[4] there appears a series of gods that are of uncommon interest as much mythologically as in relation to art history.

Among these is Sirî called "Sirimâ devata," represented in the dress and ornaments of a Hindu woman with largely developed breasts. She holds in her right hand a flower, now broken. All these figures, in imitation of Western Asian deities,[5] stand upon

[1] Manu: striyah *S*riyascha geheshu

[2] Tiruvalluvar, the Tamil poet of the weaver caste, in his *Kural* (v. 1082), styles the woman in full attire "the goddess *S*rî attacking with an army's might":—

"She of the beaming eyes,
To my rash look her glance replies,
As if the matchless goddess' hand
Led forth an armèd band." (Dr. Pope's tr.).

For *S*rî or Lakshmî, see *Vishnu Purâna*, Wilson's tr., Hall's ed., vol. I, pp. 118-120, 144-5.

[3] *Cave Temples*, p. 74, and pl. 1; Cunningham, *Bharhut Stupa*, pl. xxxvi, fig. 1; Fergusson, *Tree and Serp. Wor.*, pp. 112, 113, 120.

[4] Cunningham, *Bharhut*, pll. xxi-xxiii. Minayeff, *Recher. sur le Bouddhisme* (Ann. Mus. Guimet), pp. 93-102, 138-152, examines the divinities represented as compared with the texts.

[5] Kubera treading on a Yaksha is a type preserved even in Lamaism and Japanese Buddhism. Kubera and Virudhaka are two of the so-called Lokapâlas, again referred to. We have here the origin of the creatures called *vâhana* (vehicles) on which the Hindu gods stand or ride. Conf. the remarks below on Garuda.

their attributes; thus, Kubera, king of the demons called Yakshas, stands on a pointed-eared, thick-set demon, and the Nâga king on a piece of rock in which are seen heads of snakes, in front a pond with lotuses. Two Yakshinî, females, stand on Makaras (fig. 16). In others the attribute or cognizance under the feet is wanting, and they stand instead on elephants or on a stone fence, as it were, on detached parts of a Tora*n*a, in order to equalize them with those standing on their attributes as pedestals.[1] Two or three of these women stand under a tree, and raise their hands among the branches as if to pluck the blossoms. The same subject is met with decoratively treated under the *sûchis* of the gateways at Sâñchî.[2]

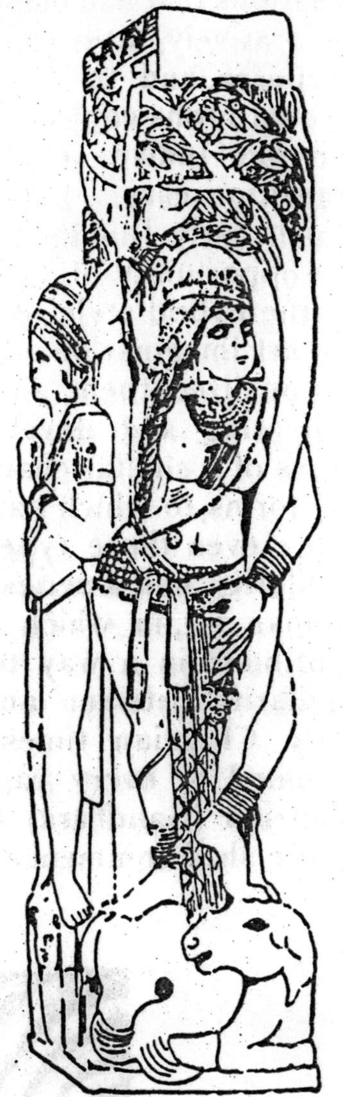

16. Pillar figure from Barâhat described in the inscription as the Yakshinî Chandâ. Cunningham's *Bharhut*, pl. xxii.

Another Hindu divinity also occurs, though rarely, among the early Buddhist sculptures. This is Sûrya, the sun-god (Gr. Helios)—evidently an importation from the north or Central Asia. He is the only member of the pantheon who is represented as clad from the feet upwards to the bosom; he wears a girdle, *avyañga* (Baktrian, *aiwyâonha*) about his waist; and is usually represented in a chariot drawn by four (or seven) horses, and attended by two females. Exampies of this divinity occur on a pillar of the old rail at Gayâ, in the early cave at Bhâjâ, and in the Ananta cave at Udayagiri.[3]

With these we terminate the types of national gods represented as human beings so far as they come under our consideration. For the sculptors of that age it was more difficult to represent the other mythological beings. The lower divinities had to be moulded after fixed types; for they play a large part in the *Sûtras* already mentioned.

[1] The reliefs of Bhûtesar (Mathurâ), Cunningham, *Arch. Sur. Ind.*, vol. III, pll. vi and xi, are certainly not Buddhist (probably Jaina). These very erotically represented groups, which Curtius has so pertinently described (*Arch. Zeit. N.F.*, Bd. VIII, 1876, Ss. 95f.) have no trees in blossom behind them. A noteworthy parallel in mediæval art is supplied by statues standing on "the evil principle;" and one that resembles the *vâhanas*, the mediæval personifications of the virtues and vices standing or riding on animals. E. P. Evans, *Animal Symbolism in Ecclesiastical Architecture*, p. 163.

[2] Fergusson, *Tree and Serp. Worsh.*, pl. xiii.

[3] See Râjendralâl Mitra's *Buddha Gaya*, pl. l; Cunningham, *Arch. Sur. Ind. Rep.*, vol. III, pl. xxvii; and Fergusson, *Archæol. in India*, p. 34. Sûrya also appears on the Lahaul Lota; *Arch. Sur. W. Ind.*, vol. IV, p. 6.

As explained above, the connexion with Irân introduced into India a series of artistic forms which became the standards in sculpture as well as in architecture. From the series of hybrid creations that had come from Western Asia and that were employed decoratively, attempts were made to adapt certain forms to native purposes and to develope them into fixed types, whilst closely related forms continued to be purely decorative. The character of the old Indian reliefs that were also decorative rendered this transition easy. Let us now enumerate the different beings for which early Buddhist art required types, and thus we shall have the opportunity of pointing out how extensive was the hold taken by the hybrid style of Western Asia, and how, on the other hand, the art imagination adapted the borrowed forms for its own needs, nationalized them, and in some cases succeeded admirably in re-animating and developing them,—evidently because indigenous types of a similar character already existed. Much inconstancy in the forms, to which names can hardly be given, is specially remarkable; even those types that we can name do not preserve their similarity, and a series of imaginary shapes crops up, as in early Roman art, in which antique elements—sirens, centaurs, &c., still continued in a way to exist, though no longer intelligible. The similarity between ancient Buddhist art and the monuments of early Christian times, without direct contact being necessarily assumed in every case—becomes greater still when the Græco-Baktrian (Gandhâra) types are introduced.

We shall commence with a type in which the human element still

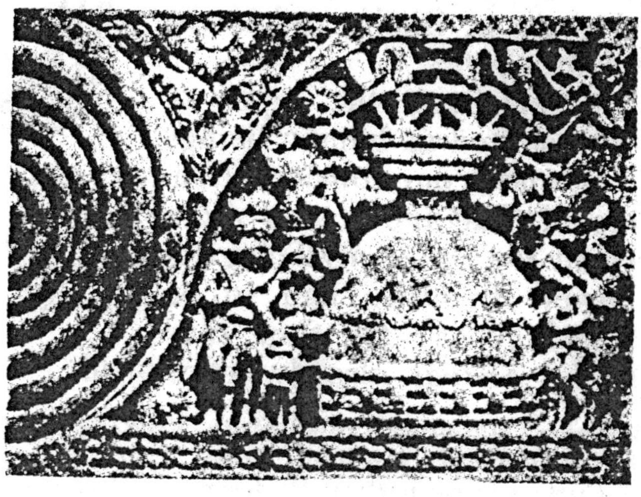

17. Gods and men (Devamanussâ) worshipping a Stûpa.
On the east gateway at Sâñchî.

plays the principal rôle,—the so-called Nâga. Indian popular belief, whose conceptions were moulded later by the official Brâhman religion, besides demons of every sort, giants, &c., recognises a much venerated class of snake-gods (Nâgas). We cannot undertake an examination of the origin of this belief, which is unknown to the Vedic age; suffice it to say that besides the world of gods and men there are eight classes of demigods which the Bauddha writings generally enumerate in the order—Devas, Nâgas, Râkshasas, Gandharvas, Asuras, Garu*d*as, Kinnaras, and Mahoragas;[1] but the Yakshas often take the third place instead of Râkshasas.

The second class form a separate snake world, the inhabitants of which have the power of assuming human forms. They are fabled to reside under the Trikû*t*a rocks supporting Mount Meru, and also in the waters of springs, lakes, rivers, &c., watching over great treasures, causing rain and certain maladies, and becoming dangerous when in anger. They are the subjects of Virûpâksha, the red king of the western quarter and probably the Buddhist form of *S*iva, who is well known in Hindu mythology as Virûpâksha as well as Nâganâtha and Nâgabhûshana. Chiefs or kings of the Nâgas are named in the legends and their deep reverence for Buddha, which puts men to shame, is specially characteristic of them. The wonderful alms-bowl of Buddha is, according to the legend, a gift from the demigod kings of the four quarters. More than once, Nâga chiefs approached the Master,—thus Muchilinda, the tutelary deity of a lake near Gayâ, protected him from the rain; Apalâla, the guardian Nâga of the source of the Swât or *S*ubhavastu river in Udyâna, was converted by *S*âkyamuni shortly before his Nirvâ*n*a; Elâpatra (Erapato, Sans. Airâvata), another Nâgarâja, consulted Buddha about rebirth in a higher condition; and Chakravâka

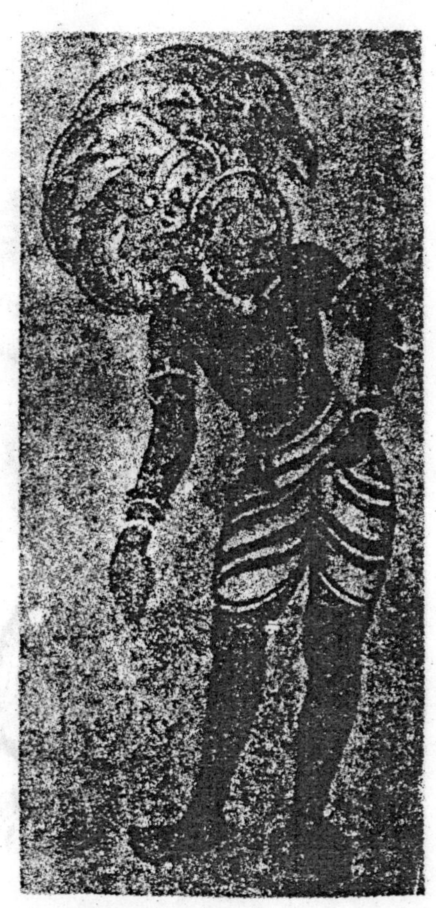

18. A Nâga râja.
From a fresco in Cave I at Ajantâ; Griffiths' *Paintings in the Ajantâ Caves.*

[1] The Jainas also enumerate eight divisions of their Vyantara-gods, viz.:—Pisâchas, Bhûtas, Yakshas, Râkshasas, Kinnaras, Kimpurushas, Mahoragas (boas), and Gandharvas. See note 2, p. 47. Each of the Tirthankaras has an attendant Yaksha and Yakshinî.

Nâga is figured on a pillar at Barâhat.[1] Even in the ritual for admission to orders, the question was introduced whether the candidate was not a Nâga.

Thus it was necessary to represent Nâgas typically in the body of the compositions illustrative of the life of the founder of the religion; and yet in the scenes in which they appear in the legends they could be properly represented only in human form. The problem was admirably solved; the Nâgas were represented as human, and, in the manner of the Egyptian Uraeus-snake, a serpent—usually many-hooded in the case of a male, but single-hooded

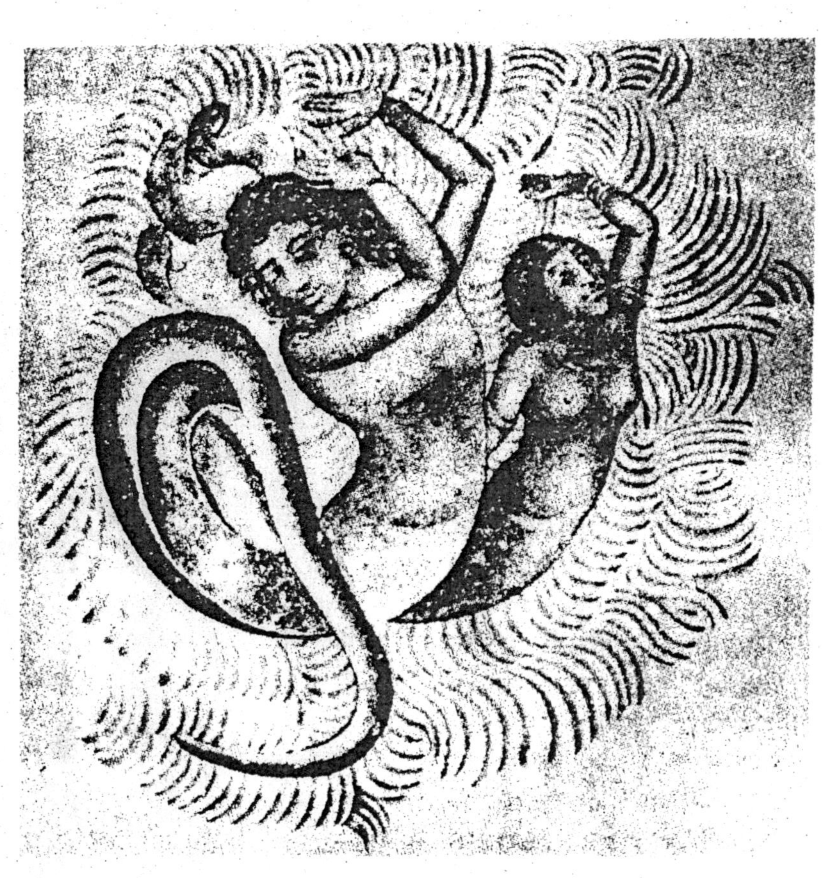

19. Nâga and Nâginî in water.
On a wall-painting in Cave II at Ajantâ; from Griffiths' *Paintings*.

for a Nâgî—was placed over the head (or rather springing from behind the neck) as ornament. (See figs. 8, 18, 20). We do not maintain that this type is to be regarded as a result of contact with western Asiatic art, but neither must we reject it unconditionally, for the Nâgas were represented in other forms also as hybrid creatures. The Nâga in human form with the snake-hood has been retained in Buddhist art in all its ramifications, and is found

[1] Beal, *Romantic Hist. of Buddha*, pp. 276ff; *Si-yu-ki*, vol. I, p. 37; Rockhill, *Life of the Buddha*, pp. 34, 46f., 244f.; Cunningham, *Bharhut Stûpa*, p. 27, &c.

also in the Chino-Japanese, where snake-kings are represented as men in Chinese costume, with a dragon on the back of the neck, whose head appears over that of the human form. Along with this human shape is also found a purely animal one. Sometimes even both appear in combination (conf. ill. 19): snakes the upper part of whose bodies are human, their heads crowned with serpents' hoods, while the lower part of the body from the hips downwards is purely animal. This is, iconographically, the proper form of the Nâga, and they are so represented whenever they appear in their proper element—water; and so we find them pictured in the Ajan*t*â wall paintings (fig. 19). These forms are employed by preference decoratively, or as accessory figures in larger compositions of the purely human Nâgas with snakes as head ornaments. But this type may certainly be regarded as derived from west Asian prototypes. It is allied to the creatures with fish tails that are represented with human bodies: apparently mostly of the female sex—the so-called Matsyanâris—'fish girls.' From this type, modern Brâhman art has evolved the representation of Gañgâ and Yamunâ, the goddesses of the Ganges and Jumna. Together with the creatures with fish tails and human busts, there are also decorative figures with animal bodies, on which a few words will be said.

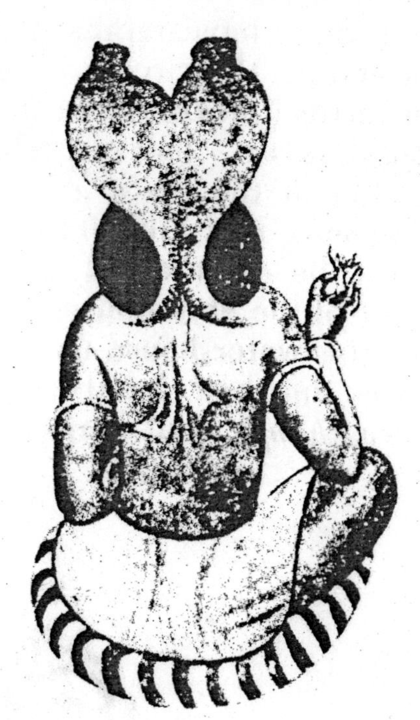

20. NÂGA, from Ajan*t*â, Cave II.

Yakshas (Pâli, Yakkhas) appear frequently in Bauddha legend and iconography, being usually enumerated as in the third rank of the secondary gods. Their king Kubera, Vai*s*rava*n*a or Alake*s*vara, is guardian of the north, and his capital is Alakâ or Alakamandâ. But the other three guardians were also styled Yakshas; and we find various individual Yakshas named, as—Alawaka, Sâtâgera, Bemâwata, Pûr*n*aka, Virû*d*aka, Gañgita, Suchiloma, Supavasa (Suprâv*r*isha), Nandaka, &c. They are always represented in human form. At Barâhat they appear as guardians or *dwârapâlas* at the gateways; at Nâsik also, one at the entrance of the Chaitya-cave is indicated in an inscription as a Yakkha, and the two figures by the door of Cave III bear the same character. At Barâhat, Yakshinîs also are figured on the pillars at the entrances, —as Chadâ (Chandâ) and Sudasava Yakkhinî.[1]

[1] Sp. Hardy, *Man. Budd*, pp. 58, 269, 265f., 271, 272n.; *Quest. of Milinda* (in *S. Bks. East*), vol. I, p. 152; Cunningham, *Bharhut*, pp. 19f.; Burgess, *Cave Temples*, pp. 268, 274, and pll. xx and xxv.

The *Dulva* (xi. fol. 34*b*) gives us a sort of key to the frequent representation of Yakshas as *dwârapâlas*: Anâthapi*nd*ada asks the Buddha how the vihâra must be ornamented with paintings (or sculptures). The Buddha answers—"On the outside door you must have figured a Yaksha holding a club in his hand; in the vestibule, you must have represented a great miracle, the five divisions (of of beings) the circle of transmigration; in the courtyard, the series of births (*jâtakas*); on the door of the Buddha's special apartment (*gandhakûti*, 'hall of perfumes'),[1] a Yaksha holding a wreath in his hand; in the house of the attendants (or, of honour: *rim-gro*), bhikshus and sthaviras arranging the *dharma*; on the kitchen must be represented a Yaksha holding food in his hand; on the door of the storehouse, a Yaksha with an iron hook in his hand; on the water-house (well-house?), Nâgas with various ornamented vases in their hands; on the wash-house (or, steaming-house: *bsro-khang*), foul sprites or the different hells (*nârakas*); on the medicine-house, the Tathâgata tending the sick; on the privy, all that is dreadful in a cemetery; on the door of the lodging-house (? text effaced), a skeleton, bones, and a skull."[2]

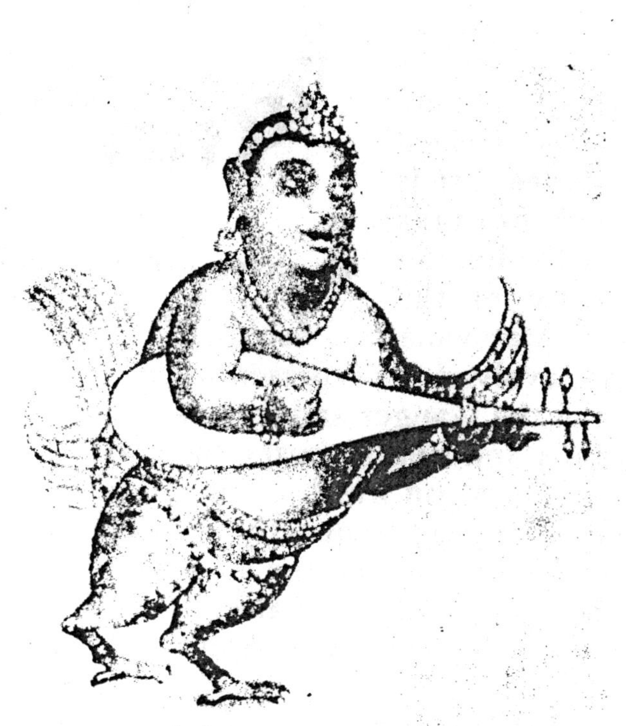

21. A GANDHARVA OR KINNARI.
From Ajantâ wall-paintings.

But if, in the representations of the Nâga, the human element predominates and so affords the principal factor in distinguishing them, the identification of the winged figures is more difficult. Winged animals occur in such numbers that it is impossible to provide them all with Indian names. A series of representations, however, stand out conspicuously from among those that are purely decorative.

Next to the human figures are the hybrid creatures with human busts, Indian head-dress and ornaments, represented so frequently

[1] Burnouf, *Introd.*, 2d. ed. p. 234; *Lotus*, p. 305; Childers. *Pali Dict.*, s v.; *Ind. Ant.* vol IX, pp. 142-3.

[2] From Rockhill's *Life of Buddha*, p. 48, note 2.

at Sâñchî. The lower part of the body is that of a bird on which the hips of the human form are set; the bushy tail, intended for that of a peacock, is treated decoratively. On the reliefs they appear flying from both sides towards the holy places,—stûpas, foot-prints, sacred trees, &c., and are hanging offerings upon these objects of worship—flowers, strings of beads, &c.—and thus frequently accompany the human worshippers (man and woman) of the under part of the relief: a well defined, oft-employed phrase, which occurs so frequently in the texts, corresponds to this—"gods and men there offered wreaths, &c." In this decorative form these winged creatures are still to be found in modern Brâhman art (Conf. ill. 15). They passed also into the Gandhâra school, but with marked differences. The antique Eros type has supplanted the early forms,—so that figures resembling the angels of Christians are found (conf. illus. Le Bon, *Les Civilizations de l'Inde*, p. 251; *Jour. Ind. Art and Indust.* vol. VIII, p. 74). The form occurring at Sâñchî (conf. ill. 4 and 17) and Barâhat is worthy of notice because its wings are really used, so that they are not simply attributes of speed.[1]

The positions assigned to these figures seem to agree best with the characters assigned to the fourth class of demigods—the Gandharvas (Pâli, Gandhabba)—the musicians of *S*akra, who join with their master to serve and worship Buddha.[2] Modern art, however, also represents the seventh class, known as Kinnaras and Kinnarîs, by the type above described, as the modern Siamese painting in fig. 23 shows. The two classes, in fact, have got mixed up or confounded.

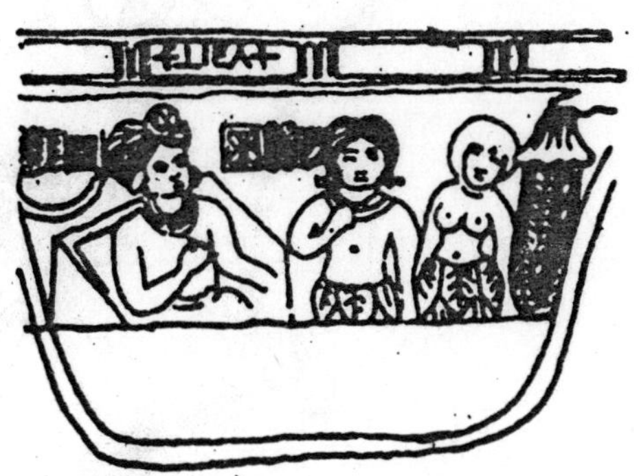

22. 'KINNARAJÂTAKA.' Cunningham, *Bharhut*, pl. xxvii, 5.

Notwithstanding the west Asian form of the wings, the type is a purely Indian one, and the time of its origin can hardly be fixed. As to the Siren form of representation of the Kinnarîs, there is a Barâhat relief which, if it were more distinct, might afford a sug-

[1] Cunningham, *Bharhut*, pl. xiii, 1, xxxi, 1.

[2] See Feer, *Avadâna-Sataka* (Ann. Mus. Guimet, t. XVIII), pp. 58, 77, 88; *Lalita Vistara*, passim. The Gandharvas or Gandharbas, in Brâhman mythology, belong also to the class of secondary gods, or attendants; this class includes—(1) Kinnaras, having a human body with the head of a horse,—musicians in the retinue of Kuvera; (2) Kimpurushas, with a human face and the body of a bird, are often confounded in later times with the Kinnaras and Gandharvas; (3) Gandharvas are similarly represented with a human bust on the body of a bird; their wives are the Apsarases, their chief Chitrarathà or Supriya, and they are the attendants of Dhritarâshtra (Dhataraṭṭha), guardian of the East; (4) Pannagas or Nâgas; (5) Siddhas, who fly in the air and can appear anywhere in a moment; (6) Vidyâdharas, the celestial students, skilled in all knowledge; and besides these, the Yakshas, Râkshasas, &c. For some of these monstrosities, see Râjendralâl Mitra, *Buddha Gaya*, pll. xxxiii, xxxiv, xxxvi, xxxviii, xliv, xlv, and xlvii.

gestion (ill. 22). In it are a pair of such creatures so represented as to be seen only to the knees and who appear to be wearing leaves of trees round the body (*parna*: leaf and feather). These secondary deities, then, may have been originally represented in the costume of the aborigines of India, which, by borrowing from the antique, resulted in the siren type.

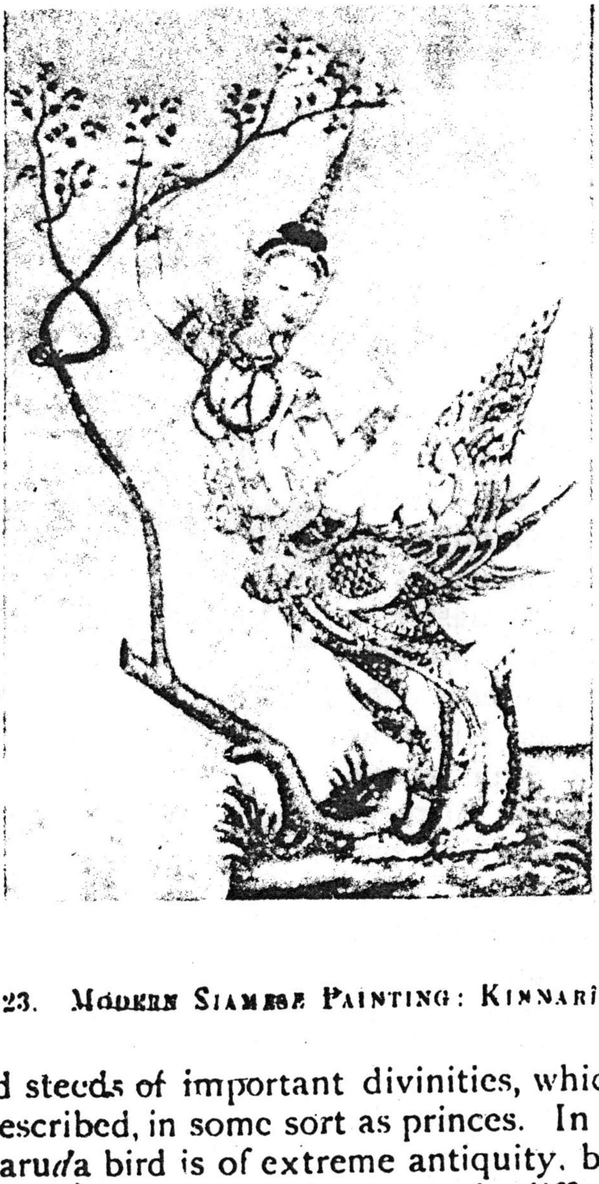

23. MODERN SIAMESE PAINTING: KINNARÎ.

The names *deva*, *devatâ*, 'divinity,' but in the sense of 'angel,' will suffice generally to designate this whole class of gods, which is apparently unlimited. The type is still retained in Japanese art, as fig. 24 shows.

Another type, the development of which may to some extent be observed in the sculpture at Sâñchî, is nearly allied in its form to these demigods. These are the sixth class or Garu*d*as, the winged steeds of important divinities, which appear among those thus described, in some sort as princes. In India the representation of a Garu*d*a bird is of extreme antiquity, but a systematic account of this mythical creature is extremely difficult; only what is certain and of value for the explanation of Buddhist sculptures need be mentioned. The Indian popular belief recognizes the Garu*d*a or Supar*n*a (Pâli: Garu*l*a and Supa*nn*a) as the king of birds; he is the deadly enemy of the snakes, the Nâgas described above, which he kills and injures when he can. A kind of vulture, called Garu*da*, and living on snakes, can hardly form the foundation of the ancient allegory: possibly it is of Irânian origin, related to the legends of the Simurg. From the myth, various birds have come to be called Garu*d*as in different districts.[1] How this representation is connected with the Vedic one, which recognizes a solar-being (!) Garutmant, has no bearing upon our purpose. Only this, perhaps—in the Buddhist *sútras* (*Játakas*) the antagonism of the Garu*d*a, Nâgântaka, or Târkshya, to the snake plays a prominent part.[2]

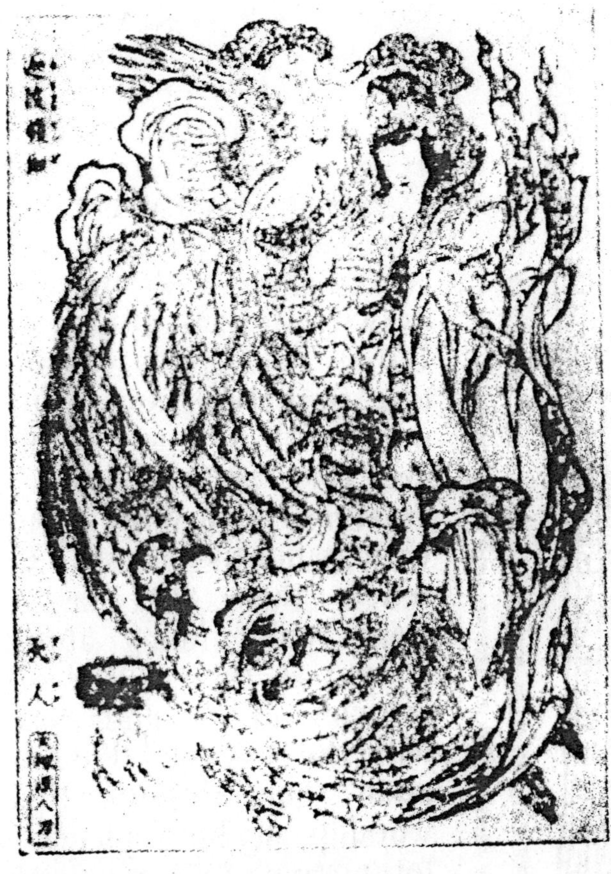

24. THE GODDESSES KARIÔBINGA AND TEN-NIN. From a Japanese woodcut.

In some places, according to the popular belief, the Garu*d*a, Supar*n*a, or Târkshya, is represented, like the Nâga, as also possessing the faculty of assuming human form. Buddha, or one of his disciples, is shewn making peace between the two creatures, and we find both at the feet of the Sage imploring better incarnations.

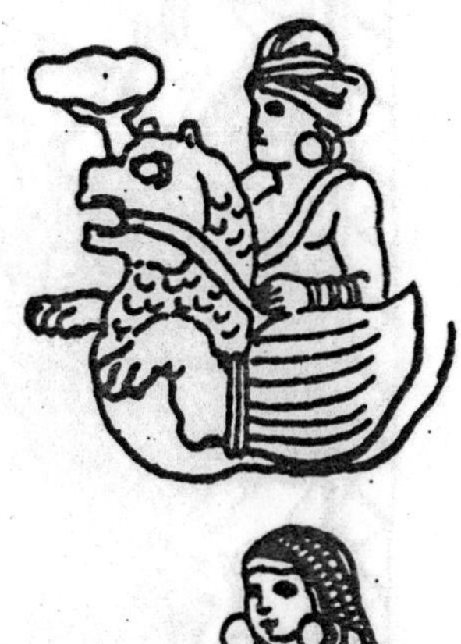

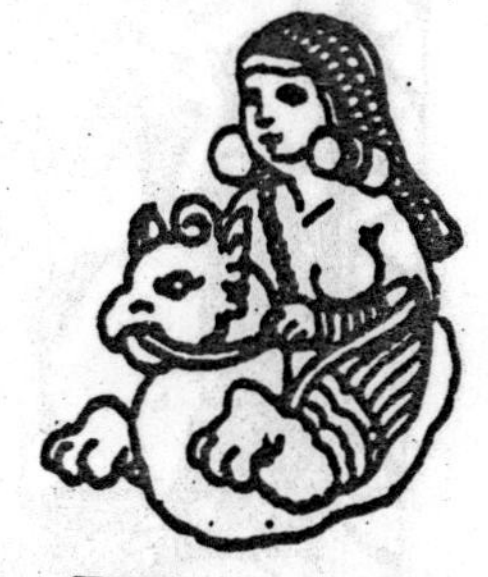

25. DEITIES RIDING ON GARUDAS. From a relief at Sâñchî.

On the relief from the east gateway at Sâñchî, given in fig. 26, the

[1] In S. India the *Falco pondischerianus* or red Brâhmani kite, which is a sort of dwarfish fishing eagle, but not probably a destroyer of snakes. Garu*d*a seems to be chiefly applied in the S. Marâ*th*a country to *Circaetus Gallicus*, a widely distributed and conspicuous bird, and certainly a snake-eating eagle. In Kanara the name is also given to the Great Hornbill (*Dichoceros bicornis*), of remarkable appearance, and which eats snakes occasionally. See Jerdon, vol. I, p. 77.

[2] For the Vedic, Epic, and other legends and allusions,—see De Gubernatis, *Zoological Mythology*, vol. II, pp. 180-195. The Buddhist drama, ascribed to king *S*ri-Harshadeva, on the deliverance from Garu*d*a, of *S*ankhachûda of the Nâga race, has been translated into English by Mr. Palmer Boyd (1872), and into French by M. Abel Bergaigne (1879).

animal kingdom is represented adoring the holy fig tree. In the corner, beside a five-headed snake, evidently the king of the Nâgas, stands a large bird with ear-ornaments and big bushy tuft, represented on the whole like a great parrot, and thus a purely Indian type, while his wings again show the artificial forms of west Asian art. This is assuredly the Garu*d*a, with the Nâga, whose mortal enemy he is. This parrot-like creature has scarcely had any successors in Indian art, but it is clearly the ancient national representation. Now, on the same relief, along with the splendidly drawn Indian animal realm—Indian buffaloes, extraordinarily true to nature, and, depicted almost with a touch of humour—are very artificial lions, leonine creatures with dogs' heads, lions with griffin-like heads. On other reliefs these last creations of west Asian fancy appear with wings, as represented above, as vehicles of the gods who, along with the so-called Kinnaras, ride upon them through the air to worship at holy places. It is interesting to notice that the artificial-like wings of west Asian art again appear here. Evidently it is the Indian feeling for Nature that reanimates these appendages that had been stiffened into a symbol. From these last-named forms the Garu*d*a was afterwards developed, as the Gryps, Gryphus or griffin, was in Greece.

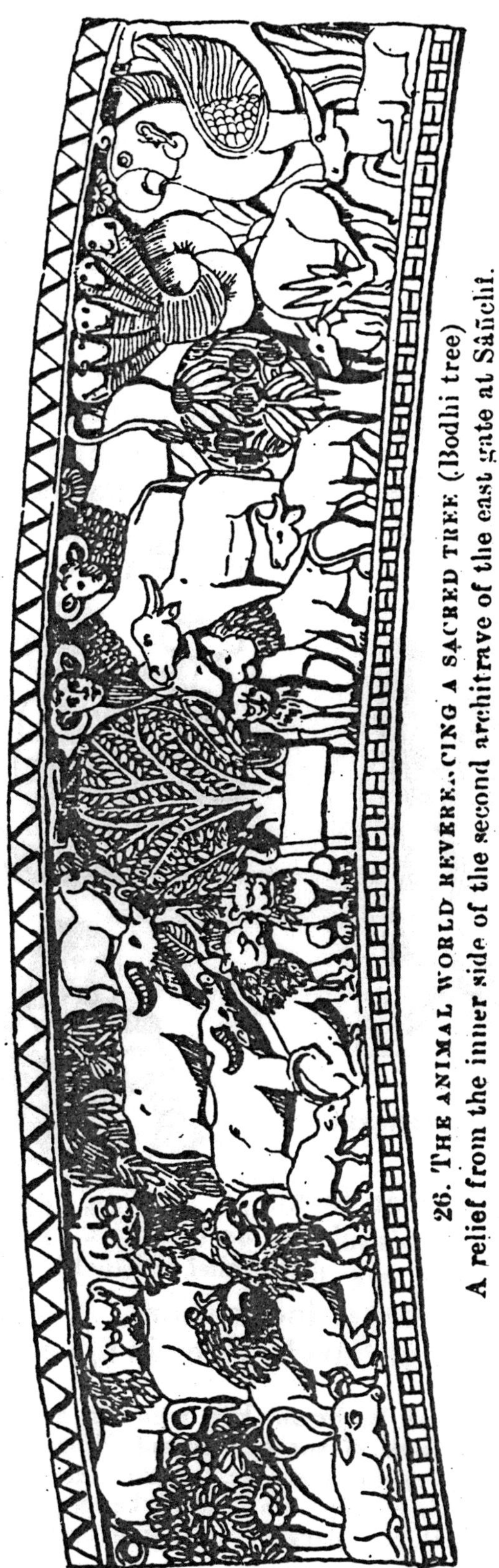

26. THE ANIMAL WORLD REVERENCING A SACRED TREE (Bodhi tree)
A relief from the inner side of the second architrave of the east gate at Sâñchî.

But the man who composed the sculpture shown in ill. 26 saw other things. In the middle of the relief we find oxen with human faces, long pointed beards and finely twisted manes, every lock of which is represented according to rule; these are derivatives of the Assyrian cherubs. They are still more like the ancient Greek river-gods. If this idea is the correct one, they serve to indicate locality and belong properly to the same category with the buffaloes always wallowing in the water. Another explanation seems more correct; a few words on this will follow in another connection.

The picture affords a new and interesting parallel with the Greek griffin in the dog-headed lions on the left side above the griffin itself. This representation reminds one of the treasure-guarding griffins of Ktesias, which I think have been correctly identified by Ball with the great shaggy Tibetan dogs: they are the prototype of the so-called Corean dog.

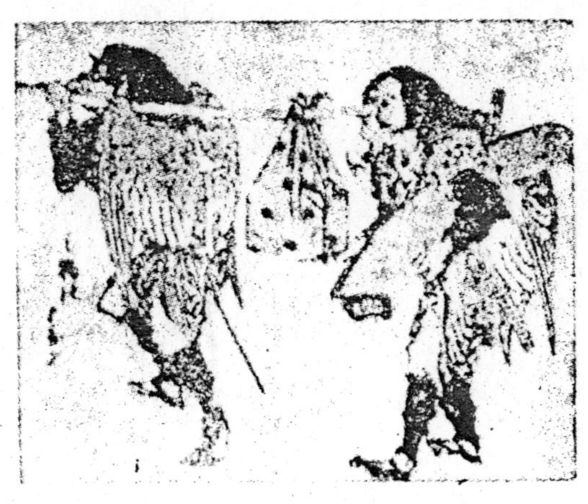

27. JAPANESE TEN-GUS (Garu*d*as). From a woodcut by Hokusai.

The relief in fig. 26 contains at any rate a series of variations upon one theme—the representation of the Garu*d*a, for which—in a groping way—foreign types have been introduced, the names of which perhaps sounded like the Indian word. The native parrot type on the one hand, the west Asian

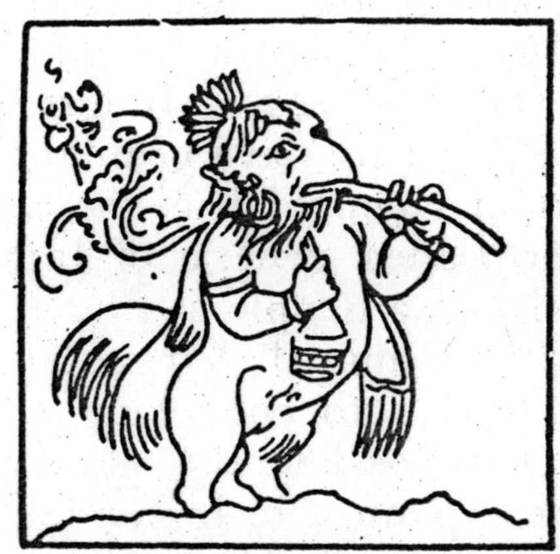

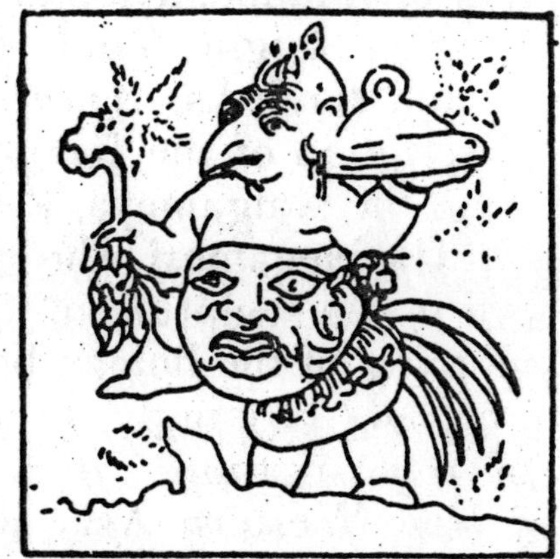

28. GARUDA FIGURES, from Aja*nt*â paintings, Cave 17.

griffin on the other, are the bases upon which more modern iconography developed its Garu*d*a.

The griffin type was retained in Buddhist art, but it soon received (when?) human arms: indeed the human element was sometimes even more prominent. Modern Brâhma*n*a art makes of it a winged man with a beak, and the Chinese form resembles it. There the Garu*d*a (Thien-kou, celestial dog) appears as a winged man, though the head generally, and the feet always, remain animal (ill. 29). The Japanese prefer to represent their Ten-gus (Garu*d*a) as fabulous animals, and two types are employed—one more animal and the other almost human (conf fig. 27). The way in which the Japanese contrive to vary these hybrid creatures, for the purposes of ritual and caricature, manifests a masterly observation of the grotesque-comic, as well as of the weird elements of animal nature. Good examples of purely human Garu*d*as with wings and demoniac expression of countenance are to be seen in the British Museum sculptures from Jamâlgarhi (conf. *Jour. Ind. Art and Indust.*, vol. VIII, pl. xxvi, or sep. ed. p. 18 and pl. xxiv). In modern Nepalese temples, two figures of Garu*d*a form the distinguishing supporters of Amoghasiddha, the fifth Dhyâni Buddha, who, like the Jaina Pâr*s*vanâtha, is depicted with a seven-headed snake as a canopy or nimbus. And in the shrines Garu*d*a is often represented with a serpent in his beak and a Nâgakanyâ in each claw.

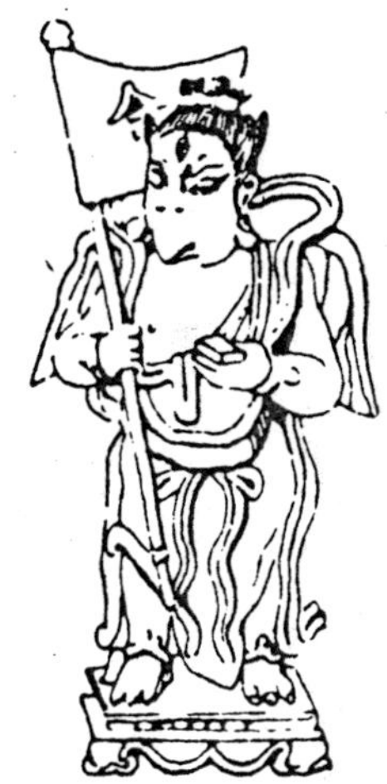

29. Thien-kou: Garu*d*a, modern Chinese bronze.

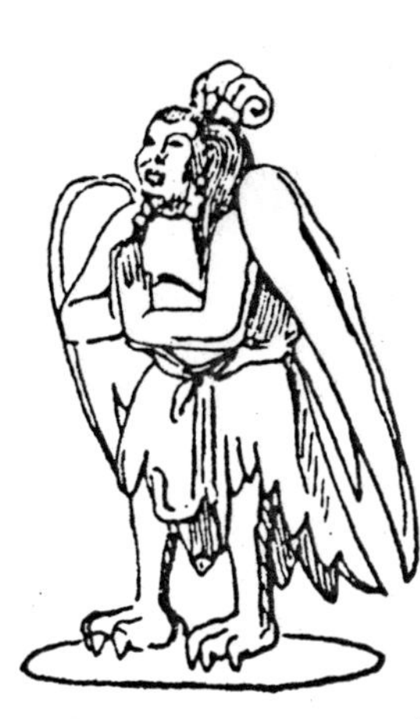

30. Khyung: Garu*d*a, Lamaist gilt bronze.

Such are the types to which names can be given among the subordinate gods in the art of the A*s*oka period, with their offshoots in modern miniature art. The horse-headed female figure on the A*s*oka railing at Buddhagayâ stands almost alone and is no doubt of purely Indian origin (conf. Râjendralâl Mitra, *Buddhagayâ*, pl. xxxiv. 2, and Griffiths, *Ajantâ*, vol. II, pl. 142). It agrees with the usual description of the Kinnaras; and we have goat and ram-headed beings in Naigameya, a sort of companion of the war-god Skanda; in Hari*n*egame*s*î, the deer-headed general of Indra; in Daksha, and in the sculpture in the Kailâsa temple at Elura[1].

The combining of the human body with animal elements seems to have been brought gropingly, so to speak, into connexion with the doctrine of reincarnation. It is not impossible that these types, introduced from Western Asia, were explained in Indian fashion—*i.e.*, in each degree of animal existence was hidden a human one which would be attained by good works, and which might then lead to deliverance. It is curious that Chino-Japanese tradition assigns to the centaur-like art-forms the name of Tiryagyonis[2] as the representatives of quadrupeds within the transmigratory gradation. It is thus not impossible that the centaur represented on the A*s*oka rail-

[1] *Epig. Ind.*, vol. II, p. 314, and pl. ii.; *Trans. R. As. Soc.*, vol. II, p. 326, and pl. i; Muir, *Or. Sansk. Texts*, vol. IV, pp. 381, 391; Wilson, *Vishnu Purâna* (Hall's ed.), vol. I, p. 132n; Wilkins, *Hindu Mythology*, p. 309.

[2] Centaur-like figures as representations of the Tiryagyonigatas (Jap. *Chiku-shô*) are found in the section on 'Buddhist effigies' in the Japanese work *Gwa-zen*, i.e. 'Picture creel,' of Hayashi Moriatsu, A.D. 1721, containing instructions for drawings and paintings, with many roughly drawn but strongly characteristic examples. The male and female Centaurs are, in Japanese fashion, distinguished by their coiffure.—Dr. F. W. K. Müller.

ing at Gayâ, and hybrid forms thereto related, simply represent such transmigratory phases. The other emblems depicted on the Gayâ railing and the oxen with men's heads in fig. 26, already mentioned, perhaps also belong to this category.

It has been stated that the Indian feeling for nature animated afresh even the fantastic forms of the western Asiatic hybrid style. A curious example of the way in which even animal forms when used decoratively were regarded as living animals may be here cited as it well illustrates the Indian character and shows off their childishly naïve and invariably humorous disposition. When speaking of the wood-carving style, we have already noticed the chairs and throne-backs in which such interesting early forms have been preserved; but along with these, as illus. 8 shows, west Asian (Persian) winged animals have been introduced among the accessory figures. The rampant lions in the corners of the back of the throne, with or without wings, continue from that time a favourite motif for the ornamentation of pillars and columns of every description. Elephants are worked from the projecting cross-pieces which are ornamented with dragons' heads, and under the rampant lion a new form, the Makara—about which we must say a few words. On the specimen from Amarâvatî (fig. 8) little human figures appear on the side pieces also. We must doubtless imagine as similar the throne of king Vikramâditya, of which the legend tells. and whose little carved figures even relate stories.[1] A fragment of a throne, fig. 31, from the ruins of Nâlanda, shows the animals still more artificially: the old Indian dragons' heads, which remind one of German forms, have entirely disappeared; and instead appears the elephant. In the mediæval style of Drâvi*d*a (S. India, Mâdura, &c.) these pillar forms have been adapted to native conceptions, *i.e.* hunting scenes of the Ku*r*umbars and the like, and have been further developed in a highly grotesque fashion.

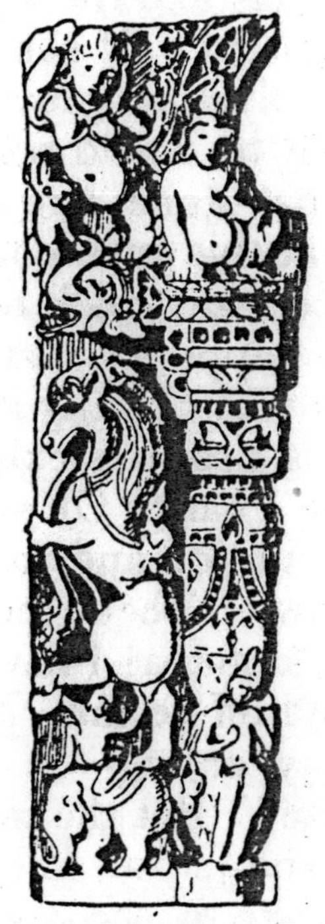

31. FRAGMENT OF A THRONE, from the ruins of Nâlanda. (Conf. Nrs. 8, 32).

The absurd story of the *Sabbadâtha-jâtaka* shows that the popular Indian mind regarded these animal figures as real animals standing one upon the other. Even though the fable only makes sport of such art creations, it is sufficiently clear from it how far the Hindu by himself was from inventing such compositions, and how, on the contrary, his own feeling led him to again reduce these overloaded foreign forms. The story, which is interesting in more ways than one, may be given here from Mr. Rouse's translation in Prof. Cowell's edition.[2]

[1] Conf. on this B. Jülg, *Mongolische Maerchensammlung Siddhikür und Ardschi Bordschi Chan*, Innsbruck 1868, xi ff.

[2] Fausböll, *The Jâtaka together with its Commentary*, vol. II, p. 243; Cowell's English version, vol. II, translated by W. H. D. Rouse, pp. 168ff.

"*As the haughty Jackal, &c.*" This story the Master told while staying in the Ve*l*uvana, about Devadatta. Devadatta, having won favour in the eyes of Ajâtasattu, yet could not make the repute and support which he received last any time. Ever since they saw the miracle done when Nâlâgiri[1] was sent against him, the reputation and allowances of Devadatta began to fall off. So one day, the brethren were all talking about it in the Hall of Truth: 'Venerable brother, Devadatta managed to get reputation and support, yet could not long keep it up.' And the Master came to them with the question: 'What story, O monks, do ye sit and discuss?' and when they had told him, he said: 'Not only now has Devadatta thrown away all chance of benefits: this happened in olden days in just the same way.' And then he told them an old-world tale:

"Once upon a time, when Brâhmadatta was king of Bârâ*n*asi, the Bodhisattva[2] was his house-priest, and he had mastered the three Vedas and the eighteen branches of knowledge. He knew the spell entitled 'Of subduing the World.' (Now this spell is one which involves religious meditation). One day the Bodhisattva thought that he would recite this spell; so he sat down in a place apart upon a flat stone, and there went through his reciting of it. It is said that this spell could be taught to no one without use of a special rite; for which reason he recited it in the place just described. It so happened that a jackal lying in a hole heard the spell at the time he was reciting it, and got it by heart. We are told that this jackal in a previous existence had been some Brâhma*n*a, who had learned the charm 'Of subduing the World.' The Bodhisattva ended his recitation and rose up, saying—'Surely I have that spell by heart now.' Then the jackal arose out of his hole and cried—'Ho Brâhma*n*a! I have learnt the spell better than you know it yourself!' and off he ran. The Bodhisattva set off in chase, and followed some way, crying—'Yon jackal will do a great mischief—catch him, catch him!' But the jackal got clear off into the forest. The jackal found a she-jackal, and gave her a little nip upon the body. 'What is it, master?' she asked. 'Do you know me,' he asked, 'or do you not?' 'I do[3] know you.' He repeated the spell, and thus had under his orders several hundreds of jackals, and gathered round him all the elephants and horses, lions and tigers, boars and deer, and all other four-footed creatures; and he became their king under the title of Sabbadâ*th*a,[4] and a she-jackal he made his consort. On the backs of two elephants stood a lion, and on the lion's back sat Sabbadâ*th*a,

[1] A great elephant, which, at Devadatta's instigation, was let loose for the purpose of destroying the Buddha, but which only did him reverence; "non facit hoc jussus nulloque docente magistro: crede mihi, nostrum sensit et ille deum." Hardy, *Manual of Buddhism*, p. 331; *Milindapañha*, iv, 4 (Sac. Bks. of the East), vol. i, p. 288.

[2] Buddha in a previous existence.

[3] Reading *âjânâmi*.

[4] The name signifies 'All-tusk,' 'All-biting.' Sansk. Sarvadam*sh*tra: a play on the word *Sabbaraththa*, Sansk. Savarâ*sh*tra—'All-ruling.'

the jackal king, along with his consort the she-jackal, and great honour was paid to them. Now the jackal was tempted by his great honour and became puffed up with pride, and he resolved to capture the kingdom of Bârâ*n*asî. So with all the four-footed creatures in his train, he came to a place near to Bârâ*n*asî. His host covered twelve leagues of ground. From his position there he sent a message to the king. 'Give up your kingdom or fight for it.' The citizens of Bârâ*n*asî, smitten with terror, shut close their gates and stayed within. Then the Bodhisattva drew near the king and said to him, 'Fear not, mighty king! leave me the task of fighting with the jackal king Sabbadâ*th*a. Except me, no one is able to fight with him at all.' Thus he gave heart to the king and the citizens. 'I will ask him at once,' he went on, 'what he will do in order to take the city.' So he mounted the tower over one of the gates, and cried out—'Sabbadâ*th*a, what will you do to get possession of this realm?' 'I will cause the lions to roar, and with the roaring I will frighten the multitude: thus will I take it!' 'Oh! that's it,' thought the Bodhisattva, and down he came from the tower. He made proclamation by beat of drum that all the dwellers in the great city of Bârâ*n*asî, over all its twelve leagues, must stop up their ears with flour (dough). The multitude heard the command, they stopped up their own ears with flour, so that they could not hear each other speak—nay, they even did the same to their cats and other animals.

"Then the Bodhisattva went up a second time into the tower, and cried out, 'Sabbadâ*th*a!' 'What is it, Brâhma*n*a,' quoth he. 'How will you take this realm?' he asked. 'I will cause the lions to roar, and I will frighten the people and destroy them, thus will I take it!' he said. 'You will not be able to make the lions roar; these noble lions, with their tawny paws and shaggy manes, will never do the bidding of an old jackal like you!' The jackal, stubborn with pride, answered, 'Not only will the other lions obey me, but I'll even make this one, upon whose back I sit, roar alone!' 'Very well,' said the Bodhisattva, 'do it, if you can.' So he tapped with his foot on the lion, which he sat upon, to roar, and the lion resting his mouth upon the elephant's temple, roared thrice, without any manner of doubt. The elephants were terrified and dropped the jackal down at their feet; they trampled upon his head and crushed it to atoms. Then and there Sabbadâ*th*a perished. And the elephants, hearing the roar of the lion, were frightened to death, and wounding one another, they all perished there. The rest of the creatures, deer and boars, down to the hares and cats, perished then and there, all except the lions; and these ran off and took to the woods. There was a heap of carcases covering the ground for twelve leagues. The Bodhisattva came down from the tower, and had the gates of the city thrown open. By beat of drum he caused proclamation to be made throughout the city: 'Let all the people take the flour (dough) out of their ears, and they that desire meat, meat let them take!' And the people all ate what meat they could, fresh; and the rest they dried and preserved. It was at this time, according to tradition, that people first began to dry meat."

"The Master having finished this discourse, identified the Birth by the following verses, full of divine wisdom:—

"Even as the jackal stiff with pride,
Craved for a mighty host on every side,
And all toothed creatures came
Flocking around, until he won great fame:

Even so the man who is supplied
With a great host of men on every side,
As great renown has he
As had the Jackal in his sovranty.

"In those days Devadatta was the Jackal, Ananda was the king, and I was the chaplain."

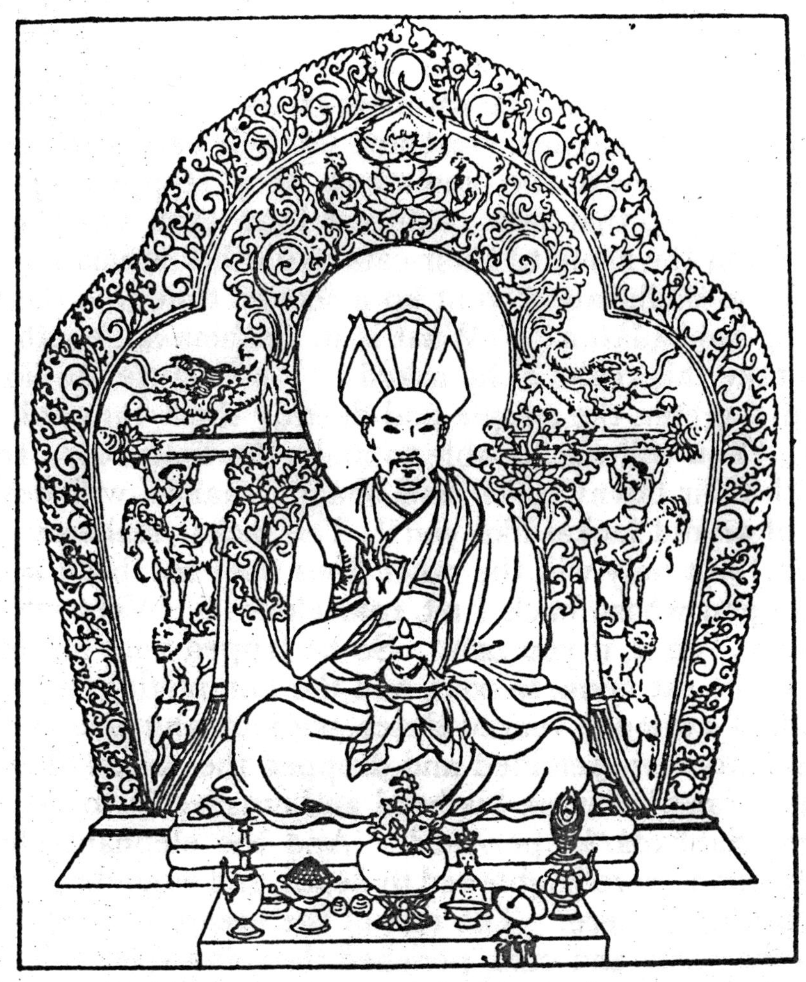

32. Changcha-Hutuktu Lalitavajra.

For the ornamentation of the throne compare ill. 8 and 31.
From a miniature on silk, 18th century.

It is clear that a throne like the one shown in figs. 31 or 32 was in the mind of the narrator of the *Jâtaka*. The ancient Oriental idea of imagining the subject, the vanquished, as lying under the feet of his conqueror, is interesting here. But this motif also originated in western Asia, where, in Assyrian reliefs for example, upright figures of gods are clumsily placed on the backs of animals, like one hieroglyph upon the other, without the slightest attempt at appropriateness. The Indian love for nature, which was only too strongly developed, gives a burlesque interpretation to the idea. The throne-seats with ornaments, just described, have been preserved even in the latest Lamaist ecclesiastical style of Tibet and China. Ill. 32 represents the throne of a Lamaic ecclesiastical prince; the original is found in a splendid work painted on silk, dating from about the middle of last century, and containing the genealogy of the so-called Changcha Hutuktu of Pekin. The holy man sits on a throne, the back of which consists of two elephants, with two lions above them, and two goats with riders above these again; higher up still are seen two elephants apparently running downwards, and in the middle a Garuḍa and Nâgas. All these are the decorative elements of ancient wooden doors and throne-backs loosely superposed on one another.

The sea-elephant, Makara, a creature formed of the forepart of an elephant with the body and tail of a fish, appears even on the reliefs of the Asoka railing at Buddhagayâ, along with winged elephants and hippocampi,[1] &c. It has been retained everywhere in Indian art, though later the fish-tail was made into an ornament. When, later still, it became the ensign of Kâma, the Indian god of love, it was due, as has long been recognised, to Greek influence: the dolphin of Aphrodite supplied the model.

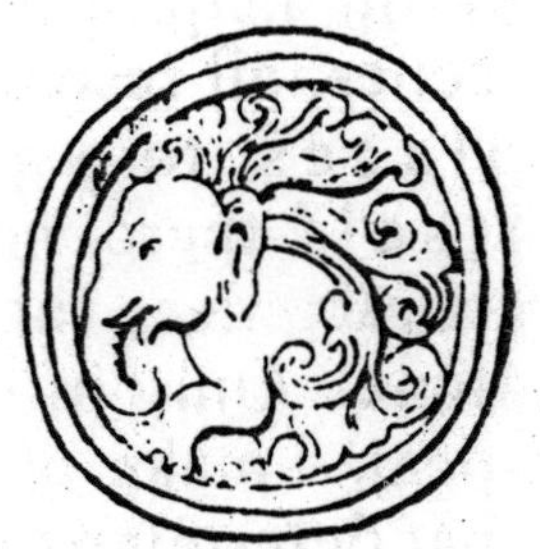

33. **Makara.** From the pattern on the dress of the old Javanese Mañjuśrî.

All the Greek elements found within the Asoka period, even counting the Sâñchî monuments, follow throughout, as it were, in the steps of the west Asiatic forms. Altogether there are not many: representations of centaurs, and water-gods (oxen with human faces). Of more importance is the question whether the thunderbolt as an attribute of gods, was introduced by Greek influence, or whether the streaming sheaf of lightning-flashes of the Babylonian-Assyrian gods should be considered as the model; though the former seems to me the most probable, no certain proof is forthcoming. This must depend on the date of its introduction and the extent of the western influence at the time.

I cannot here enter upon the subject of the representation of the dwarfish creatures, which are regarded sometimes as real human dwarfs and sometimes as evidently demi-gods, nor upon so much that is connected therewith. But I would like to point out that the

[1] Râjendralâl Mitra, *Buddha Gayâ*, pl. xlvi; Cunningham, *Mahâbodhi*, pl. ix, 15; another as a pillar ornament, Burgess, *Cave Temples*, pl. xvi, 6.

type is the same as that of the antique pigmies. (Conf. above, p. 34). It is interesting to observe that the account of the pigmies, like that referred to on p. 49 of the griffins of the west, is given us by Ktesias,[1] who was physician to the Persian king Artaxerxes Mnemon (405-362 B.C.).

This concludes the series of the types found in older Buddhist art. The question now is, how the composition is to be executed. The form of composition, with which every art begins, is the pure narrative. In what follows we shall try to discover how far the art of the Asoka period (including Sâñchî) represented this narrative tendency, and how the national character made itself felt thereby.

On the reliefs of the great gateways of Sâñchi is a series of representations of different kinds. Many are purely decorative, others represent perfectly definite historical events. Very few have, as yet, been fully explained, and for those that have been correctly explained, the convincing proof is not yet forthcoming; but they may be divided into two distinc categories. The first category, by the help of numerous figures in a series of formally composed scenes, all resembling one another, depicts—processions to holy places, to sacred trees, to stûpas, etc. On the panel itself there nowhere appears an indication which sufficiently characterizes the incident to enable us to determine it from itself alone. Only inscriptions, like those found at Barâhat, could—so to speak—make of those incidents historical events. The elements that determine the incidents are solely external, as we shall see below. Along with the representations of human beings (of which those seen in illus. 4 and 17 are, as it were, conventional abridgements), we meet with others in which forms of existence other than human come to worship at the holy places. Here, again, a national Indian element makes itself felt—the fondness for the repetition of ritualistic phrases, which thereby become more sacred and efficacious.

The animal world, again, shares also in the worship of the sacred places. Along with animal-representations, that are uncommonly true to life, come in throngs the monsters of mythology, to adore the places where a saint has lived, in order to obtain a better incarnation. The juxtaposition of mythical and real animals has a highly startling effect: it looks as if the uncommonly animated and characteristically represented animal world was intended to impart a greater probability of existence to the fantastic creatures of very varied styles depicted beside them. While the latter, the Tiryagyoni-type, Garu*d*a, etc., stand stiffly in rows (conf. illus. 26), the life of the real animals makes itself felt; alongside a Garu*d*a, adorned with earrings and carrying a lotus-flower, an antelope (*cervi capra*—Indian gazelle or spotted antelope, Skt K*r*ish*n*asara), in a curious position, is trimming itself. The religious act—in a truly Indian fashion—becomes a Nature-scene.

[1] Lassen, *Ind. Alterthumskunde*, Bd. II, Ss. 644. 661; *Ind Ant.*, vol. X pp. 229-331

If, owing to the objects represented, this change appears a very natural one, neither is it lacking in the representations of human beings. Ill. 34 shows the end of a long procession leaving a thickly peopled city. The gate of the city is of the same form as the gates of Sâñchî, though much simpler; the great volute looks almost like the rolled-up tongue of a dragon; the houses of the town are provided with open galleries, from which the inhabitants (men and

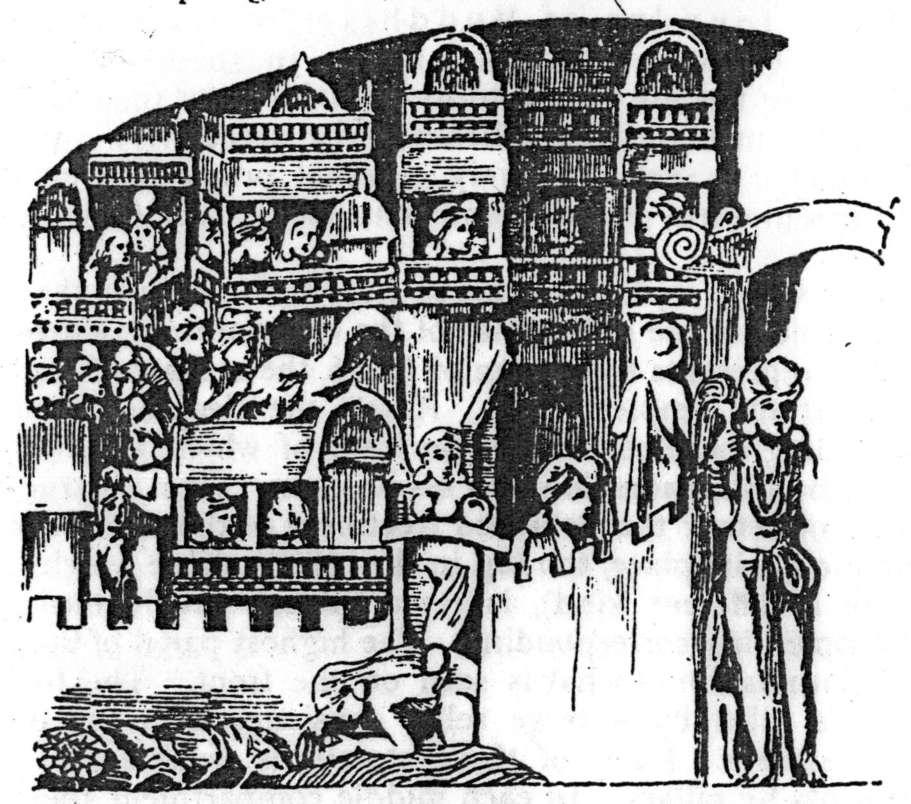

34. Representation of a city.
From the second architrave of the east gateway of the great stûpa at Sâñchî.

women) look down. This looking down from house-terraces is an element that became frequent in Greek art—very late, it is true—for the animation of the background; it belongs essentially to the old Indian art, which owes this form to the representation of towns in west Asian art. It forms a part of the composition—the rejoicing of the inhabitants of the town, who are witnessing the procession, is thus presented, exactly as ancient and modern Indian texts—and the Chinese pilgrims also—describe such feasts. The separation into little groups, each of which has its own interest, also begins here. The Indian character cannot endure the stiffly historic, and breaks up the whole into a series of genre-scenes.

The thickly-peopled terraces are the models of the superimposed storeys of the different heavens in the Buddhist universe.

A genre-scene in ill. 34, which has nothing to do with the main incident, shows a woman who has come through a postern in the city wall to fill her lôtâ with water from a pool. In the pool are growing water-lilies in flower; a second woman comes down the same street to the pool, and this figure is made so large that the gate lintel passes right across her body like a paling. It is difficult to determine whether the elephant rider, or mahaut[1], coming along the street on an elephant, belongs to the end of the procession (conf. ill. 39), or is taking the elephant to the water; but the latter is more probable. I shall return to these narrative-reliefs again.

The second category represents scenes from the life of the founder of Buddhism, or from his previous existences, the Jâtakas. In the case of these reliefs also, very few are satisfactorily explained, for the characteristic elements almost disappear beneath the accessories. We are therefore obliged to seek for purely external proofs (the arrangement of the sculptures on the monument itself); and the result is curious.

Few of the scenes represented are so clear and simple as the relief on the inner side of the right pillar of the east gateway, above. It undoubtedly represents the dream of Mâyâ, the mother of Buddha, in the briefest and simplest form. Above the sleeping woman is seen descending the elephant, in the form of which, according to the legend, Buddha came down to his mother. One is struck by the paucity of detail: the detached treatment of this really notable representation. Its place, too (up in the corner above a rich composition of a different kind), is remarkable. Involuntarily one seeks for something corresponding. The highest panel of the inner side is a continuation of what is seen on the front. The front of the pillar is filled by a large relief consisting of three double stages, *i.e.* storeys. Each of these storeys is divided into three compartments by pillars. In each middle compartment there sits a god with the thunderbolt and a round bottle as attributes. The space behind the god shows a second god, clearly subordinate, and 'daughters of the gods' with sunshades and whisks (Hind. *chaurî*). In these divisions there is always a group of dancing girls playing on instruments before the principal divinity. The background is filled up with fruit trees.

Ill. 1 shows the fourth storey, counting upwards. The two below it are much injured, but still it may be clearly seen that the representation of the second storey corresponded with those that have been preserved, while the lowest of all was filled with weeping and mourning figures seated in a circle. At the very top of the relief there is, on the roof, a group of gods and goddesses. Unfortunately, this group is also much injured. If this highest terrace, the roof of the whole structure, is not counted, one is naturally reminded of the six Devalokas, the six inferior heavens[2] of the gods. All six form the so-called Kâmâvachara heavens, the

[1] Hind. *Mahâwat*, Sansk. *Mahâmâtra*; the German has *Kornak*, Fr. *Cornac*. See Yule and Burnell's *Glossary*, s.v.

[2] As to the heavens of the gods, the Kâmâvacharas and Suddhâvâsas (Tib. Gnas-*gtsan*-mai-lha)—an obscure expression—are attested at Barâhat by inscriptions. Conf. Hultzsch, *Zeit. d. Deut. Morg. Ges.*, Bd. XL, S. 65, Nrs. 47, 48, 49.

abodes of the gods in which desire is still potent. Now it was supposed that when a Bodhisattva, a pre-existent Buddha, attained the lowest heaven, great lamentations broke out among the gods, who feared the end of an earthly period. A thousand years afterwards the cries of the guardians of the world (Lokapâladevatâ—the gods of the lowest terrace) proclaim that in a thousand years a Buddha will be born upon the earth: the so-called Buddhahalâhalam. The gods of the lowest terrace are represented lamenting; the subject must, therefore, be the birth of a being who is to become a Buddha. The panel is thus the beginning of all the pillar reliefs, and is continued on the inner side of the same pillar. The heavens are to be named as follows, beginning from below: the heaven of the Chaturmahârâjika-gods, *i.e.* the four great kings or guardians of the world; the heaven of the Tâvati*m*sa-gods (Sk. Trayastri*ms*at), the so-called 'three and thirty' superior angels over whom Sakka presides; the heaven of the Yâmâs, where there is no change of day and night; the Tusita-heaven (San. Tushita), where all Bodhisattvas are born before appearing on earth, and where Maitreya now is; the heaven of the Nimmânarati (Sk. Nirmâ*n*arati), who create their own pleasures; and of the Paranimmitavasavattî-gods, who indulge in pleasures created for them by others, and over whom Mâra presides. These mighty terraces of the gods, mounting one above the other, over which again rise the meditative steps, belong to the grandest ideas which Buddhism has produced. The whole representation—this is not the place to examine it fully—with the ways of deliverance and the cataclysms which destroy whole worlds and put new creations in their place, had to be specially noticed here, for it is capable of affording us the necessary explanation of the representation on the other pillar (front side).

If we return to the reliefs which represent scenes from Buddha's life, we shall find that some of those on the left pillar of the east gateway are highly instructive as regards ancient Indian relief-composition. The first of them which is found on the middle of the inner side of the pillar (conf. ill. 35) has already been correctly identified, so far at least as determining the incident is concerned, although the naming of the individual figures may not be quite correct. Towards the bottom and to the right on the panel is seen a bearded man with bands of hai (*jatá*) twisted about his head turbanwise; the knees of the crouching figure are held together by a band. This man (from his costume, evidently a Brâhma*n*a doing penance) is seated on the threshold of a hut thatched with leaves. Before him is a pond with aquatic birds and shell-fish; lotus-flowers are in bloom upon the water. Buffaloes and an elephant come to quench their thirst. A bearded ascetic is bathing, another is drawing water, with which to sprinkle his body in the bath, in a vessel shaped like the *lótá*, which even at the present day answers this purpose. What has already been described is a rough representation (on a remarkably small space, though it is fairly broad) of a Tîrtha or bathing-place at a river flowing past a Brâhma*n*a hermitage. Higher up, in the middle of the relief, may be seen a temple-like house, before which a fire burns upon an altar; a second vessel containing fire lies further forward, with tongs and fuel; on the left side, approach unbearded figures carrying fuel; the ordinary occupations of the Brâhma*n*a-disciples are thus represented. A row of Brâhma*n*as stand round the temple in the attitude of adoration; the background is composed of fruit trees, on which monkeys are climbing. Towards the man sitting before the leaf-covered hut, comes another Brâhma*n*a from the right to announce what is going on in the fire-temple; in the middle of the temple sits a seven-hooded snake; flames burst forth from the windows in the roof.

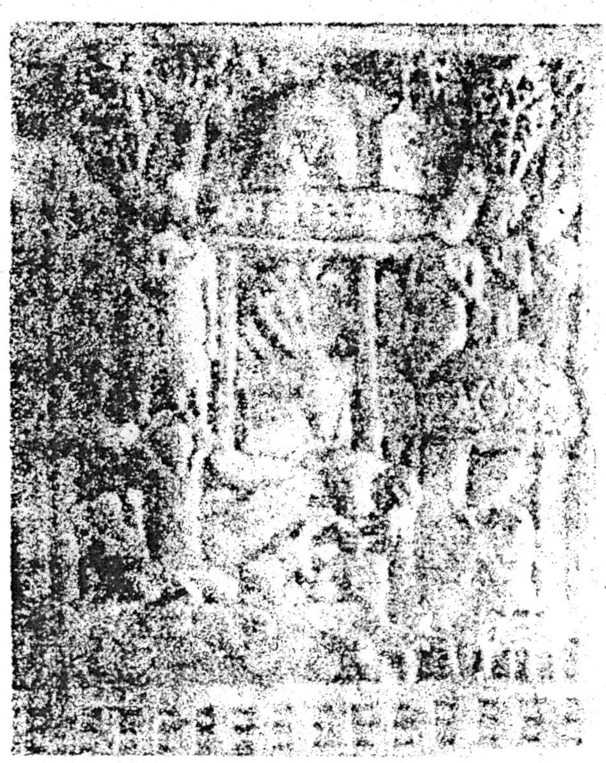

35. RELIEF OF THE EAST GATEWAY AT SÂNCHÎ.
Left pillar, middle of the inner side. The first scene of the conversion of Uruvilvâ-Kâ*s*yapa.

This relief represents a scene from the story of the conversion, at Buddha's hands, of Kâ*s*yapa (Pâli, Kassapa) of Uruvilvâ (Pâli, Uruvelâ), a Brâhma*n*a ascetic, with his brothers and disciples. The figure sitting before the hut is Kâ*s*yapa; to attempt to name the other Brâhma*n*as would be useless. The legend is somewhat to the following effect: When Buddha wished to lead all in the right way, he went to Uruvilvâ and begged for permission to dwell in the fire-hut. It was granted him; though Kâ*s*yapa warned him of a mighty snake that lived in the temple. Buddha caught it in his alms-bowl and sending forth flames of fire, which burst out at the roof, left the hut unharmed.[1]

In the main, the whole incident is well rendered on the relief,

[1] On the Kâ*s*yapa legend, conf. Fergusson, *Tree and Serp. Worsh.*, pp. 143f.; Beal, *Rom. Legend*, pp. 292f.; S. Hardy, *Man. of Bud.*, pp. 193f.; Bigandet, *Legend of Gautama*, vol. I, pp. 138f.; and Cunningham *Arch. Sur. Ind.*, vol. XI, pp. 149f.

though at the first glance there seems to be a great deal that is superfluous. The Brâhma*n*a disciples are not necessary to the representation of the incident; the Brâhma*n*a bathing is quite superfluous, and the one with the *lótá* just as unnecessary, unless one supposes—what seems hardly probable—that he is fetching water to extinguish the fire. In short, the whole prolix and idyllic representation of the pond is a superfluous accessory. But the main point is—Buddha himself is not present at all.

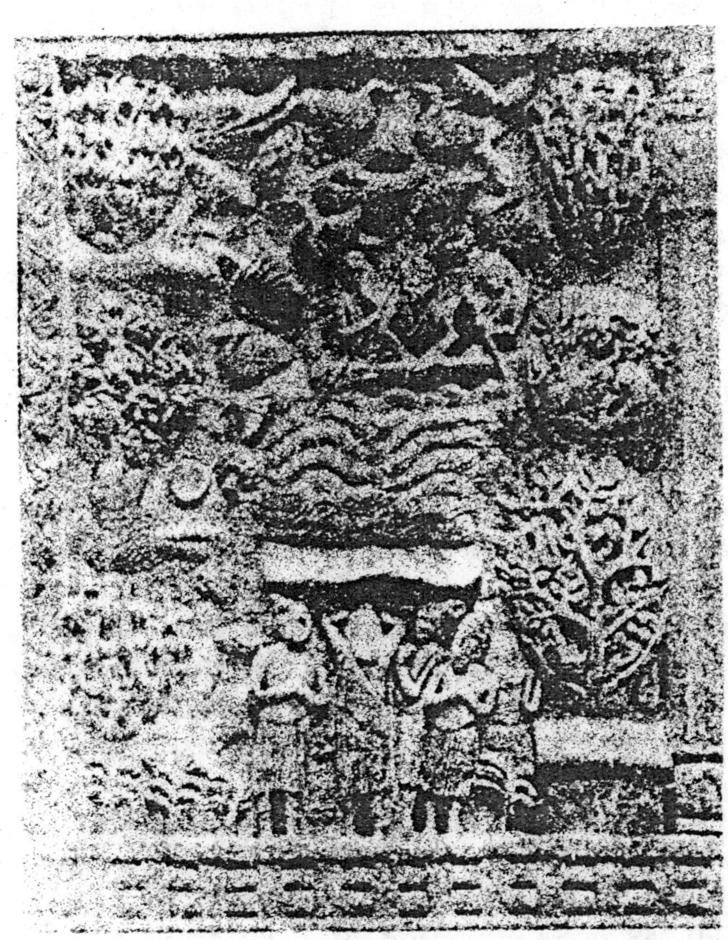

36. RELIEF FROM THE EAST GATEWAY AT SANCHÎ.
Left pillar, middle of the front side. The second scene in the Kásyapa legend.

More remarkable still is another and allied relief on the middl panel of the face of the left pillar (ill. 36). If one looks for nothin but the depicting of the situation, and puts aside any thought of representation of Buddha, the incident can be explained as on th previous relief. The locality is determined by six large fruit tree: to which, though roughly outlined, botanical names can neve theless be given. On one of these trees are perched two ape one occupied in plucking fruit. But the trees are standing in water; the surface of the water is full of animation; aquatic birds are swimming about upon it; one dips its head under; another, with neck bent backwards, is preening its wings; and a pelican is devouring a fish. The waves, on the relief itself, rise very high indeed over the outer lines of the fruit trees; lotus-flowers, with very animated-looking leaves that do not lie flat, appear on the water, and a snail is tossed about on the waves; above, in a corner, is seen an alligator. The water is thus in continual movement; the aquatic birds behave as if they had just gone into it. This must represent the overflowing of a river, or, at any rate, the flooding of a place planted with fruit trees.[1] In the middle of this landscape, three men are sailing in a boat. The one sitting in the middle is bearded, and his hair is twisted about his head turban-wise; he is therefore a Brâhma*n*a. A bearded man, like the former, and one without a beard but with long hair,—therefore Brâhma*n*as too,—are rowing in the boat, which is made of planks roughly joined together. This shape of boat is still in use in India, on the Madras coast and elsewhere.

Now among the miracles by which Gautama Buddha is said to have converted Uruvilvâ-Kâsyapa and his school, it is related that the river Nairañjanâ was very much swollen, and that Buddha passed over the flooded place as if there had been no water there. The amazed Kâsyapa followed him in a boat, but did not become his convert yet. The situation is thus broadly depicted here—but Buddha, the principal figure, is wanting.

On the lower part of the same relief, before a high stone plinth, are seen four men; behind them is a stone bench before a tree hung with votive offerings; it is therefore a second composition, which is connected with the former. The men, to judge from their dress, are Brâhma*n*as. The hands of the middle figure, which are raised over its head, as well as the peculiarly high placed heels of the feet (unfortunately, these are partly broken off), prove that the figure is conceived as lying full length on the ground: the touching of the ground with eight limbs (*ash*t*ânga*) is hereby intended. The flowers near the figure, seen from above, seem to indicate that it is to be regarded as in a recumbent attitude. Similarly, the slab of the altar in ill. 38 is represented as seen from above, so that the flower offerings on it are shown. The Brâhma*n*as standing beside the recumbent Brâhma*n*a in an attitude of prayer have upright growing plants beside them to indicate that they are standing upon the ground. On the cast in the Museums, behind the figure in the *ash*t*ânga*-position and below the projecting stone, no wavy line is to be seen, as on Col. Maisey's drawing (Fergusson's *Tree and Serp. Worship*, pl. xxxi, 2, p. 141). As the water which fills the middle ground is regarded as a surface seen from above, it thus happens that the background of the worshipping Brâhma*n*a is

[1] S. Beal, *Romantic Legend of Sakya Buddha*, pp. xi, note, and 302.

looked upon as a platform. But this platform, with its far-projecting edge, is, it appears, mentioned in the legend of the conversion of Kâ*s*yapa of Uruvilvâ. Buddha, as the story goes, found a hempen garment which he picked up and wanted to wash in the river. Sakka presented him with a flat stone for the purpose.

Now with these explanations, in which justice is done to all the figures represented, and the characteristic common to all of which is—that they only witness to Buddha's existence, but do not actually represent the sage himself, it is possible to connect a third relief belonging to the same cycle of legends.

Below the representation of the miracle of the snake, on the inner side of the pillar, is another relief (conf. ill. 37), the place of which on the pillar and the Brâhma*n*as represented therein, clearly characterize it as being connected therewith. In a wood, planted with fruit trees, three Brâhma*n*as are busy kindling sacrificial fires; a Brâhma*n*a disciple is bringing wood for fuel; a second carries a pole (H. *bahangi*, S. *vihangikâ*) supporting vessels in a network.

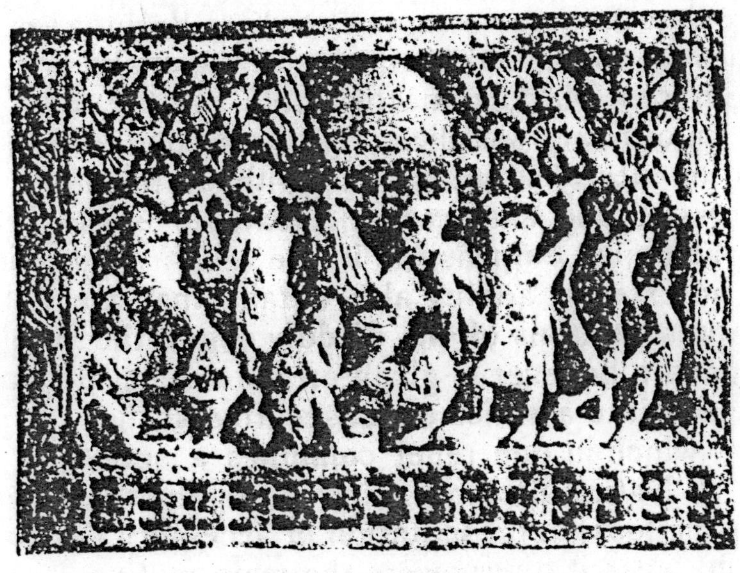

37. Relief on the east gateway at Sânchi.
Left pillar, inner side, under relief No. 35.

Two other bearded Brâhma*n*as are splitting wood with heavy (stone?) hatchets. A round hive-like building decorated with shells and enclosed by a railing forms the background. Whether this building, as I am inclined to think, represents merely a hermit's hut thus railed in as a protection from wild beasts, or something else is uncertain. The whole is a genre picture, and without the reliefs explained above, it would be impossible to determine its nature, so far as the persons and the occasion of the sacrifice are concerned.

The legend of Kâ*s*yapa's conversion relates that, after the miracle of the snake, a sacrifice was offered. When the Brâhma*n*as tried to light a fire the wood, owing to Gautama's power, would not burn. They made their trouble known to Kâ*s*yapa, who entreated Gautama to let the fire kindle. When Gautama gave his consent the wood took fire, and there was nothing to prevent the sacrifice.

Now these three reliefs give one a good insight into the relief-composition of ancient India. It stands on a level with that of the Middle Ages in the Western world. The same legend is continued on one relief; the same figures may therefore be repeated on the same panel. Land and water are always represented as extending horizontally; in consequence of this, the figures are of the same size throughout. The limits of land and water are indicated by sharply defined outlines; flowers and plants are employed to determine whether the figures represented are supposed to be lying or standing. Along with this may be noticed a naïve aptitude for converting the area into a landscape in which the principal groups occupy the centre. External details alone explain the incident depicted. Thus the only certain determining factor to explain the three panels examined above is the circumstance that the persons represented are Brâhma*n*as. Then the first relief may be explained by means of the snake and the flames bursting from the window in the roof; all the rest represents nothing but an ordinary sacrifice, and the second, or even the third panel, would be utterly unintelligible without the first. One way of laying stress on the characteristic features is the decided prominence of the object emphasized in the relief. The reliefs narrate the incident in extenso, adding also details that are not essential. As in the representations of the Middle Ages, the whole story of the sufferings of a believer is given on one relief or one picture, which is divided into a series of consecutive scenes: so is it in the Buddhist art, which in one relief combines a series of continuous events into a Nature-picture. Now the admirable rendering of nature, with the loose representation of accessory details, is apt to lead astray, because it overpowers the main motive.

Something exactly analogous occurs in Indian literature, especially in the so-called *Kávyas* and the half-epic, half-lyric works related to them. The treatment itself becomes merely an opportunity for introducing descriptions of nature, and comparisons with nature that are broad and sensuous—often delightful though sometimes repulsive, or at least bizarre. In this law—the rudiments of which are perceptible in ancient Indian reliefs, but which reigns supreme in the literature of a later period—chiefly lie the difficulties to the ordinary European mind in understanding their modes of thought; but, at the same time, to it is due the peculiar beauty of this tropical life, bursting forth so luxuriantly on every side. In the art of the Asoka period—on which that of

Sâñchî was modelled—everything is still naïve, and no trace of refinement exists.

As already mentioned, no picture of Buddha appears on the reliefs of this older period. Only the signs of his activity were represented; the footprints (*padah*) which he left behind him, or the sacred tree beneath which he, or one of his mythical predecessors, obtained enlightenment, or even a Stûpa erected in memory of him, are represented as being universally venerated. To these are added the symbols of his miracles: as snake and fire in the case of Kâsyapa, and so on. The wheel (*dharmachakra*), as already mentioned, was adopted by Buddha's disciples as the symbol of his doctrine, and combined with other symbols—a trident placed above it, etc.—stands for him on the sculptures of the Asoka period.[1]

From the Buddhist literature it clearly appears how irreparable was the loss sustained by the death of the Sage. Schisms soon broke out: there was no proper cult. Everything had to be developed, and it was a slow process. The wonderful growth of the more modern religion must not cause us to forget its simple and small beginnings. As long as the doctrine of the 'Overcomer' was pure, a Buddha cult could not be thought of; the tendency to this first made itself felt when the figure of the Sage was deified. Originally, Buddhism was only a philosophy, no religion: but therein consisted the weakness of the Buddha doctrines, which speedily became unpopular on that account.[2] When in the course of time the religion fell back into a worship of gods, the cult picture appeared. The countless legends which are related of the oldest Buddha pictures describe plainly the embarrassment occasioned when such a representation had to be made. The ability

[1] In these different scenes, Bharhut, with its reliefs determined by the inscriptions, is very characteristic as compared with Sâñchî and even Amarâvatî. The *Dharma* or *Chakra* symbol is adored by gods and men, who approach with offerings or with folded hands; purely external accessories determine the scene: thus the wheel and two gazelles are the representation of the discourse at Bânâras, in the deer-park; *Tree and Serp. Wor.*, pl. xxix, 2 (Sâñchî); pl. lxxi, 2 (Amarâvatî), etc.—even in modern Lamaist art, cf. the emblem on the roof of a Mongolian temple at Pozdneev, *Zap. geogr. Obshch.*, XVI, 1887, pl. on p. 38; the *Dharma* symbol with fire pillars surrounded by Brâhmaṇas, the representation of the conversion of Kâsyapa (*Tree and Serp. Wor.*, pl. lxx). Another emblematic representation is the celestial ladder, with footprints above and below, for the descent of the Bodhisattva from Tushita; *Bharhut*, pl. xvii (middle), also at Sâñchî, *Tree and Serp. Wor.*, pl. xxviii, 3; conf. S. Beal, *ut sup.*, p. 183. From this comes the idea that the descending elephant beside the sleeping Mâyâ is a dream. The Bodhisattva descending on the ladder, appears, however, also in Gandhâra sculptures. To this subject also belongs a modern picture from Kamboja in the Berlin Museum.

[2] If in Buddhism the proud attempt be made to conceive a deliverance in which man himself delivers himself, to create a faith without a god, it is Brahmanical speculation which has prepared the way for this thought. It has thrust back the idea of a god step by step; the forms of the old gods have faded away, and besides the Brahma, which is enthroned in its eternal quietude, highly exalted above the destinies of the human world, there is left remaining, as the sole really active person in the great work of deliverance, man himself, who possesses—inherent in himself—the power to turn aside from this world, this hopeless state of sorrow.—Oldenberg, *Buddha, &c.*, p. 53.

to create an ideal type was lacking, so a portrait was chosen which the artists beautified beyond nature, and which they tried to make authentic by tales of miracles that Buddha had wrought. Thus the *Divyâvadâna* relates that Bimbisâra, king of Magadha, desired to have a representation of Buddha painted on a cloth. The artist tried and failed. Then Buddha let his shadow fall upon it, commanded that the outlines should be filled in with colour, and that the chief articles of the faith should be written upon it. This is an artistic authentication of a modern picture, as clearly no portrait was extant.[1] This point will be found of value in a subsequent chapter, for it proves that there was no desire to create an ideal type. In a modern branch of Buddhist art, in the miniatures of the Lamaist church of Tibet and China, notwithstanding the narrow limits of the canon, the individual appears surprisingly beautiful. It is, indeed, the only really artistic point in the endless series of absurd rites of the degenerate hierarchical representations. But the ideal type of Buddha—which spiritualized the simple monk's figure, and, notwithstanding the want of ornament, stood out from all else,—was created for Buddhist art by foreigners.

The doctrine of Buddha's Nirvâ*n*a can hardly be taken as affording the reason for the fact that on the reliefs of Barâhat, Gayâ, and Sâñchî the Buddha does not appear. The doctrine of the Nirvâ*n*a, in its present canonical form, was probably not developed at all at that time. Later, when statues of Buddha were already in existence, the legends paid no attention whatever to the dogmatic conception: according to a legend handed down by the Chinese pilgrim Hiuen Tsang, for example, Buddha, who long before had disappeared into Nirvâ*n*a, came down from heaven to exhort the statue of Buddha, which king Udayana had made to serve the faithful as the symbol of the doctrine that brings salvation.

In the ancient Buddhist art, so far as the representation of the founder of the religion is concerned, the conditions are the same as in ancient Christian art: symbols, such as the fish, the lamb, etc., were employed at first by the early Christians, as types reminding them of Christ. The type of the Christ was long a fluctuating one, until that of Byzantium became universal. So it was in Buddhist art: the Gândhâra type, which will be examined in greater detail below, became the prevailing one.

The single panels become comprehensible only by virtue of their connection one with another. For the chief figure does not appear in their composition.

If we return to the reliefs of the left pillar, we are struck above all by the fact that these three reliefs of the Kâ*s*yapa legend, the scene of which was at Gayâ, are so much separated from one another. From what was said above (p. 60) about the manner in

[1] Udayana Vatsarâja of Kau*s*ambi, and Prasenajit of Ko*s*ala are said to have had statues made of Buddha before his death. Beal, *Si-yu-ki*, vol. I, pp. 235-6; Eitel, *Handbk. of Chin. Buddhism*, pp. 137-8.

which the heavens are represented, we expected something compensating sufficiently on the left pillar.

As middle panel on the left pillar we have a representation of a great tree so built about by a chapel, that the main branches grow out of one of the windows. Rows of men, in the attitude of prayer, stand round about it; gods are flying towards it through the air to crown it with garlands. By means of rows of men at prayer, which fill the upper panel, the composition is made to balance, to some extent, that of the right pillar, even as to form. Now the tree, the worship of which is so important, that it could be placed opposite the palace of the gods on the right pillar as a counterpoise, and in fact in such a way that the Kâśyapa legend had to be divided in two, can be none other than the Bodhi tree of Gayâ with the chapel which king Aśoka had built round about it. The representation of the fig tree at Buddha Gayâ, which is shown on the reliefs of Barâhat, is indeed identical with our Sâñchî representation (fig. 38).[1]

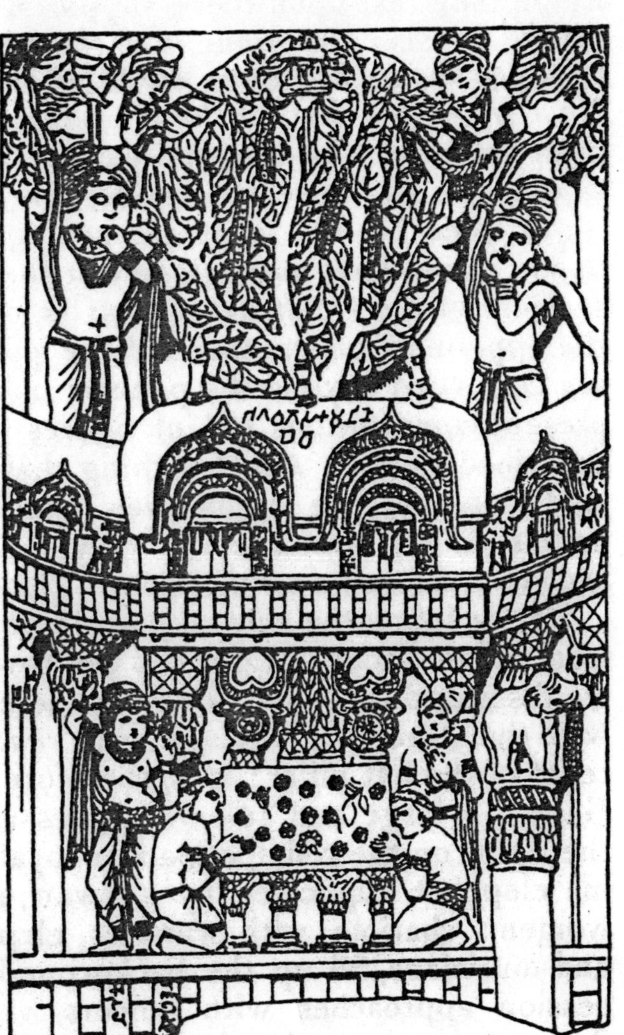

38. Relief from the so-called Prasenajit Pillar from Barâhat.

(Cunningham, *Bharhut*, pll. xii and xxx). In the middle is the Bodhi-tree of Gautama Buddha. The inscription above reads: "Bhagavato Sakamunino bodho"—the Bodha (for Bodhi) tree of the exalted Śâkyamuni; the one below: "Râjâ Pasenaji Kosalo"—the King Prasenajit, the Kośala.

We see, therefore, that the desire for symmetry in composition also prevailed among Indian architects, though not in the strict form in which we are accustomed to it from Græco-Roman art.

The reliefs, so far as their explanation is concerned, always refer one to the other. The main difficulty for us consists in separating the decorative elements from those that are important in the composition. Now those external determining points in the com-

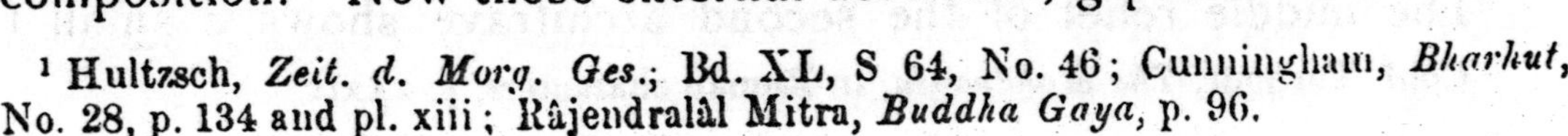

[1] Hultzsch, *Zeit. d. Morg. Ges.*, Bd. XL, S 64, No. 46; Cunningham, *Bharhut*, No. 28, p. 134 and pl. xiii; Râjendralâl Mitra, *Buddha Gaya*, p. 96.

positions are most apparent and most interesting on the architrave of the east gateway. Above the pillars there rise three transoms, which we shall call architraves; the lowest of them rests upon the capitals, while the next two are laid upon supporting blocks, which are about as high as the architraves themselves. At the places where they rest upon these supports, the beams are covered with carved panels: the whole is of the nature of a timbered scaffolding in which the cross-beams are fitted in beneath ornamented panels. Now we notice that, of the six panels on the front, the two uppermost are carved each with a pair of zebu-riders, and on the other side all the six represent similar mounted groups. Only the two lower ones on the front are sculptured each with three winged lions. If we look more closely at them we see that all the carved surfaces of the architraves—that is, of the three on the back and the uppermost on the front—have purely decorative reliefs, which are continued beyond the panels; only the two lowest on the front present compositions full of figures and of the processional kind described above. Another thing that strikes one is that the representations on the architraves, which project beyond the inlaid panels, do *not* continue the central compositions of the first and second architraves on the front. (Conf. ill. 39).

The relief on the central portion of the first architrave, reckoning from below (front), belongs to the narrative representations, which we discussed on p. 57. In the middle is to be seen a large fig tree with the same kind of building (a *chaitya*) encircling it as on the relief of the left pillar: it is, therefore, once more the Bodhi tree at Gayâ. A large and solemn procession is winding round it. To the right, on the relief, a man in royal garb is getting down from his elephant, supported by a dwarf, surrounded and attended by women; chariots with warriors, elephants with mahâuts, archers and musicians, fill up the background. On the left, a great procession approaches with flowers, vessels with perfumed water, flags, etc.; a large band of music, with drums of different kinds, fifes, and conch shells as trumpets, fill up the rest of the relief. It is therefore a procession to the Bodhi-tree at Gayâ, perhaps on the occasion of Mahinda's embassy to Ceylon (conf. p. 26). The winged lions in the inlaid panels may possibly be intended to suggest this. Lions are the armorial bearings of Ceylon: 'the lion island,'—Si*m*haladvîpa (Pâli, Sîhaladîpa). The ends of the architraves, in the corners under the volutes, have a pair of peacocks of unusual size in their reliefs on both sides. On the right end a pair of lovers is represented behind the peacocks. In Pâli the peacock is called Mora (Sansk. *Mayûra*); and as peacocks are the symbol of the Maurya[1] dynasty, their representation on the first architrave might indicate that the central incident, which refers to Ceylon, takes place in India.

The middle relief of the second architrave shows a small fig

[1] Conf. Turnour, *The Mahâvansa*, in Roman characters, p. xxxix.

tree in the centre; this—if the previous relief has been correctly explained—may indicate the newly-planted slip. Again a great procession appears, just leaving a city. The princes have dis-

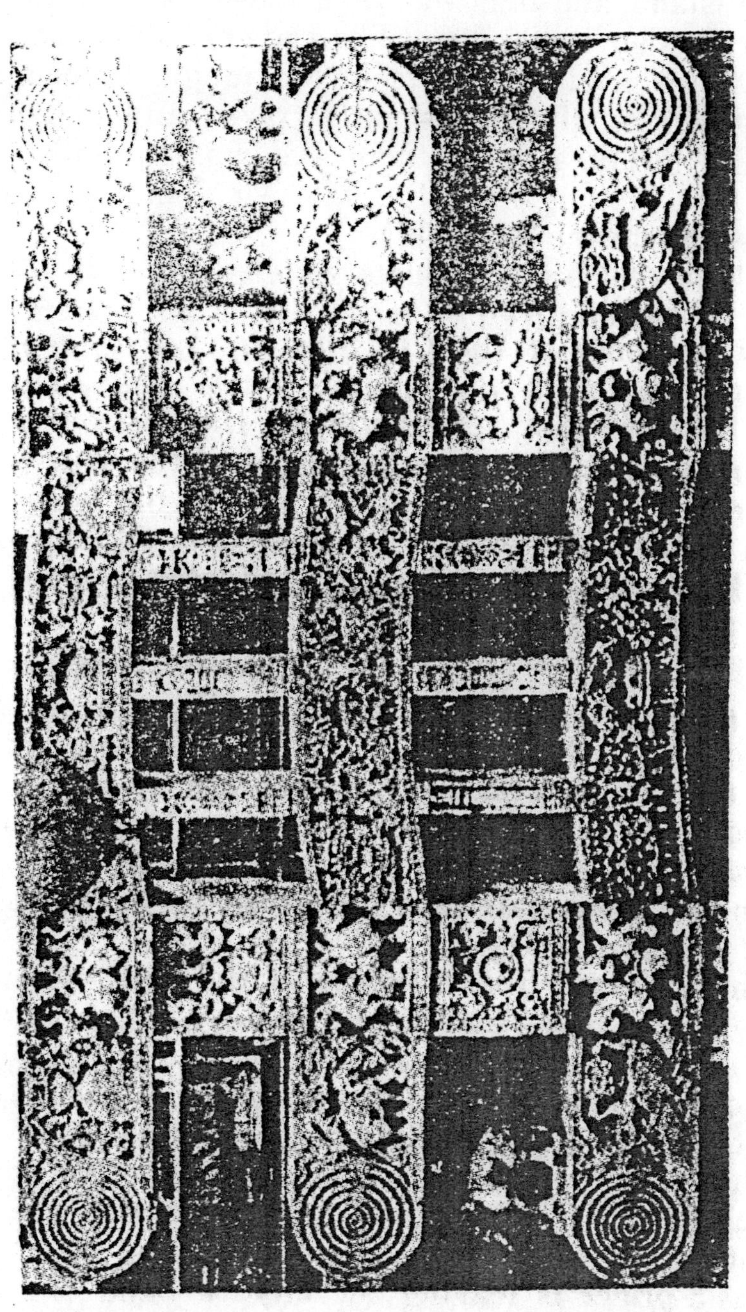

39. ARCHITRAVES OF THE EAST GATEWAY OF THE GREAT STÛPA AT SÂNCHÎ.

mounted; their horses are following the procession. The right side of the relief shows a king kneeling before footmarks[1]—presumably Buddha's—surrounded by servants with sacrificial vessels,

[1] Yule, *Travels of Marco Polo*, vol. II, p. 260.

umbrellas, etc.—evidently the worship of the Buddhapâda, the footprints of Buddha, which he is said to have left on the Sumanakûṭa (Adam's Peak) on the occasion of his mythical visit to Ceylon. There a giant footprint has been regarded as sacred from ancient times and for all the religions prevailing in Ceylon.[1] On the reception of Buddhism, it became a proof that Buddha had walked upon the island, and thus was taken as a pattern for similar footprints in Further India, &c. The ends of the architraves, next the volutes, show wild elephants in the jungle as companion pieces to the peacocks of the first architrave; and to correspond with the pair of lovers, a naked man and woman, both with bow and arrows. As, judging from the wild elephants, we are in Ceylon, these may be meant for Veddâs.

Thus both reliefs are intimately connected with the story of the building at Sâñchî given on p. 26. It is an extremely interesting fact that, not only at the Christian era, but even in the days of Aśoka, the footmark on Adam's Peak was considered as the print of Buddha's foot. No doubt, for the missionaries of the faith sent from India, it was a decisive proof of the true doctrine, when so striking an instance of Buddha's visit to the island was given to them on the occasion of their bringing over the slip of the Bodhi-tree. The Buddhapâda, which existed later at Gayâ, is now worshipped as the footprint of Vishṇu.

Reliefs of the east gateway at Sâñchî.

Casts of this gateway were made in 1869 and are set up in the S. Kensington, Edinburgh and Dublin Museums of Science and Art, in the Royal Ethnological Museum at Berlin, at Paris, &c. (See above, p. 25). The following is a brief description of the sculptures upon it. The only representations we yet possess of those on the other gateways are given in Fergusson's *Tree and Serpent Worship* (1873).[2]

Right pillar, front: Palace of the gods. Inner side: worship of a sacred tree—the fig-tree at Gayâ, where Buddha obtained enlightenment; below, the dream of Mâyâ; the Bodhisattva comes down from the region of the Tusita gods in the form of a white elephant. Below, a large relief presents a great town, in the streets of which meet riders and men on elephants. The windows of the houses are full of people, women with parrots in their hands look down into the streets. A chariot with a young man clearly characterised as a prince is leaving the city: a band of musicians goes before. Archers and an elephant with its *mahâwat* accompany the chariot of the prince. It is perhaps the procession of the youthful

[1] Locally known to the Tamils as Śivadippâtham (Śiva's footprint) and Dharmarâjâkkal (Buddha's rock). The Muhammadans say Adam alighted on it when expelled from Paradise, and call it al-Rahun See E. Tennant, *Ceylon*, vol. II, pp. 132-6; and Skeen, *Adam's Peak*.—J.B.

[2] Since p. 25 was printed off, Mr. H. Cousens has sent me his re-measurement of the Sâñchi stûpa. The diameter of the dome at the top of the ramp or plinth is 106 feet, and of the encircling rail, outside measurement, 143 feet from E. to W. and only 146½ from N. to S.—J.B.

Gautama on which the four appearances mentioned above (p. 13) were met with. This view is to some extent supported by the fact that on the lowest relief a fig-tree is again represented (the later Bodhi-tree, or the other one at Gayâ, under which Gautama, according to the legend, first meditated?). Before the tree are five men in lay costume, worshipping (Fergusson, *Tree and Serp Wor.* p. 145 and pll. xiii, xvii and xxxiii). The under half of the inner side represents a large figure of a man, in royal dress, resembling that on the left pillar. These figures appear to correspond to the Yaksha at the entrance of the Nâsik chaitya temple (p. 36).

Left pillar, front: above, two rows of men worshipping. Below, the Bodhi-tree surrounded by the chapel over an altar or table bearing the tri*s*ula symbol (conf. p. 69). (Fergusson, *Tree and Serp. Wor.*, pll. xiii, xvi and xxv, 3). Below that, the water miracle of Uruvilvâ (p. 63). The lowest panel is uninterpreted. The representation is divided into two scenes: on the right is a thickly peopled city, through whose streets pass a rider and a *mahâwat* on an elephant. The smaller half, clearly defined as a separate incident, shows two men in rich dress,—one in the attitude of a teacher, the other in a listening, devotional pose with folded hands. Inner side, upper panel: in the foreground is a pond with lotuses; buffaloes, zebus and goats stand on the bank, two buffaloes are up to their necks in the water. Beyond the pond is seen a large stone slab with an awning and two men worshipping. A young man with a sling-pole for carrying vessels (*bahangî*) stands behind the pond or river surrounded by women; a woman draws water with a lo*t*â, others hold their lo*t*âs in their arms. The middle ground is occupied by a large house with adjoining buildings; near it are women engaged in preparing rice: one woman pounds the rice in a mortar, another cleans rice on a winnow, a third makes cakes, a fourth, who is occupied in the same way, is talking with a man (*Tree and Serp. Wor.*, p. 150 and pl. xxxv, 2): probably the meal which Sujâtâ, with the help of the gods, prepared for Gautama, and the stone slab on which he partook of it, before he began the last decisive meditation which was to bring him enlightenment. The panels beneath represent the fire-miracle at Uruvilvâ (conf. above, p. 62, 66). The lower half of the inner face is filled by a man (or Yaksha) in royal dress.

The backs of the pillars, right at the top only, have each a small relief; on the left with a stûpa, on the right with a sacred tree which is worshipped by gods and men.

The outsides of both pillars show rich patterns of lotus-flowers; on the right side is a flower pattern only (conf. p. 19); on the left side, a large garland which is alive with little aquatic birds and springs from the jaws of a large *makara*.

The capitals of the pillars are filled with men richly dressed, bearing flags and seated on elephants. Outside and joined to each capital is a dancing girl, or a *Devî*, on a large scale, under a tree—the one on the right being quite preserved (conf. p. 42).

The first architrave: front, inlaid panels,—winged lions; middle relief: Mahinda at Gayâ, see p. 70 (*Tree and Serp. Wor.*, pl. xv, 2). Outside: peacocks.

Second architrave: front, applied panels: winged lions; see ill. pp. 18 and 71. Middle relief: the Bodhi-tree at Anurâdhapura (?), adoration of the Buddhapâda; see p. 69. Outside: wild elephants; see p. 72 (*Tree and Serp. Wor.*, pl. xv, 1).

Third architrave: front—applied panels: zebu riders. Middle and ends of the beam: five stûpas and two sacred trees, worshipped by gods and men.

The blocks supporting the architraves bear on the front the following reliefs: between the first and second to the left,—a wheel (*dharmachakra*) adored by gods and men; to the right, the goddess Sirî on lotus flowers, &c.; see p. 39; between the second and third, to the left, the goddess Sirî; to the right, a sacred tree with gods and men.

First architrave: back, applied panels: on each a man and a woman with peculiar coiffure, riding on goats. Middle relief and ends of beams,—elephants bring offerings of flowers (lotus-flowers) to a stûpa (*Tree and Serp. Wor.*, pl. xv, 4).

Second architrave: back, applied panels,—on each a man and a woman riding on dromedaries. Middle relief and ends of beams,—the animal kingdom adores a holy tree, the different animals bringing branches, flowers and blossoms; see p. 48 (*Tree and Serp. Wor.*, pl. xv, 3).

Third architrave: back, applied panels,—on each a man and a woman riding on horned and winged lions, clearly foreign types (conf. ill. p. 34). The middle and the ends of the beams show seven holy trees adored by gods and men, evidently the Bodhi-trees of the six predecessors of Buddha and that of the Buddhas—Vipassî, Sikhi, Vessabhû, Kakusandha, Ko*n*âgamana, Kassapa and Gotama which are also represented at Barâhat, as the inscriptions witness.

The blocks supporting the architraves show, on the back the following reliefs: between the first and second architraves,—groups of lotus flowers; between the second and third architraves,—on each a stûpa with gods and men.

Between the ends of the architraves stand figures, some of which are still preserved: statuary groups of men on elephants and dancing-girls under trees. The small pillars which support the architraves bear in their reliefs lion-pillars (see p. 20), or simply ornaments. How the remaining spaces between the small middle pillars, or the highest architrave between the wheel-symbols, was further ornamented we do not know. On the other Sâñchî gateways, small figures of riders and statuettes of different sizes are employed as additional decorations: motifs that remind one of the throne of Vikramâditya (see p. 29).

Above each pillar there was once a symbol of Buddhism: the wheel with the trisula over it (see p. 19 and note 2).

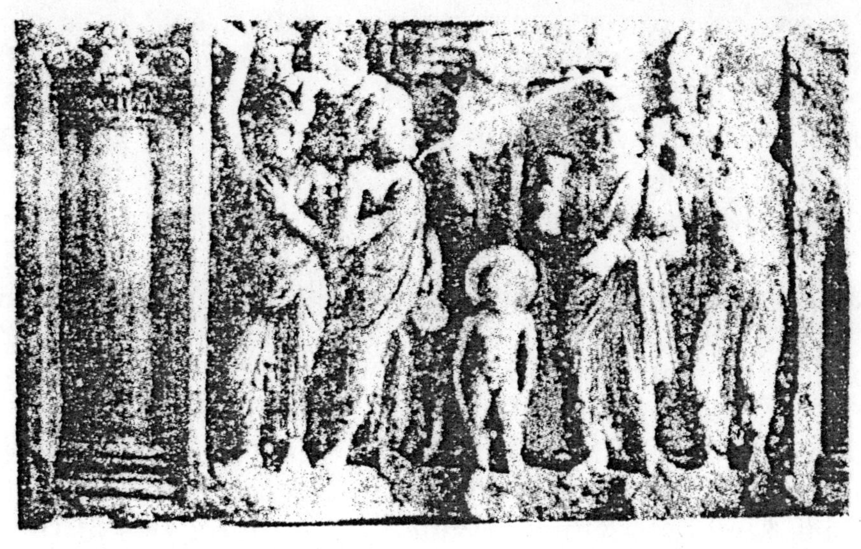

40. THE INFANT BUDDHA TAKING THE SEVEN STEPS (from Swât).

CHAPTER III.

THE GANDHARA SCULPTURES

(SO-CALLED GRÆCO-BUDDHIST SCULPTURES).

By Gândhâra sculptures are designated the numerous images, carved friezes, pillars, &c., excavated from the ancient ruins of Buddhist monasteries and stûpas on the north-west frontier of India. They have been variously styled Græco-Buddhist, Aryan, Indo-Greek, and Indo-Baktrian—terms which are open to the objection of implying a theory respecting their art origin. They are all but entirely connected with Buddhist iconography, and many of them manifest some western or classical influence. And since they are found almost exclusively in the country which early writers named Gandhâra, they may very properly be characterized by the area of their origin. The country of the Gandarioi, Gandaræ and Gandaritis is mentioned by Herodotos,[1] Hekataios, Ptolemy and Strabo. The Gandarioi furnished their contingent to the army of Darius in the invasion of Greece. Their country occupied the whole lower valley of the Kâbûl river—the ancient Kophen or Kubhâ—from the Kâu or Alingar river near the meridian of 70° W. longitude to the Indus, and from the Safid Koh range and the Kohat Toi river on the south to the borders of Kohistân, Chitral and the Hindu Kush on the north. It thus embraced the whole of the modern Afridi and Momand country, Swât, Bajaur, Bunêr, &c. At one period, at least, it seems even to have included

[1] Herodotos, bk. vii, c. 65, 66; conf. bk. iii, c. 91; iv, 44.

within its limits the great city of Takshasilâ in the Râwal Pindi district, to the east of the Indus,—forming an area 170 miles from east to west, and above 100 miles from north to south.[1] The province between the Swât and Indus rivers, or the modern district of Yûsufzaï and northwards to Kohistân, was known as Udyâna or Ujjâna (Gr. Suastênê), and sometimes probably formed a separate principality. It was through the northern districts of this country that Alexander led his army into India. On the rise of the Græco-Baktrian kingdom, in the middle of the following century, Gandhâra was included in it.

The political events which followed the short reign of Alexander the Great in India terminated with the founding of two great states—the kingdom of the Prasioi with its capital Pâṭaliputra (Gr. Palimbothra, the modern Pâṭnâ) in the east; and the Græco-Baktrian kingdom, which retained for a time parts of India, the Panjâb, and portions of the North-Western Provinces of to-day. The heirs of the Græco-Baktrian kingdom and of its hybrid civilization, formed of Iranian and Greek elements, were the Yueh-chi or Indo-Skythians (cir. B.C. 126). The struggles which the Indian states carried on with them continued till the sixth century A.D., and thus form the political background for the further development of Buddhism on Indian soil.

With the fifth century begins the darkest period of Indian history, political as well as religious. When, after centuries, the veil is lifted again, and Indian sources are once more fully at our disposal, Buddha's doctrines have largely disappeared from the continent of India, foreign influences are overcome, and, whilst a complete transformation has taken place in Brâhmanism,—which organizes the national worship and moulds it into an important system,—an entirely new development of the languages is in progress.

In detail, the following had probably been the course of affairs. After the death of Alexander the Great, his generals had divided his vast empire among them; his Indian possessions had fallen to Seleukos Nikator, king of Syria. But as the supremacy of Seleukos was immediately subjected to attack, and as he saw that western Asia would call for his utmost exertions,—convinced of the extreme difficulty of retaining the eastern lands of his empire—he ceded the Indian provinces to Chandragupta of Magadha (cir. 305 B.C.) in return for a supply of war-elephants. A daughter of the Macedonian was married to the king of India, and a permanent ambassador, Megasthenes (whose narratives of Indian affairs, though only fragmentary, are of great value),[2] remained at the

[1] It still retained the old name in the thirteenth century. The capital at different times was Pushkalâvati, Purushapura, and Udakhâṇḍa or Waihand (Ohind).

[2] The Fragments of the *Indika* of Megasthenes have been collected by E. A. Schwanbeck (Bonn, 1846) and by C. Müller. They have been translated into English by J. W. McCrindle in *Ind. Ant.*, vol. VI, 1877, and also separately (Bombay and London).

Indian court at Pâṭaliputra. About a century later (B C. 260–230) Asoka did his best officially to propagate Buddhism within his wide domains, and also sought to procure an entrance for it into neighbouring states. About the year B.C. 246, we learn that a Buddhist mission was sent to Kashmîr and Gandhâra by the great Council held under king Asoka. It was led by an elder or monk named Majjhantika (Madhyântika) of Dahala, who found a savage Nâga king, Aravâla, ruling the country. After strong opposition, the monk is said to have converted the king and gained over the whole population. "From that period," says the *Mahâvansa*, "to the present day, the people of Kashmîr and Gandhâra have been fervently devoted to the three branches of the faith, and [the land] has glittered with the yellow robes [of the priests]." And the testimonies of the early Chinese pilgrims, together with the numerous remains of Buddhist monasteries and stûpas still found, amply confirm the statement that such was once the case.

King Asoka mentions in his inscriptions that he had carried on negotiations in reference to this object with the kings of the Yavanas—Antiochos of Syria, Ptolemy Philadelphos of Egypt, etc. The alliance with the Seleukidæ continued, and about the year 256 B.C. Antiochus Theos concluded a treaty with Asoka.

But this condition of things was soon altered. Between the two great states there arose a new power which drove the Syrian monarchy from the Indian frontier for ever. The Græco-Baktrian kingdom, which was founded at the expense of the Syrian satraps, waxed powerful, and Eukratides, king of Baktria, took up arms against India (cir. 170 B.C.).[1] His armies seized upon the Panjâb and perhaps made their way as far as Sindh and Gujarât. The Baktrian kingdom, however, was attacked by the Yueh-chi, a Skythian tribe, who drove the Baktrians, under their king Heliokles, over the Hindu Kush (B.C. 125).[2] Somewhat later his successor, Menandros, whose dominions could no longer have included Baktria, had his capital at Sâkala (Sangala or Sânkala) in the Panjâb, somewhere near the Hydraôtes or Râvî river, and made considerable conquests in north India.[3] A generation after Menandros, the Yonakas or so-called Greeks were again subjected to the onslaughts of Yueh-chi tribes, and Hermaios, about B.C. 25, seems to have shared his kingdom with Kadphises, the Yueh-chi chief of the Kûshan tribe.

Among the kings of the Baktrian dynasty—whose contemporaries in India were the Sunga and Kânva dynasties—M e n a n d r o s is

[1] Justin, *Hist.* lib. xli, 6; Strabo, lib. xv., 1, 3; xi, 9, 2, and 11, 2; Wilson, *Ariana Antiqua*, pp. 234ff.

[2] Ptolemy, *Geog.* vii, 1, 46; Wilson, *Ariana Ant.* pp. 280ff; Duff, *Chronology of India*, p. 16.

[3] Sylvain Levi, *Quid de Græcis vet. Indorum monum. trad.* p. 17; Beal's *Si-yu-ki*, vol. I, p. 166, note 5; and *Ind. Ant.* vol. XV, p. 246; Specht in *Jour. Asiat.*, 8me Ser. t. II (1883), p. 348; Sylvain Levi, *ibid.* t. XV (1890), pp. 237-9; McCrindle, *Invas. Ind.* pp. 347-8, 411; *Sac. Bks. of the East*, vol. XXXV, p. 23.—J.B.

by far the most important. He is doubtless identical with the Milinda of the Buddhists; and seems, according to Plutarch, to have gone over entirely to Buddhism.[1] A Pâli work, *The Questions of King Milinda—Milindapanha*[2] (first rendered accessible to English readers through the Singhalese version, *Milindaprasnayâ*), which belongs perhaps to the first century after Christ, represents the king in conversation with a Buddhist monk who expounds to him Buddha's philosophy in a style almost Platonic; whereupon the king is converted. In any case, this work is an important Indian testimony to the interest of the Greeks in Indian philosophy, on which subject Greek authors are so well informed.

Hermaios, the last of the Yonaka or Græco-Baktrian dynasty, was dispossessed of part of his power by the Yueh-chi about 25 B.C. Other tribes—Ye-tha or Sakas—had also pressed into the same region; Maues had previously established himself there and was succeeded by Azes, Azilises, &c., who were perhaps Skythic or Sakas; and a little later we have names that seem to be Parthian. such as Gondopharas or Gudapharas, Abdagases,[3] Orthagnes, &c. Gudapharas must have ruled about A.D. 25-50, and is the king mentioned in Christian tradition as having received the Apostle Thomas. A little later Kanishka the Kûshan became supreme from Kâbûl to the Ganges.

In those days a vast interchange of ideas was carried on between the east and the Hellenic and Roman worlds by means of the newly opened highways. It is, of course, impossible within the limits of this work more fully to describe this period, so highly important for the east as well as for the west; but a few cardinal points in connexion with the artistic efforts of the Indian world may be mentioned. The Greeks sought and found in India traces of their own gods; the tendency of the Hellenes, noticed as early as Herodotos, to identify the gods of barbarian races with their own, led to the recognition of the ancient conquests of Dionysos in India.[4] Just as Alexander the Great, impelled by the exigencies of Oriental court etiquette, assumed the title of a god; so, to reverse the process, the gods who, according to the legends, had performed such miraculous feats in India, were soon represented as deified conquerors. The sages of Egypt and India had to furnish pretended proofs that the personages of their national mythology were only deified heroes. The Indian doctrine of the transmigration of souls was adopted, and in the Occident was utilized in a Puritanic

[1] Strabo, *Geog.* xi, 11, 2; Plutarch, *De Rep. Ger.* p. 821; Lassen, *Ind. Alt.* Bd. II, Ss. 313f., 340f.; *Hist. Baktr. Kings*, 150-158; *Sac. Bks. of the East*, vol. XXXV, p xix f.

[2] Translated by Rhys Davids, *Sac. Bks. of the East*, vols. XXXV, XXXVI.

[3] There is no ground whatever for Cunningham's hypothesis (*Jour. As. S. Beng.* vol. XXIII, pp. 711-12) that Abdagases is the Parthian who led the revolt against Artabanus III.—J.B.

[4] Herodotos, ii, 50, &c.; Diodoros, iii 63; Strabo, xv, 1, 58; Polæn, *Strateg.*, i, 1, 1-3: Arrian, *Ind.*, cc, 5-7

direction in order to sift the fast increasing crowds of gods and forms of worship which had been the result of the confusion of ideas, or to prove directly the incorrectness of the ancient legends, —the so-called Euhemerism.

The story of the campaigns in these tropical lands created an interest in adventure and travel, and gave birth to tales of adventure, which, by means of foreign names, romantic descriptions and strange themes, ventured to surpass reality. Greek ideas and narratives find their way into the Buddhist texts; and Indian similes, fables and legends appear in the literature of the West. Whether Greek dramatic art merely influenced the Indian, or founded it, may be left an open question. These attempts continued until the time of the later Roman emperors—about the fifth century.[1]

With regard to India and the influence of Buddhism at this period, stress should be laid on the fact that an exactly analogous flood of Indian ideas, which had a much more powerful effect than in the case of the Græco-Roman civilized world, set in at the same time towards the East and especially towards China and the lands east of India, and that this went on for centuries. About 65 A.D. the Han Emperor Ming-ti had Buddhist books brought from India; in the succeeding centuries Buddha's religion made gigantic strides in East and Central Asia. Fah-hian, who visited India about A.D. 400, was acquainted with a set form of prayer to the Bodhisattva Maitrêya: the Buddhists outside India were thus, throughout this whole period, constantly in touch with the development of the doctrines in the mother-country. But the same Chinese pilgrim saw on Indian soil representations of the founder of the new religion for which Western art had afforded an ideal type.

Under the heirs of the Greek power in India, the Yueh-chis, Turushkas, or Indo-Skythians, Greek or Western civilization still prevailed; but coupled with the interest of the ruling houses in Buddha's doctrines, the Indo-Skythians may perhaps have become disciples of Buddha in their own country. The most potent of these kings was Kanishka,[2] the Kûshana. He ruled over a powerful kingdom including Kâbûl, Gandhâra, Kashmîr, the Panjâb, parts of Râjasthân, and the present N.W. Provinces. About the year 100 A.D., at his instigation, there met, at Jâlandhara in the Panjâb, a council of Buddhist teachers, which set itself the task of collecting and arranging the sacred writings and bringing about an agreement and a reconciliation between the different sects. At this council the sacred texts were no longer written in the ancient Pâli or

[1] On this see Reinaud, *Relations politiques et commer. de l'Empire roman avec l'Asie orientale* (Paris, 1863); and Priaulx, *Indian travels of Apollonius of Tyana, and the Indian embassies to Rome* (Lond. 1873).—J.B.

[2] The Greek form of the name was formerly read Κανέρκης, but see Burgess, *Ind. Ant.* vol. XIII, p. 58, and M. A. Stein, *ibid.* vol. XVII, pp. 94f. Senart considers the form Kaneshka as the correct one; *Jour. As.* 9me Ser., tom. VII (1896), p. 11. Hiuen Thsang calls him Kanishka Râja of Gandhâra; Beal, *Si-yu-ki*, vol. I, p. 56.

Mâgadhi tongue, probably spoken by Buddha himself, but in Sanskrit. By this means the split between the now separating northern and southern schools became decided and lasting. The southern school does not recognise the council of Jâlandhara in its traditions; its own canons are in the Pâli language; the numerous heterodox works emanating from the sects that had been more or less influenced by Brâhmanism, and which the northern school received for conciliatory reasons, are also unknown to the southern church, which now went its own way, and was in consequence removed from Hindu influences. This southern church thus represents in her sacred canons the older and purer exposition of Buddha's doctrines.

Now-a-days, since the extinction of Buddhism on Indian soil, besides the countries of Farther India—Burma Siam, and Kamboja, only Ceylon is still Buddhist, and it is regarded as the seat of the southern church. The northern school has gained Tibet, Nepâl and China, with the neighbouring countries, but it has also made some way in Farther India, and in Java it has got a footing side by side with Brâhmanism. In Northern India, between the sixth and seventh centuries, Buddhism declined rapidly; in Kashmîr it held out longest. What it lost in the land of its birth it gained in Central Asia; twice it penetrated into Tibet, and there it not only brought all religious life into subjection, but contrived by means of its powerful hierarchy to gain also the political supremacy. In China, Buddhism is found in two sects—Foism, which was introduced from India, and Lamaism, which came from Tibet—side by side with other forms of religion; but it has lost much of its prestige. Japan received the Bauddha religion from Korea. In the Indian Archipelago Buddhism is almost extinct.

Buddhism of the Mahâyâna school continued to flourish in Gandhâra including Udyâna, down to the close of the fifth century. When Fah-hian visited the country about A.D. 404, he found 500 monasteries and the people devoted to the Bauddha Path; but about 515 A.D. Mihirakula, a Hûna, overran Udyâna and Kashmîr, killed Simha the Buddhist patriarch, and massacred the Buddhists. In the seventh century Hiuen Thsang, passing through the country, found the religion decadent; but fully a century later (A.D. 757-764) U-K'ong, who resided for some years in Udyâna, speaks of over 300 monasteries of the Sarvâstivâdin or Vaibhâshika school of Mahâyânists in this district, and the then ruling princes zealously patronised the monks.

When, after long struggles, the Yueh-chis had been driven out of India proper, the dynasty of the Gupta emperors became the dominant one. Under their rule (A.D. 319-530) Buddhism began to fall decidedly into decay. It had at an early date become divided into numerous sects or schools, which decidedly contributed to its loss of power; and the mass of the people, who could not follow the hair-splitting dialectics of these various schools,—who had regular argumentative combats among themselves,[1]— fell back into the older and more eclectic cult of Brâhmanism, which they had never altogether forgotten. The strong and continually increasing intrusion of Brâhma*n*a elements into philosophical statement and into ritual gradually but completely transformed the old doctrines of Buddha. Unfortunately, with the fifth century the darkest period of Indian history begins; native sources of information cease almost entirely. What we do know we owe to foreign writers: the Chinese pilgrims already mentioned—Fah-hian (cir. 400 A.D.), Sung-yun (cir. 518 A.D.), and Hiuen Thsang (629-648 A.D.). While the first of these found the Bauddha religion still pretty generally observed in India, Hiuen Thsang laments its decline.

We have still to note the changes effected about the third century by the Christian religion, which, from western Asia, was spreading in all directions. Through Syrian sources, Christendom had become almost the immediate neighbour of Buddhism.[2] Alongside of the Christian religion stood the theories of the Zoroastrians; and from these two Manichæism had been evolved, which had already adopted certain Buddhist ideas also: everywhere a lively reaction of the old religious forms had set in against the new doctrines. For our purposes it is specially noteworthy that the Paraclete plays a prominent part in Mani's doctrine, for, as we shall see, in the Gândhâra sculptures of the Peshâwar district, the Buddhist Messiah, Maitreya, seems to be reverenced almost more than the founder himself.

Returning to Buddhist art, we find traces of Greek influence in Asoka's buildings, in particular elements which neither the richness of form of the so-called Orientalising tendency, nor Persian influences, suffice to explain. (Conf. above p. 57). The elements in question are essentially decorative, and quite in the Persian style; they consist of particular forms of creatures with fishes' tails (*Matsyanâris*), hippocampi, *makaras*, centaurs, river-gods with human faces and the bodies of oxen, the thunderbolt, etc. Unfortunately, the miserable ruins of ancient Irânian art are altogether insufficient to represent the whole range of the influence which ancient Irân must have exercised in India. It is particularly regrettable that there is no answer to the question to what extent Greek hands may have been employed in the buildings of the Achæmenides. That Persian ideas were at work for a much longer time in India, and that they had a special influence on the

[1] Notices of such competitions, almost in the monastic style of mediæval times, occur in plenty in Târanâtha (Schiefner's transl.). Even still, the Lama religion prescribes similar competitions as school exercises. Conf. Huc et Gabet, *Souvenir d'un voyage dans la Tartarie, etc.* (Paris, 1850), tom. II, pp. 117-8.

[2] How influential the Christian communities were is evidenced by the fact that the Christians (651 A.D.) buried with great ceremony the shamefully murdered Persian king Yazdigard.—Ibn Athîr, iii, 96, quoted by E. Kuhn, 'Barlaam und Joasaph,' *Abhand. K. B. Acad. Wiss.* (1893) 1 Cl. Bd. XX, i, S. 37; also Nöldeke in *Zeitsch. d. D. M. Gesch.*, Bd. XLIV, S. 521.

later Buddhism of the north, is shown by what follows. The cuneiform inscriptions of the time of the Achæmenides refer to the Indian peoples under two names, adopted by Herodotos also, as Hindu (Indoi) and Gandârâ (Gandarioi).[1] These designations are peculiarly suitable for the two periods of Buddhist art; if the style of Asoka and the Indian style that sprang from it are comprised under the name Indian (Indo-Persian), the name Gandârâ (Skt. Gandhâra and Gândhâra) remains to designate the style adopted in the kingdom of that name, whose geographical position we have defined above. The designations Græco-Buddhist, Indo-Baktrian, &c., which have been applied to them, are all, for various reasons, incorrect and misleading.

Yet, of course, there is no lack of transitions and opposing tendencies. Thus, in India proper (at Mathurâ) are to be found traces of what Mr. Vincent Smith styles an Indo-Hellenic school, which represents subjects purely Greek. The best known relief, which belongs to this group, is the so-called Silenus, now in the Calcutta Museum; a second represents Hercules with the Nemæan lion.[2] To this little known school, which ought possibly to be somehow connected with the stay of Megasthenes at Pâtna, belongs the representation of Mâra with bow and arrow, and also some similar older Greek elements which differ entirely from the Gândhâra sculptures, and are still to be found even in Brâhmanical art. Both the sculptures mentioned above are Greek in form, but the figure of the woman in Grecian dress, represented on the Silenus relief, shows Indian influence in its exaggerated outlines. To this group also belongs an Athene found in the Gandhâra territory,[3] and described by Vincent Smith. It is now in the museum at Lahor.

The rich antiquarian remains of the Kâbûl valley and Indian frontier were brought to notice between 60 and 70 years ago by Mr. C. Masson, Dr. Hönigberger, General Ventura, and Captains Court and P. T. Cautley. The Manikyâla and other stûpas were opened and large numbers of Græco-Baktrian and Saka coins were collected, together with some sculptures. These excited much interest among scholars at the time: and after the Panjâb came under British rule in 1849 wider scope was afforded to investigators; the ancient sites, particularly in Yûsufzaï, became accessible, and soon yielded numerous sculptures which have, in various ways, reached our Museums. The late Sir E. Clive Bayley obtained the first collection made at Jamâlgarhî, but,—placing these valuable

[1] Inscriptions of Persepolis and of Nakhsh-i-Rustam, in *Jour. R. As. Soc.*, vol. X (1847), pp. 280 and 294.

[2] Silenus, Anderson's *Archæol. Cat.*, pt. I, pp. 169-176f. Nemean lion, ibid, pp. 190-1; *Ar. Sur. Ind.*, vol. XVII, p. 109. Another Silenus was found by Mr. Growse at Mathurâ; *J. A. S. Beng.*, vol. XLIV (1875), pt. i, pp. 212-15; and references above on p. 34, note 2.

[3] *Ind. Monuments*, pt. I, pl. 91, 1; conf. also the pedestal in Lahor Museum, represented in *Jour. Ind. Art, &c.*, vol. VIII, pl. 20, 7, and *Jour. R. I. Br. Arch.* (1894), p. 138.—J. B.

sculptures in the Crystal Palace for exhibition,—they were destroyed by the fire in November 1866, and this before they had even been photographed.[1] In November, 1885, General Cunningham shipped a large and important collection to England, which was lost in the steamer "Indus"[2] off Ceylon. A very large number were excavated for the Government of India in the Yûsufzaï district, and were distributed among the various Museums in India, much to the detriment of their proper study. The largest collections are in the Museums of Lâhor and Calcutta.[2] Numbers have from time to time been acquired by private individuals, and some have found their way to the British Museum, the Berlin Ethnographical Museum, the Louvre, Vienna, the Edinburgh University,[3] &c., &c.

In the numerous reliefs thus found, a quite new and very remarkable development is presented. The ruins are found in the neighbourhood of Peshâwar, the ancient Purushapura, at one time the capital of the Gandhâra kingdom, at Jamâlgarhi, Takht-î-Bâhî, Shahr-î-Bahlol, and places in the Swât (Suvâstu, Gr. Soastos) district. Monuments of a similar style are found farther to the west, such as the colossi of Bâmiyân and so on, and also farther to the east.

It is to the late Mr. Jas. Fergusson (1808-1886) that we owe the first scientific discussion of these monuments and of the Indian art represented by them; and whatever advances we have made since, have been largely due to his work as a remarkably skilful and wise pioneer, abreast of the knowledge of his time. Serious attention was first drawn to the subject by his writings, and the materials have since been largely increased.[4] We are thus in a position now to attempt to advance a step and to arrange the results attained and apply them to the further interpretation of our materials.

The antiquities discussed by Fergusson, Cunningham, Bailey, and others, and made known to the public in part by Cole,[5] have since been treated more in detail in the excellent paper of Vincent Smith

[1] All the record we have of them is a short descriptive note by Sir E. C. Bayley, with eleven rough lithographed sketches in *Jour. As. Soc. Beng.*, vol. XXI (1852), pp. 606-621.—J.B.

[2] Besides those sent to Lahor and Calcutta Museums, smaller collections were sent to the Victoria and Albert Museum at Bombay, to Madras, and even to Rangoon.—J.B.

[3] Sixty-three pieces, largely from Swât, are in the Berlin Ethnographical Museum, and it was chiefly to explain and illustrate them that the following portion of the *Handbuch* was written. The late Dr. Leitner, while at Lahor, formed a splendid collection, which he brought to Woking. In other private hands there are numbers, which, unfortunately, are generally unknown and practically inaccessible to students while unpublished.—J.B.

[4] *Hist. Ind. and East. Archit.*, pp. 72-83, 169-184.

[5] Major H. H. Cole published thirty plates of *Græco-Buddhist Sculptures from Yûsufzaï*, as a fasciculus of the work on 'Preservation of National Monuments' (1885). This work is out of print; but twelve of the plates were reproduced in the reprint of *Preservation of National Monuments in India* (London, 1896), and other seventeen, (with sixty-four additional) in the *Ancient Monuments, &c., of India*, Part I (London, 1897). In the *Journal of Indian Art and Industry*, vol. VIII, a further series of twenty-five plates and thirty-eight cuts have been published.—J.B.

and in an important article by M. Senart.[1] Both discuss, from different points of view, the period to which the sculptures belong; the former would extend them over the first five centuries of our era, placing the most flourishing period in the third and first half of the fourth century; the latter does not incline to extend the period to so late a date, and regards the second century and earlier half of the third as its principal period. Mr. V. Smith lays stress on certain features of the art as being Roman rather than Greek. This distinction, however, must not be carried too far: it is one of age rather than of origin. Roman art had always been influenced by Greek taste and models, through the races of Greek descent in Southern Italy; and finally—

> Græcia capta ferum victorem cepit, et artes
> Intulit agresti Latio.

Roman art in sculpture and decorative invention was primarily Hellenic; the Greeks developed Roman architecture in their own facile creative way, ever inventing new forms of ornament and lavishing upon it their wealth of decorative taste. We may call the art of the early Christian centuries Roman, as being produced under Roman rule, but it was Greek minds that inspired and Greek hands that executed it. Greek artists, in their wanderings, carried with them the types and style of the age to which they belonged. And during the first three centuries of our era, Greek art was an article of exportation, and artists—art practitioners—also seem to have travelled everywhere in search of employment. Naturally, they would copy or adapt the models of their native art to meet the demands of their foreign clients of whatever religion.[2]

The few inscriptions found in connexion with the Gândhâra sculptures or on the same sites are dated from 103 to 384 of an undetermined era. The first, that of Gondophares, is in his 26th year, and he is otherwise placed in the first century A.D. This would refer the epoch to about the middle of the previous century, and the 'Samvat' era dates from 57 B.C. If, then, we adopt this for all the dates, —and there is no reason for supposing the use of more eras than one among these inscriptions, unless indicated, nor for supposing another era than the Samvat one beginning in the same century, —we may thus place the accession of Gondophares in A.D. 21-22, and his 26th year in A.D. 47; the Theodorus inscription would fall in A.D. 57; the Pañjtâr inscription in 65; that of Loriyân Tangai in 262; and that of Hashtnagar in A.D. 328.[3] All these dates are within the limits otherwise indicated for the age of the sculptures.

[1] Smith in *Jour. A. S. Beng.*, vol. LVIII (1889), pt. i, pp. 107ff; Senart in *Jour. As.*, 8me Ser., tom. XV, pp. 139-163. An outline of M. Senart's argument was reproduced in *Jour. Ind. Art and Ind.*, vol. VIII, pp. 25-29. Conf. also Bühler, *Anz. d. K. K. Acad. Wiss. zu Wien* (1896), Ss. 44ff.—J. B.

[2] Conf. Foucher in *Rev. de l'Histoire des Relig.* tom. XXX (1894), pp. 365-68.

[3] See Senart, in *Jour. As.*, 9me Sér. tom. XIII (1899). pp. 526-537, 555. It may be remarked here that if we assign the inscription of Mogas of 78, to this era, it falls just at the accession of Gondophares; but see *Jour. Asiat.* 8me Sér. t. XV, p. 128.—J. B.

The period of development is limited then between the birth of Christ and the fifth century A.D. In the seventh century, as stated above, the Chinese pilgrim Hiuen Thsang found the buildings in ruins, with clear traces of long decay. The most ancient of all the sculptures are, of course, those which represent purely Greek subjects, such as the Athene mentioned above. A further development revealing an idealistic and a realistic tendency, but at the same time a series that is more Hellenic and one more Indian, is very noticeable in different pieces of sculpture which, unfortunately, cannot possibly be examined in Europe. One seems to recognise a great many of the borrowings made: Greek elements, Roman, and even Christian. The Gândhâra school has consequently a certain analogy with the old Etruscan. Even here an indigenous naturalism is found side by side with the influence of the architectural styles of west Asia—the Etruscan intermixed with the Greek. But as Italian art gradually passes into Christian, and endeavours to derive from the old types models for the saints of the new religion which has overthrown heathenism; so, in the Gândhâra school, extraordinarily similar types are developed for the Buddhist saints. A wide range of homogeneous resemblances is apparent here: both religions, Christian and Buddhist, have in their ethical doctrines much that is related; the same external means, outrunners of ancient art, contribute to the development of the types, and, in addition, direct borrowing is evident. By its representation of forms, the school of the Gândhâra monasteries is only a daughter of ancient art; but, as it represents none but Indian subjects —the saints and legends of a purely Indian religion,—it belongs entirely to Indian life: and this so much the more that it forms the groundwork for the canonical representation of the founder of the religion and several other personages, especially of the northern school; so also the Greek art of composition, as will be shown more in detail below, from this time onward, is apparent in Buddhist art in all lands.

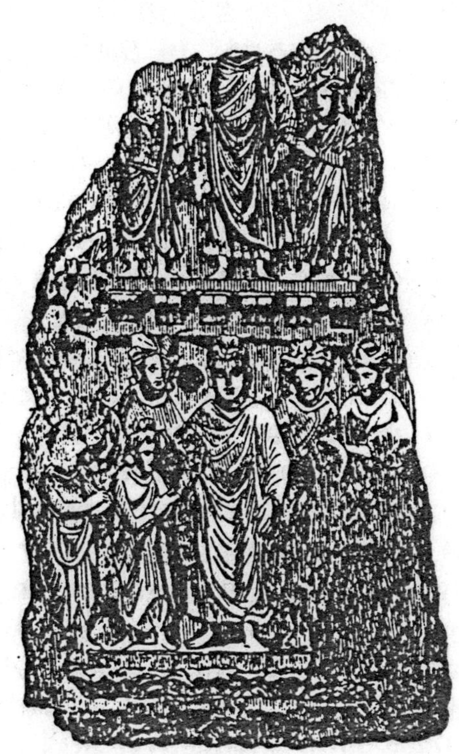

41. Relief with scenes from the life of Gautama Buddha (Takht-i-Bahi). Original in Berlin Museum, 20 inches high.

In what follows we shall try to indicate the types occurring in the Greek sculptures, to fix their names as far as possible, and generally to sketch their genesis and further development.

As the central figure of most of these compositions (though also occurring frequently by itself), the representation of the founder of the Buddhist religion appears as a finished type (fig. 41). He is given again in the form of a young man, in a long robe which covers both shoulders. The face, in the older and more ideal conceptions, shows features resembling those of Apollo, while on the more modern and more stereotyped pieces the features are distinctly Hindu. The representations in Chapter IV. show the extremes fairly well. The hair is arranged in a krobylos: sometimes the figure is represented sitting, Indian fashion, with legs drawn up; at others standing with the right hand uplifted, or striding towards the right, and so on. The draping and treatment of the garments is thoroughly Hellenic; on the more ancient slabs it is often very delicate, and here and there it has quite a distinctive character; but on the later representations the different garments, which have become conventional and stereotyped, are arranged in a fashion that is decidedly not Indian. The position of the hand, and the arrangement of the garments, bear a certain relation to the treatment represented, and become typical in their portrayal of particular crises in Buddha's life. As the symbol of his claim to adoration, there appears a large nimbus surrounding the head (Sans. *bhâmandala, prabhâmandala*). On the reliefs of the Asoka period, and the sculptures on the gates of Sâñchî, which are related, the nimbus, as a symbol of the gods, is not quite unknown (Buddha does not appear in them at all); on the other hand it appears at Amarâvatî, and, with some other elements, belongs to the interesting evidences which point to contact between these sculptures and those of the Gândhâra school (see ill. from Amarâvatî in ch. iv).

The nimbus is borrowed from the Greek school, yet it appeared very late in Greek art—in the time of Alexander.[1] Together with the kindred halo, it belongs originally to the celestial deities; it is interesting to note that, in this sense, it is not wanting in the Gândhâra sculptures. On the relief from Jamâlgarhî the deities of the sun and moon are represented with the nimbus. But that Gautama, not merely as Buddha, but also as a prince, receives the nimbus, proves that at that time his deification was already generally accepted. For such an attribute—which can properly be given only to a god of light,—must necessarily have separated him from the other figures, and put him on an equal footing with the deities there represented with the nimbus. That the Persian fire-worship facilitated the transference of the attribute is an important point, to which we must call attention, as, at a later date, Persian influences show themselves still more strongly. The nimbus is a purely artistic element which, executed in stone, presents a strange appearance, and points in the clearest way to an old school of art. In connection with this, the fact is to be noted that in reliefs

[1] See Stephani, *Nimbus und Strahlenkranz*, in *Mém. de l'Acad. St. Petersbourg*, 6me Sér. t. IX; and conf. Gardner, *Coins of Greek and Scythian Kings*, pll. xiii, 9; xvi, 4; xxvii, 7; xxviii, 22, 23; xxvi, 8, and xxxii, 14: Senart, *Jour. As.* 8me Sér. t. XV, p. 146.

which go back to the ancient types of plastic composition (*e.g.* ill. 41, 57, 70) the nimbus is not found, while in artistically executed representations it exists (conf. ill. 50, &c.). But for the solution of this difficulty more data are necessary. In reliefs which represent scenes from the life of Gautama before he had left his home and obtained enlightenment, he is represented in royal garb, in the same manner as gods and kings are represented on the Sâñchî sculptures. It is true that there the figures are Greek also, and the nimbus makes him clearly conspicuous in the later works of art. In the fourth chapter the Buddha-type will be treated in detail.

As concerns the gods,—as was indicated above (p. 38), they retain the regal type, though sometimes with the addition of a nimbus (conf. ill. 50); and if, in the sculptures of the Asoka period, a characterization of the individual divine figure does not exist, expressing the rôle of a deity by his bodily presence, on the other hand we may observe that the Gândhâra sculptures exhibit, in this respect, a rich individualization. Let us remember, first, then, that in the former, only attributes—the thunderbolt, lotus, and flowers —and in pillar figures the vâha*n*as of the gods are determinative; and now let us look somewhat more closely at the individual types of divinities.

Brahmâ (or the Brahmâ gods as a class), who, from the description given in the *Avidûrenidâna*, cannot be mistaken on the relief above-mentioned, has a kind of krobylos—a *jâta*—on his head, and, so far as can be seen from the somewhat damaged relief, is bearded. He is also represented as a Brâhma*n*a. The figure of Brahmâ on this relief, which is probably of later date, reminds one thereby in a remarkable way of Peter. The garments are quite Grecian. The divine attributes, mentioned above —thunderbolt, flowers, &c.—are wanting to him (see also fig. 40).

The most important personality of the older Bauddha Pantheon —Sakka (S. *S*akra)—should, however, be expected to bear his attribute of the thunderbolt (conf. fig. 40). In fact, many thunderbolt bearers appear, but varied to a remarkable extent.

On the reliefs, which represent scenes from the life of the great Teacher as he moves about among his fellow-men—teaching, reconciling, healing, and working wonders—the Gândhâra sculptures almost invariably show, close to Buddha himself, a strange figure, the explanation of which has occasioned much discussion. In more highly decorative compositions this figure appears also, but in a corner of the whole, and not directly beside Buddha. The sketches in ill. 42 show some of the numerous variations in the representation of this being on earlier and later reliefs. One attribute, however, is common to all—a peculiar club-like object which the figure sometimes grasps by the middle with his right hand, and sometimes holds upright on his palm. In the case of the more modern reliefs (*e.g.* Nos. 2 and 5), one gets the impression that the sculptor has not known exactly what the object was intended to represent. On the earlier and better composed reliefs, like the one from which No. 1 is copied, this object is more distinct, and it is always grasped by the middle (as in ill. 40).

This figure General Cunningham regarded as Devadatta, and others have agreed with this identification. According to the

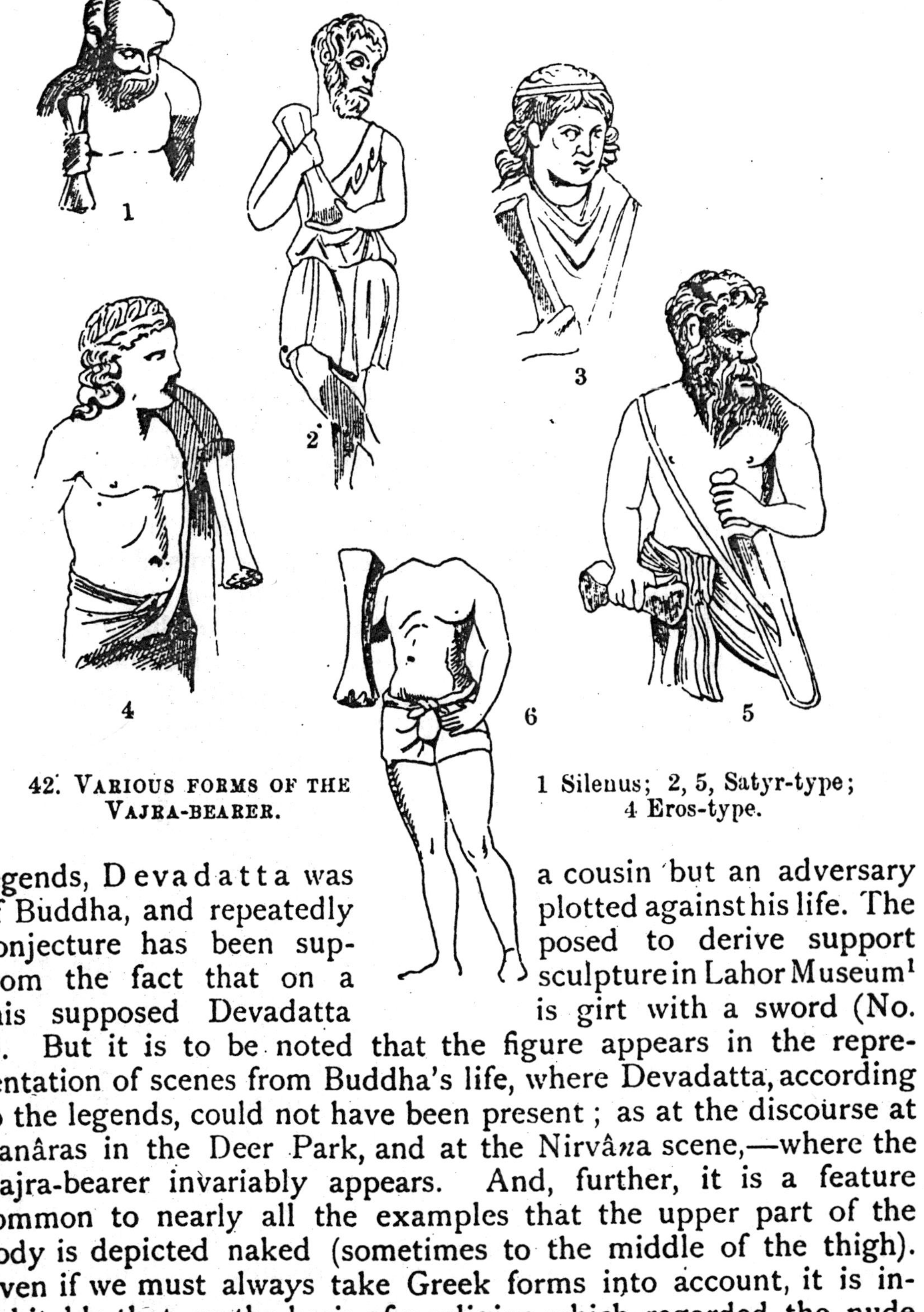

42. Various forms of the Vajra-bearer. 1 Silenus; 2, 5, Satyr-type; 4 Eros-type.

legends, Devadatta was a cousin but an adversary of Buddha, and repeatedly plotted against his life. The conjecture has been supposed to derive support from the fact that on a sculpture in Lahor Museum[1] this supposed Devadatta is girt with a sword (No. 5). But it is to be noted that the figure appears in the representation of scenes from Buddha's life, where Devadatta, according to the legends, could not have been present; as at the discourse at Banâras in the Deer Park, and at the Nirvâ*n*a scene,—where the Vajra-bearer invariably appears. And, further, it is a feature common to nearly all the examples that the upper part of the body is depicted naked (sometimes to the middle of the thigh). Even if we must always take Greek forms into account, it is indubitable that, on the basis of a religion which regarded the nude quite as unfavourably as did the Christian religion, this almost

[1] *Indian Monts.* pl. 132. A scene in the Kâsyapa legend.

invariable nudity must have a meaning. Even if Devadatta was really the *Guru* of a sect of naked monks, the partial covering is unintelligible.[1]

Next it has been argued that Mâra, the evil one, is represented by this figure; and for this view the argument stands thus:—The head of the figure, where preserved, differs widely in character. On the old and beautifully composed relief from which No. 1 is taken, the head is like that of Silenus, with tonsure, sensual face, and thin, streaky beard. On another (No. 6) he has bristling hair and a full beard, and is somewhat wild and demoniacal in look and bearing. In representation No. 4, which is taken from a relief representing the one given in fig. 57, the club-bearer is represented with a youthful appearance and with a wreath upon his hair. No. 5 is taken from a rougher replica of the same composition. The features of the head shown in No. 3, from a representation of the discourse at Banâras, which forms part of a pointed arch, express malicious joy. The club-bearer, it is inferred, therefore, is a being who looks with an unfriendly eye upon all Buddha's miracles and upon every practical proof of his ministry, who lies in wait continually, but is careful not to enter into direct opposition to him. In one instance this figure is represented (ill. 57) with a fan (Hind. *chauri*), with which he fans the great Teacher. The lying in wait and the mockery seem expressed on the relief represented in ill. 70 (from Natthu, near Sanghâo), which depicts Gautama Buddha's death. In the centre of the composition, behind the couch of the dying, is seen a bearded figure which raises high his left hand with the club-like attribute. On a rough replica of the same representation (ill. 74) this divinity stands at the head of the Buddha entering Nirvâ*n*a. On this relief he is naked but for a short loin-cloth, and unbearded; in his left hand he holds his club-like attribute, and with the right he points to Buddha's head. The relative size of the figure varies in different sculptures; while on some it is of the same size as the other figures, there are instances where it is of dwarf-like diminutiveness. It, however, is admitted that on some reliefs at least (ill. 44, &c.), he manifestly stands in a position as if a protecting guardian.[3]

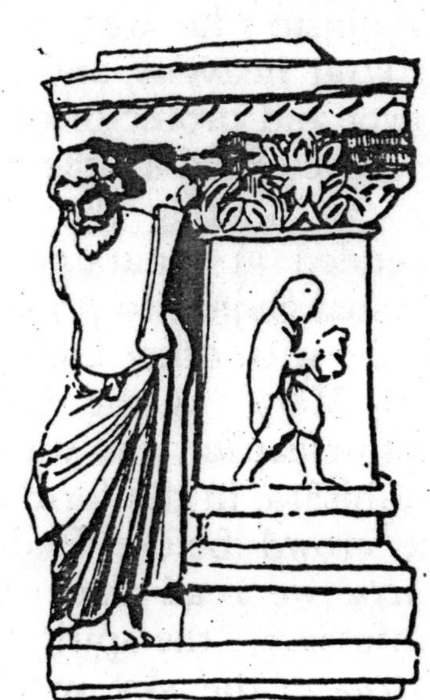

43. THE THUNDERBOLT-BEARER. From Natthu near Sanghâo.[2]

[1] Monier Williams, *Buddhism*, pp. 52, 474.

[2] Cole, *Pres. Nat. Mon., Gr.-Bud. Sc.* pl. 17; Burgess, *Monts. Ind.* pl. 115, 7.

[3] That the same figure may appear on a combined slab in two different forms within the different relief areas—here bearded and again unbearded—need not surprise us in the case of the Gândhâra school which, exercising its art mechanically, always repeats certain compositions.

Now the figure may represent the old thunder-god Sakka, and, indeed, ought to represent him in all the instances where he appears in a protective and sympathetic way. For Sakka is the *Deus ex machina* of the Bauddha legends; when anything important is about to happen on earth, his throne in heaven grows warm, and he hastens down to interfere in the interests of right and truth.[1]

But, further, apart from the features as they now exist in these sculptures, the appearance of the figure is nowhere represented as distinctly inimical; and we may pause before regarding it as in any case representing Mâra—the implacable enemy of the Buddha; —in fact, it would be entirely against all Buddhist ideas that he should ever appear among the followers of the Vanquisher.[2]

In the different representations of the Nirvâ*n*a scene, too, the personage in question appears to be clearly identified by the legends as Sakka, *S*atamanya, or Vajrapâ*n*i—the bearer of the thunderbolt. In a former birth, they relate, he had been the son of a Chakravartti, or universal ruler, and had taken a vow to defend Buddhism; he was then born king of the Devas of the Trayastri*ms*at heavens, and as such is the representative of the secular power and protector of the Sa*m*gha or church. Hence he came to be represented as the constant attendant of Buddha and ever at his call, holding the *vajra* as ready to crush every enemy. He attended at Gautama's birth, and at his flight from home; he assisted Sujâtâ to prepare his meal on the attainment of Buddhahood; with other Devas he congratulated Buddha on his victory over Mâra; at the Muchalinda tree he brought Buddha fruit, a tooth-cleanser, and water to bathe his face; on the conversion of Bimbisâra, in the form of a young Brâhma*n*a, he advanced through the crowd before Buddha, singing his praise. In the *Ambattha Sutta* we read that, when Gautama was forcing Amba*tth*a to a confession, 'the spirit who bears the *vajra*[3] stood over above Amba*tth*a in the sky with a mighty mass of iron, all fiery, dazzling and aglow, with the intention, if he did not answer, there and then to split his head in pieces. And the Blessed one perceived the spirit bearing the thunderbolt, and so did Amba*tth*a the Brahma*n*a.' Lastly, when he saw Buddha was about to depart, Sakka exclaimed in grief,

[1] I reluctantly differ from Professor Grünwedel as to the weight of his argument outlined above. We must bear in mind that this figure in all these sculptures is carved in most refractory material, on a very small scale, has been weathered by more than a millenium, and was, almost certainly, originally covered by a thin coating of plaster and painted. Such considerations should make us chary of laying too much stress on the features left on these small figures. Then the theory that the thunderbolt is an attribute of Mâra and of the Devas generally is one for which I know of no sufficient evidence.—J.B.

[2] In this and the following paragraphs, I state the view which to me seems most consistent with the legends and the reliefs.—J.B.

[3] Buddhaghosa identifies the Vajrapâ*n*i here with Indra. Conf. *Sac. Bks. of the Buddhists*, vol. II, p. 117.

'The Tathâgata is about to leave us to enter the great Nirvâ*n*a he will no longer teach us, he will no longer protect us. The poisoned shaft hath entered deep, the flame of sorrow riseth up.' Then letting fall the diamond sceptre, in despair he rolled himself in the dust, and rising again full of grief and compassion he exclaimed, 'In the vast ocean of birth and of death who shall be our boat and our oar? In the darkness of a long night, who shall be our lamp and our watch?' Both Fah-hian and Hiuen Thsang refer to this and to the stûpa raised on the spot.[1] Now this Nirvâ*n*a scene is one of the most frequently represented, and in most, if not all, the reliefs Sakka appears there—often as a burly, bearded man, naked to the waist—either fallen to the ground, or standing by the dying teacher in an attitude of grief. The hand upon the head, or raised in the air, or pointing to the dying, are attributes expressive of grief or dismay.

The Nirvâ*n*a subjects thus explained lead us to conclude that in the others,—whether he appeared as a comely young Brâhma*n*a (fig. 40) or in the burly form reminding us of a copy of a Zeus,—we have the same *S*akra in all, distinguished as the thunderbolt-bearer or Vajrapâ*n*i; and as Strabo and his authorities regarded Indra as identical with the Jupiter Pluvius[2] of the Greeks, we can readily imagine how an artist at all familiar with the classical forms, on being called upon to represent the Indian ruler of the atmosphere, would naturally take some well-known type of Zeus as his model, and with the bushy locks he would copy also the nude trunk and even the beard of his originals.[3] When a form was demanded representing the Deva 'as a young Brâhma*n*a,' more or less modification and adaptation would be introduced; but the refractory character of the material would interfere with the nicer details of feature and the like. Whether the appearance in the earlier Gândhâra sculptures of a god bearing a thunderbolt always seen near the person of Buddha may, at a later date, have originated the Bodhisattva V a j r a p â *n* i of the northern school,[4] must remain a probable conjecture.

[1] Sp. Hardy, *Man. of Bud.* 198, 298f., 355f.; Beal, *Si-yu-ki*, vol. II, p. 36; Remusat and Klaproth, *Foe-koue-ki*, p. 239; conf. Bigandet, *Legend of Gaudama*, vol. I, pp. 141-2, 154-5, II, p. 75; Rhys Davids, *Bud. Birth Stories*, pp. 67, 86, 109, 116-17. In Legge's translation of Fah-hian the illustration (No. 8) of the Nirvâ*n*a scene, from a Chinese work, shows *S*akra fallen to the ground beside his sceptre.—J.B.

[2] Strabo, lib. xv, c. 1, § 69; conf. Lassen, *Ind. Alter.* Bd. II, S. 702-3; Muir, *Or. Sansk. Texts*, vol. V, p. 77.

[3] Conf. *Globus* (1899), vol. LXXIII, No. 2, p. 170, fig. 2. There is another replica of No. 44, on which the bearded figure holds the thunderbolt—which is wanting here. Conf. *Jour. Ind. Art*, vol. VIII, pp. 78 and 35, pl. 10, fig. 4.

[4] Further, as Vajrapâ*n*i swears to Buddha's doctrine, so Buddha—his master and defender—must have at his disposal Vajrapâ*n*i's weapon, the thunderbolt. Thus the legend of Buddha's thunderbolt arises, and also the use of the small brass *vajras* (r*Do·rje*, Mongol: *Ojir*) which to this day are among the most indispensable attributes of a Lama. But that pictorial representations have exercised a very important influence on the creation of Bauddha legends has been mentioned when speaking of the

Mâra Pâpiyân, or Vasavarti (p. 39), rarely, if ever, appears in Bauddha sculptures, except in the representations of the temptation scene. There, among the weapons that he and his host threaten to hurl at *S*âkyamuni, his sceptre javelin or vajra may appear, but not specially as an attribute, for the bow and arrows are rather his distinctive symbol.

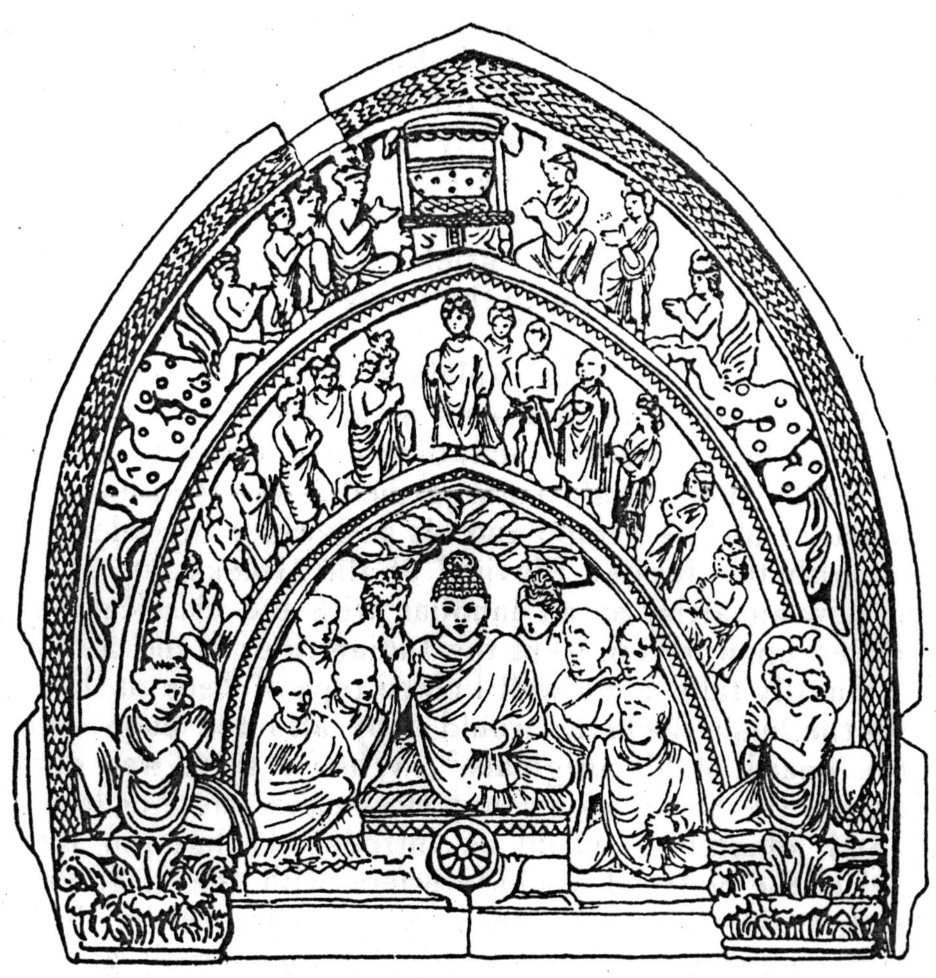

44. Gandhâra relief. From a photograph.

On the relief (ill. 44)[2] Buddha is represented with the wheel symbol, supported on the *trisula*, therefore preaching and surrounded by disciples. He sits under the Bodhi tree; and among his surroundings, a bearded figure appears on his right hand and

throne supports of the Lamas, and can hardly be sufficiently emphasised. With reference to the spread of Buddhism and the intercourse between different countries, it is interesting to note that the thunderbolt worshipped in Se-ra near Lha-sa originated in Persia (conf. Laufer, *Sitzungsber. der Phil. Kl. Bayer-Acad.* 1898, III, S. 591). I would remark that Mâra has been received into the system at least of the red-capped Lamas (Padmasambhava's school) as Tse-ma-ra. He is the tutelary deity of Sam-ye, the most ancient monastery of Tibet, where he enjoys a strange ritual: *Jour. Buddh. Text Soc.*, vol. V (1897), ii, pp. 3-4. But there a tutelary deity also—Kin-kan, *i.e. vajra*—is worshipped; conf. Jäsche, *Tib. Dict.* s.v. However, these remarks are not decisive for our reliefs, though they may be of value for the later history of this type.—A.G.

[2] In Lahor Museum; see *Ind. Monuments*, pl. 96; and conf. Rhys Davids, *Buddhist Birth-Stories*, p. 100.

one without beard to the left. As to their persons we can say nothing, as almost nought but the shoulders are seen. The identity of the bearded head with that of the thunderbolt-bearer on the Nirvâ*n*a reliefs (No. 70) is evident; but we can hardly assume that the attitude here is inimical to the Teacher, or that the two heads represent a good and an evil divinity. In the line of sculptures above, we see the vajra-bearer on Buddha's left—here, too, with a sword—while another *deva* kneels on the right.

The designation Vajrapâ*n*i which we assign to these figures in the reliefs, suggests other conceptions—quite a new phase in the development of Buddhism. We have before us a descriptive term or poetical appellation which has crystallized into a special deity:[1]—the term itself was perhaps taken from a *Stotra*, such as the verses of the *Lalita-Vistara*,—a term, indeed, which may even go back to the sculptor's studio. Let us fancy how the artist receives his commission: According as there is more or less space available, the pious donor will pay more or less; a Buddha, a thunderbolt-bearer, a few Nâgas, &c., will be brought together from the ready made figures and grouped as desired. Thus we see that we must everywhere work with a history of the types employed, and that these artist's types, in details as well as in whole compositions, may be used for different individuals and different events. Doubtless, in the development of the Gândhâra period, changes of interpretation may have taken place, even through the artist himself. Let us remember that the huts of the Middle Ages were often the birthplaces of new doctrines: thus the idea strikes us that the Græculi and their disciples, who executed the first reliefs in Gandhâra, were not without their influence on the religion. The artist is surely the first exponent of his own work. In the circumstances we have here, such must have been the case, when a mythology had to be first created from fixed types. No one has described this better, with reference to the circumstances in Gaul, than M. A. Foucher:[1]—"Do you want a Hesus, a Teutâtes? We can give you a Mars, a Mercury, and you can worship them under other names. We do not know your goddess Sulcis—you people of Aquæ Solis (Bath), but how would it do to make this representation of Athena stand for her image? . . ."

If now we consider more closely the early materials from which the Gândhâra sculptor chose to represent the Indian legends, there offer themselves as the basis of his types—Zeus represented with the eagle (=Garu*d*a); the eagle with the thunderbolt (*vajra*); the eagle with Ganymede[3] (Garu*d*a with the Nâgakanyâ: conf. p. 109).

[1] On the genesis of new gods from epithets, conf. G. de Blonay, ***Materiaux pour servir à l'histoire de la deese Târâ***, Paris, 1895, p. 64.

[2] 'L'Art Bouddhique dans l'Inde' in ***Revue de l'histoire des Religions***, tom. XXX (1894), pp. 366ff. Conf. for Hesus or Esus and Teutâtes, Lucan, i, 445; Lactantius, i, 21.

[3] The employment of this type in the Persian style plays an important part at the period of the migrations of peoples. Conf. Hampel, ***der Goldfund von Nagy Szent***

If we call the figure Vajrapâ*n*i, what is it to be called when it appears twice on the same relief? We must decide (ill. 45),—

(1) Whether we should call the one Vajrapâ*n*i, the other, Mâra or Indra (*S*akra). The latter is quite possible, since the texts often indicate both (as well as *S*iva and Rudra) as different gods side by side; or,

(2) Whether we should think of the old Indian panoramic scenes which would permit two representations of the same person to appear on the same panel: but, so far as our evidence goes, panoramas are usually divided by pillars. The figures also are here so varied in appearance, dress, and attitude that we might readily suppose they are different.

The representation relates to the snake king Elapâtra.[2] Elapâtra the Nâga appears before Buddha in human shape, in order to hear his teaching. Buddha requires him to show himself in his true form as a snake. The Nâga answers that he is afraid of the Garu*d*as, the hereditary enemies of the Nâgas. Then Buddha commands Vajrapâ*n*i to protect him. Vajrapâ*n*i does so and the Nâga appears as a gigantic snake. The relief shows a small Vajrapâ*n*i in the background, who raises the thunderbolt threateningly, while in the foreground the Nâga king, accompanied by his wife, stands before Buddha in water and a second thunderbolt-bearer walks behind the Buddha. The indication of the Nâgas is the usual snakes appearing over the heads of the hero worshippers.

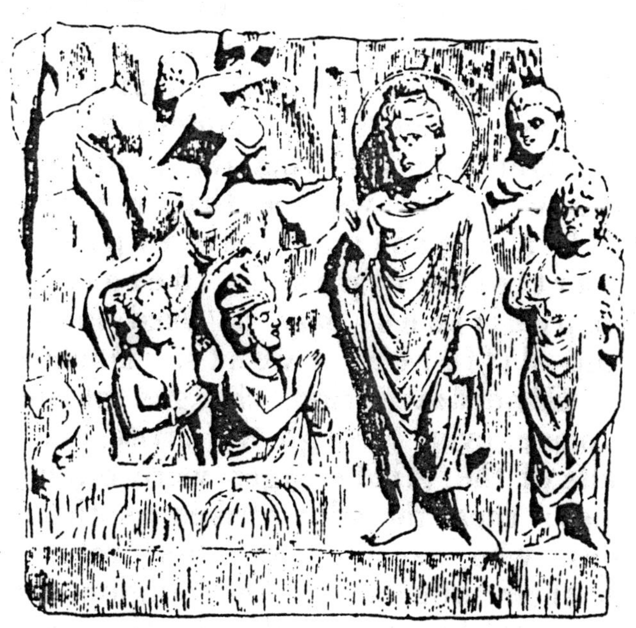

45. Relief from Rodh Monastery, near Sanghâo. (Cole, *Pres. Nat. Monts.* pl 8).

Sakka, converted into a Vajrapâ*n*i, loses his old Hindu character as a nature god; and, as is common with the Buddhists, he is multiplied into a class of Devas: thus, when Buddha returned to Kapilavastu, "the eight Vajrapâ*n*is surrounded him as an escort," and "divine *S*akra, with a multitude of Devas belonging to Kâma-

Miklós. Budapest, 1885, figs. 4, 10, 11, 39. Compare, further on, for example, the bronze medallion in Speier, *Jarhb. des Vereins der Alterthumsfreunde im Rheinlande*, Hft. lviii, Tf. 1. This combination of the Vajrapâ*n*i with the Garu*d*a still lives in Lamaism: there is a Vajrapâ*n*i accompanied by Garu*d*as, the Vajrapâ*n*i-âchârya.—conf. *Globus*, 1899, S. 170*b*; and one with Garu*d*a wings, Khyun-shog-chan.

[2] Conf. Schiefner, *Tibet. Lebensbeschreibung des Sâkyamuni*, S. 19 [S.A.]; the same, 'Mahâkatyâyana und König Tschandrapradyota,' in *Mém. de l'Acad. de St. Pétersbourg*, tom. XXII (1875), p. 11.

loka, took their place on the left hand." Vajrapâ*n*i thus got separated from *S*akra and was converted into a distinct god, or into a Bodhisattva; lastly, *S*akra sinks into a Yaksha.[1]

The later Indian art retained the thunderbolt bearer: we see him as Sakka, for example, on the Amarâvatî relief (in ch. iv.)[2] where he is present when Râhula, Buddha's son, demands his inheritance from his father, and is clothed as a monk. Another figure which, though many handed, we must call Vajrapâ*n*i, is carved in the Vi*s*vakarma Buddhist chaitya cave at Elura, and is here given as an example in fig. 47.

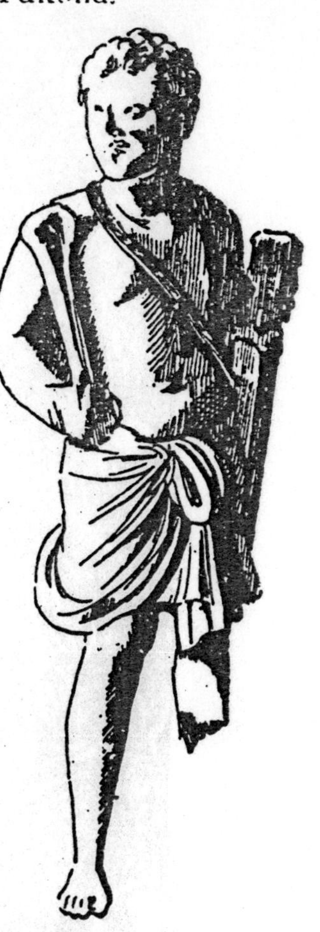

46. THE THUNDERBOLT BEARER. From a relief in Lahor Museum.

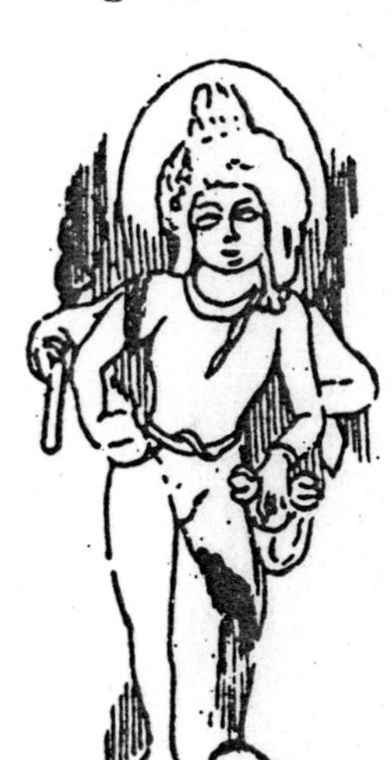

47. VAJRAPÂNI. From Vi*s*vakarma[3] rock temple (Elurâ)

Though different sculptors may have taken their own ways of representing Mâra, still there was a fixed type also for this Deva. He appears, at a later date, in full festal attire, youthful in figure, with b o w a n d a r r o w; and in this type (fig. 49) he appears at Buddha's temptation. He is thus brought into comparison with K â m a or S m a r a, of the Hindu pantheon, who also bears the names of Mâra and *S*amâ*n*taka. The worship of this latter god seems to have been much cultivated in mediæval India. His attributes, bow and arrow and Makara, ill. 33 (Dolphin) suggest that there is some connexion with the Greek Eros.[4]

On the relief on ill. 50, the lower subject presents Gautama on his faithful horse Ka*nth*aka, riding out of the gate to spend his life as a begging ascetic. At the gate, from which the guards are fleeing, stands a kingly form with a nimbus, the d i v i n i t y (perhaps) of the p a l a c e g a t e (*dvare adhivatthâ devatâ*), and, if so, a local divinity, quite in the style of later Hellenic art. With regard to the Hellenic influence under which the composition originated, it is of interest, further, to note that the right hand of the divinity stretches out into the frame and so points forcibly to what is following.

[1] In Japan the two temple guardians called Ni-ô, and habitually found at the entrances, are named as Indra and Brahmâ; but their type is derived from Vajrapâni (Shoméi-kongo). Vassilief, *Le Bouddhisme* (tr. par M. La Comme), pp. 197, and 163; Schiefner, *Tib. Lebensbeschr*. S. 14.

[2] From Fergusson, *Tree and Serp. Wor*. pl. lix, p. 189.

[3] Burgess. *Elura Cave Temples* in *Ar. Sur. W. Ind*. vol. V, pl. xix, 4.

[4] The Holî or Hûli, the spring festival in honour of K*r*ish*n*a's sporting with the Gopîs, may perhaps be indirectly connected with Kâma,—but this is doubtful.

If we now look at a replica of the same subject in the Lahor Museum,[1] we find there that, in the place occupied by the gate

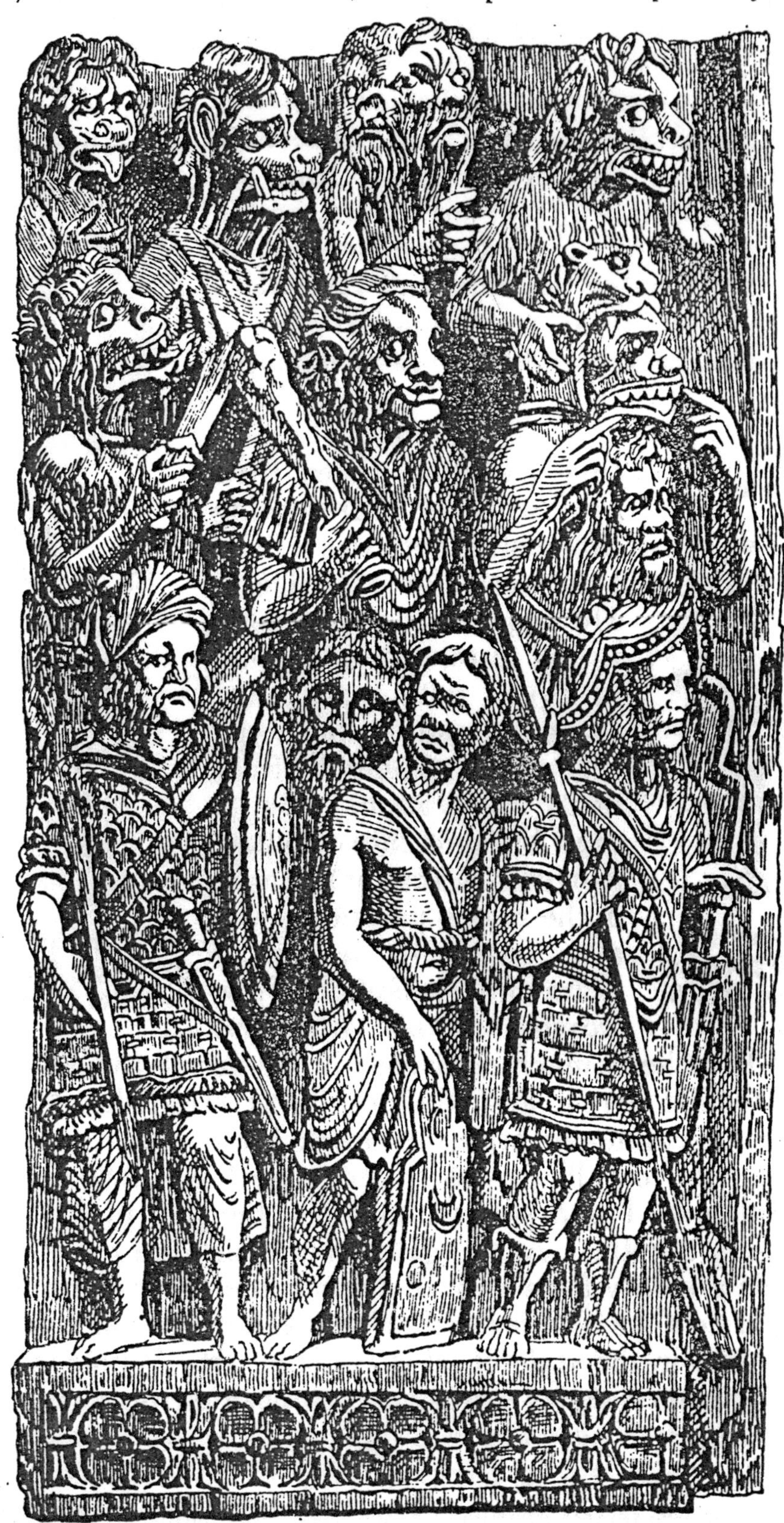

48. GÂNDHÂRA RELIEF IN LAHOR MUSEUM.

divinity, in the first representation, is an archer—perhaps Mâra. In the *Avidûrenidâna*, it is related how, at the moment the gate *devata*

[1] Burgess, in *Jour. Ind. Art and Ind.* vol. VIII, pl. 19, 1, or sep. ed. pl. 17, 1; Simpson in *Jour. R. Inst. Br. Arch.* 3d ser. vol. I (1894), p. 106.

opened the door, Mâra came with the intention of stopping Gautama; and, standing in the air, he exclaimed, "Depart not, my lord! in seven days from now the wheel of empire will appear, and will make you sovereign over the four continents and the two thousand adjacent islands." When Gautama asks who he is, he receives the reply "I am Vasavatti" (Sk. Vaśavarti—'acting under the will of another') Gautama's victory over the tempter is well represented by the immovable attitude of the chief figure here, as also by that of the umbrella-bearer stepping out vigorously over the relief.

It must be admitted, however, that any quite accurate apportionment of names for the accessory figures in this composition can hardly be given, since it has to do with a more or less extended scheme.

Mâra's army, which combats Buddha and seeks to drive him from the "diamond seat" under the Bodhi-tree at Gayâ, is effectively represented in the Gândhâra school by means of popularised figures of demons which have received at Greek hands a powerful characterization (conf. ill. 48). The original of this—one of the oldest and finest reliefs—is now in the Lahor Museum. The three lowest figures are soldiers, equipped partly like Greeks,[1] but with peculiar accessories—one wears an Indian loin-cloth and turban, another a kind of three-cornered helmet or hat which suggests the well-known whitey-grey felt caps of the Tibetans and Khwaresmians: to the heads, represented as quite human, a decidedly demoniacal expression is given by the great staring eyes and the wild hair of head and beard. It has been doubted whether this relief represents Mâra's army, but its agreement with the Ajanta picture given in ill. 49), which, with the sculptured representation in Cave XXVI,[2] at the same place, must be considered. The relief arranges these frightful figures in tiers in a

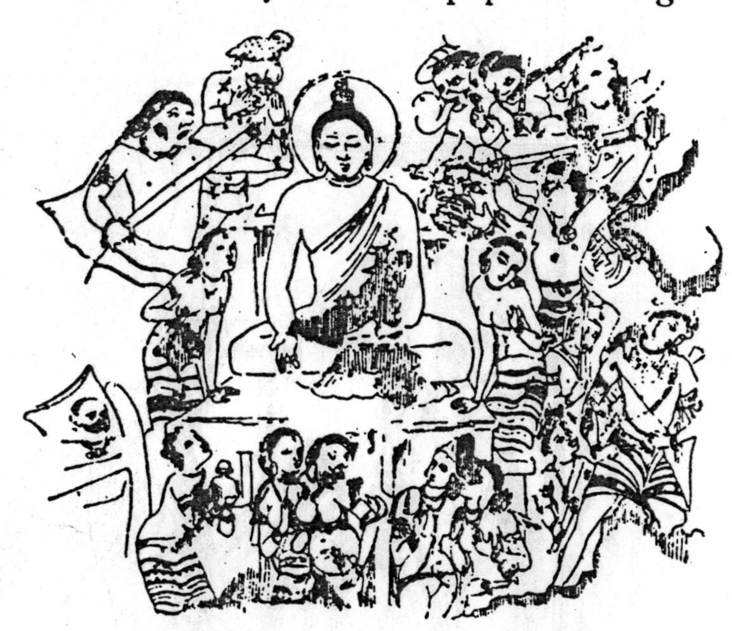

49. Mâra's attack on Gautama.
Painting in Cave I at Ajantâ, from Râjendralâl Mitra's *Buddha Gayâ*, pl. ii; conf. Griffith, *Ajantâ*, vol. I, pl. viii.

[1] It suited the stone-cutter who produced this relief, in representing the coat of mail—unintelligible to him—to put the scales with the rounded ends (openings) upwards. Whoever would use these sculptures, therefore, for the history of costume and armour, must be careful.

[2] Burgess, *Cave Temples*, pl. li and p. 345. There are also two other fragments of temptation scenes in Lahor Museum: *Ind. Monts*. pl. 133.

very clever way. In the first row are seen ordinary soldiers; behind them, in the second row, are the real demons, whose grotesque faces rise one above the other in a most effective way. On the Ajaṇṭâ representations, also, soldiers appear in the first row, and the

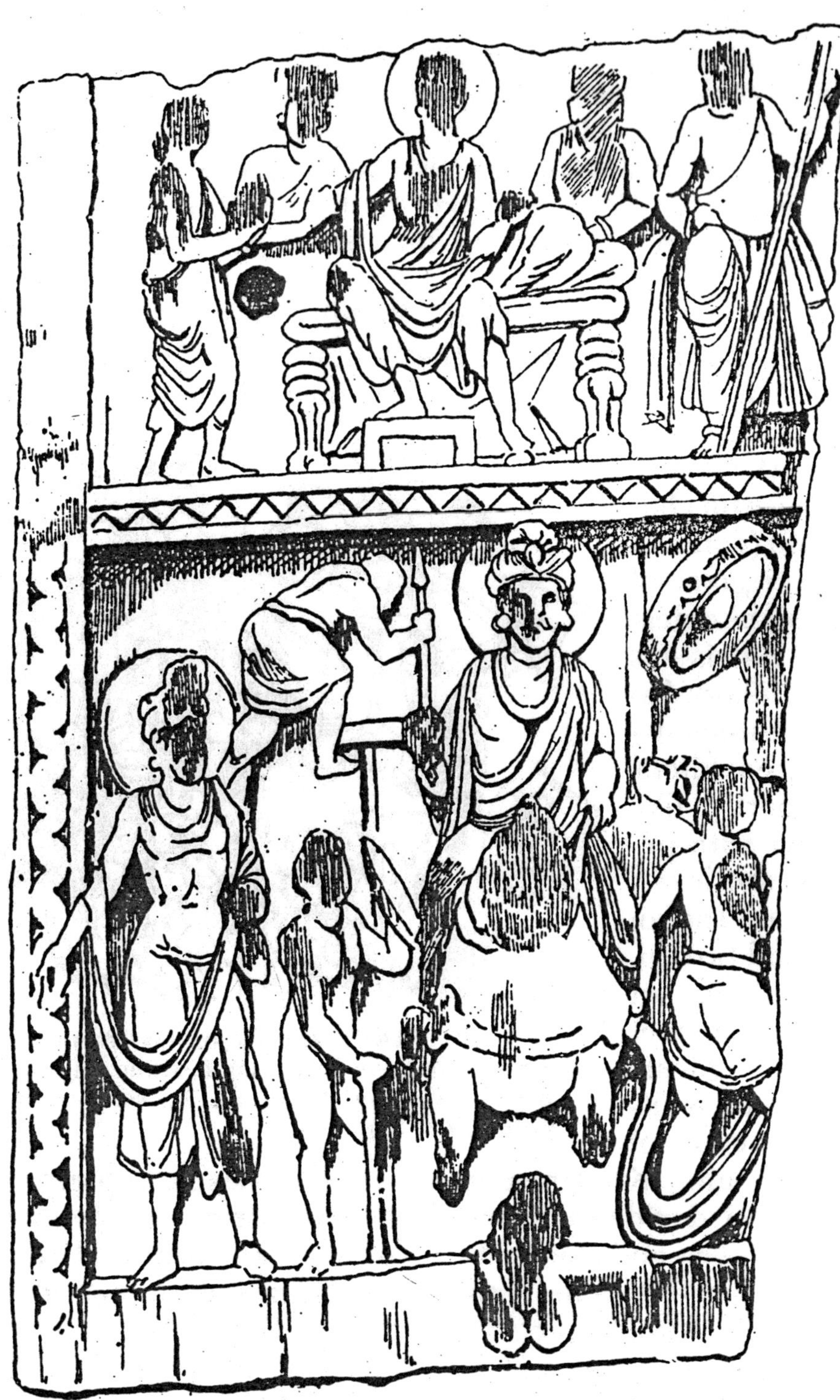

50. Gândhâra Sculpture (Lahor Museum),
The Bodhisattva Gautamâ leaving home.

hob-goblins behind them only. This graduated arrangement produces a quite peculiar effect in the relief. One figure, the first of the second row, the ample dimensions of which bind the whole group into a sort of scaling-party, shows this cumulative arrangement in a grotesque fashion. The almost fleshless mask, which is evidently intended for a death's head, grins broadly, while the hairy hands are thrust into the corners of the mouth; on the body of the demon appears a wild bearded face, and over the bare skull there rises a grinning animal's head that forms the end of a skin cap. Detached elements of this powerful figure are to be found in the art of a later day: figures with faces on their bodies, or with half-macerated skulls, or with animals' heads over the real head of the figure, have been preserved even in the modern art of the Lamas. It would be an interesting but difficult task to find out how far these

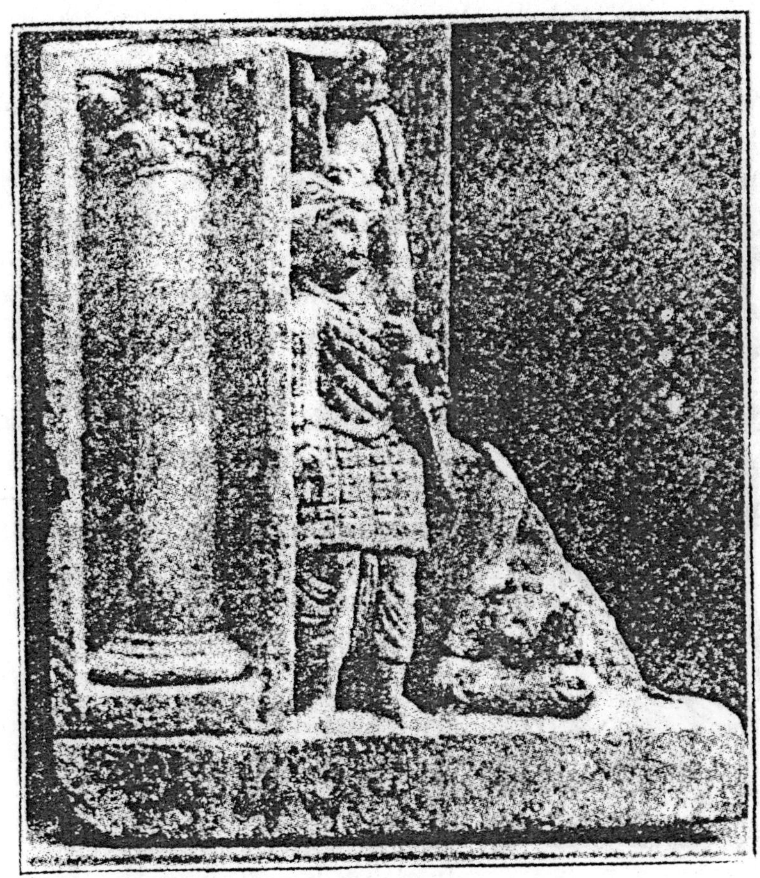

51. FRAGMENT OF A GÂNDHÂRA SCULPTURE.
The Earth-goddess bearing upon her shoulders the feet of the horse Kanthaka. Before are two men (guards), one in quilted mail with bow.

Gândhâra forms are shown in the Oni-types, so popular in Japan. The second figure of the second row is very striking. The clubs and peculiar fold of the sleeve are purely Greek; indeed, were it not for the fangs and the demoniacal features, one would be reminded of a Hercules. The three heads of the leader of the group are almost surpassed by a bearded figure in the third row: only a Greek could have succeeded in combining these skulls, which evidently belong to three faces (though only two are recognisable). This form is unique, and the Hindu artists of later times were incapable of repeating the motif except by placing side by side three disconnected faces. The little flame on the tip of the tongue of the demon, who is represented with two swords, is also interesting.

On the reliefs given in ill. 50, 51 there appears a female figure which calls for special mention. Under Gautama's horse the upper part of a woman's body (much destroyed) is seen rising out of the earth. In Greek art the female figure rising thus from the ground is known as Gê or Gaia, the goddess of the earth. On the Buddhist relief, also, it is evidently the goddess of the earth that is intended. This is clear from a description of the situation in the *Avidûrenidâna* of the Jâtaka book. There it says, after the description of the repulse of Mâra, literally this: "When Gautama desired once more to look back upon the city, the wish had hardly arisen in his mind when the great earth (Pâli, Mahâpathavî; Skt. Mahâp*ri*thivî) turned round like a potter's wheel, as if to say: 'thou needest not to turn round in order to look,' and so let him see the town once more."[1] On the relief the feet (now broken off) of the horse Ka*nth*aka evidently stood on the forearm of the Mahâpathavî (ill. 50). Another incident of the Buddhist legend, in which also the goddess of the earth is represented as speaking, is of interest in connection with the question how far art has influenced the sacred texts. When assailed by Mâra, Gautama, who is sitting under the Bodhi-tree, calls the Earth to witness that he has acquired the right of sitting in this place (on the "diamond-throne"—Vajrâsana) by reason of his liberal alms-giving in a previous existence. The description of the incident in the *Avidûrenidâna* says merely that Gautama laid his hand upon the Earth, whereupon the Earth (Mahâpathavî) testified to his beneficence by a loud rumbling[3]. Now the description which the much

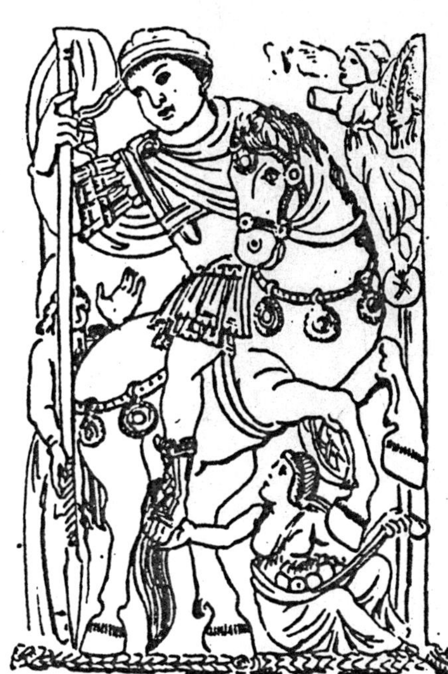

52. CENTRAL PART OF AN IVORY RELIEF, in the Casa Berberini, Rome. For comparison with No. 50.[2]

[1] Rhys Davids, *Buddhist Birth Stories*, p. 84. Conf. Foucaux, *Lalita-Vistara*, pp. 186f; A. C. Warren, *Buddhism in Transl.* pp. 61f.

[2] *Materialen zur Archäologie Russlands, herausgbn. von der k. archäol. Komm.*, No. 8, St. Petersbourg, 1892, Taf. 14 (Russ.). Conf. below, note on coin of Demetrios.

[3] Rhys Davids, *Bud. B. Stories*, p 101. Conf. also the Gândhâra relief in Arnold's *Light of Asia*, illust. ed. p. 19, where the earth-goddess is represented under the Bodhi tree; and a pedestal in Lahor Museum, *Jour. Ind. Art and Ind.*, vol. VIII, pl. 18, 1, or sep. ed. pl. 16; Foucaux, *Lalita-Vistara*, pp. 271-2.

later *Lalita Vistara* gives of this scene, seems to correspond exactly with the illustrations which show the earth-goddess introduced in the Gândhâra sculptures. "The great earth-goddess, named Sthâvarâ," it says there, "not far from Buddha, showed half of her body with all her ornaments."

This antique design is best represented by a copy on an ivory relief preserved in Rome[1] (ill. 52). In this instance it has to do with an Emperor-type developed from coin-types (conf. ill. 56 and coin of Demetrios).

Now the representations which show the event in profile are

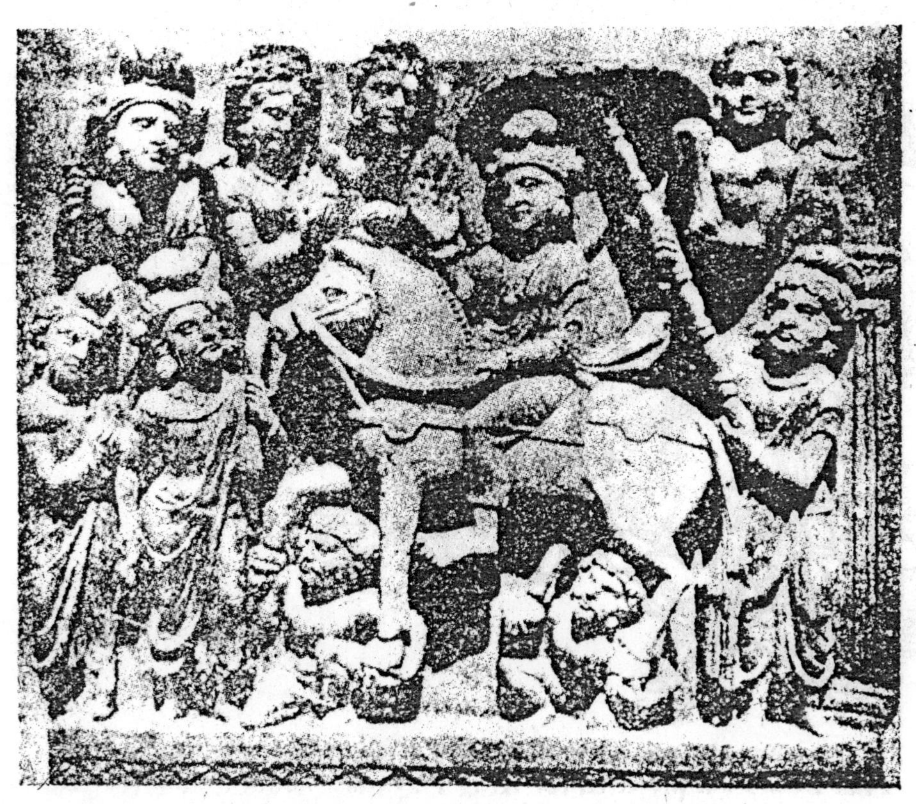

53. Gautama's Mahâbhinishkramana, or Renunciation.
A relief from Loriyân Tangai, in Calcutta Museum.

remarkable in this that below the hind legs also a figure rising out of the earth supports the horse. Thus, according as it is viewed from the front or from the side, we have two phases, one of which is due entirely to artistic considerations. It appeared to the artist irregular to place the horse in the side representations merely with the forefeet on a supporting figure (P*ri*thivî), and so he places

[1] The composition is thus directly connected with the late Roman so-called 'giant riders,' *e.g.* on the pillar of Marten; Duruy-Hertzberg, *Gesch. d. röm. Kaiserreiches*, Bd. IV, S. 58; F. Hettner, *die römisches Steindenkmäler des Prov. Mus. zu Trier*, 1893, S. 21, Nrs. 31, 32, 33.

the hind-legs also on a figure,—later art has even a supporting figure for each foot of the horse. The real explanation, however, of this artistic phase is something different: we must, in the majority of the figures, think of the deities who raise the horse

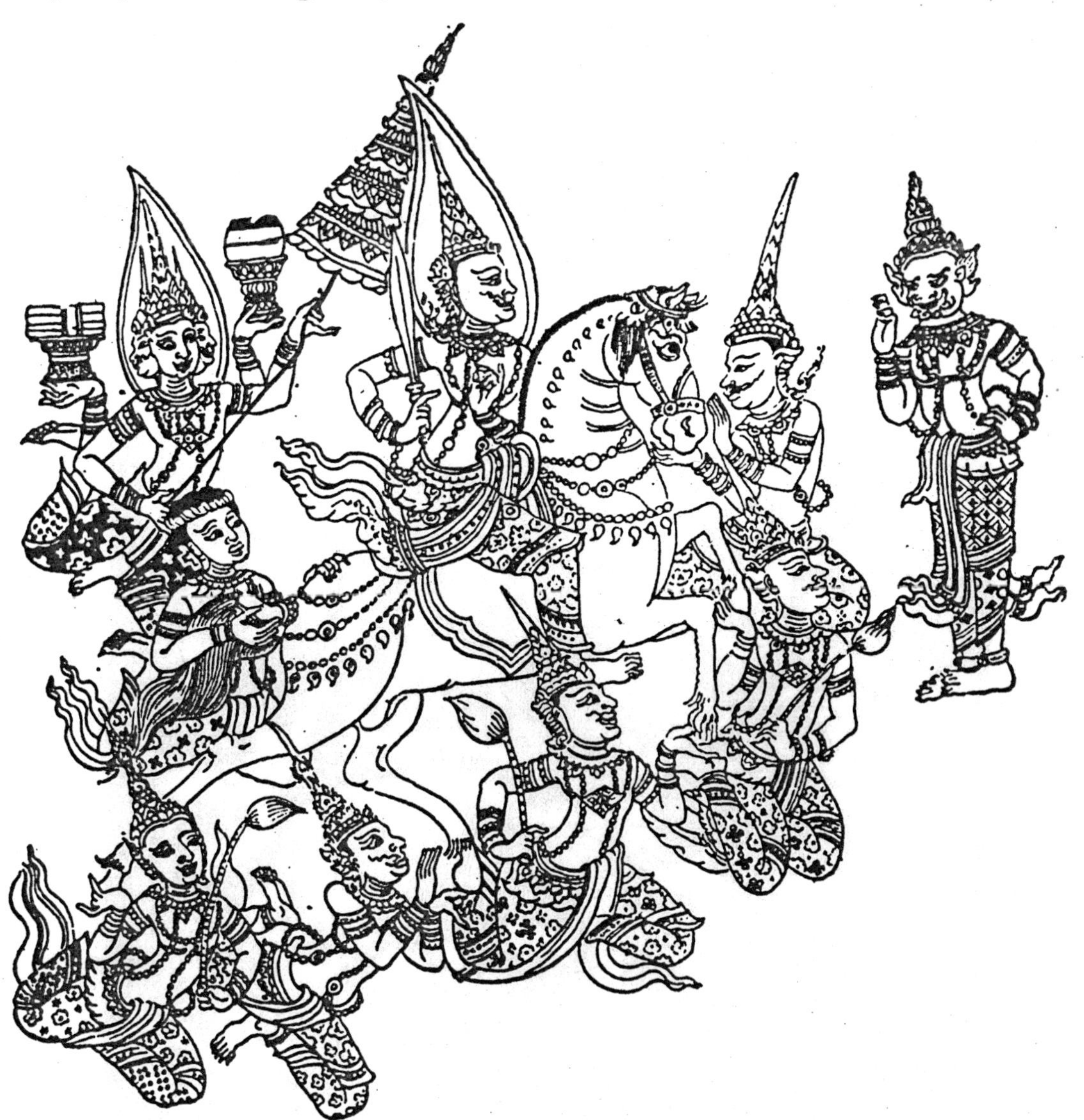

54. THE BODHISATTVA LEAVING HIS FATHER'S PALACE.
From the *Trai-p'um* prepared for King P'aya-tak, about a hundred years ago.
(Original in Berlin Museum).

Ka*nth*aka. Indeed, in a relief found at LoriyânTangai, the beings that uphold the horse have moustaches (fig. 53).[1] This sculpture,

[1] The legend (*Avidûrenidâna*) represents Gautama as considering whether he cannot leap over the gate while Channa hangs on to the tail of the horse, and it would have happened so if the gate-deity had not opened the gate. We must recognise in the bearded figures the Yakshas which lift high the horse's hoofs so that their tread may not awaken the sleeping citizens (Beal, *Sac. Bks. of the East*, vol. XIX, p. 57; *Romantic Legend*, p. 136; Rhys Davids, *Birth Stories*, p. 83). But on a sculpture at Lahor, represented in *Jour. Ind. Art and Ind.* vol. VIII (1898) pl. 22, 1 (or sep. ed. pl. 20, 1, conf. also pl. 11, 2), it is clearly two female figures who support Ka*nth*aka's hoofs. We have thus a transition from the one to the other, *i.e.* we see how the Yakshas have had their genesis in the Gê motif. In the legend of Padmasambhava, which borrows the whole story of the flight from the Buddha legend, the Dâkhinîs and Jinns, which bear the enchanted horse, take their origin in this way; conf. *Ein Kapitel des Ta-sé-sun*, Berlin (1897), S. 5.

which measures 19 inches each way, is in the Indian Museum at Calcutta and is exceedingly well preserved. The representation of the Mahâbhinishkrama*n*a or renunciation here given, shows the white horse Ka*nth*aka, as at Amarâvatî,[1] on the flank, and we can note the trappings. Here his feet are borne up by two Yakshas, as mentioned in the Chinese *Buddhacharita*.[2] Sakra, with the *vajra* on his palm, follows close behind in the air, and, as usual, is nude to the waist: Chhandaka holds the umbrella over his master's head; three other Devas,—one bearing a short sword,—appear in the air in front; and two figures, one of them holding a bow (possibly Mâra), stand in front, apparently addressing Siddhârtha.

Later Buddhist art has retained the uplifting of the horse. Fig. 54 gives an outline sketch of a beautifully finished, though mechanically composed representation from the Siamese *Trai-P'um* book, painted for king P'aya-tak about 1780 A.D. Indra leads the horse, four Yakshas bear his feet, Channa holds firmly by the tail, Brahmâ (of Hindu type) follows with an umbrella, the Vedas and drinking vessel. Before the group stands Mâra represented as the prince of demons.

Reference may here be made to two goddesses, to the first of which we cannot yet attach any name in Bauddha iconography. Along with a small stûpa, carefully excavated by Major H. A. Deane, at Sikri in 1888, were found two sculptures of considerable interest, now in Lahor Museum: a very emaciated form of Buddha, and the female figure ill. 55. These were first published by M. Senart:[3] the western influence in the female figure is quite pronounced. It is 3 feet 0½ inch in height, but the feet are broken off. Whether she be a symbolic representation or a divine personage, is difficult to determine; she may even be allied to the earth-goddess in some Mahâyânist form; or she may possibly represent Hâritî, who will next be noticed. She is accompanied by three children, one of which sits astride on her right hip in Indian fashion, and which she is about to suckle.[4] The head-dress and crown surmounting it have also a classical appearance. In other respects, the bracelets on the arms and the anklets are after the Indian fashion: and the pad that appears under the robe near the middle of the body corresponds, no

[1] Burgess, *Amarâvati*, p. 81, fig. 22; the representation of this scene must have been frequent at Amarâvatî; besides the one just referred to, see also pll. xvi, 4, xxxii, 4, xxxviii, 5, xl, 1, xli, 6, and *Tree and Serp. Wor.* pl. xlix, 1, or lix, 1.

[2] *Sac. Bks. of the East*, vol. XIX, p. 57: conf. vol. XLIX, pt. i, p. 61.

[3] *Jour. Asiat.* 8me sér. t. 15, pll. ii and iii; reproduced in *Ind. Monts.* pl. 145, and in *Jour. Ind. Art and Ind* vol. VIII, pl. 3. The illustration No. 55 is the sketch of Mr. J. L. Kipling, in *Jour. R.I.B. Arch.* (1894), p. 136, by kind permission of the Institute.

[4] A statue at Lahor, accompanied by small attendant figures (*Ind. Monts.* pl. 85) will be noticed later on. Among the sculptures in the Lahor Museum is another, which may be compared with this (*Jour. Ind. A. and I.* u.s. pl. 5, 1). It is a statue of a woman, completely draped, and holding on her left arm a child. Unfortunately, the head and right arm are wanting, and the whole fragment is much worn and abraded. But the draperies are quite Western in disposition, and the general appearance at once recalls to one's mind a mutilated statue of the Virgin suckling her child (Senart, *J. As.* u.s. pp. 141-2).

doubt, to the girdles which formed a feature of female attire, in a great many cases, at Mathurâ, at Sâñchî, at Amarâvatî, and elsewhere. On the forehead hangs a jewel, in the form of a star, the cord holding it is clearly indicated coming from the hair. It may be noted that in the cutting of the eyes, the pupils are marked with the care observable in other works from the same source.

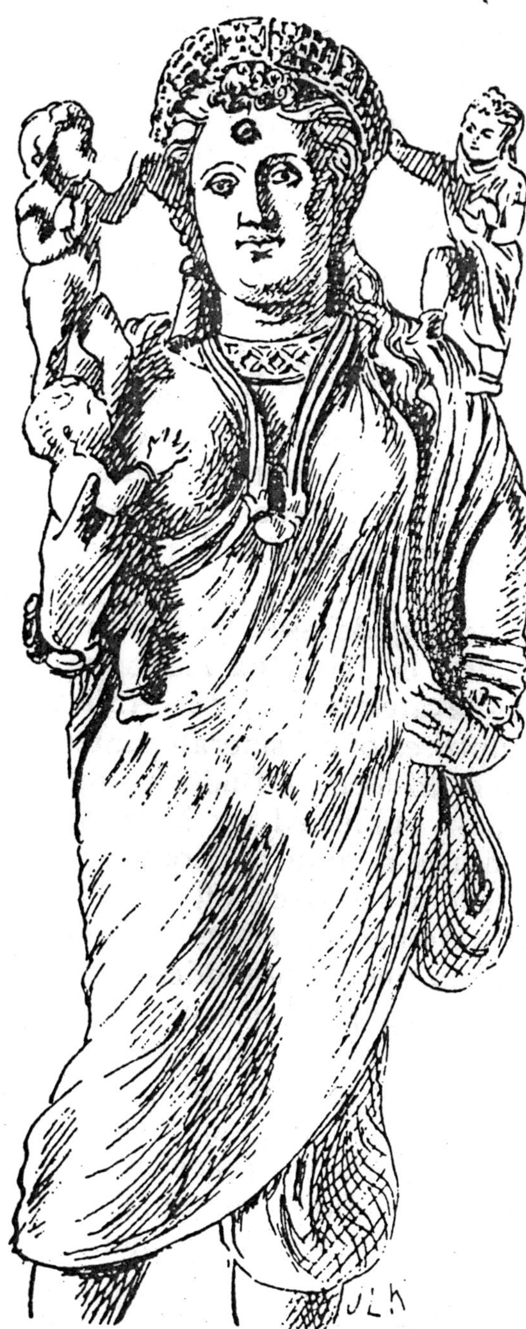

55. Female figure with children. From Sikri, Yûsufzai.

The other goddess referred to is a sculpture in the British Museum, about 28 inches in height, also representing a female divinity.[1] She has one child in her lap, one between her feet, and three at each side, of whom two on the left are wrestling,—recalling the expression in the *Ratnakûta-sûtra*, that each of Hâritî's children "was possessed of the strength of a great wrestler." The Sikri figure just described, it may be suggested, is possibly another form of this Yakshinî,—or, at least, of some allied being. For we can hardly fail in identifying the British Museum figure as Hâritî—'the mother of demons.' The Yakshas (p. 45) are described as devouring human beings, and they possibly represent the aboriginal local divinities; and, if so, are a survival of demonolatry. This Hâritî is described as having made a vow in a former birth to devour the children of Râjagriha, and was accordingly born as a Yakshinî, and became the husband of the demon king Prajñâka. She became the mother of 500 children,[2] all very strong. To nourish these she daily took a child of Râjagriha. The people having appealed to Buddha about this, he took her youngest child Pingala—"the loved one"—

[1] *Jour. I. Art and In.* vol. VIII, pl. 4, 2; or sep. ed. pl. 2, 2, and p. 9. There is a smaller replica of this relief in the Edinburgh University Library.

[2] Some versions of the legend say "ten thousand;" the Japanese say "a thousand;" but consistency in Bauddha traditions is not to be looked for. From *Lalita Vist.* u.s. p. 177, we might infer that the demon king—chief of the Yaksha army—was called Pañchika.

and placed him in his bowl. The mother sought for him seven days and, failing to find him, applied to Buddha for information. He addressed her—"Do you so tenderly love your child? yet you have 500 of them. How much more would persons with only one or two love theirs?" On this she was converted and became an Upâsikâ, or lay disciple; and to feed her children Buddha said to her, "The Bhikshus, who live in their monasteries, shall every day offer you food out of their portion for nourishment." Hence, I-tsing tells us, the image of Hâritî was found either in a porch or in a corner of the dining hall of Indian monasteries, holding a babe in her arms, and round her knees three or four children. An abundant offering of food was daily made before it. This "demon mother of children" is described as one of the subjects of the Chatûrmahârâja devâs. In Japan, she is known as Kishimojin, the protectress of the earth, and is represented carrying her youngest child Bïngara in her arms, or sometimes with six daughters.[1]

Another Indian goddess must also be mentioned, though she does not appear in the body of a relief itself, but is only employed decoratively: this goddess is represented (in a defaced sculpture in Lahor Museum) sitting sideways on a lion and holding on her knees a musical instrument in the form of a lute (fig. 56). This can only be intended for S a r a s v a t î, the goddess of music, while it remains enigmatical why the goddess, who plays no part at all in the older Buddhist texts, appears here beside the Hindû gods known by the Buddhists. This figure is possibly meant for a local deity. Perhaps, as goddess of Vedic poesy, she received the attribute of the lute. Siri (Skt. *Srî*), the local goddess of the Asoka period, is not found in the Gândhâra sculptures, and later she disappears from the Buddhist pantheon. But Sarasvatî is very prominent not only in Chino-Japanese Buddhism—as the goddess B e n t e n she belongs to the gods of fortune,—but in the Buddhism of Tibet, the so-called Lamaism, she has taken a prominent place among the goddesses of that degenerate form of the old doctrine. She is the only one of the female Energies of the Bodhisattvas whose characteristics are pronounced and well-defined; she is the Energy (*S* a k t i) of the Bodhisattva Mañjughosha or Mañjusrî,[2] with whom we shall deal in a

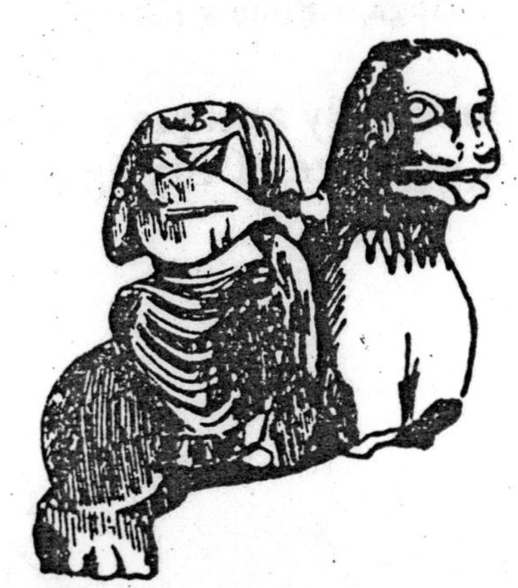

56. SCULPTURED FRAGMENT FROM GANDHÂRA. A goddess playing the Vînâ, sitting on a lion: a type of the goddess Sarasvatî.

[1] I-tsing's *Record of the Buddhist Religion*, p. 137; Beal, *Si-yu-ki*, vol. I, p. 110; Bigandet, *Leg. of Gaudama*, vol. I, p. 245; *Archæologia*, vol. lviii, p. 241; *Mahâvagga*, I, 6, 30; *Vinaya Pit.*, *Samyuktavastu*, ch. 31; and *Samyuktaratna-sutra*, vii, 106; *Guide au Musée Guimet*, 1897, p. 208; *Catal. au M.G.* 1883, p. 218.

[2] Grünwedel, *Mythol. d. Buddhismus in Tibet*, &c., Ss. 152, 155; Schlagintweit, *Buddhism in Tibet*, p. 66, n.; conf. Oldfield, *Sketches from Nepal*, vol. II, pp. 177, 186, 267. *Srî* is one of the names of Sarasvatî; it is also applied in Nepal to Mañjusrî himself. Waddell says no female energy is allotted to Mañjusrî; *Bud. of Tibet*, pp. 355-6.—J.B.

subsequent chapter. The figure of Sarasvatî thus forms an additional proof of the connexion of the iconography of the northern school with the Gândhâra sculptures.

In the Gândhâra school the Nâga has preserved the same type which the older Indian art has created for him. The relief shown in ill. 57,—other replicas of which are known,—represents the Nâga-king behind an altar, before which stand Buddha and Vajrapâ*n*i The snake-hood over the head is hardly visible in the illustration, but on the replicas it is clearly seen. The relief represents the scene in which a Nâga wishes to be admitted into the order. Evidently the lower part of the Nâga's body, which is to be imagined behind the altar, should terminate in that of a serpent. This is a thoroughly antique refinement which seeks to mitigate the repulsive appearance of the figure, and makes the human form possible for the Nâga as far as the figure is visible. From the time when a Nâga managed to introduce himself, in human form, into the

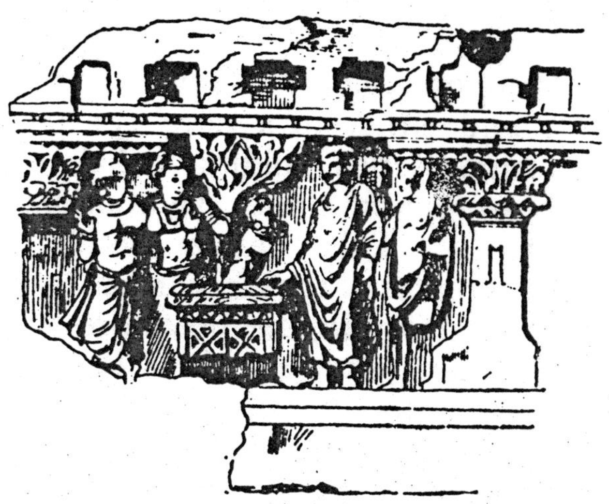

57. Gândhâra relief, Lahor Museum.
Buddha attended by Vajrapâ*n*i, talking with a Nâga. From a photo.

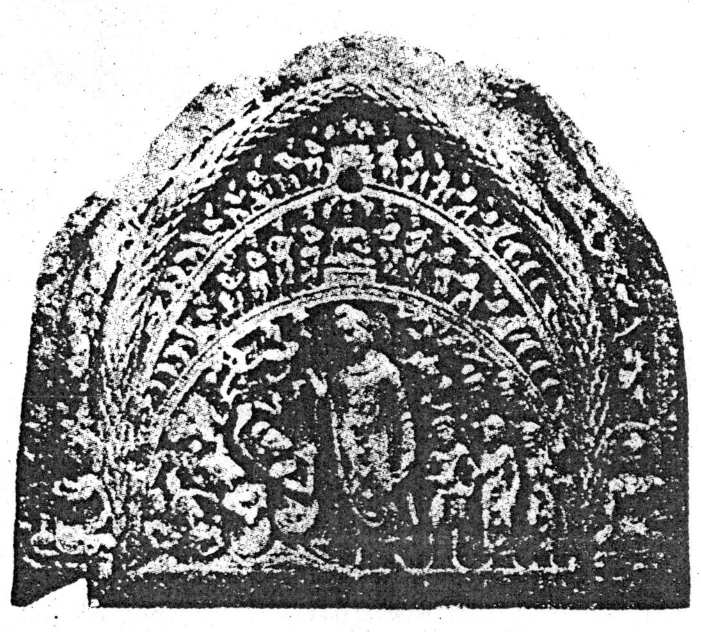

58. Relief from Loriyân Tangai, 1. Calcutta Museum.
Buddha attended by Vajrapâ*n*i, gods and men, teaching the Nâgas.

monastery till in sleep or at Buddha's command, his true form was recognised, the question—whether the novice was a Nâga—was

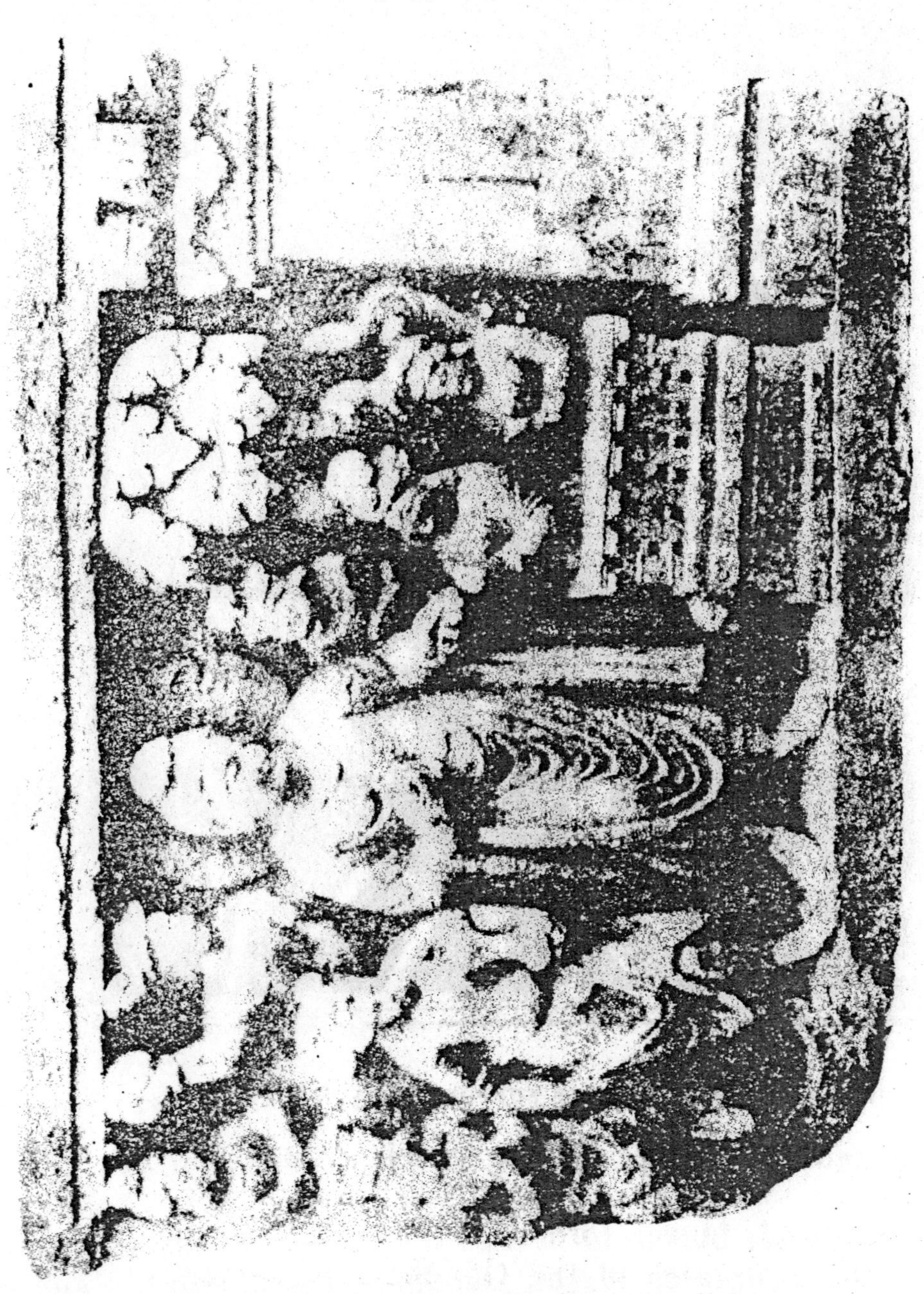

59. Buddha, Vajrapâni and Nagas (Takht-i-Bâhi).

embraced in the formulæ for admission to the order (*Kammavâchâ*), and to this day the ritual is thus completed. Ill. 58, from Loriyân Tangai, is almost a replica of the same, only the Nâgas appear in it to be rising out of water; and fig. 59, from Takht-i-Bahî, is a third example, in which a good representation of Vajrapâni appears.[1] In many sculptures, in the rock-temples, figures of Nâgas, both with the full human form, and also showing only the trunk, are represented upholding the Padmâsana or Lotus-throne of the Buddha. With the lotus stalk growing out of water, it is not inappropriate as a decorative device. This is exemplified in fig. 60 from the Kanheri Caves.[2] The Nâga seems at a later date to have

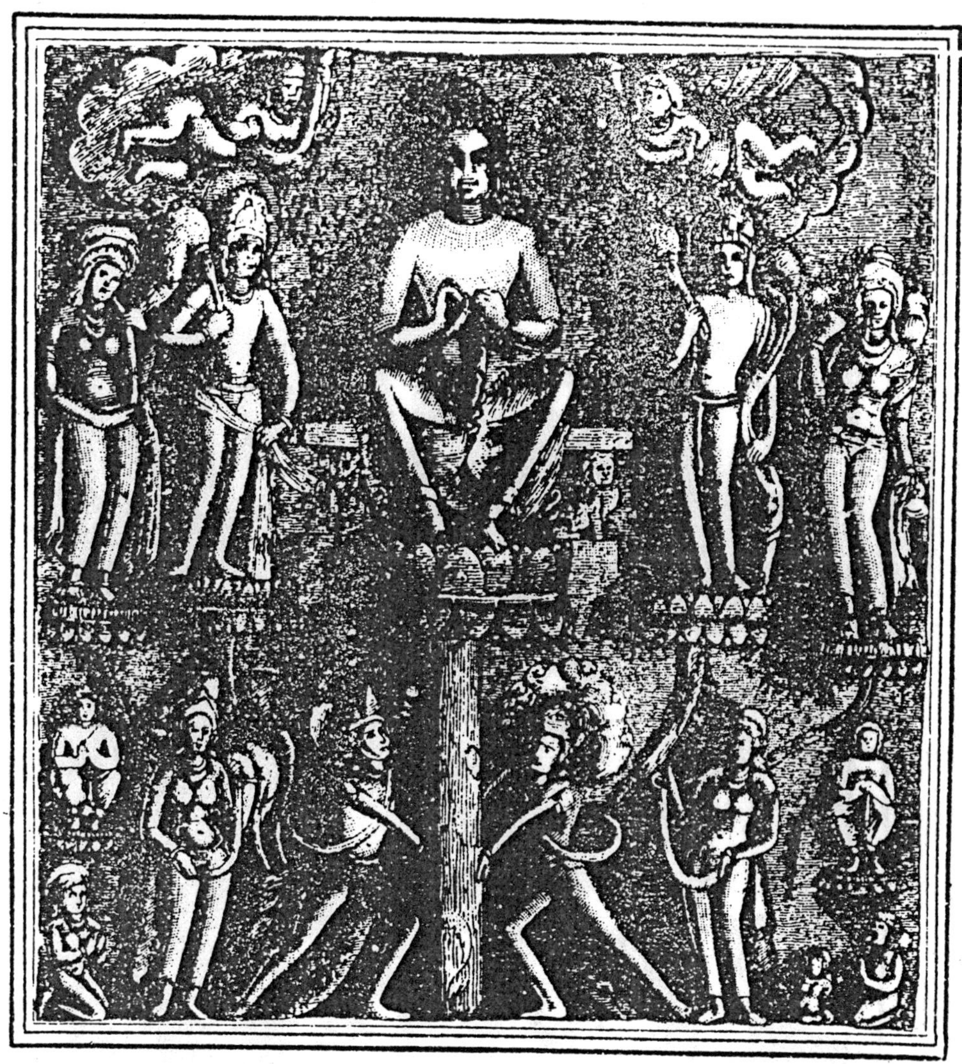

60. Buddha's lotus throne supported by Nâgas (Kanheri Caves).

been looked on as a protecting power (Burgess, *Cave Temples*, pl. xxxix).

But the purely human form with the snake over the head appears also on the sculptures of the Gândhâra monasteries. The most remarkable representation of this kind, which evidently was popular as a decoration, has been quite misunderstood by its interpreters. A group—in which an imitation of the Ganymede of Leochares

[1] *Jour. R. A Soc.* 1899, p. 422.

[2] The numerous sculptured panels in the Kanheri Caves, if carefully delineated, would form an important chapter in Bauddha iconography.

(B.C. 350)[1] has been, with reason, recognised,—appears in the Gândhâra sculptures in several replicas (conf. ill. 61).[2] A rather coarsely executed female figure, from the back of whose neck, on the best preserved relief, rises a long snake, is borne into the air by a great eagle. The features of this female figure, whose uncovered right breast escapes from the otherwise ample garments, are distorted with pain: the eagle's beak tears at the serpent. The bird itself has a cap with a kind of fillet and ear-rings! Cunningham tried to explain the group as the ascension to heaven of Mâyâ, Buddha's mother, who according to the legend, died seven days after the birth of her son. Apart from the fact that the legends do not speak of an eagle thus carrying off any one to heaven, or even of any sort of ascension, but only of re-birth,—it seems clear from the representation itself that it is intended for a Nâgî, *i.e.* a female snake-demon who is borne off into the air by a Garu*d*a,—for the great bird decked with these ear-ornaments can be none other than the Garu*d*a or Supar*n*a with the golden wings. Legends of such acts are frequent in Buddhist literature, so that representations of them cause no surprise. The Bauddha drama of *Nâgâ-nandâ*, already mentioned, will at once occur to the mind in connexion with the representation; but in the *Jâtakas* there are two or three that speak of the Garu*d*a king carrying off a beautiful queen from her husband;[3] and it seems here as if he had taken

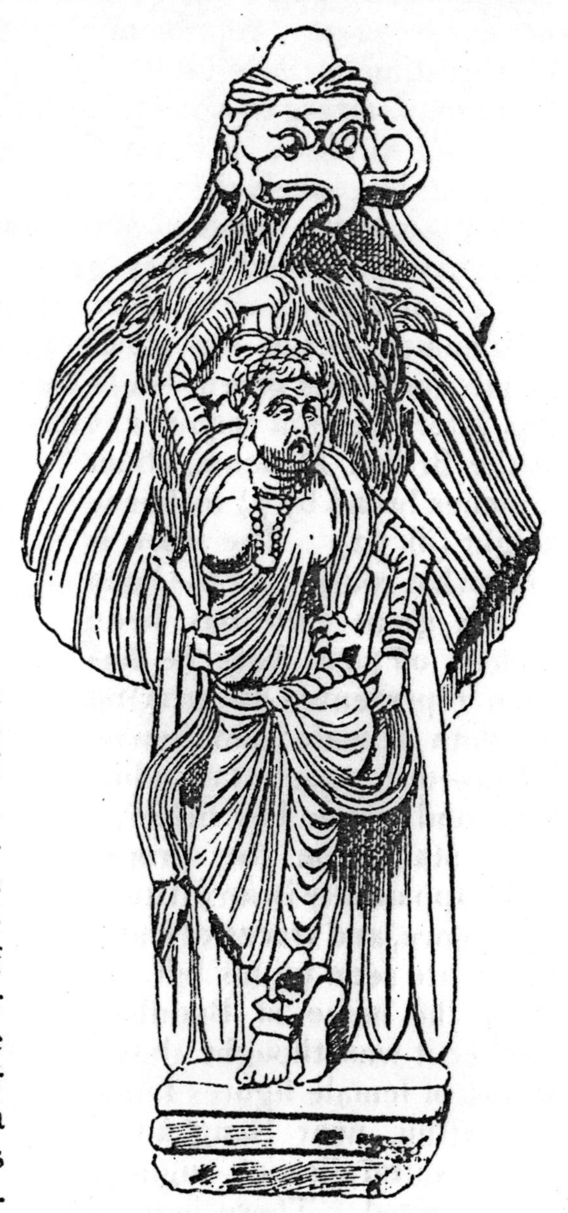

61. RELIEF FROM SANGHÂO.
Cole, *Pr. Nat. Mon.* pl. 3.

[1] Visconti, *Mus. Pio-Clement*. vol. iii, p. 49; Müller, *Denkmäler d. alten Kunst*, vol. i, pl. 36; Zanetti, *Statue*, vol. ii, pl. 7; Stuart's *Athens*, vol. iii, pls. 2 and 9; Lübke's *Hist. of Sculp.* vol. i, p. 187.

[2] Cole's *Pres. Nat. Mon. Ind.—Græco-Bud. Sculp.* pl. 3;—and *Anc. Monts. Ind.* pl. 113. This important sculpture disappeared at Lahor. Two less perfect examples are represented by Cole. *ibid.* pll. 4 and 17, or *Anc. Mon.* pll. 114 and 115. Conf. V. Smith, *Jour. A. S. Beng.* vol. LVIII, pp. 133-35.

[3] *The Jâtaka*, ed. Cowell, vol. III, No. 327—*Kakati Jâtaka*, No. 360—*Sussondi Jâtaka*, and No. 536—*Kunala Jâtaka*.

hold of a Nâgî by the neck of the serpent, and is carrying her off, his talons holding her by the waist. The Garu*d*a represents the type that still exists in the northern school (Tibet), and here too it is very frequently represented as tearing a snake-maiden in pieces by thrusting both its talons into her breast. As a decorative motif this group, arranged somewhat differently, is very frequent on gates, in apses, windows, and on throne-backs (conf. ill. 32, &c.). It is quite easily conceivable that the replica of the Leochares group, which was at the disposal of the unknown stone-cutter of Gandhâra, must have produced a very great impression. That very attitude of the Garu*d*a (which is represented quite as an animal) to its helpless human victim—to which, in order to heighten the pathos, a female form was given,—was quite in the spirit of Buddhism. If this interpretation requires confirmation, it is found in a fragment in the British Museum, about 6 inches broad by 7½ inches in height (ill. 62). The work is somewhat coarse and the head of the great bird has been broken off; but here he has been represented as carrying off both a male and female Nâga—one in each claw, while a second female lies below, a male stands on the proper right, apparently in an attitude of defence, and traces of a fifth figure are seen on his left.

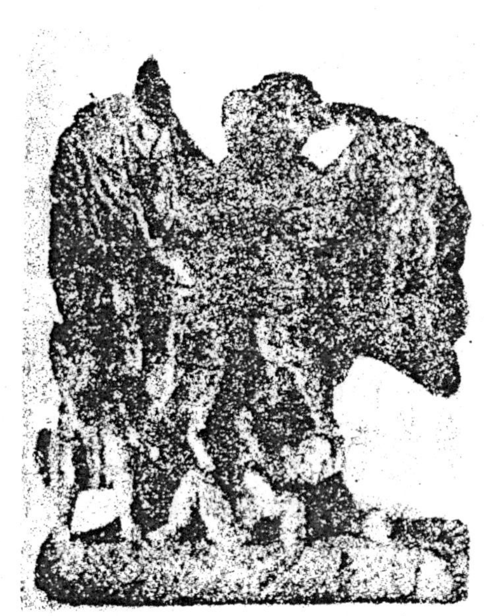

62. GARUDA CARRYING OFF NÂGA YOUTHS. (British Museum).

By the name of Buddha's mother it was thought that a series of female figures found in Natthu, near Sanghâo in the Yûsûfzaï district, ought to be described. These figures, which are mostly very gracefully and pleasingly executed, stand, with one leg crossed over the other so that one hip protrudes, under trees whose branches they grasp with one hand. One arm is always posed somewhat coquettishly on the protruding hip. Besides the drapery round the legs, three of the four examples recovered wear a sort of jacket, one of which is open down the front; three have scarfs over the shoulders; and three wear bead-girdles round the loins, with a clasp suspending a leaf-shaped ornament. The hair is waved over the brow and plaited into a wreath above, terminating in knobs; and all wear earrings, necklaces, torques and bangles round the wrists and ankles. The costume proves at once that M â y â cannot be represented thus: all these women wear Persian trousers and long jackets with sleeves; in their hair are fresh lotus-flowers;

like the dancing girls on the ornaments of the architrave of the gateway at Sâñchî, they may represent Nâch-girls employed for side decorations on reliefs of larger groups, or on portions of façades.[1] Conf. ill. 63, and above pp. 40, 41. But the pantheon was too numerous to require, even for a decoration, to resort to the merely human or secular individual. The Yakshinîs are Dryads as well as spirits of the air; (the Yoginîs or sorceresses of Hindu myth may possibly be only a modification of the same, of whom six appear in the iconography of Tibetan Buddhism—always dancing naked); and we may regard these figures as probably analogous to such *devatas* as Chulakoka Devata and Chundâ Yakshinî, found at Barâhat. Similar figures are found on mediæval temples, and even on modern ones.[2]

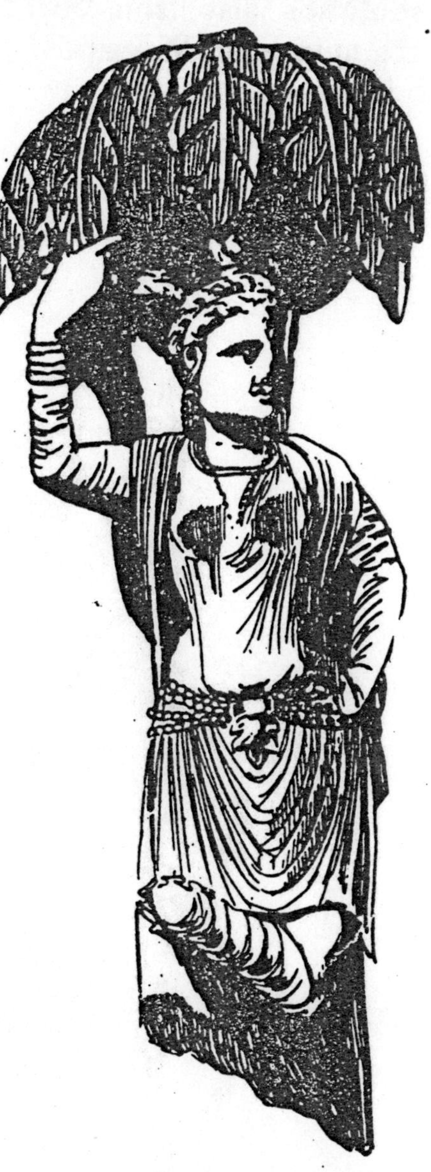

63. DANCING FIGURE.
From Natthu Monastery.
Cole. *Pr. N. Monts.* pl. 15.

Mâyâ, the mother of Buddha, and her sister Prajâpatî are depicted on the reliefs in Greek dress—upper and under garments; but with Indian ear-ornaments (Hind. *Karanphûl*), and large anklets (*ghunghru*) on the feet. The female figures are remarkably coarse; Indian exaggerations appear much more distinctly and with a more unpleasant effect in the contours of their figures than in those of the men. A favourite subject is the scene already mentioned, of Buddha's birth in the Lumbinî garden. As Mâyâ is stretching out her hand to grasp the blossom of a sâla-tree, the child springs from her right side, is received by Brahmâ, and being set down, advances seven steps with the boast, "I am the best in the world." On this relief (ill. 64), from Loriyân Tangai, now in the Calcutta Museum, we may note the appearance of the child twice to indicate both the birth and the assertion of greatness. The legends mention *châmaras* and a *chhatra* appearing in the air; and

[1] Conf. Cole, pll. 10 and 15, 2; or *Pres. Nat. Monts.* (1896), pl. 93, and *Anc. Mon.* pl. 116, 2; and Fergusson, *Tree and Serp. Wor.* pll. iii, 1, ix, and xiii.

[2] Among Buddhists a woman representing a goddess to be worshipped is also styled a Yoginî. For the Yakshas, see above p. 45; Burnouf, *Introd.* (2nd ed.), pp. 480, 536-7; *Notes on Ajanta Paintings, &c.* p. 103 and figs. 32-36; *Arch. Sur. W. India*, vol. III, pll. xx, 4; xxi, 5-7; and xxvi, 4-6.

in this relief a *châmara* is represented above the head of Brahmâ. *S*akra and other gods were also present. This sculpture is about 18 inches high. On the relief shown in ill. 64 an ancient Nike type has supplied the prototype for the figure of Mâya Another representation also from Swât (fig. 65) includes two of the women in attendance on Mayadevî together with the same three Devas as before.

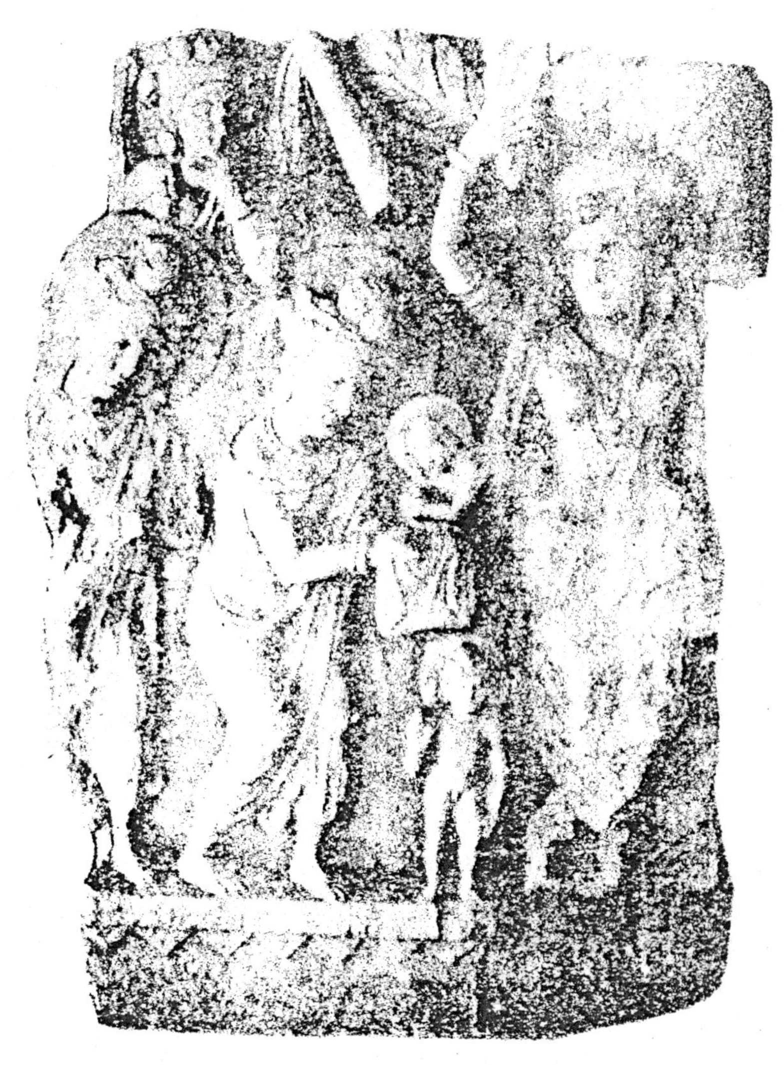

64. Scene in the Lumbinî Garden.
From Loriyân Tangai. In Calcutta Museum.

This mode of representation of Gautama's mother continues in later art. The Tibetan figure sketched in No. 66, so far as the Mâyâ is concerned, rests distinctly on the Gândhâra form; but in later Indian reliefs (as at Amarâvatî, Fergusson, *Tree and Serp. Wor.* pll. lxv and xci) the Mâyâ looks exactly like the Nâch girls mentioned above. It naturally occurs to one that here we have to do with an instance of Buddhist myth formation, which has been developed in connexion with a special artistic type. The application of an existing model to a distinct legend gives rise to a want of clearness, which unfortunately we too often meet with. In Gandhâra the model is artistically differentiated by modification of the costume and by the manifest adaptation of an ancient Nikê for the representation of Gautama's mother. As regards the origin, we have here one of the instances where archæology aids in explaining the texts by pointing to the source of Indian myth formation.[1]

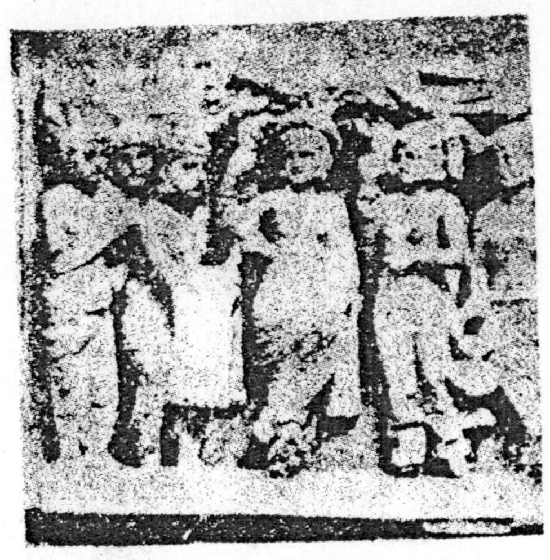

65. THE LUMBINÎ SCENE.
Fragment, from a photograph.

A peauliar figure, the signification of which it is difficult to fix, appears on the reliefs which represent Buddha's death (conf. ill. 70 and the fragment No. 77), at the foot of the victor as he enters Nirvâ*n*a. A fully-clothed, earnest-looking, unbearded man, whose head is so enveloped in a close-fitting cap or cowl that only the face is visible, holds in his left hand, on the different replicas of the

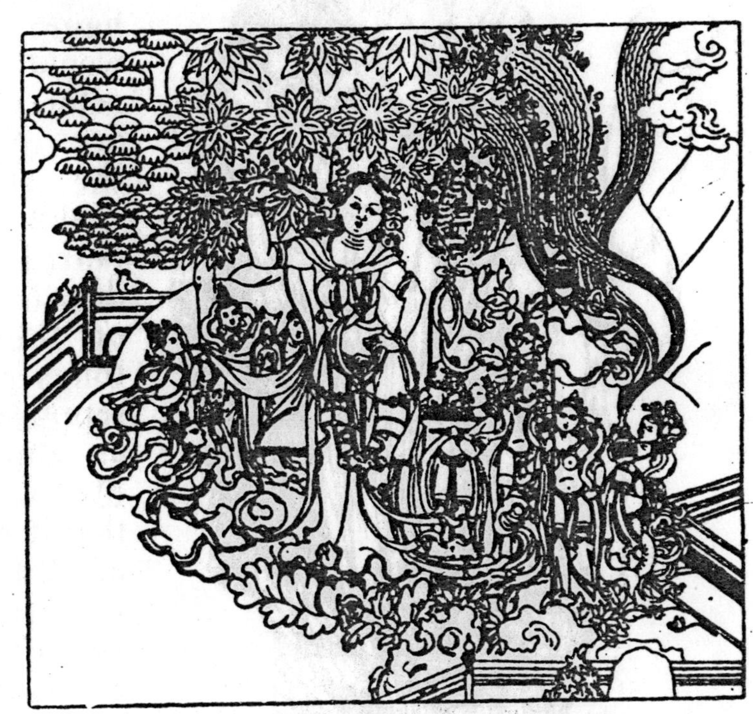

66. MÂYÂ IN THE LUMBINÎ GARDEN.
The infant Siddhârtha springs from her right side and the gods receive him. From an old picture (companion to Nirvâ*n*a picture ill. 75).

[1] On this compare the pertinent remarks of L. de la Vallée Poussin, *Bouddhisme, Etudes et Matériaux* (Lond. 1898), pp. 169f. The Devadâsî dancing under the tree has, moreover, continued in Brâhma*n*a art. Thus one is found represented on the Brâhma*n*a Picture of the World in the Tanjor Library, of which a copy is in the Berlin Museum.

scene,[1] a staff with what might be intended for a sort of noose or loop at the upper end of it. Might this represent the mendicant friar's jingling staff—the hi-ki-la, (Tib. *h*Khar-*g*sîl) carried by the *bhikshus* of the northern schools;[2] or was that introduced so early as to appear in these sculptures? Though the dress may possibly give the figure the appearance of a messenger, we can hardly take it for the messenger of Yama, the god of death; nothing in the legends would suggest this; and in Buddha's Nirvâ*n*a there is clearly no question of a death,—though such a figure, typifying the event, would agree with the character of the latest Hellenic art. Nor can it be Chunda the smith, who supplied Buddha with his last feast (*kari* and pork),—for neither does he figure in the legends on this occasion, and his tongs could hardly be misrepresented by such a staff as appears in his hands. May we not then conjecture that it was intended for the monk Kâ*s*yapa who, though not actually present at the *parinirvâna* scene, arrived afterwards and, asking that he might see the feet with the marks that had prognosticated Buddha's destiny, was honoured by the prodigy of the feet appearing of themselves? Kâ*s*yapa and Ananda are the two personages pious Buddhists would expect to be repre-

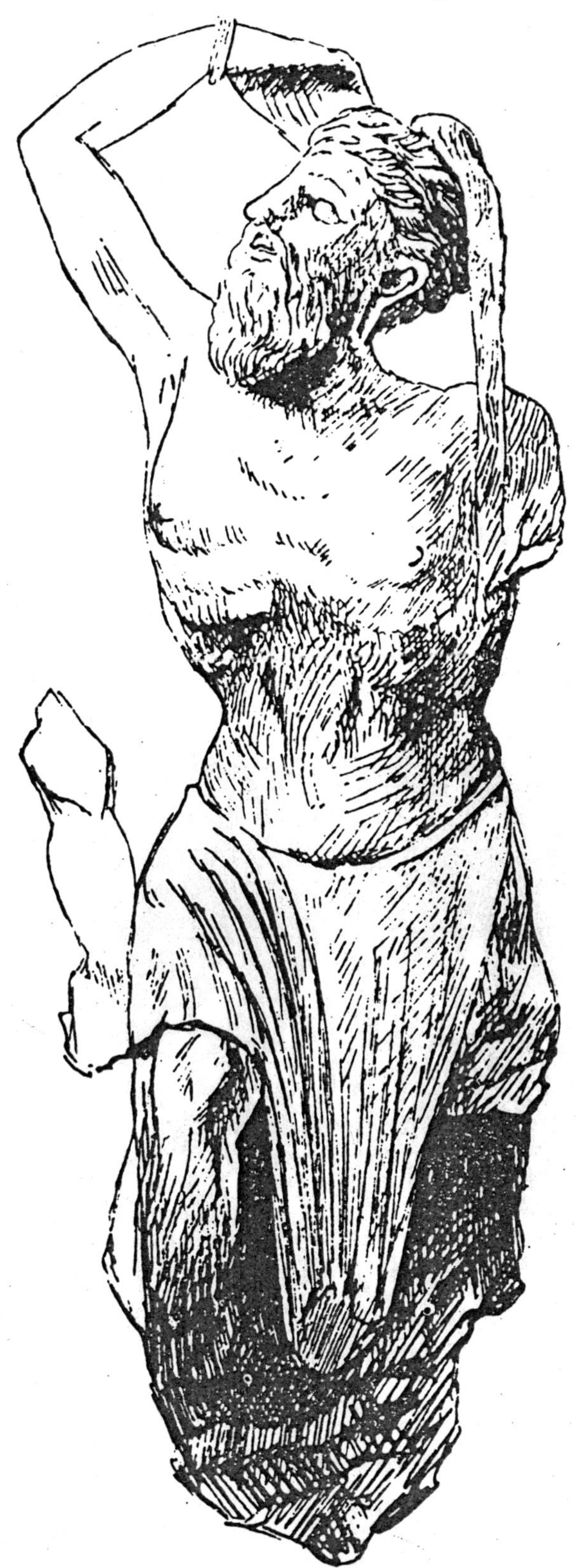

67. FIGURE OF A BRÂHMANA.
Gandhâra: from a photo.

[1] *Anc. Monts. Ind* pll. 121, 2; 115, 4; 122; or Cole, *Græco-Bakt. Sculp.* pll. 16, 2; 17, 4; and 22; *J. Ind. Art and Ind.* Vol. VIII, pl. xiii, 5; or sep. ed. pl. xi, 5; also figures 70, 72, 74, and 77.

[2] The Singhalese monks follow the early orthodox fashion—making no appeal for alms. Copleston, *Buddhism*, pp. 448f.

sented in the scene. Kâsyapa learnt of the decease by seeing some one (Subaddha?) carrying one of the Mandârava flowers that had fallen at Kusinâra. Might he not, further, be indicated by such a flower on the head of his staff? In some, perhaps later, replicas this figure has disappeared, as it were, among the mourners, without being assigned any other special rôle.

I have now enumerated those gods and demi-gods of the Gândhâra sculptures known to me. As regards the mortals, the Brâhmaṇas take the first place (conf. ill. 67, 68). Generally speaking, the type must be the same as that of the Asoka period, making allowance, of course, for its further development. They are represented as bearded men simply dressed; the hair is not dressed turban-wise in plaits about the head, as at Sañchî, but fastened together like a *krobylos*, in a wavy tuft on the top of the head. Most frequently they are represented as old men leaning on a staff or led by their disciples, and several of the older of these Brâhmaṇa representations (a blind old man occurs frequently) are of uncommon artistic merit. See also below, fig. 93.

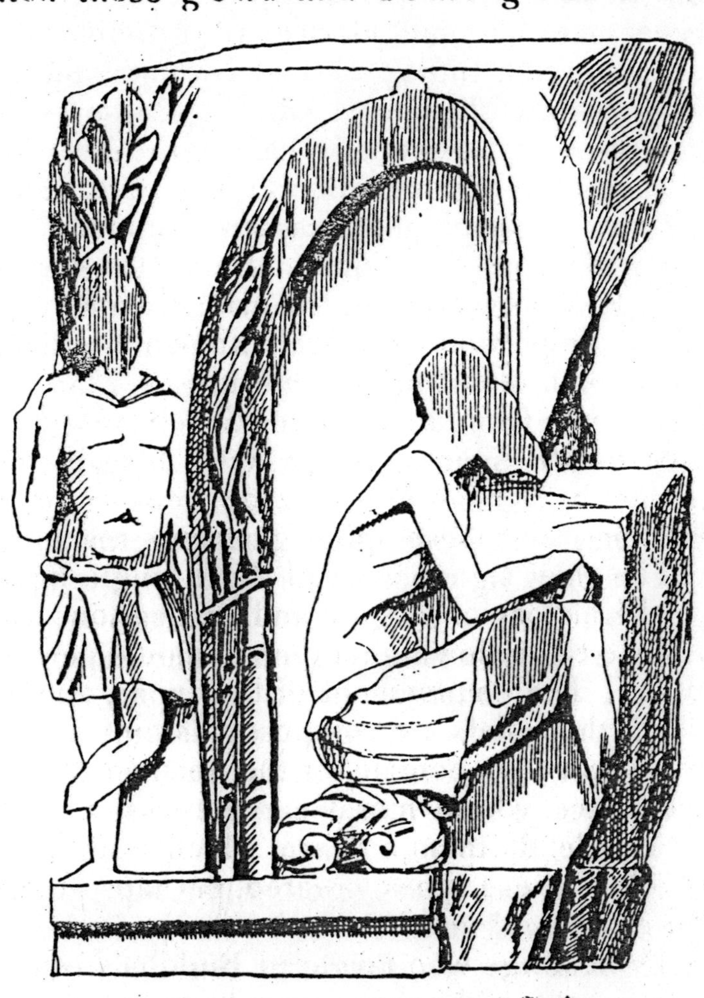

68. Relief fragment from Swât.
An old Brâhmaṇa sitting on a pillow of straw under a leaf hut, a scholar behind. Original in Berlin Mus.

Among the other figures—men and women of different conditions—apart from the fact that different races are represented, there occur two kinds of types from a stylistic point of view: beside purely Hellenic forms, the Indian element is very prominent. Generally speaking, the principal figures, Buddha, kings, gods, and so on, have on the whole rather the ideal Greek types, while the other figures are less and less conspicuous according to their importance. But, among uncouth and coarse figures of inferior composition, there would also seem to appear a purely Greek type, which haply may have suggested itself as appropriate. The representations of royal figures (conf. ill. 88, and in ch. iv) are of great interest from an antiquarian point of view, especially as regards ornament and dress. Long breast-chains, the clasp of which lies on the breast and ends in two animals' heads, festooned cords with square appendages, which now-a-days would be called *Ta'wîz* (*tâbîj*)—amulets—are especially striking. In the more important types the old Indian costume is always found. Along with these barbarian types, men of small stature are prominent—with features that are certainly not Indian and heavy moustaches, clad in trousers and long coats with sleeves; and again horsemen and camel-drivers in costumes that are not Indian, and others of the same kind.

It has already been mentioned that the dress of the women, where the principal figures are intended, is mostly Greek, although the ornaments—earrings and anklets—are Indian. An interesting feature is presented by the armed women, the female body-guards of the kings, who were well known to the ancient historians and are spoken of in Indian literature as Yavanânîs—Ionian women, *i.e.* women from lands under Greek rule (conf. ill. 81). Among the subordinate figures, as we have already mentioned, there appear women in Persian dress: wide trousers, sleeved tunics reaching to the knee, and loose upper garments resembling shawls.

The chief significance of these single figures lies in their bearing on the history of religion and civilisation; as regards their artistic value the following judgment should perhaps be pronounced upon them. The employment of the types, above described in detail, of which the reliefs are composed, is only a more or less clever adaptation in a new domain, of the finished phrases of an art already in decadence, whose moral earnestness, as seen in particular modifications, lends them a charm which rests indeed only on this change of rôle. These types, created, perhaps at the word of command, by the dynastical interests or by the personal initiative of one of the Hellenic kings who favoured Buddha's religion, have a certain development which, as we pass from replica to replica, ends with a degeneration in which individual ideal forms, preserved as by miracle, appear beside creations which are childish and coarse. But that their genesis was accomplished with great ability and intelligent deliberation will be seen by the treatment of the relief as regards its composition. The permanence of single types, as well as of whole compositions in the sacerdotal sculptures of the northern school, proves how greatly native interest has been excited thereby.

In truth, the tradition of the northern school proves very reliable. Later on, in speaking of types of Buddha, we shall have occasion to point out that the miniatures of Tibet (paintings and bronze casts) are capable of affording very substantial and unexpected aid in correctly explaining not only the single figures but also the compositions as such. Unfortunately, space does not allow me to enter into all the consequences of this fact: all that I may hope to attempt is to represent convincingly the facts and thereby to explain correctly the sculptures to be noticed.

As a preliminary to entering upon this subject, it is further necessary to compare the Chinese and Japanese pantheons, as well as their favourite compositions, with those of the Lamas, in which case a history of the types, going back to the sculptures of the Gândhâra school, must be attempted. It is a troublesome task, but only in this way is a scientific archæology of Buddhism made possible. Many interesting results may be obtained from a special study of the Gândhâra sculptures by themselves combined with tentative efforts to trace those types which are already known to us from the history of Hellenic and other art; but this investigation will always have to cope with the greatest difficulties, and be exposed to strange mistakes. A remarkable proof of this was the supposed seizure of Mâyâ by the eagle! To leave the ecclesiastical tradition of the northern school out of account is absurd.

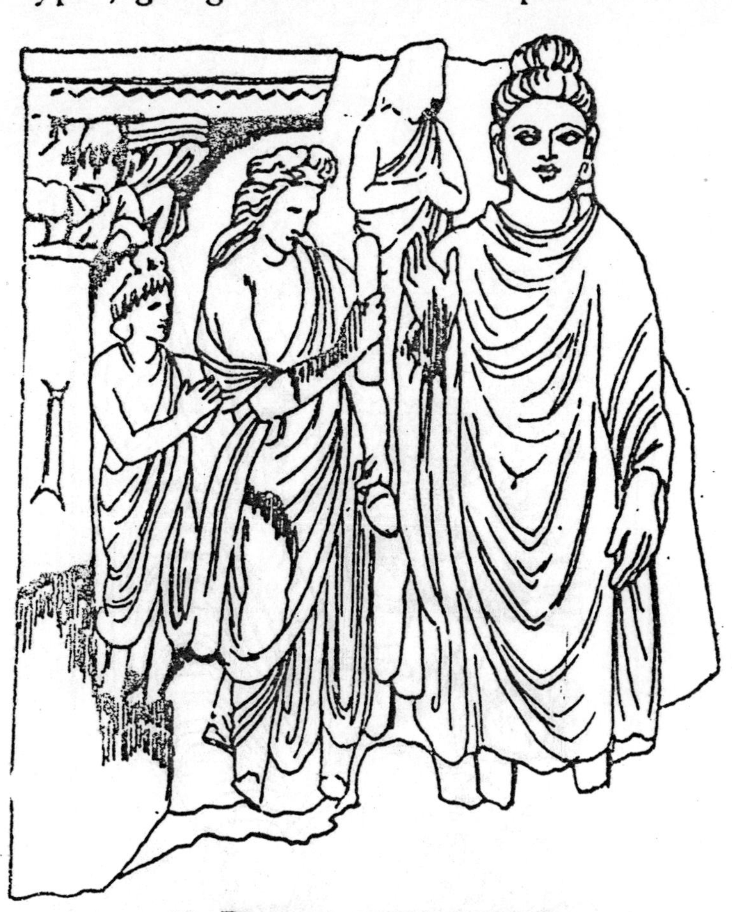

69. **Buddha with disciples.**
Relief from Takht-i-Bâhi: original in Berlin Museum.

That certain forms became quite changed in their development, were absorbed again into ecclesiastical art, and obliged to give place to new formations, is explained by the evolution of new sects; and if we take into consideration the constant equalizing efforts of Buddhism, we cannot wonder that individual elements again become models for new arrangements; and fresh interpretations are always possible. But I must defer the detailed discussion of this and many other questions.

If we now pass to the compositions,—one of the most interesting and frequently repeated is the death of Buddha (the *Mahâparinirvâna*, ill. 70-74, 77). We shall treat this representation in some detail, and it may be well to remember that the legends ought to be our guides in attempting to interpret the scenes, we ought in the first place to look for the personages referred to in the literature. We may not import others that are not mentioned, in order to explain what we may not quite understand.

In the middle of these reliefs the dying teacher lies on a raised couch (Hind. *chârpâi*); the deities and monks stand round him.

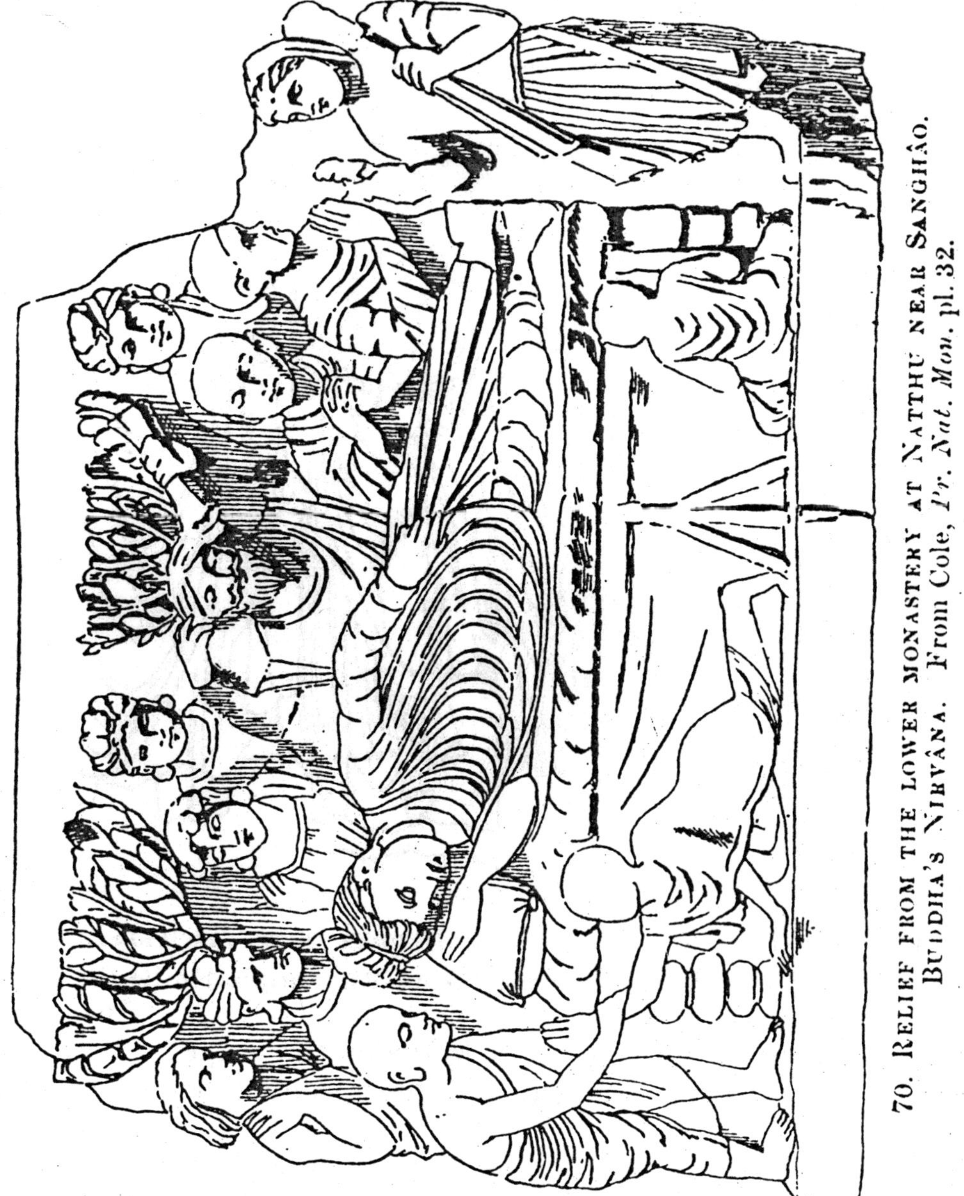

70. RELIEF FROM THE LOWER MONASTERY AT NATTHU NEAR SANGHÂO. BUDDHA'S NIRVÂNA. From Cole, *Pr. Nat. Mon.* pl. 32.

In ill. 70 the vajra-bearer stands beyond, lifting his arms in despair. One of the monks (Ananda) has fallen to the ground in his distress, while another, at the head of the couch, raises him by the hand. The figure at the feet,[1] who has already been mentioned (p. 113), has his robe (*chaddar*) drawn over his head, somewhat as women wear

[1] In the Ajantâ sculpture (Burgess, *Amarâvati*, p. 99) this personage seems to be represented by the large figure behind the feet of Buddha, and there he has no rod. In the Bombay V. and A. Museum is a much damaged replica, 14 inches by 11, of ill. 74, and another in better preservation (21 inches by 15) without the fallen monk, and with Vajrapâni behind the figure at the feet. Both are from Marjan tope near Mâyan Khân. There is also another copy, about 20 inches by 15, from Chinglai Stûpa, much like the two figured in ill. 70 and 72.—J.B.

the *sári*; he carries a thick rod or staff,—sometimes it is represented as a number of thin rods bound together (*fasces*),—the upper end being thicker or broader than the shaft. Whoever he

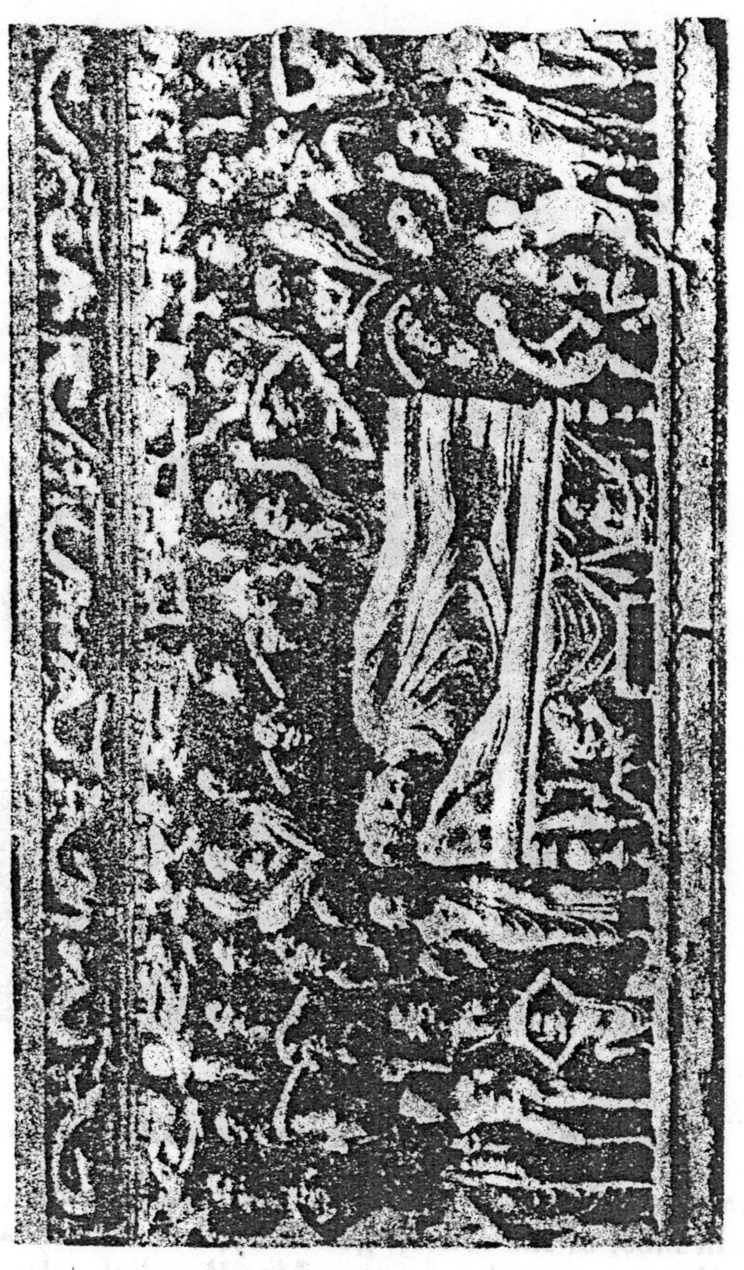

71. Mahâparinirvâna scene from Loriyân Tangai: in India Museum, Calcutta.

may represent, he is deeply interested in the decease: can it be Kâsyapa? The background of the compositions is almost always filled in by the traditional two sâla trees of the little wood of Kusinâra, and among their foliage we usually find represented the Devîs who resided in, or watched over them, and who, on the occasion of the decease, are said to have thrown down beautiful flowers on the Buddha and sung in his praise. Devatâs, Nâgas, and other supernatural beings also showered Mandârava flowers (*Erythrina fulgens*) till they were knee-deep. This is probably the meaning of the flying figures in the upper part of the relief ill. 71.

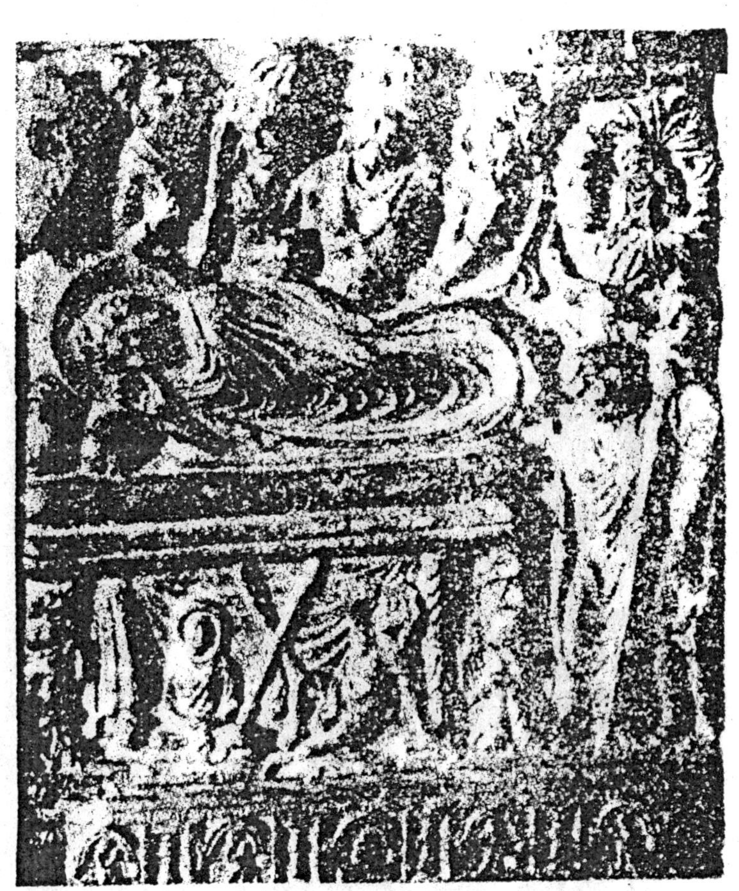

72. MAHÂPARINIRVÂṆA SCENE FROM LORIYÂN TANGAI.

The monk sitting in front beside the tripod water-cooler (ill. 71) appears in most of the reliefs, generally, but not always, facing the couch. He appears also in the Aja*nt*â relief. In the sculpture from Loriyân Tangai, in the Calcutta Museum, measuring 2 ft. 4 in. long by 1 ft. 4 in. high, we have one of the most artistic representations as well as the most elaborate in detail (ill. 71). In this, and in another from the same locality (ill. 72), we observe that the fallen figure is Vajrapâ*n*i. The replica (ill. 73) from Kâfarko*t* in Swât, and now in the British Museum, is on a slab 16 inches long by 10 high, and there Vajrapâ*n*i is represented standing at the head of the couch, holding up his right hand in dismay and grief at the demise of the Master whom he had constantly followed to protect. The relief from Natthu (ill. 74) is almost a copy of this.

The representations of this subject differ in minor details, but the general features seem to persist down to modern times: these permanent features must have been regarded as essential. In most

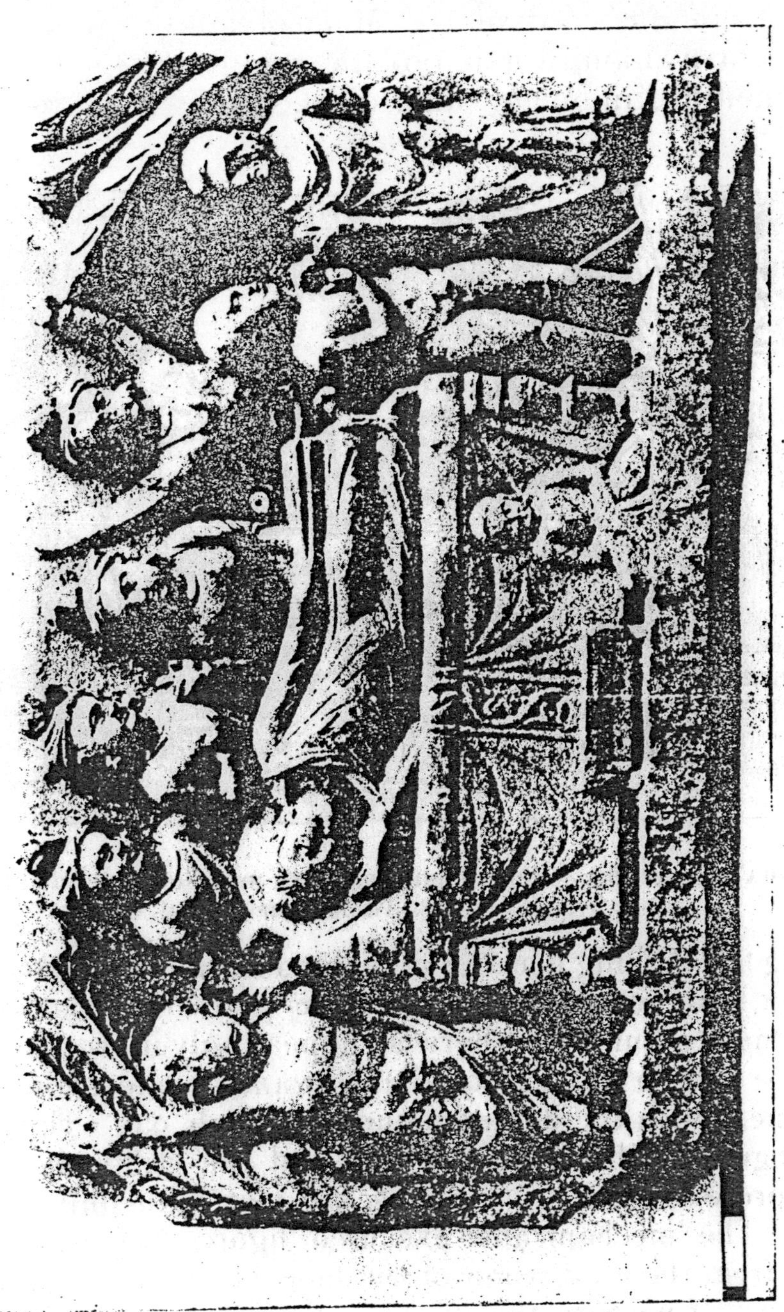

73. Buddha's Nirvâna. Relief from Kâfarkot, Swât Valley. In the British Museum.

of the copies of this scene we find these,—(1) the small figure of an ascetic seated in front of the couch on which the dying *S*âkyamuni lies; (2) Vajrapâ*n*i—the bearer of the *vajra*; (3) a naked figure close by; (4) the Sâla trees, between which the couch was placed, usually with the Tree Spirits (females) rising among the foliage and adoring the Teacher; (5) the robed figure with (or without) a rod or baton, at the foot of the couch; and (6) the gods and other attendants. Careful study may yet determine satisfactorily who are intended by each of the individuals thus represented; but the legends must be our guide. We read of Subhadra, the Brâhma*n*a heretic (possibly a follower of the naked Tîrthakas) being converted by the dying Buddha and immediately entering Nirvâ*n*a; of Ananda, Aniruddha and Upâvana attending the dying Master; of Vajrapâ*n*i's great grief; of the visit of the Malla chiefs of Kusinâra; and of Kâ*s*yapa's arrival and worship of the sage's feet.[1] Possibly these may be identified in one or other of the reliefs.

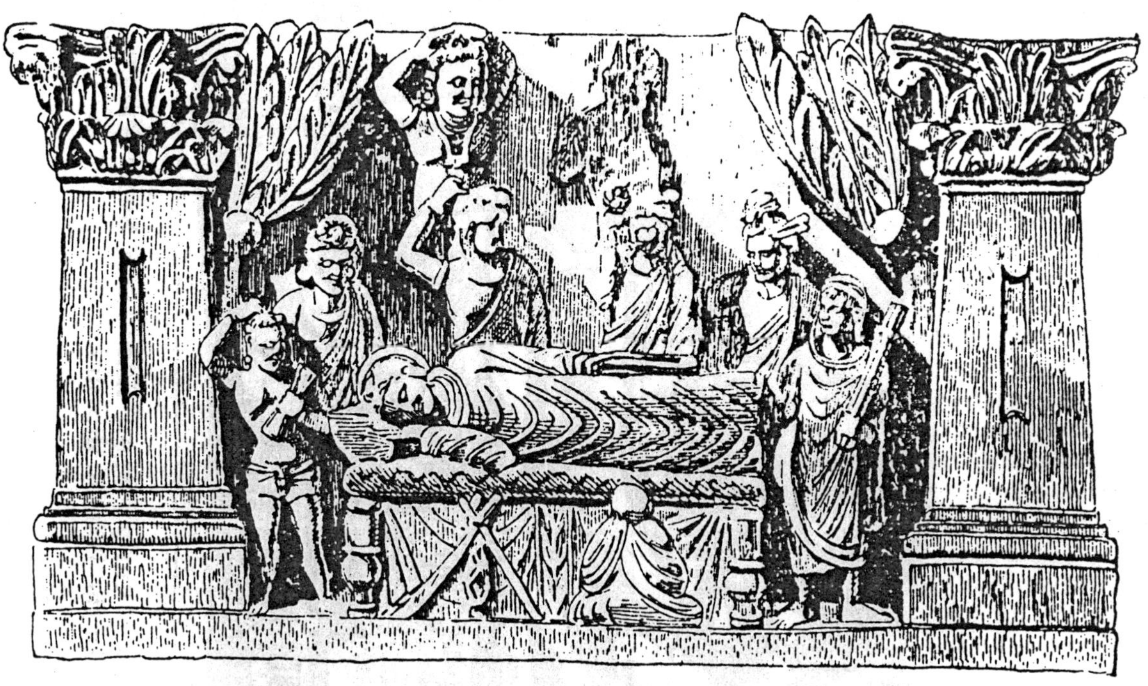

74. Buddha's Nirvâna. Relief from the upper monastery at Natthu (Yûsufzâi). From Cole, *Pr. Nat. Monts.*, pl. 16.

Among the striking features presented by the Gândhâra sculptures is the fact that, beside figures of quite perfect formation, cases of awkwardness occur that otherwise appear only in works of primitive art. The sketch (ill. 74) of the Nirvâ*n*a scene shows the usual arrangement with the deities round the couch, &c. Here the well-formed figure at the Buddha's feet and the stiffly depicted monk alone represent contrasts such as are met with only in the decay of art. The mechanically executed figure, too, of the reclining Buddha, from the expression of the face, is simply a standing figure laid down. If we turn the picture round, we have simply the upright statue before us.

This composition—two other replicas of which are found in Cole's collection[2]—gives evidence of having been long in vogue, for modern

[1] Rockhill, *Life of Buddha*, p. 138. The *Avadâna Sataka* (x, 10) mentions that on the occasion of the Nirvâ*n*a, a Bhikshu, *S*akra, Brahmâ, and Aniruddha each chaunted a separate verse. [In the above descriptions I have not quite followed Professor Grünwedel's text.—J.B.]

[2] Cole, u.s. pl. 16, 2; or *Ind. Monts.* pl. 121; conf Cole, pl. 17, 4, and 22.

Tibetan and Chino-Japanese representations (conf. ill. 75 and 76) still show clear signs of having been based on the old Gândhâra reliefs.

Clearly the entourage of Buddha's death-bed has grown with the embellishment of the Buddha legends. Along with Buddha's chief disciples are assembled as mourners not only representatives of all classes of the gods, but of all the demons: Nâgas, Garu*d*as, all sorts of monsters, and representatives of all living creatures. Particular figures, still clearly defined in Gandhâra, as we have already mentioned, have disappeared from the number of the mourners. It is one of the ingenious suppositions of Vincent Smith that the subject-matter of this most expressive composition of old Buddhist art has been derived from Greek and Roman sarcophagus reliefs.

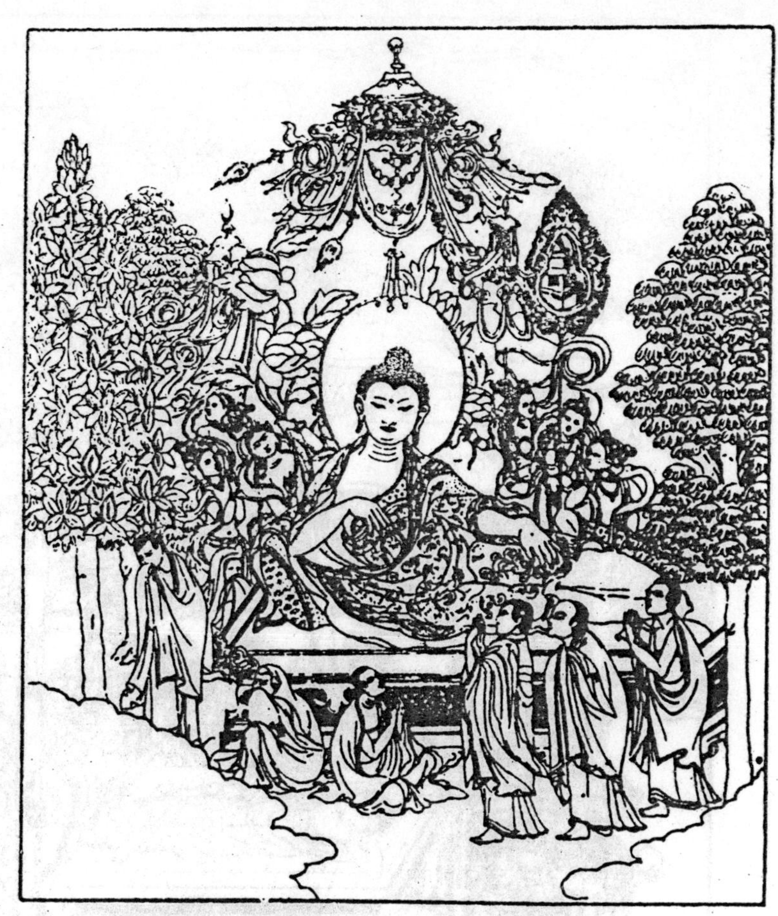

75. NIRVÂNA (MYA-NGAN-,DAS) OF GAUTAMA (SHAKYA-THUB-PA). From an old Tibetan painting. Original in Berlin Museum.

The composition of the reliefs of the Gândhâra monasteries is throughout based upon ancient models. The relief itself is set deeper than was the case in the older Indian art: for the sculptors of the A*s*oka period, and of the schools that sprang therefrom, executed hardly any but flat reliefs. The individual figures of the Gândhâra reliefs are types of statuary arranged beside one another, starting from the middle, and groupd always according to the importance of the individual figure (conf. ill. 45, 69, &c.).

The same figure can even be used in the representation of different scenes: thus the figure of Buddha in the different scenes of his life is based upon a reproduction of a few statuary motifs; this adaptability is remarked in the case of accessory figures, *e.g.* (ill. 46 and 48) gods, disciples, spectators, devotees, soldiers and servants. We at once think of model figures brought together in the mechanical execution, more or less numerous according to the means which the donor wished, or was in a position to spend on a relief. Side figures would sometimes change their rôles: a figure that in one relief throws down flowers, in another may throw stones—even at Buddha.

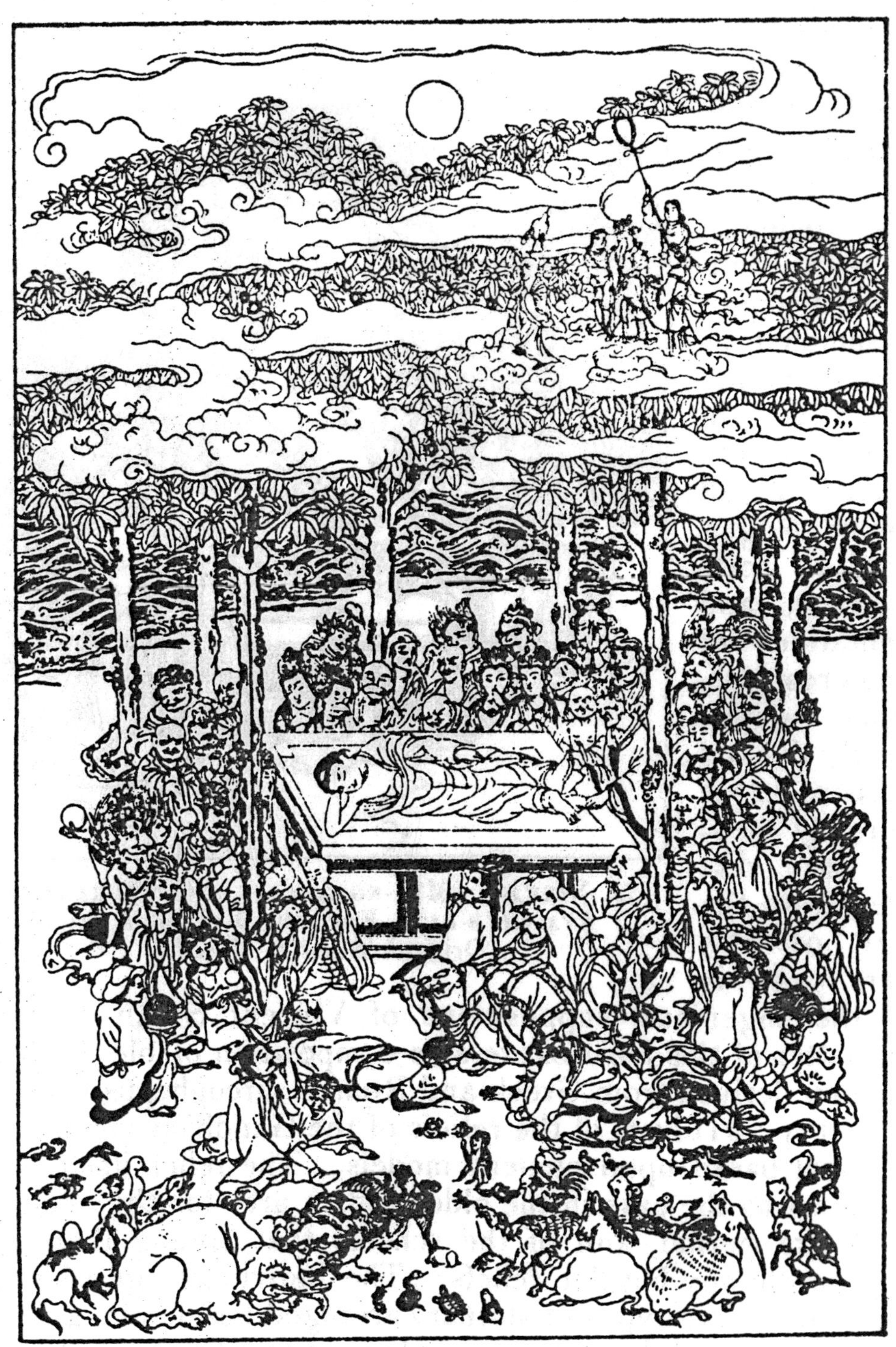

76. NIRVÂNA OF GAUTAMA BUDDHA. A Japanese painting from a Chinese copy. The couch of the dying is surrounded by his disciples, gods, and representatives of all classes of living beings. Above the Sâla trees is the weeping mother of Buddha, descending from heaven. Conf. Hofmann, *Buddha-Pantheon von Nipon*.
Original in Berlin Museum.

This form of composition, due to ancient influences, is retained in Buddhist art and is powerful and permanent in the northern canon; on the reliefs of Boro Bu*d*ur, in Java, the compositions are also put together according to this plan. From these reliefs, which have been constructed purely on antique models, and which, separated from one another by small columns and pillars, have served as gallery decorations, a series of scenes is afforded by slabs known to me, which are either model compositions (this is more rarely the case), or which have been copied from still older ones. It thus happens that the composition in its principal features varies only slightly in the replicas; but that besides slabs where the figures are numerous—a 'scriptio plena' as one might say—there is often found a 'defectiva,' which retains the main design but curtails the rest, thus frequently omitting just what is most important. Of the following scenes more or less complete replicas are to be found—I shall mention only a few—the birth of Gautama in the Lumbinîgarden, in full composition—Mâyâ, Prajâpatî, Brahmâ, Sakka behind Prajâpatî, girls with palm-branches and pitchers (conf. ill. 64, 86, and Cole, pl. 11, 2, 10 [only two girls]; Vincent Smith, pl. 9). Gautama leaving his palace, in full composition: Gautama on horseback on the shoulders of the earth, before him the palm-bearer, beside him Mâra, guards in flight, and god of the gate (conf. ill. 50, 51 and 54). The simplest form of this representation shows only the Bodhisattva riding out from a gate.[1] In this composition the artistic element is striking (conf. p. 27). Further, a series of scenes from the miracles of Gautama while he sojourned upon the earth. The construction of these last-named reliefs is usually thus:—In the centre stands Gautama coming from the left, near him Vajrapâ*n*i alone or with disciples and people also near; Gautama

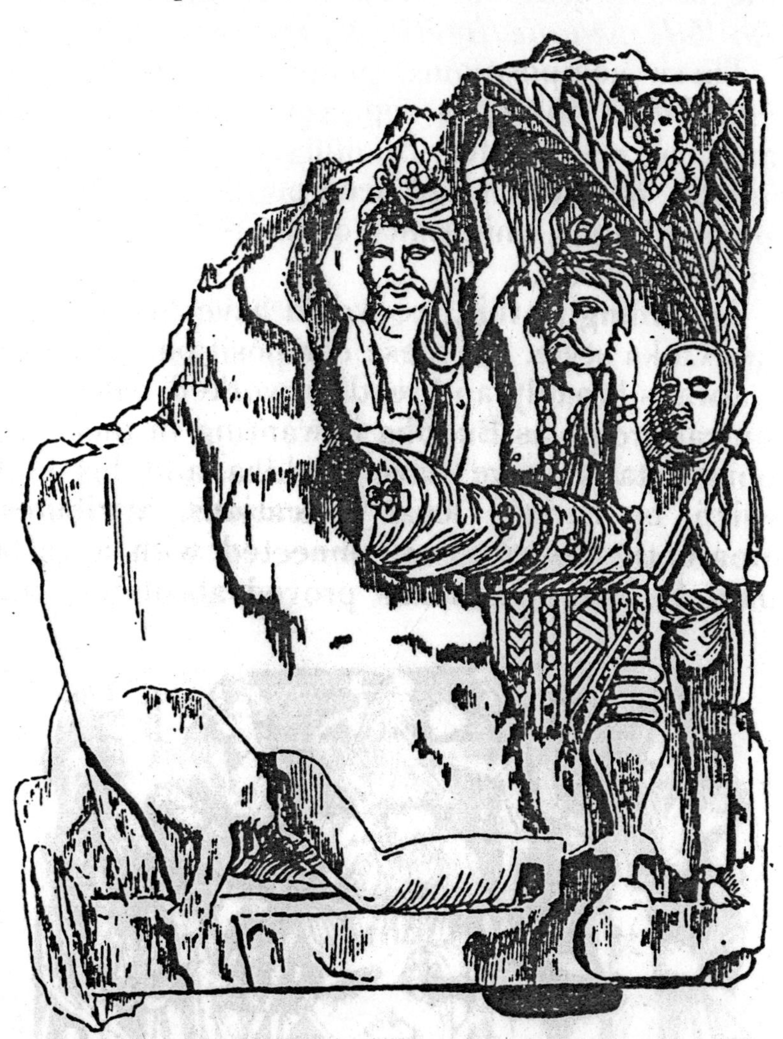

77. **Fragment of a relief with representation of Buddha's Nirvâna.** Swât district. Original in Berlin Museum.

[1] Conf. Arnold, *Light of Asia*, ill. p. 86; Burgess, *Amarâvatî*, p. 81.

opposite then Gautama with his entourage, converts or devotees (conf. ill. 57, 69).[1]

Gautama usually takes a position reminding us of the ancient sacrificing commanders, the alms-bowl (*pâtra*) taking the place of the patera (conf. ill. 79 and *Veröffentlichungen aus d. Kgl. Mus. für Völkerkunde, Berlin*, V, 130).

These compositions, generally very similar, must no longer be regarded, I think, as representations of a fixed legend, but as a mark of respect for Buddha on the occasion of a conversion, a miracle, &c., which had been performed by him. From architectural considerations, uniformity of the relief may have been the standard for these forms.

According to this, we would have before us the very reverse of the Asoka style. In these compositions (conf. pp. 65ff.) the situation is always broadly and readily worked out, but generally without a central group, as Buddha is wanting in them. But in the Gândhâra representations we have Buddha and his entourage as a model, which, by certain local indications, attributes, and such like, is apparently described as connected with a certain legend. Unfortunately, this model has proved absolutely indestructible in later Buddhist art.

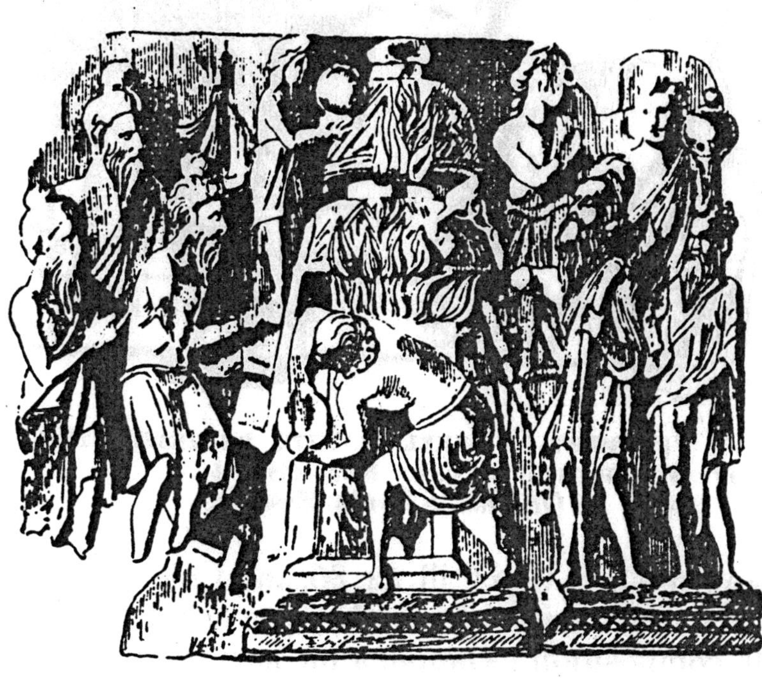

78. Uruvilvâ Kâsyapa and the fire wonder. Grünwedel, *Buddh. Stud.* S. 8, Abb. 10.

As an example, let us select some reliefs representing a legend that has already been brought under notice, from which the differences will be made more distinct.

Besides these reliefs, composed so as to constitute a series, each of which gives by itself a complete and self-interpreting representation, we very frequently find a blending of two or more compositions on o n e slab.

I have treated in detail the representation of the conversion by Buddha of Uruvilvâ Kâśyapa as it is pictured on the reliefs of the east gateway at Sâñchî (above p. 61). The theme is also a favourite one in Gandhâra.

The first part of the legend (the fire-miracle, conf above p. 62) is

[1] These last-named compositions, therefore, take the place of the schematic representations of the Asoka period characterized in note 1, p. 67.

also represented in detail on the relief from Gandhâra sketched in ill. 78. The disciples endeavour to quench the fire with their lô*t*âs filled with water, while Kâ*s*yapa arrives leaning on his staff. Buddha stands behind him with the snake in his alms-bowl.

But this relief belongs to the detailed narrative panels, forming the upper portion of a larger slab, the under half of which is almost completely destroyed.[1] The sketch of the thunderbolt-bearer on

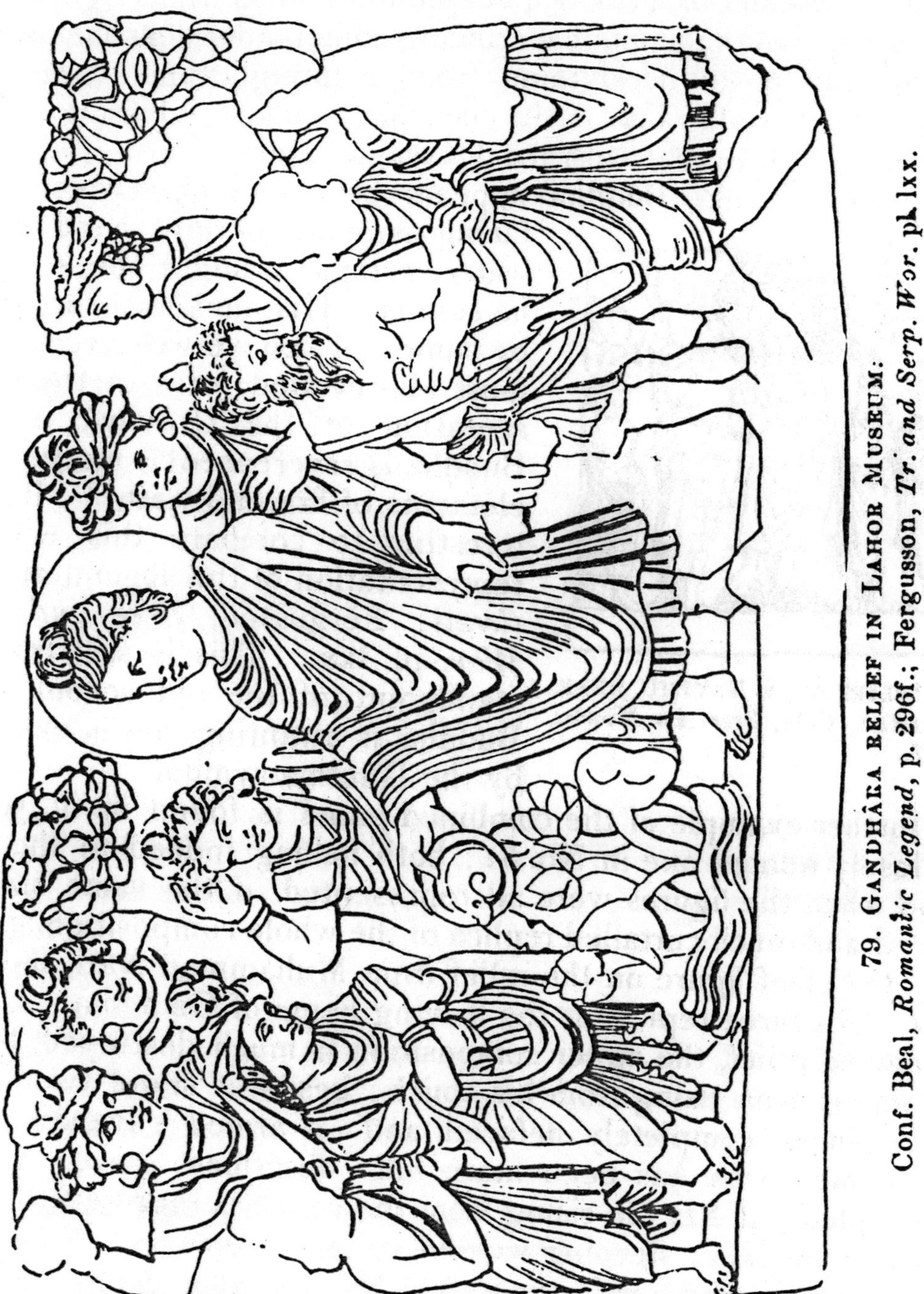

79. Gandhâra relief in Lahor Museum: Conf. Beal, *Romantic Legend*, p. 296f.; Fergusson, *Tr. and Serp. Wor.* pl. lxx.

ill. 46 is taken from the lower part, which is very interesting in connexion with the Kâ*s*yapa legend.

The story relates further that Kâ*s*yapa still did not bow. Then Buddha caused the whole precincts to be flooded, and walked away over the water in presence of the Brâhma*n*as. Both phases of the

[1] See *Ind. Monts.* pl. 131, fig. 1. Conf. Beal, *Romantic Legend*, p. 295.

legend seem now to be employed in order to celebrate Buddha as master "over fire and water." To this belong two reliefs which are among those running continuously: ill. 79, 80. On ill. 79, Buddha is seen standing, turned slightly to the right, surrounded by laics—men and women; the bearer of the thunderbolt—in this instance, a bearded figure—follows him; water springs up before him in which stand lotus flowers. It might be doubted whether this represented the water wonder of Uruvilvâ, but Buddha holds in his right hand his alms-bowl,—as the ancient sacrificing commander does the patera,—but,—owing to its derivation from a foreign type,—it is represented very small, and in it lies the snake. This proves the connexion of this relief with the Kâsyapa legend.

In relief No. 80, Buddha appears between eight worshippers, facing us, with his right hand raised; water springs up under him, on which he stands. His nimbus is surrounded by flames. I believe we have here the most abbreviated form of the representation of the Uruvilvâ miracle: Buddha is reverenced as master of the elements of fire and water.[1] It is interesting to compare this with the representation of this legend at Amarâvatî: Fergusson, *Tree and Serp. Wor.* pl. lxx. This is still from the standpoint of the old school: there Buddha is awanting, but is expressed by the Dharma symbol.

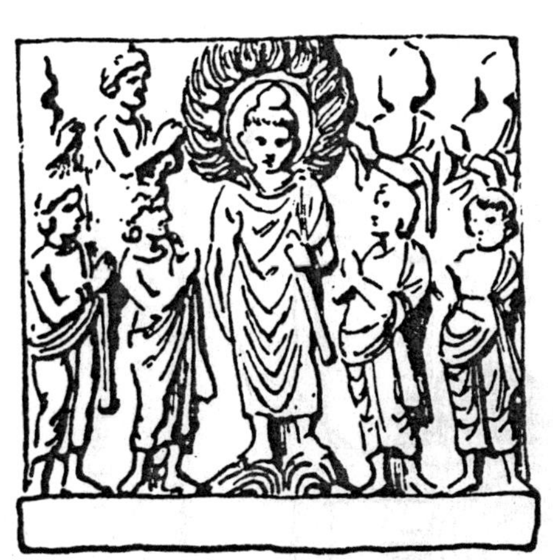

80. Relief from Natthu, near Sanghao. Cole, *Pres. An. Monts.* pl. 17.

A further example of the combined panel is found in ill. 50, and the closely related one in No. 81; both belong indeed to the older period when the figures were all represented of the same size. A reduced and much curtailed replica of the whole composition appears above the chief figure on the relief from Muhammad Nâri, shown in ill. 82. All three represent the leaving home of Gautama. On the first-named relief, the upper composition is much destroyed, though Gautama is seen rising from his couch; beside it stand two female figures almost completely defaced, and n armed Yavanânî. The lower composition has been more full described above. On the small replica (ill. 82) the rising from the couch is represented in the lower composition: sleeping women sit in the corners. The upper representation, which unfortunately is injured also, shows Gautama, and under him the Mahâpa*th*avî on whose shoulders Gautama himself stood; before him, as it appears, his faithful Channa, and behind him the head of his horse Ka*nth*aka.

Better preserved and quite distinct in all details is the relief from Jamâlgarhî, now in the Lahor Museum, represented in ill. 87. It gives two stages of the story, and is also specially interesting from

[1] *Zeitsch. d. Deut. Morg. Gesells.* 1898, S. 460, note 1.

its architectural forms in which we find such a mixture of styles,—the alcoves panelled on the roofs in the later Græco-Roman style, the pillars with Persepolitan capitals and Indian bases, the Buddhist rail pattern of frieze, and the ornate Hellenic or Roman torus. The

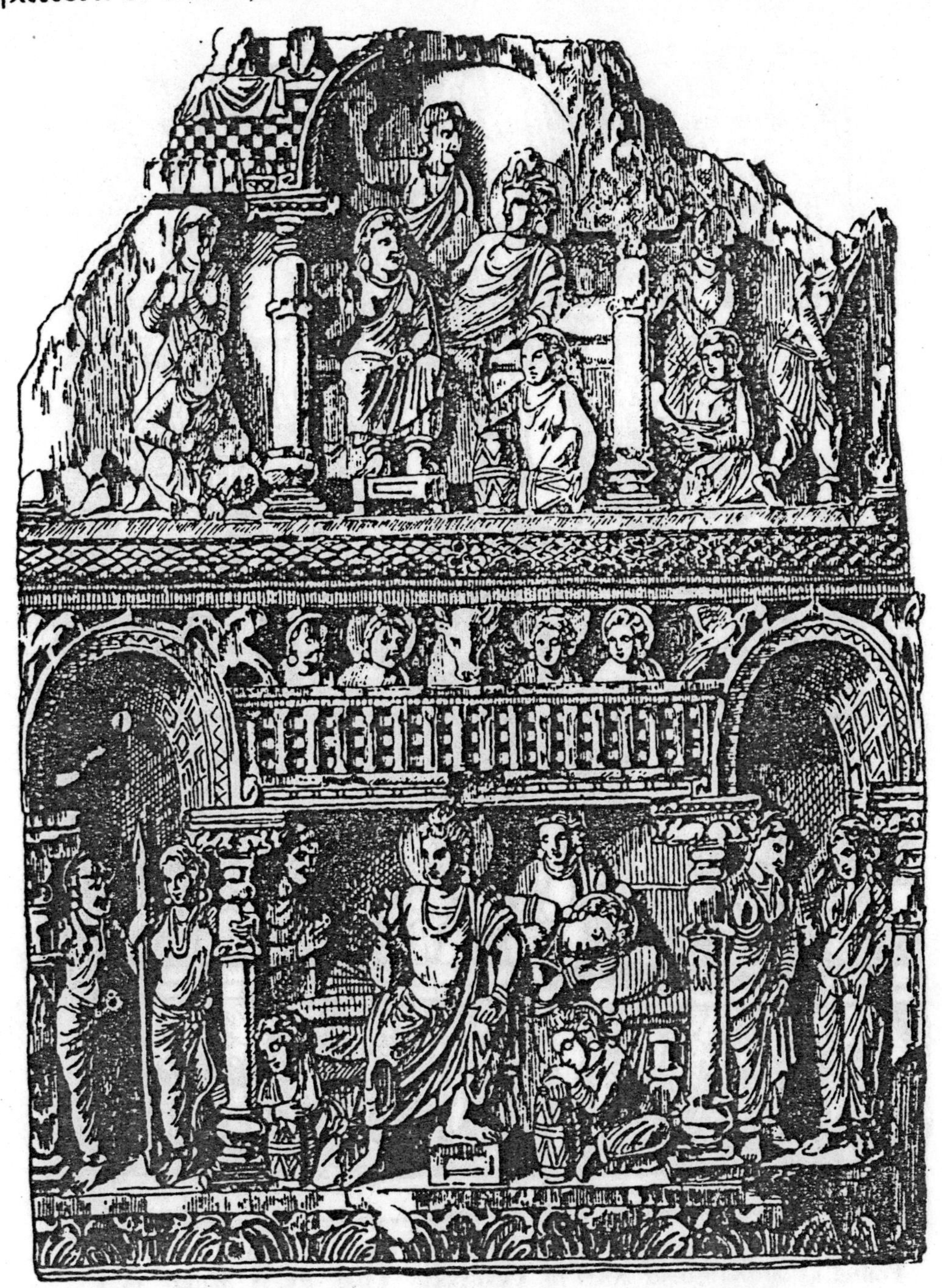

81. Gautama Buddha about to leave home.
Relief from Jamâlgarhî in Yûsufzâï. (Lahor Museum).

upper portion of the sculpture shows Gautama reclining on a couch, attended by women, one of whom sits on the front of the couch with her feet on a stool (*pádapítha*), and one behind seems to fan him, and girls are performing on musical instruments—a flat harp (such as is still used in Burma), drums, a flute, and cymbals (*tálas*); while two dancing girls (*kañchukiní*)—one on each side—beyond the pillars, shew their performances. The lower half of the slab presents Gautama seated on the front of his wife's couch, contemplating the sleeping musicians. He then felt more disgusted, we are told, with the vanities of life, and determined to accomplish the renunciation (*abhinishkramana*). Behind the couch are two spirits,

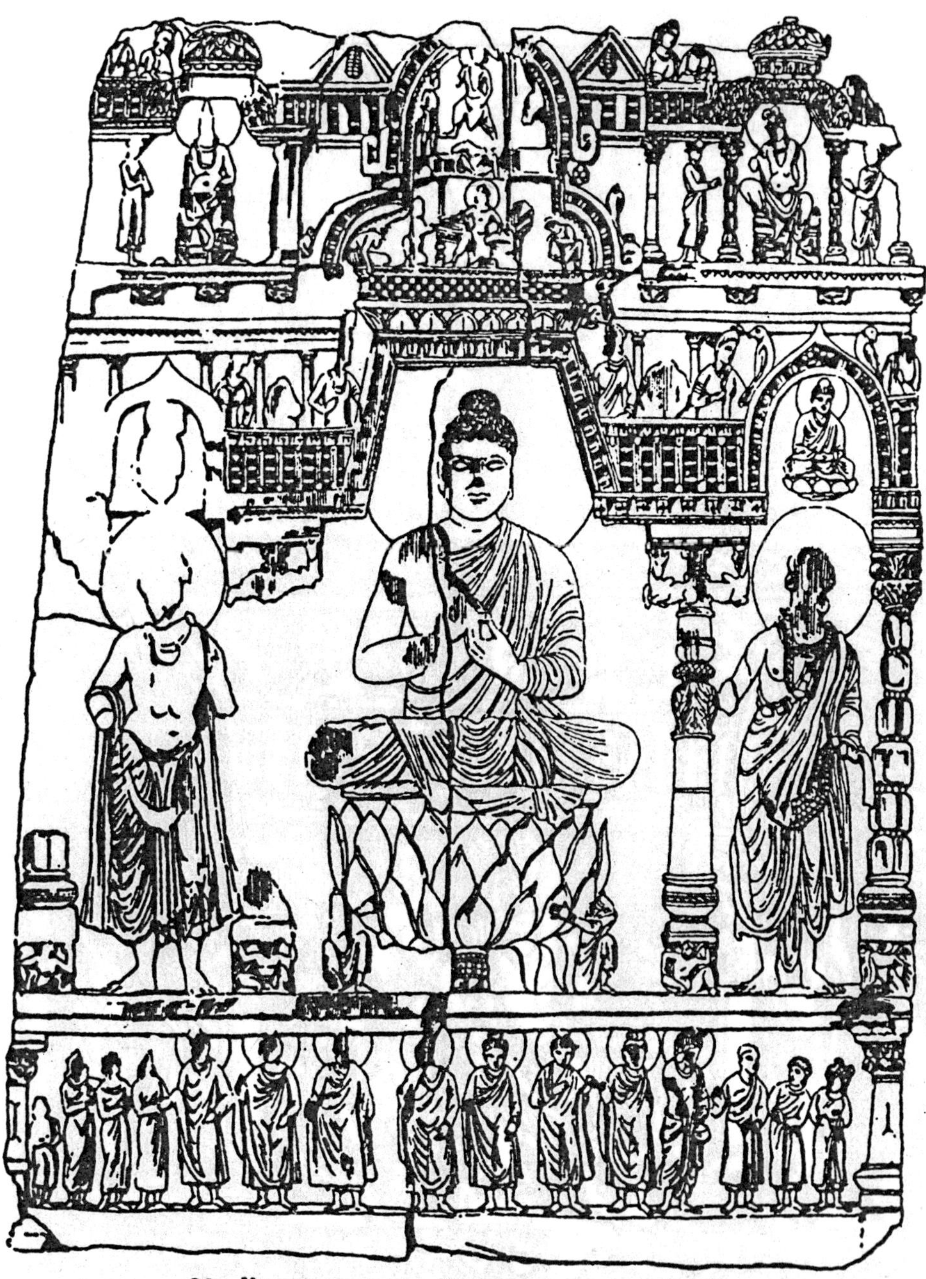

82. RELIEF WITH BUDDHA ENTHRONED.
Found at Muhammad Nâri in Yûsufzâï. Cole, *Pr. N. Monts.* pl. 1.

one in the form of an old man, possibly Dharmachârin, who made all the sleepers contort themselves, or Lalitavyûha, who prevented all sounds from being heard. To the right and left, in niches or windows, are Yavanânîs, or Ionian female guards—two of whom are armed with spears. Above, from a balcony, the gods look down: Sûrya (the sun) to the right and Chandra (the moon) to the left of a bull, that is the sign Taurus (*Tâvuri* or *Vaiśâkha*) It was on Tuesday, at the full moon of Vaiśâkha in the Nakshatra or asterism of Viśâkhâ, that the legends say Gautama was born, and this representation would agree with that date. But the conception and renunciation are both placed at full moons of Ashâ*dh*a (June-July) in the Nakshatra Uttara-Ashâ*dh*a, when the sun would be in Karka or Cancer, and in conjunction with Pushya (Tishya) "the king of stars."[1] The representation then seems intended to show the sun in connexion with the constellation of the Bull, perhaps between two personified "houses" of the moon in the month Ashâ*dh*a: evidently the night of that month on which the moon was full was thereby intended. Perhaps this is an indication of the date when, in the artists opinion, Gautama's flight took place; but it does not agree with the tradition, but with the date of the birth. But this is by the way. What is important here is the similarity of the whole composition to early Christian ivory tablets.

By the combination of different scenes in one relief, the old principle of composition is thus again reverted to, according to which the complete representation of the different phases of an event was related, as it were, by the repetition of the same figures. Yet, owing to regularly arranged decorative elements, the different groups remain separated. The influence of ancient art was also strong enough to preserve the prominence of the principal scene or of the chief figure, to which the others had to be subordinated. Many reliefs contain a representation of Buddha as principal figure enthroned in the centre, and on the left, on a smaller scale, stand servants or worshippers; and smaller compositions, often only rows of figures, are found under and above the central group. Among the reliefs from the monasteries of Gandhâra are semi-circular pediments containing a principal scene below, and two concentric arches over it, filled with smaller figures (ill. 58, 84). One of the most richly carved of these pieces in the Calcutta Museum is a pediment slab from Loriyân Tangai (fig. 83), measuring 3 feet wide by about 25 inches high,—a portion having been broken from the top. On the capitals of pillars that appear at each side, sit Devas adoring the Buddha who occupies the centre. In a band just inside the outer moulding of the arch are figures, perhaps also of Devas, one above another; within this is a torus covered with leaf or scale ornament, and inside this again two arches divide the area into a lower semi-circular and two upper lunulate spaces. The narrow ends of the lunular areas are occupied by dragons or Nâgas having snake bodies, fish tails, wings, forefeet, and human busts. Above them are human or divine figures worshipping Buddha enthroned at the apex of each arch. In the scene below, Buddha sits under

[1] The *Lalita Vistara* in one place (pp. 54-55) fixes the conception at the full moon of Vaisâkha, in the nakshatra Visâkhâ, and "when in conjunction with Pushya"; but Pushya (δ Cancri) being scarcely 70° east of Taurus, the full moon must have been fully seven hours behind it; and if the conception were not in Âshâ*dh*a, the birth could not have been in Vaisâkha, as is always stated. Conf. S. Hardy, *Man. Budh.* pp. 144, 149, 163; *Lal. Vist.* pp. 26, 74, 185, 191, 193; Kern, *Man. Buddh.* pp. 13n., 17. J. B.

a canopy and preaches his Law to a group of females on his right and males on his left, while figures (Devas?) look down from balconies above on each side. Buddha in the Tushita heavens,

83. Relief from Loriyân Tangai. In the Indian Museum, Calcutta.

whither he is said to have gone to teach and convert his mother, may be suggested by this scene: but the identification is altogether uncertain.

Terraces are also occasionally carved to separate the different parts of a relief, and then the whole scene reminds one of a festal procession marching through a crowded street in which the cult-picture is shown as stationary or is being carried along. The Chinese pilgrims describe such festivals in which the faithful upon the roof-terraces showered down wreaths of flowers upon the great idols.[1]

The construction of the sacellum in the temple, with the image of Buddha in the middle and the ornamental reliefs round about, provided another model for these compositions. The steles, in the centre of which Buddha stands or sits, are then much reduced; beside him are disciples and monks: above rises a pointed arch, in which a conversion-scene—as replica of some much employed composition—is represented (ill. 84).[2] Pillars—before which stand followers of Buddha, or groups reduced from larger compositions—make a complete whole of the slab.

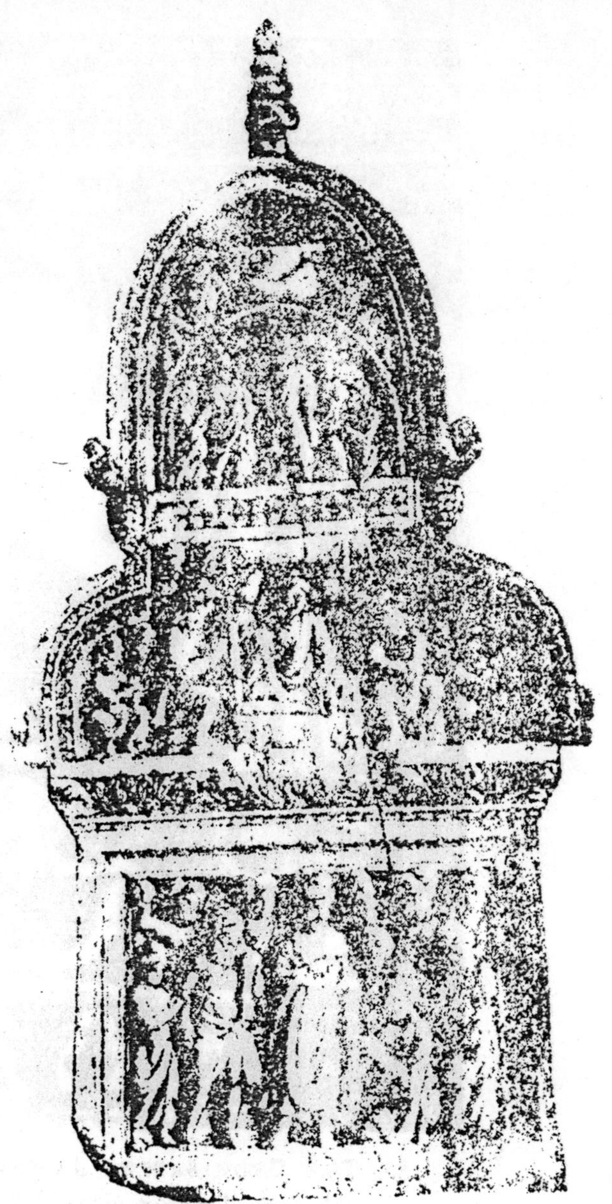

84. STELE FROM JAMÂLGIRI.
From a sculpture in S. Kensington Museum.
From Fergusson and Burgess, *Cave Temples*, p. 138.

It is very interesting to find that this kind of stelé composition is still stereotyped in the style of the reliefs, and especially of the pictures of Tibetan ecclesiastical art and of the Buddhist school of Japan. This is most strikingly shown by a comparison of ill. 82 with the modern Tibetan picture from Nga-ri-Khor-sum (ill. 85): the connection is very striking. At any rate, the transitions mentioned prove once more in regard to this that in the main the Gândhâra sculptures dominate the art of northern Buddhism, so that we may justly hope that an acquaintance with the iconography

[1] The splendour of these ancient feasts, as well as many characteristic features still to be found in Tibet, Mongolia, and especially in Siam and Japan even in modern times, shows that Buddhist pessimism cannot have been so very terrible: we might just as well speak of Buddhist optimism. Conf. A. Pfungst, *Ein deutscher Buddhist*, S. 43.

[2] The illustration affords a characteristic example of this class of reliefs. These steles have been taken to be conventional representations of the fronts of cells or small shrines. This may be so; but they seem to have been employed decoratively as pediments of a sort. The lower scene in fig. 84 presents Buddha addressing a kneeling figure with two attendants. On Buddha's right is *S*akra with the *vajra* and behind him a figure in reverential attitude, while above are four Devas throwing down flowers. The middle is occupied by Buddha teaching, seated under a square canopy—an unusual form,—with two attendants,—perhaps Devas,—and worshipped by three figures on each side and Devas above. The third storey also represents Buddha and attendants; and above all is the *Pâtra* or alms-bowl worshipped by the Nâgas.—J.B.

of this modern school may provide valuable material for the explanation of the old Gândhâra reliefs.

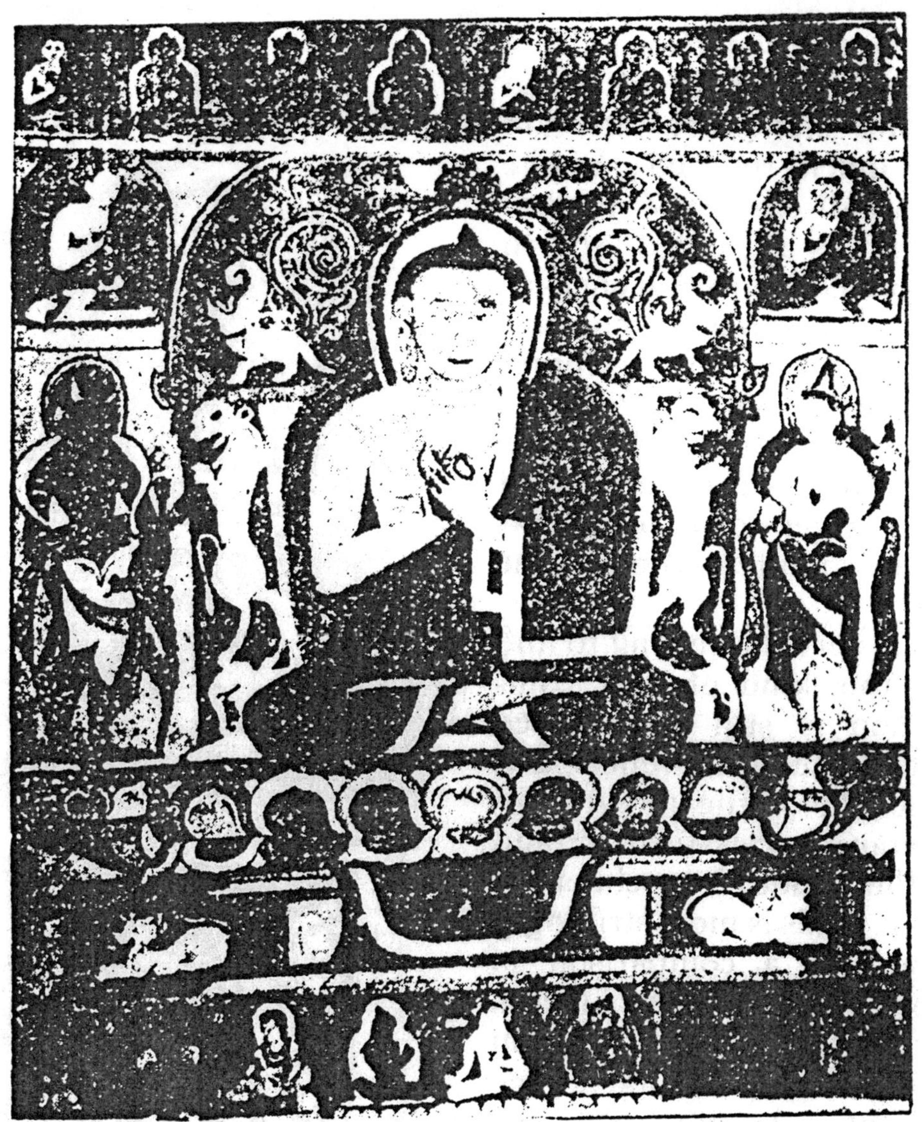

85. THE BODHISATTVA JAMBA (Byams-pa): MAITREYA.
Modern Tibetan picture from Nga-ri-Khor-sum.
Original in Berlin Museum.

The decorative elements which serve as framework or border to the reliefs contain a series of figured and purely ornamental forms of very varied origin. Along with such as have been borrowed from the older Buddhist art, appear quite a number of antique motifs. It is impossible to examine these individually; therefore only the most noteworthy will be mentioned. The giganto-machia relief published by Vincent Smith is only a reproduction of a Greek motif, but it is also a unique example.[1] A giant, seen from behind, similar to the one in the Zeus group from Pergamon, threatens with his club a naked man, who with his right hand tears at the left snake-foot of the giant. These snake-feet are

[1] *J. As. Soc. Beng.* vol. LVIII, pt. i. p. 131f. and pl. ix, 4; Anderson, *Ar. Cat. Ind. Mus.* pt. i, p, 240; and *Ind. Monts.* pl. 102, 6.

so coarsely executed that they look almost like fish-tails. Smith was the first to give the correct explanation, and he is of opinion that the fame of the great work at Pergamon may easily have led to some small replicas, of which an example came to Gandhâra. The crouching Atlases (otherwise Garu*d*as, see above, p. 52) are ilkewise purely antique: (the Royal Museum at Berlin possesses a fine example of these). They serve as supports to the beams; on the relief from Muhammad Nâri shown in ill. 82; they appear,—even furnished with wings,—beneath the slender pillars which are partly of an older order. It is a favourite feature, as has been already mentioned, to set before the broad pillars and columns which border the reliefs, a figure of Buddha alone, or flanked by upright forms of worshippers,—as a curtailment of a larger relief,—or a single worshipping figure, and so on. Of quite special interest is the figure

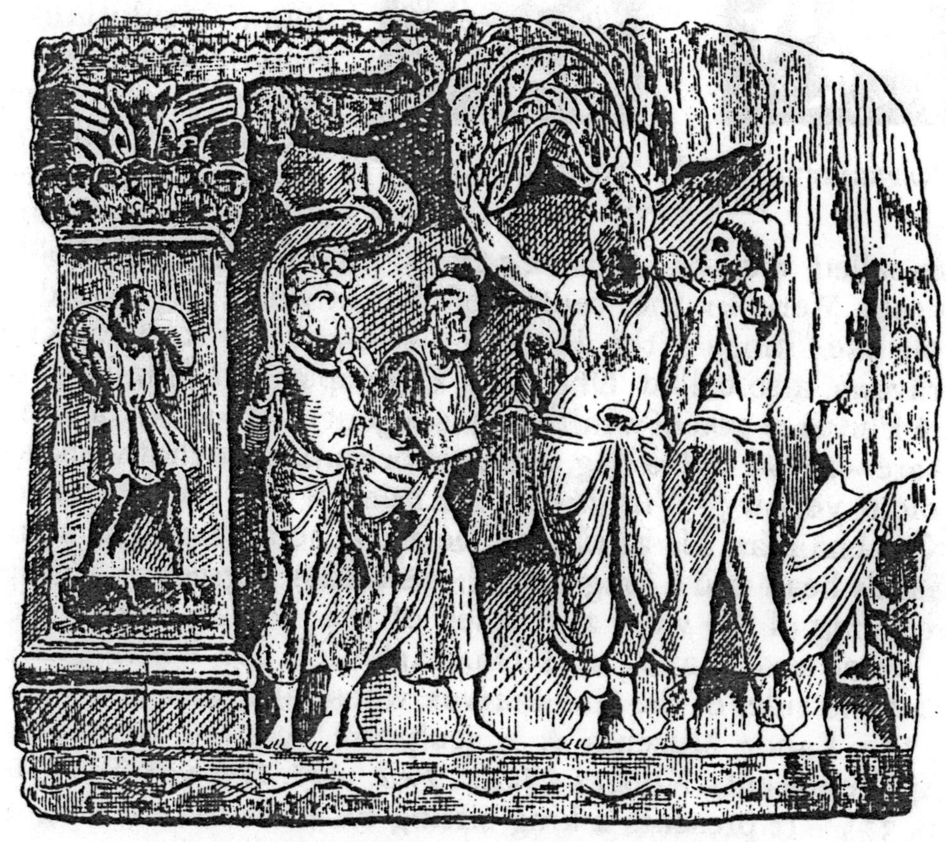

86. BUDDHA'S BIRTH IN THE LUMBINÎ GROVE.
Mâyâ and Prajâpatî before Brahmâ and *S*akra.
From a Gândhâra relief in Lahor Museum.

employed as a pillar ornament in ill. 86:—the Ram-bearer, the Kriophoros. It is perhaps, more than a strange coincidence that this Hermes representation (which, in ancient Christian art, was adopted as a symbol of the Good Shepherd) appears on a Buddhist monument and in evident reference to the founder of Buddhism. Smith's attention has been chiefly drawn to the contact that has taken place with Christian art. If one compares with the Rambearer the statue of the Good Shepherd in the Christian Museum of the Lateran (conf. Spencer Northcote, *Roma Sotteranea*, p. 299).

one cannot fail to remark a certain resemblance. The clothing is the same, and among the Gândhâra sculptures known to me it nowhere else appears.

What the figure carries, however, cannot be quite made out. We may perhaps derive a hint from a sculpture in the Lahor Museum of a man pouring out what may be meant to represent money at the feet of a seated figure, as described by Dr. J. Burgess (*Jour. Ind. Art and In.* vol. VIII, pl. 14, 3, and p. 37; or sep. ed. pl. 12, 3, and p. 15).

It is the so-called "tribute bearer" of the late antique art, so often appearing on ivory diptychs, which we must so generally draw upon as important parallels for the explication of our Gândhâra sculptures.[1] At Ajanṭâ also the "tribute bearer" is employed decoratively (ill. 87).

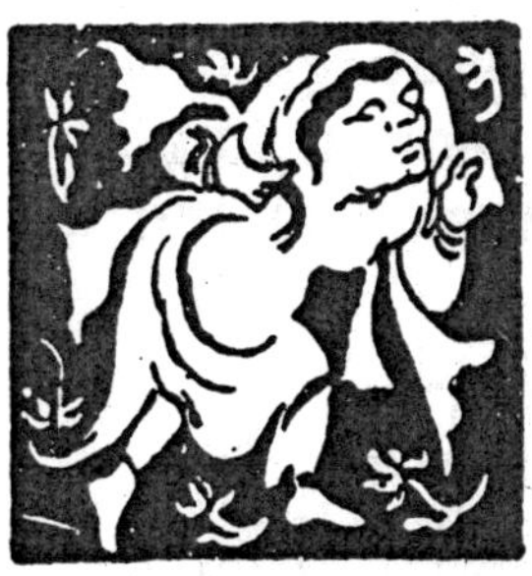
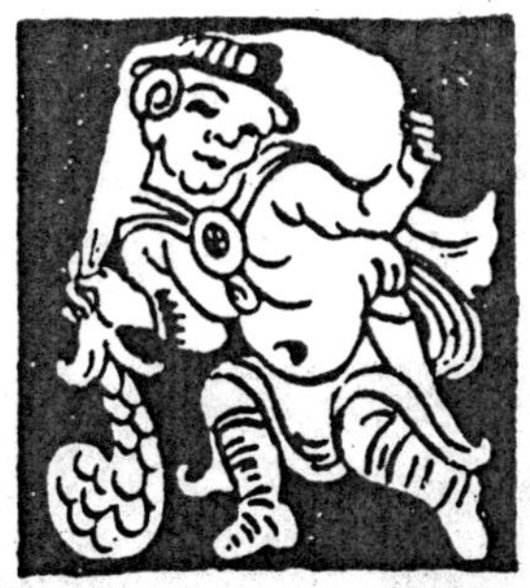

87. Representation of "Tribute-bearers," from Ajanṭâ.

The representation of the tribute-bearers brings us to the so-called world-protectors. In Bauddha mythology, the mountain Meru, in the centre of the universe, is guarded by four "heroic like" kings of the demons. These are :—Kubera, Kuvera, or Vaiśrâvaṇa, also called Dhanada, Dhanapati, Yaksha-râja, &c., the Hindû Plutus or god of wealth; he is regent of the north, and his attributes are—a pike with a flag, and a rat or mungoose that vomits jewels; his colour yellow;—Virûḍhaka, the ruler of the south and chief of the Kumbhâṇḍas, his attributes being a helmet of the skin of an elephant's head and a long sword; his colour is green;—Virûpâksha, the red king of the west and ruler of the Nâgas, whose attributes are a jewel and snake; and Dhṛitarâshṭra, the white guardian of the east and ruler of the Gandharvas, whose attribute is a mandoline.[2]

In the Lahor Museum is a sculpture, referred to above, which perhaps represents Kubera (*Jour. Ind. Art, &c.* vol. VIII, pl. 14, 3, and p. 37). It presents a king sitting on a throne, wearing a richly ornamented turban; beside him is a smaller figure—a Yaksha. Further, at his feet is the tribute-bearer, who is emptying out a bag

[1] Conf. Duruy-Hertzberg, *Gesch. d. römischen Kaiserreichs*, Bd. V, S. 409. So far as the correlation between Christian and Indian art is concerned, I can only indicate some of the modes in which the Indian may have influenced the Christian: first of all, the "folded hands" already noticed by Curtius (*Archaol. Zeit. N.F.* Bd. VIII, Ss. 90ff.) and the Indian *añjali* must be mentioned; the lions of St. Barlaam, Buddha's *siṁhâsana*; St. John's cup with the snake, the alms-bowl with the Nâga in Buddha's hand,—are matters I can only mention in passing.

[2] In China these Chaturmahârâjas, or four great kings, are placed as guardians at the temple gates. In Japan they are respectively,—Bishamon, holding a club in his right hand and a chaitya-shaped casket in his left, with his feet on two demons; Zôchô-tennô, seated on a dragon, and holding a scroll and brush; Kômoku, holding a *vajra* with three points, and sitting on a demon; and Ji-koku, also seated on a demon.—J.B.

of gold. This sack with the gold rolling out, is replaced, in modern pictures, by the rat, or rather ichneumon or mungoose (Sansk. *nakula*; Hind. *nevalá*; Tib. *neu-le*). The reason for this we know not.[1] Kubera is by far the most prominent of the Lokapâlas: in Japan he is placed among the seven deities of fortune. Even in the Asoka period he is represented, and at Barâhat he is named in the epigraph to a statue on a gate-pillar, as a guardian Yaksha. (Cuningham, *Bharhut*, pl. xxii).

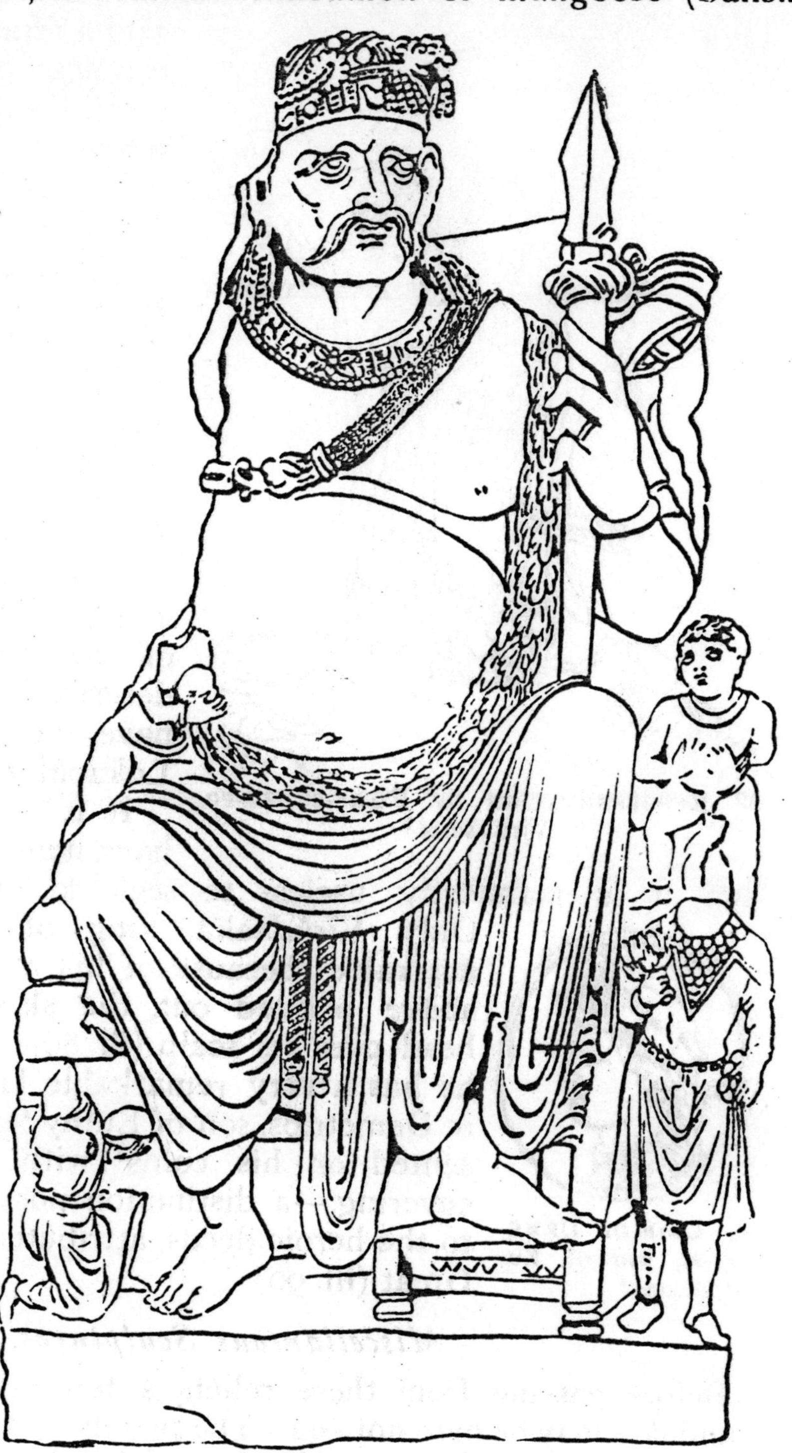

88. THE SO-CALLED INDO-SKYTHIAN KING.
From a cast in the S. Kensington Museum and in the Mus. f. Völkerkunde, Berlin.

Another sculpture, represented by Burgess, has also been identified as a Lokapâla (*ib.* Pl. 13, fig. 1, and pp. 31, 37). It is in the British Museum and is about 18 inches in height, but somewhat damaged. The principal figure wears a richly jewelled turban after the Râjpût style, and holds a pike in his left hand; the right hand is gone. His right foot rests on the regal footstool, and a small figure stands by each knee. On the base one attendant,

[1] If the Gallic divinity represented by Duruy-Hertzberg, *Gesch. des römischen Kaiserreiches*, Bd. I, S. 148, is to be depended upon, we have the same motif before us. The god sits between Hermes and Apollo, with legs crossed in Indian fashion; from a sack he shakes out what appear to be beech nuts before a couple of stags; on the gable above him is a rat! Conf. the explanation of A. Foucher, *Rev. de l'Hist. d. Rel.* tome XXX, p. 366f.; and see *Globus*, 18 Mar. 1899, Ss. 169ff.

in the middle, sits on an animal; another, on the left, presents some offering; to the right, one addresses the figure in the middle; and a female kneels behind in a precatory attitude.

89 REPRESENTATION OF P'AGS-SKYES-PO, Virû*dh*aka.[1]

With this we may compare a figure at Lahor (ill. 88), which is usually described as an Indo-Skythian king. Two things here are of special interest:—1. The little attendant figures which surround the chief one. This is a peculiarity of the declining antique, which represents the portraits of emperors as larger than the surrounding soldiers, servants, and tribute-bearers; 2. The portrait-like character of the heads of the figures described. Could actual kings have been represented as Lokapâlas?

If it is probable that we have here a figure of Kubera, then it is manifestly useless to seek to identify the others. Only Virû*dh*aka, king of the south, is remarkable because of his attribute, wearing, as above pointed out, the skin of an elephant's head over his scalp (ill. 89). In this, moreover, he has a very remarkable Hellenic counterpart in Demetrios, son of Euthydemos I, who is represented on his coins[2] with just such a head-covering,—a distinction possibly referring back to the heroic deeds attributed to Alexander the Great (ill. 90).

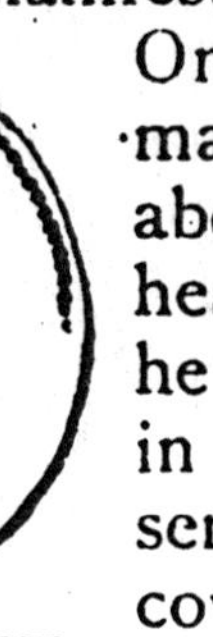

90. COIN OF DEMETRIOS, son of Euthydemos.[3]

Miscellaneous Sculptures.

Before passing from these reliefs a few other sculptures from Gandhâra may be here noticed. The two illustrations 7 and 40 are of sculptures from Swât and evidently have belonged to the same monu-

[1] From an original Pekin Lamaist miniature on silk in the Berlin Museum für Völkerkunde. Conf. *Originalmitteilungen aus dem Kgl. Mus. f. Völkerk.* Bd. V, S. 110.

[2] Coins play an important part in the development of the north Buddhist types. Notice, for example, the derivation of the *S*iva type from the ancient Poseidon (conf. Goblet d'Alviella, *Ce que l'Inde doit à la Grèce*, p. 30; and P. Gardner, *Catalogue Ind. Coins: Greek, &c., Kings*, pl. v, 1); the same type meets us in the bronze from Khoten in *Vostochnyja Zametki*, p. 364, pl. xi, 6. The victorious emperor represented in ill. 52 is likewise a coin-type; the Sarasvatî type in ill. 56 also appears on Gupta coins (V. A. Smith). Conf. *Globus*, 18 Mar. 1899, Ss. 169ff.

[3] Conf. P. Gardner, *Cat. of Ind. Coins*, 1886, pl. ii, 9-12.

ment and to the same frieze or dado. The Corinthian pillars sunk into the dividing spaces at the ends of the panels are identical. The individualization of the faces is particularly marked. In fig. 7 the central figure is a royal personage seated upon a throne with a very antique style of back. Overhead is a large canopy hung with tassels; below is a footstool; and at each end of the throne stand *chauri* bearers,—the face of one of them being destroyed. In front, at each side are two persons, seated on what seem to be cushioned stools carved with considerable care. Each holds a round bottle or vessel with his left hand; and the one on the king's left, who is the older, raises his hand in addressing him. This scene naturally suggests the story of the Brâhma*n*a explaining to Suddhodana the dream of Mâyâ previous to the birth of Gautama, or perhaps the omens after his birth.[1]

Ill. 40 represents separately the second part of the scene in ill. 64, or the seven steps (*saptapadâni*) taken by the new-born Bodhisattva. Here the gods only are represented as present. *S*atakratu or Sakka, the legend says, had dispersed the attendants by a storm of wind and rain; and here he stands on the infant Gautama's left, clad much as a Brâhma*n*a, with a high turban and holding the *vajra*[2] in his right hand.) Brahmâ, bearded, with his hair in a *jatâ* and with the *kama*nda*l*u or ascetic's water vessel, stands on his right. Other Devas appear behind, and a canopy is held over the infant, who alone has the nimbus. In the relief, fig. 64, the infant Buddha is represented pointing with the right hand up to heaven and with the left to the earth, in sign of taking possession of the world. This is the legendary attitude still preserved in China and Japan.[3]

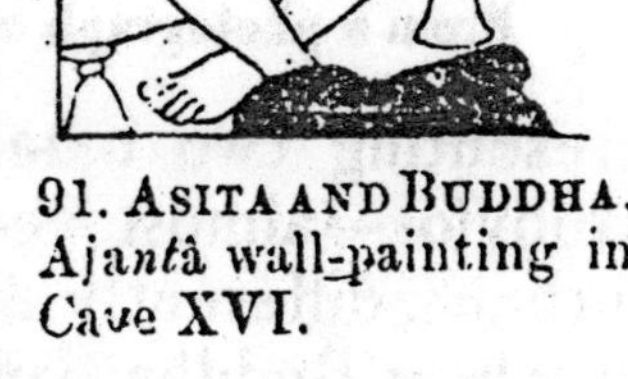

91. ASITA AND BUDDHA. Aja*n*tâ wall-painting in Cave XVI.

Connected with the scenes from the infancy of Gautama we might expect the incident of the visit of the ascetic or *R*ishi Asita to Suddhodana; and among the wall-paintings at Aja*n*tâ was one on the right side of Cave XVI which was long pointed out as representing the old hermit[4] holding the child in his hands (ill. 91). Unfortunately, this and neighbour-

[1] Rhys Davids, *Buddh. Birth Stories*, p. 63; Bigandet, *Leg. of Gautama*, vol. I, pp. 29f.; Beal, *Fo-sho-hing-tsan-king*, in *Sac. Bks. East*, vol. XIX, p. 8.

[2] In these Gândhâra sculptures the *vajra* is not forked at the ends, as is usual in Nepâl, Tibet, &c. The *vajra* with single-pointed ends is still in use in Japan, and known as the *dô-kô*, as distinguished from the *san-kô*—with three prongs, and the *go-kô*—having five points.

[3] See a bronze figure of Tanjô Shaka (the infant *S*âkya) in the Musée Guimet.—*Petit Guide ill.* (1897) pp. 196, 198. In Tibet called *lha 'bebs*, 'the god who came down.'

[4] Burgess, *Notes on Bauddha Rock Temples at Ajantâ*, p. 60; *Rock Temples*, p. 308. Conf. J. Muir in *Ind. Ant.* vol. VII, pp. 232f.; Beal, *Rom. Leg. of Buddha*, pp. 56f.; Griffiths. *Paintings of Ajantâ*, vol. I, pl. 45; and Mrs. Speir's *Life in Anc. India*, pp. 248-257. With this picture compare the sculpture of Silenus and the infant Bacchus, in the Louvre Museum: Seemann, *Die Götter und Heroen*, p. 187.

ing scenes were ruined by natives about the time Mr. Griffiths was copying these paintings.

Still another of the infancy stories is given on the lower part of the panel figured in ill. 92. This may be compared with a small relief, about 8 inches by 4, in the British Museum, probably from Sikri,[1] which represents the child taken to the Vimalavyûha garden to be decked with the royal jewellery, of which event we have so detailed an account in the ninth chapter of the *Lalita Vistara*: "All the gems on his person were lost as the glow-worm's spark in the light of day."[2] Two attendants here pour water on his head to bathe him: this service is ascribed to the gods immediately after his birth. Two nurses hold him or put on the ornaments; and two Devas behind them pay reverence with joined hands. Above this is another compartment representing two bare-headed figures, the front one with nimbus and krobylos—almost certainly Buddha,—meeting four others wearing turbans, differently dressed and perhaps bearing presents,—the first of whom Buddha converses with.

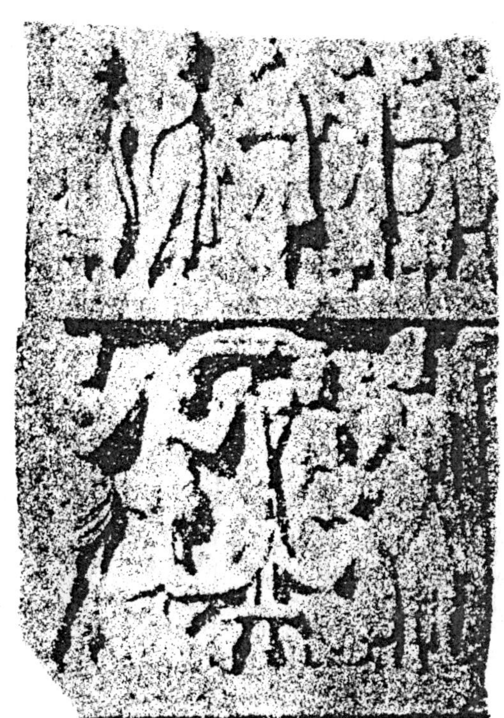

92. Bathing the infant Gautama, &c.
From a photograph of a relief from Swât.

For comparison with the figures 67 and 68,—the latter in the Berlin Museum—we may here add a representation of a remarkable relief from Swât (ill. 93). It presents Buddha addressing an ascetic Brâhma*n*a, sitting in his *pânsâla* or leaf hut, while behind the former stands Sakka as his protecting genius, in his usual scanty clothing and abundant hair, clasping his mace or *vajra* in his right hand. The meeting here might suggest that with Gayâ Kâ*s*yapa; but the absence of any indication of what neighbouring reliefs may have represented prevents any certain identification. Possibly this is from the same place as fig. 40.

In the Indian Museum at Calcutta is a fine relief from the Lorivân Tangai stûpa. The subject is the visit of Indra to *S*âkya Simha at

[1] *Jour. I. Art and Ind.* vol. VIII, pp. 35, 76, and pl. 10, fig. 2.
[2] Foucaux, *Le Lal. Vist.* pp. 110f.; and Beal, *Romantic Legend*, pp. 64-66.

the Indrasaila hill (ill. 94). It is on a slab 3 feet 10 inches high by 2 feet 8 inches wide, and represents the scene in a much more developed form than as it appears elsewhere, in an archaic style,—on an

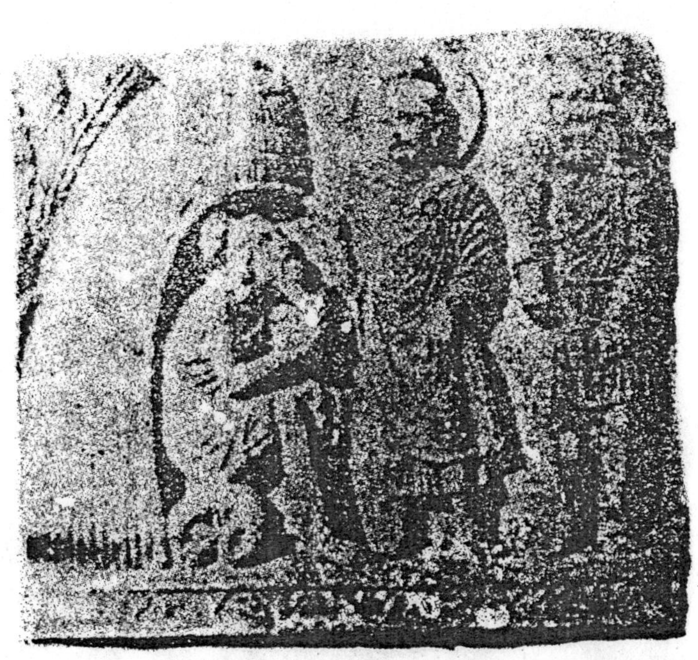

93. Buddha and Ascetic Brâhmana.
Relief from Swât; from a photograph.

inscribed fragment from Barâhat, on the north gateway at Sâñchî, at Gayâ, and in another sculpture, in the Calcutta Museum, from Mathurâ.[1] A comparison of these versions is very instructive as helping us to trace the influence of the original Hindu conceptions on the Gândhâra art, which took over the models and modified them according to a higher artistic standard. The story of Indra desiring to reverence Buddha at Indrasaila hill is well known,[2] and the Barâhat sculpture is labelled as "Indasâlaguha." The Swât sculpture represents the visit of Sakra and his retinue, with the Gandharva harper Pañchasikha, to the Buddha whilst he was living in the Indrasailaguhâ—a cave near Buddha-Gayâ. The entrance of the cave is surrounded by flames to represent the glory of the Teacher "replendent with a halo of many colours, proceeding to a fathom's length all round his person." Above and below,

[1] The Loriyân Tangai sculpture has been noticed, along with the others, by Dr. Th. Bloch in the *Proc. A. S. Beng.* (1898), pp. 186f. See also Cunningham, *Bharhut*, pl. xxviii, 4, and p. 88; *Mahâbodhi*, pl. viii, 6; Fergusson, *T. and Ser. Wor.* pl. xxix, 1, and p. 138; *Ind. Monts.* pl. 60, 1; and Anderson, *Arch. Coll. Ind. Mus.* pt. i, p. 182; S. Hardy, *Man. Budh.* pp. 298f.

[2] Beal, *Si-yu-ki*. vol. II, p. 180; *Trav. of Fah-hian*, p. 110; *Foe-koue-ki*, pp. 262-3; S. Hardy, *Man. Budh.* pp. 298f.; conf. Rhys Davids, *Buddh. Birth Stories*, p. 125.

the birds, beasts, and trees indicate the isolation of the place. Indra appears as a royal personage on the right, doing reverence to the ascetic, with his parasol-bearer close behind, and the Devas of his train beyond on both sides. His peculiar crown or headdress

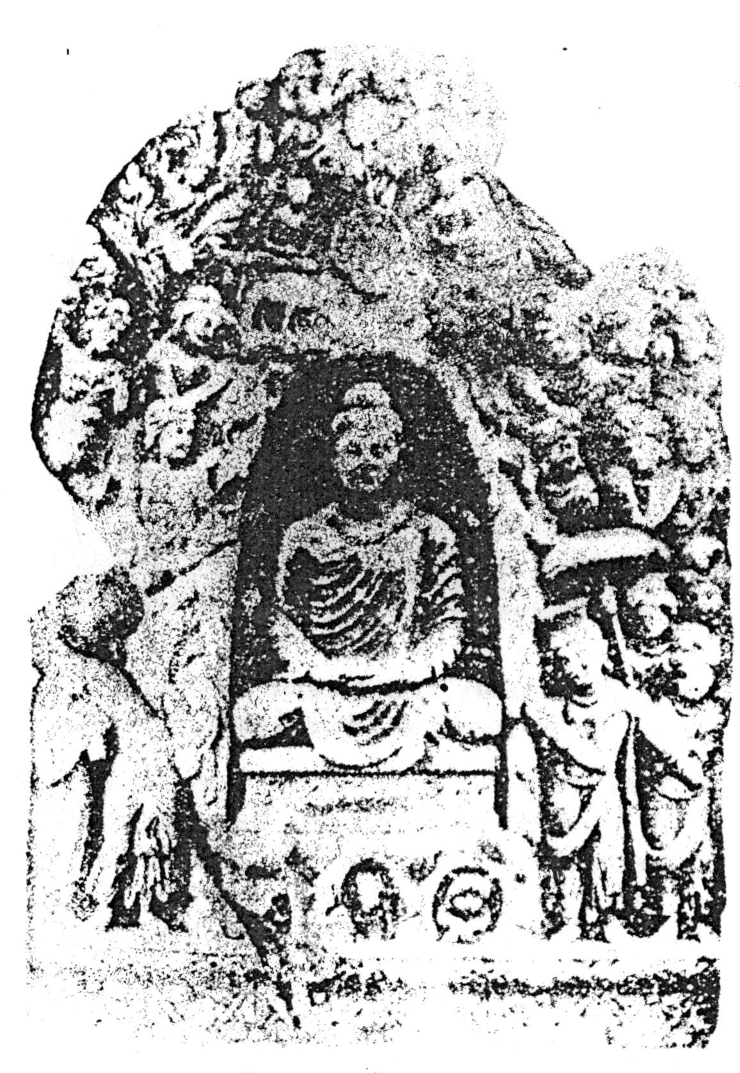

94. Buddha visited by Sakra at the Indrasaila Cave.
A sculpture from Loriyân Tangai in the Calcutta Museum.

is very similar to what we find also in the Mathurâ sculpture. The figure of the Gandharva musician, on the other side, has been much damaged by the fracture of the stone, but his harp is still visible. This sculpture may well be ascribed to the best period of Gândhâra art.

Among the Jâtaka representations, perhaps the favourite is that of Sumedha or Megha, who lived in the age of Dîpankara Buddha, the twenty-fourth predecessor of Gautama. The legend tells how Megha, the disciple of Ratna (*i.e.* of Maitreya Bodhisattva in a previous birth), obtains from Bhadrâ, a water-girl, some stalks of the Utpala flower or blue lotus, she has secured to present to Dîpankara; these he throws into the air over the Buddha's head, and then places his deer-skin covering in a muddy place, unrolling his long hair for Dîpankara to pass over, and so obtains his wish—that in a future age he shall be *S*âkya Muni, and in intermediate births Bhadrâ shall be his wife. Megha then ascended into the air and did reverence to Buddha. In two sculptures, one in the British Museum (17 inches by 16) and the other at Lahor, we have most of the details. In the first, Megha or Sumedha is represented a second time, on a plaque in the air, worshipping the Buddha. Among the Mahâyâna sculptures in the Ka*n*heri caves also, we find the sāme scene represented (ill. 95),—Bhadrâ with her *lotâ* and flowers; Sumedha throwing his flowers up, which remain in the air over Dîpankara; and then prostrating himself with his *jatâ* unrolled at the feet of the Buddha.[1]

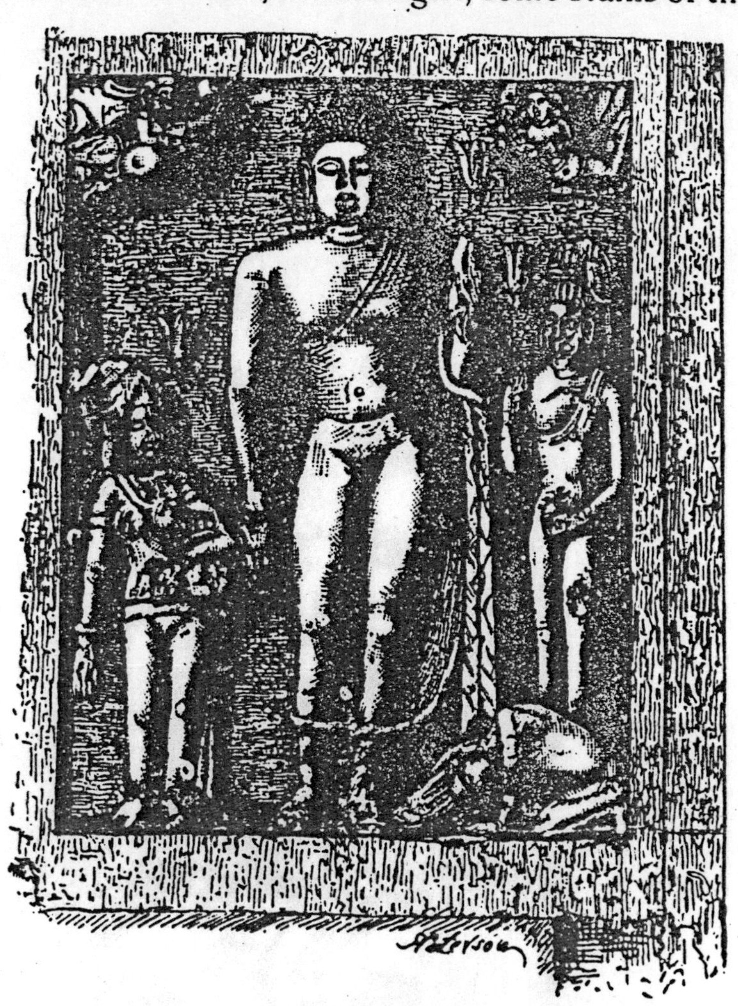

95. DÎPANKARA BUDDHA AND MEGHA.
From a wall relief in Cave XXXV at Kanheri.
Arch. Sur. West. Ind. vol. IV, p. 66.

One of the favourite subjects of Buddhist art was the first sermon in the Deer-park (M*ri*gadâva) at Isipatana in the vicinity of Banâras.[2] "To listen to the first proclaiming of the law, evening—

[1] Conf. *Arch. Sur. W. Ind.* vol. IV, p. 66. For the story see *J. R. As. Soc.* vol. VI (1873), pp. 385ff. The southern version is given by Rhys Davids, *Bud. Birth Stories*, pp. 8-28, where the future Buddha is called Sumedha. For other examples, in the Calcutta and Lahor Museums, see *Ind. Monts.* pll. 101, 114 (6), 140, and 147; *Jour. Ind. Art, &c.*. vol. VIII, pl. 11, figs. 1, 2, and p. 36.

[2] The four sacred places to which pilgrimages were to be made by pious Buddhists were,—the scene of Buddha's birth or the Lumbinî garden; the place of his enlightenment or the Vajrâsana at Buddha-Gayâ; the place where he first preached his *Dharma*

like a lovely female—came; the various beings in the world all assembled, that they might receive the ambrosia and nectar of Nirvâ*n*a." Then "Buddha opened his mouth and preached the

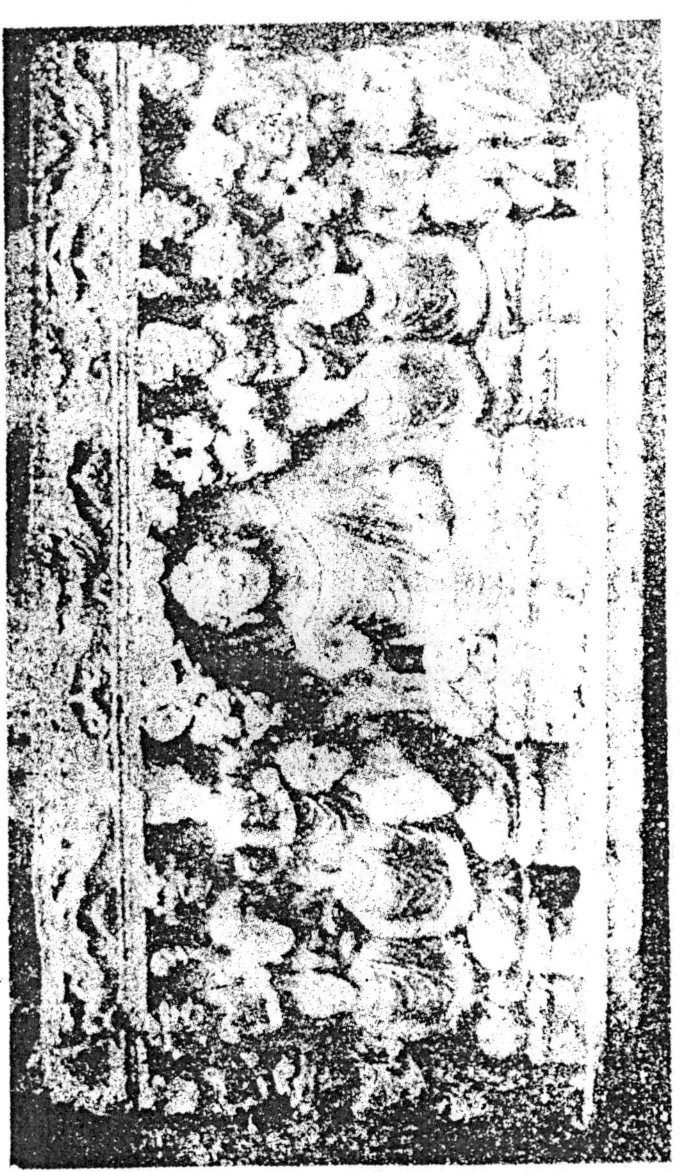

96. The first Sermon at Banâras.
A relief from Swât, in the Indian Museum, Calcutta.

Dharmachakra Sútra," and the "oldest of the five ascetics, Kau*n*d*i*nya, entered the first path as did an *asañkhya* of Devas, &c." The illustration fig. 96, is on a relief from Swât, on a panel measuring 27 inches wide by 16 in height. In this large group

at Isipatana; and the place, near Kusinagara, where he passed away "in that utter passing away which leaves nothing whatever behind." Hence these four scenes are naturally among the most frequent subjects of representation in the sculptures. Conf. Rhys Davids, *Buddhist Suttas*, in *Sac. Bks. of the East*, vol. XI, pp. 90, 155.

some faces are injured as well as the rich floral cornice, but the scene is, as a whole, animated and artistic. We have here the five ascetics seated listening to Buddha; the deer below his seat indicate the place; the pillar between them supports the *trisula* and wheel representative of the religious law (*dharma*); and behind appear the representatives of the Devas, some throwing down flowers on the Teacher. On his left we cannot fail to recognise

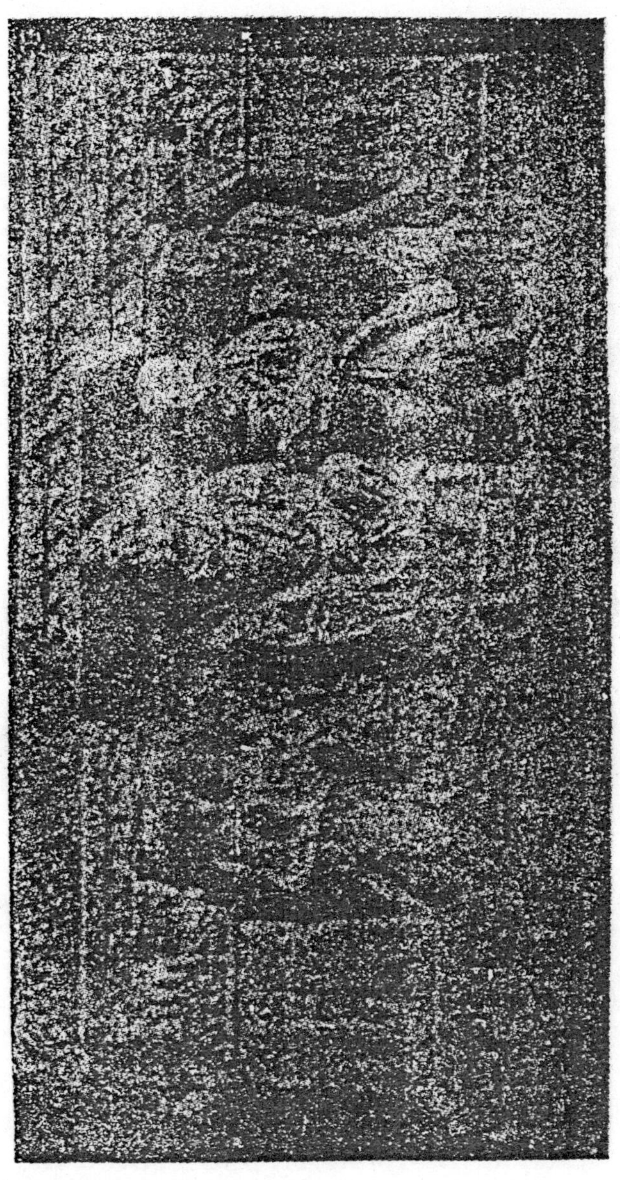

97. WASHING THE MASTER'S FEET.
A Gândhâra relief in Lahor Museum.

his constant attendant *S*akra with a large carefully moulded head, distinguished by the beard and moustache.

The story relates that when Siddhârtha arrived at Isipatana the five ascetics who resided there "were compelled to come before him and worship. They afterwards washed his feet, and enquired familiarly about his health; but Gautama informed them that they must not address him as an equal: he was now a supreme Buddha." The somewhat inferior relief, ill. 97, apparently represents this part of the story, or some similar scene.

The next illustration (fig. 98) may naturally be supposed to represent the sequel of the attainment of supreme knowledge (*bodhi*). The first food offered him after his temptation was by two merchants and consisted of honey and wheat. But Gautama reflecting

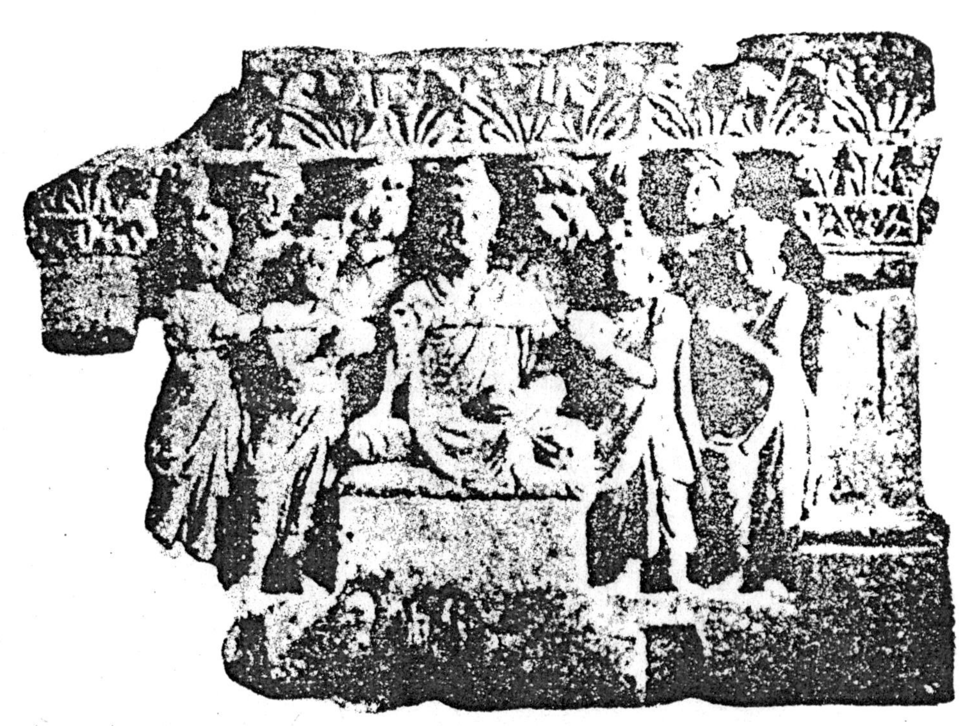

98. Supposed presentation of Buddha's Pâtra.
A Gândhâra sculpture in Lahor Museum.

that he must have an alms-bowl (*pâtra*), the four Mahârâjas each brought one of gold, which he refused; then they brought silver, emerald and ruby dishes, which were also refused; lastly, each brought an earthenware bowl, and Buddha "causing them to unite in one (lest there should be jealousy), accepted the one from all." The legend of the *pâtra* is a long one: it is now said to be kept in Sâgara's palace at the bottom of the sea, but on the advent of Maitreya, it will divide into the original four, each of which is to be guarded by a Mahârâja, as it is the palladium of Buddhism.

One other sculpture may be referred to, as of quite remarkable character among these reliefs. It is on a small slab in the British Museum, about 16 inches long by 6½ high (see *Jour. Indian Art and Industry*, vol. VIII, pl. 17, fig. 1). With a quasi-Corinthian pillar at the right end, it represents six men, carved with unusual life, bareheaded, with beards and moustaches, very muscular, and with boots or thick socks; but what serves as clothing reminds us of the Roman military tunica or kilt, growing down from their waists, as if parts of themselves. Each carries a spade or shovel over his left shoulder, except the left one who leans on his; and the second from the right carries some round object (a skull?) in his right hand. Nothing of Indian origin resembles this unique relief.—J.B.

A. Foucher has remarked (*Rev. de l'Hist. des Relig.* tome XXX, p. 359) that I have failed to point out in my account of the Gândhâra sculptures, that the entire development of this period of art belongs to the Mahâyâna school. I had, however, taken in hand to treat the art forms independently of, and uninfluenced by the religious and theoretical development, whilst I favoured the opinion that the monuments must be examined, first of all without, and unconfined by, any fixed religious system. The forms of art, moreover, give so much of which the texts know nothing, and they can help us to nothing; while the texts themselves only become intelligible by access to the forms. The saying that art speaks her own language is just as true in Indian archæology as in western. But it cannot be denied that just the consideration of the decisive word "Mahâyâna" would have had certain advantages. My chief object was to demonstrate that the Gândhâra period was really the mother of all later Buddhist (as well as Brâhmanical) creations in art; that a definite history might actually be established on this basis, which would also rectify the history of international influences and the modifications of the interpretations that Buddhist monuments have undergone through other religions.

Now, in China, the four protectors of the world, along with the so-called "fat-bellied Buddha," or Ho-shang "with the sack," represent a pentad, which are so arranged in the entrance halls that the four protectors (Chaturmahârâjas) hold the four corners of the hall while Pu-tai Ho-shang sits in the middle.

Ho-shang is the representative of the Mahâyâna system, thus it occurs that the peculiarities characterizing the old Mahâyâna art, *i.e.* the Gândhâra school, have been applied to him. Further, it strikes one, that the figures of children, which surround Ho-shang, are the survivals of the diminutive attendants in the late antique model, and that his bare stomach, which has earned for him the European epithet of "fat-bellied," goes back to the peculiar arrangement of the robe, as shown in our accepted Gândhâra Lokapâlas. The peculiarity of his dress, which, according to eastern Asiatic ideas, borders on the indecent, tended to make the figure ridiculous and gave rise to those entertaining caricatures in which the Japanese especially excel, and among which the seven gods of fortune[1] and

[1] Ho-teï (the Chinese Pu-tai, "calico bag," Ho-shang, "priest" or "monk"), commonly known as Mi-lê P'usa, was a Chinese priest under the Liâng dynasty, (A.D. 502-557), who is regarded as an incarnation of Maitreya; he is always represented as

even Ho-teï appear. The hemp sack of our fat monk is then perhaps the sack of our ancient "tribute-bearer."

These last remarks are to be regarded as purely hypothetical, and merely a suggestion which may possibly contain a grain of truth about things which are so entirely puzzling.

If we pause at the numerous little decorative figures from Gandhâra, an aspect of late antique art is there presented to us which perhaps accompanies the types above spoken of, the Pygmies,—the little cupids,—that appear with or without wings. They are represented on string courses, plinths or friezes, as boyish figures carrying garlands or playing between garlands, climbing, wrestling, or performing on (Indian?) musical instruments. In the intervening portions the old lotus-flowers, which remind one of palms, are again introduced; or the intervals are filled in with symbols, animals, or birds. The ancient classic garland was, it appears, quite incomprehensible to the Indian: it resolved itself into roll-ornaments resembling snakes (ill 99, 100). On the sculptures of the Amarâvatî rails these garland-bearers belong to those elements which bear evidence to the influence of the Gândhâra school. The boys at play have turned into men who, bearing huge snake-like bodies, advance in studied and graceful attitudes (ill. 101). The heads of the dragons (they are evidently intended to be placed one beside the other), which grasp the ends of the

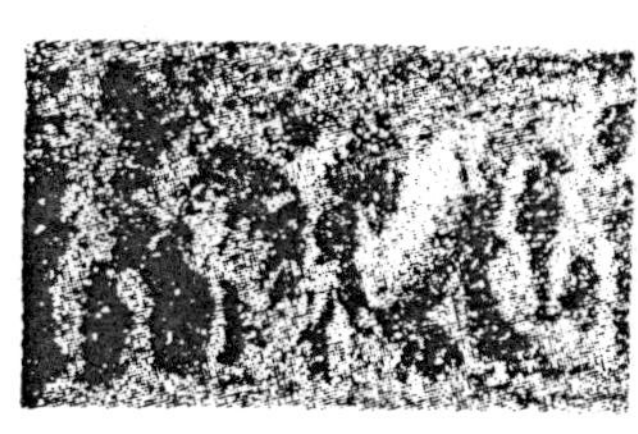

99. PART OF A FRIEZE.
From Loriyân Tangai.

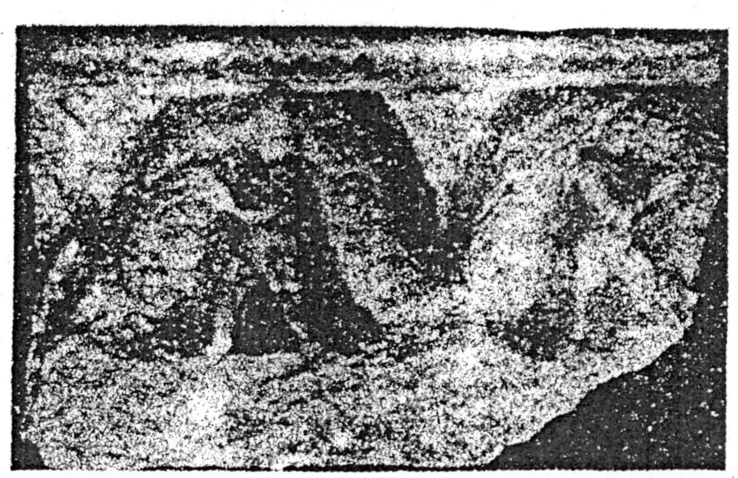

100. RELIEF WITH GARLAND-BEARING BOYS.
From Swât. Original in Mus. f. Völkerkunde, Berlin.

very fat and lazily resting on his sack. Edkins, *Chin. Buddh.* p. 143; *Cat. du Mus Guim.* (1883), p. 257; *J. R. As. Soc.* (1898), p. 346. The seven gods of fortune are:—Ben-ten (Sarasvatî), Bishamon (Vaisramana or Kubera), Daï-koku, Ho-teï, Yebis, Fuku-roku-jiu, and Jiu-rô-jin,—an eclectic series.

bodies in a curious way, present the antique appearance of the dragons' heads on the chair-backs described above (conf. ill. 8).

Among the pairs of dallying figures in the borders of many Gândhâra reliefs (*Jour. Ind. Art, &c.*, vol. VIII, pl. 7, figs. 2, 3) groups of gods and goddesses occur whose erotic excesses are a development of the ancient nude;—compare the copies in Burgess, *Cave Temples*, pll. xx, xlii, xlv, xlvii.

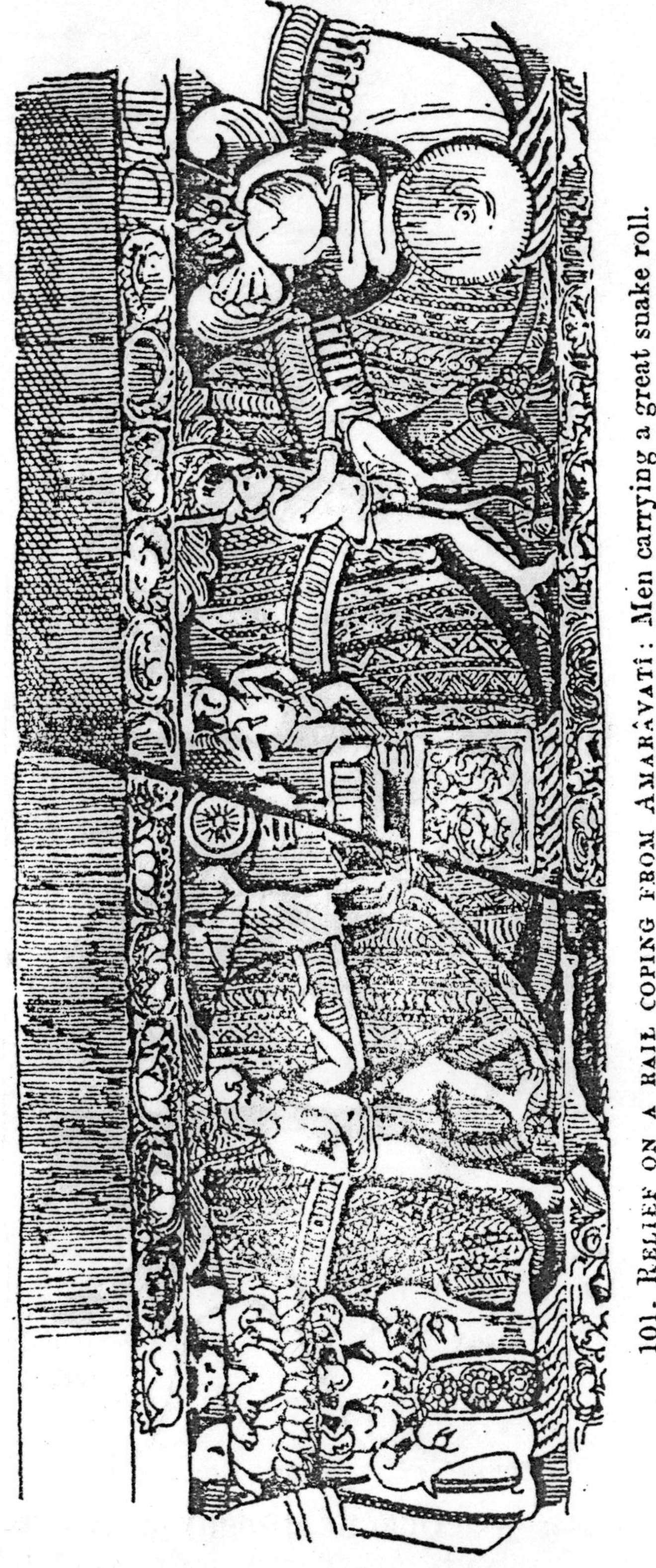

101. Relief on a rail coping from Amarâvatî: Men carrying a great snake roll. Fergusson, *Tree and Serp. Worsh.* pl. lvi.

The bases and pedestals of statues are largely used for decorative sculptures. These are very varied,—worshippers before a lamp, the Nirvâ*n*a scene, figures of Buddhas and Bodhisattvas with attendants, &c.—and it is often hard to see what relation, if any, exists between the decorative scene and the principal image (see ill. 82).[1] The ill. 102 represents one of these bases in the Lahor Museum; the figure it supported is now unknown, but this pedestal is decorated with sculpture that we should hardly associate with a highly ethical religious cult. It represents some Bacchanalian orgy, and might recall the appearance of some Roman sarcophagus, with its lion's head and claws; even the men on whose knees the women are seated look more like Romans than

[1] See *Jour. Ind. Art, &c.*, pl. 3, fig. 1; pl. 8, 2; pl. 9, 1; pl. 13, 4 and 5; pl. 23, 7; *Ind. Monts.* pll. 83, 86, 88, 112, 145.

Orientals, while the women wear the usual heavy Hindû anklets.[1]

Again, the fronts of the steps on the stairs leading up to stûpas or shrines were elaborately decorated with sculptured reliefs. This at least was the case with fronts of the sixteen steps ascending to the stûpa at Jamâlgarhî, considerable portions of which are now in the British Museum. They vary in height from about $4\frac{1}{2}$ to $5\frac{1}{2}$ inches, and the reliefs on them seem mostly to represent Jâtaka scenes, among which General Cunningham identified certain episodes[2] of the *Sâma* and *Visvantara* or *Wessantara Jâtakas*. But others are of a more convivial character. The illustration 103 seems to picture "a vintage scene, in which," as Mr. Kipling remarks,[3] "boys, leopards, a scene of dalliance, Bacchus on a leopard, and the wine-press of Europe (unknown in India, but common in Persia), are framed in a distinctly Byzantine arrangement of the grape-vine." Both of these examples are evidently strongly influenced by Western ideas.—J. B.

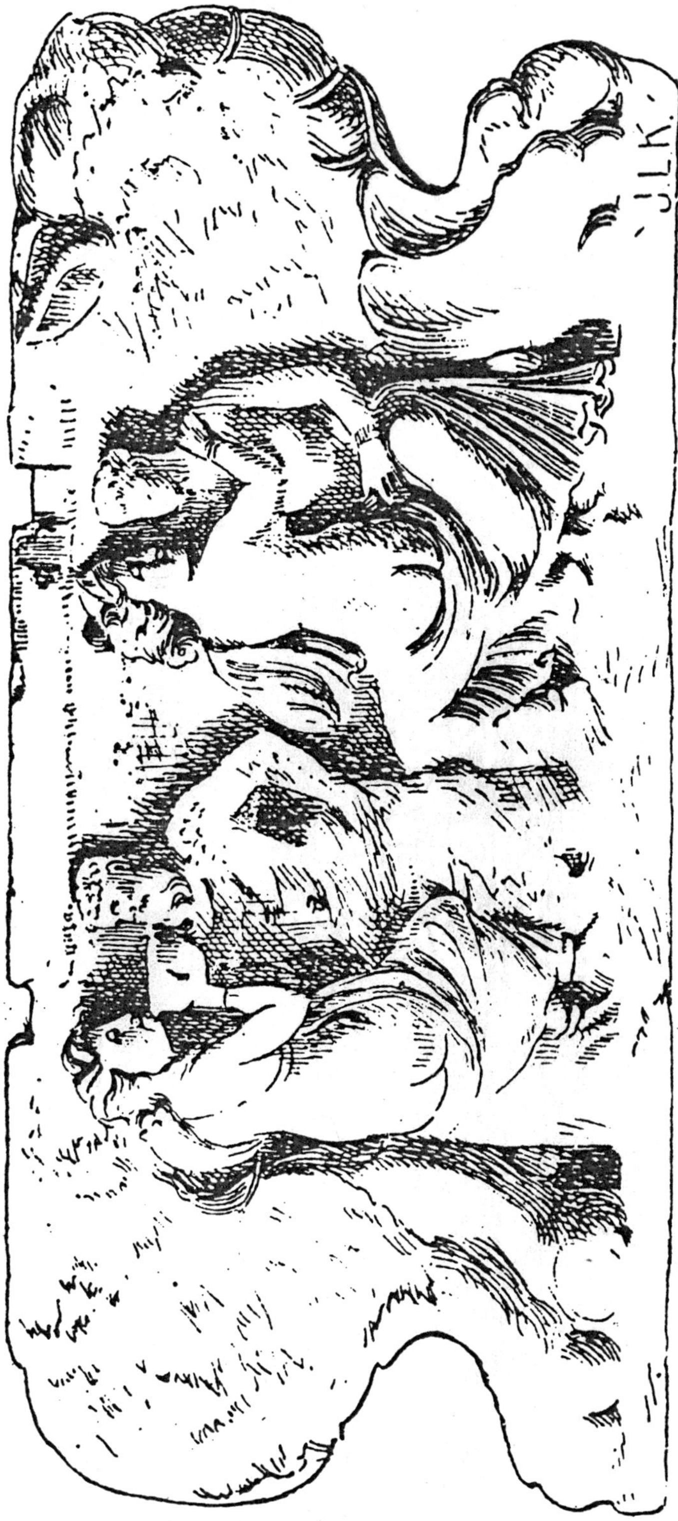

102. Pedestal of a Gândhârâ sculpture: an orgy. Original in Lahor Museum.

[1] J. L. Kipling in *Jour. R. I. Br. Arch.*, vol. I (1894), p. 138, from which illustrations 102 and 103 are borrowed.

[2] Cunningham, *Rep. Arch. Sur. Ind.* vol. V, pp. 199f.; *Ind. Monts.* pl. 151; conf. Sp. Hardy, *Eastn. Monachism*, p. 275; and *Man. Budh.* pp. 118ff.; Beal, *Fah-hian*, p. 194; *Jâtakas*, No. 540; *J. R. As. Soc.* vol. V (1870), p. 107; Burnouf, *Lotus*, p. 411; Upham, *Hist. Buddh.* vol. III, pll. iv and v; Fergusson, *Tree and Serp. Wor.* p. 126.

[3] *Jour. R. I. Br. Arch.* ut sup.

The wheel symbol, mentioned above pp. 68, 145. with or without the trident upon it, representing the doctrine of Buddha, belongs also to the decorative elements which the Gândhâra sculptures have in common with other Indian ones. This wheel—which with two couchant gazelles beside it, has become, we may say, a hieroglyph for the first sermon in the deer-park at Bârâ*n*asî,—appears in compositions full of figures, in front of the preaching Buddha, as a presentation of the phrase: *dhammachakkam pavattesi*,—"he turned the wheel of the sacred doctrine." This representation is still continued in the northern school; in modern pictures it almost looks like a sort of monstrance or pyx. Indeed, the custom prevailing in the northern school of setting in motion a cylinder filled with printed or written prayers, instead of repeating them orally,—the so-called *Ch'os-kor: dharmachakra*, "wheel of the law," can hardly be other than a materialized putting into practice of the old symbolical representation which was quite as current in the sculptures of Peshâwar, as in those of the Asoka period (conf. ill. 96).

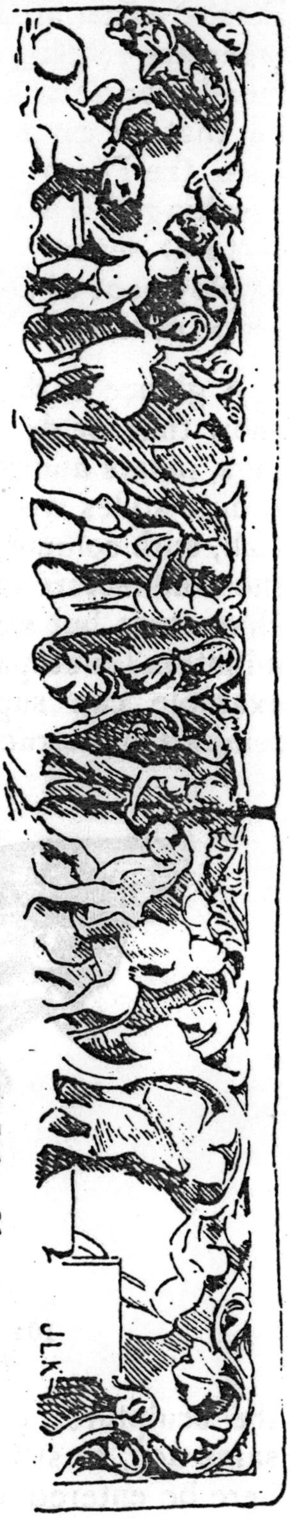

103. VINTAGE SCENE FROM A GÂNDHÂRA SCULPTURE. Original in Lahor Museum.

The architectural elements which are employed in the decoration of the reliefs likewise still show in part the older Perso-Indian forms (conf. ill. 81, 82); above them rise the terraces with round dormer-windows disposed according to the old Indian pattern, as on the reliefs of Barâhat, Sâñchî, &c., but with more members. Little attention has been paid to the strength of these, often very slender, pillars: the crowded bell-capitals of the older art have become thin and light; new forms have even been given to the animal figures represented on the capital. In ill. 82 the zebu has become a kind of goat. The pillar itself, on which a double terrace rests, is placed on the backs of crouching figures with wings. It is exactly the same absurd combination as is found in Byzantine art, which placed pillars on bodies of animals or of winged creatures; and a like practice was long continued also in Dravidian architecture.

Along with these Perso-Indian elements which still sppear, partly modified, in Gandhâra, we have western forms of pillars and columns. Frequently pillars of the later Corinthian type are represented on one and the same relief along with Perso-Indian zebu-pillars. This is seen in ill. 82; beside the Buddha-figure in the centre, stand the Perso-Indian, outside the Hellenic. Variations of this Corinthian order are employed, almost as on the façades of modern buildings, merely for decorative purposes. V. Smith is right when he points out that the circumstance that these forms,—so completely different from the Perso-Indian pillars, represented beside them,—forbid us speaking of a Romo-Corinthian order in a strictly technical architectural sense. The question of the nature of the architectural employment of the Indo-Corinthian pillars, however, is beyond the scope of this work.

A glance at the Gândhâra panels represented in this book will show that for decorative purposes and the representation of buildings, pillars and other architectural forms of the Perso-Indian and Indian styles were employed side by side, sometimes on the same slab, with columns having Hellenic capitals and bases. Structurally the architecture of the same age may have shared in this hybrid character; but we have not much evidence to guide us to a determination; a stûpa such as the best preserved at Ali Masjid,[1] for example, can supply but little aid in recovering the features of temples and structures for occupation. What we see pictured in

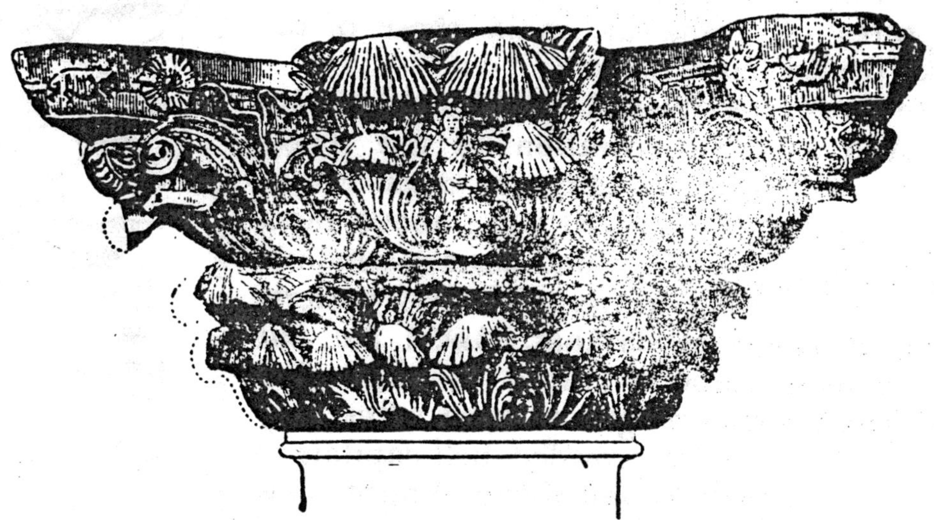

104. CORINTHIAN CAPITAL FROM JAMÂLGARHI.
Fergusson, *Ind. and Eastn. Archit.* p. 173.

the sculptures, combined with the cave architecture of about the same age, must be our chief guide. But while the question cannot here be entered upon in detail, the singularly rich capitals found at Jamâlgarhî and elsewhere in the Peshâwar valley can hardly be overlooked when speaking of the art of Gandhâra. Numerous examples exist in the Lahor, Calcutta, and British Museums.[2] The capital given in ill. 104, from Jamâlgarhî, measures 35 inches across

[1] Conf. Simpson, *Trans. R. I. Br. Arch.* 1880, p. 55 and pl.; *ibid*, 1894, pp. 94f., &c.; Fergusson, *Ind. and East. Arch.* pp. 173f.

[2] *Ind. Monts.* pll. 76-78, and 109-111; Cunningham, *Ar. Sur. Ind. Rep.* vol. V, pll. xlvii-l.

on the top, the lower section being 6 inches thick, and the upper 8 inches. It will be noted that the leafage is not of the classical acanthus, but more like one of the palms similarly treated: it is an imitation with divergencies,—not a strict copy. Then on one face, both of this and of the capital given on ill. 105, as well as on others, there appears among the foliage a small figure of Buddha, standing or seated. These figures have been regarded as a possible indication of age. The first prominent example of this practice, in classical art, as Mr. Fergusson pointed out,[1] seems to be found in the Baths of Caracalla at Rome (cir. 215 A.D.); but before such a feature was applied in an imperial work, it had doubtless been previously used elsewhere. And, in fact, we find a Nikê introduced

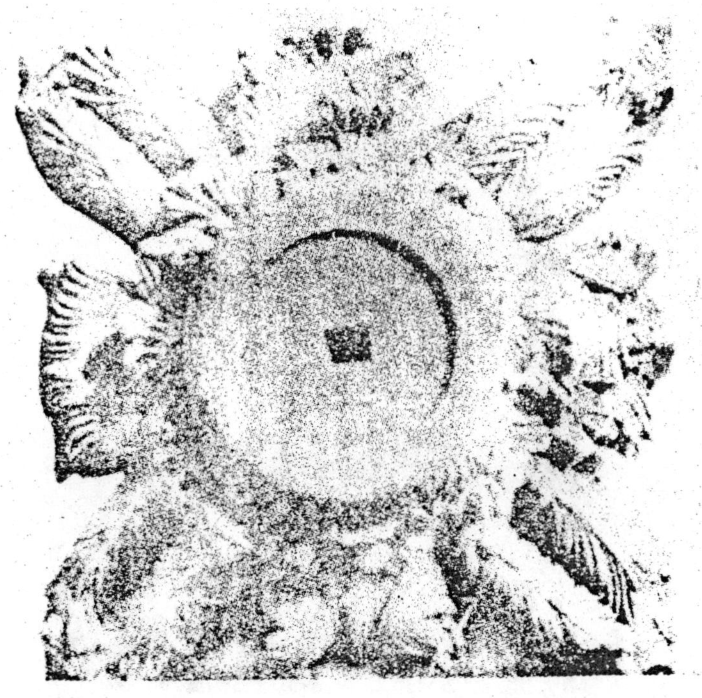

105. Indo-Corinthian capital from Loriyân Tangai.
Original in Ind. Mus., Calcutta.

among the acanthus leaves on the Corinthian capitals of the antæ of the temple of Augustus, built by Greek artists at Ancyra about A.D. 10; and another example is found on the capitals at Priene. These are of earlier date than the sculptures in Gandhâra, and its use would come to the east with the other models of the Hellenic artists who executed these reliefs.[2]

[1] *Ind. and East. Arch.* pp. 174–8.

[2] Texier and Pullan, *Prin. Ruins of Asia Minor*, pll. xxii and xxv, reproduced in Bose, *Dict. gén. de l'Archæol.* fig. 36; Dilettanti Soc., *Antiq. of Ionia*, pt. I, ch. ii, pl. 14; pt. III, ch. ii, pll. 5, 7; J. Durm, *Die Baustile*, Bd. I, S. 191.

The second capital (ill. 105) came from Loriyân Tangai, and is in the Calcutta Museum. The Jamâlgarhî examples are usually in several pieces; this is in one block, but we have no scale from which to judge of its size. The figure of Buddha occurring on one side only of these capitals is indicative that they were used in a façade or the front of a projecting porch where the other sides were less exposed to view. All these capitals were apparently originally gilt, and some of them—as well as some of the best preserved sculptures—still show traces of gilding or of colour, so that, when entire, the effect of the whole must have been gorgeous in the extreme.[1]

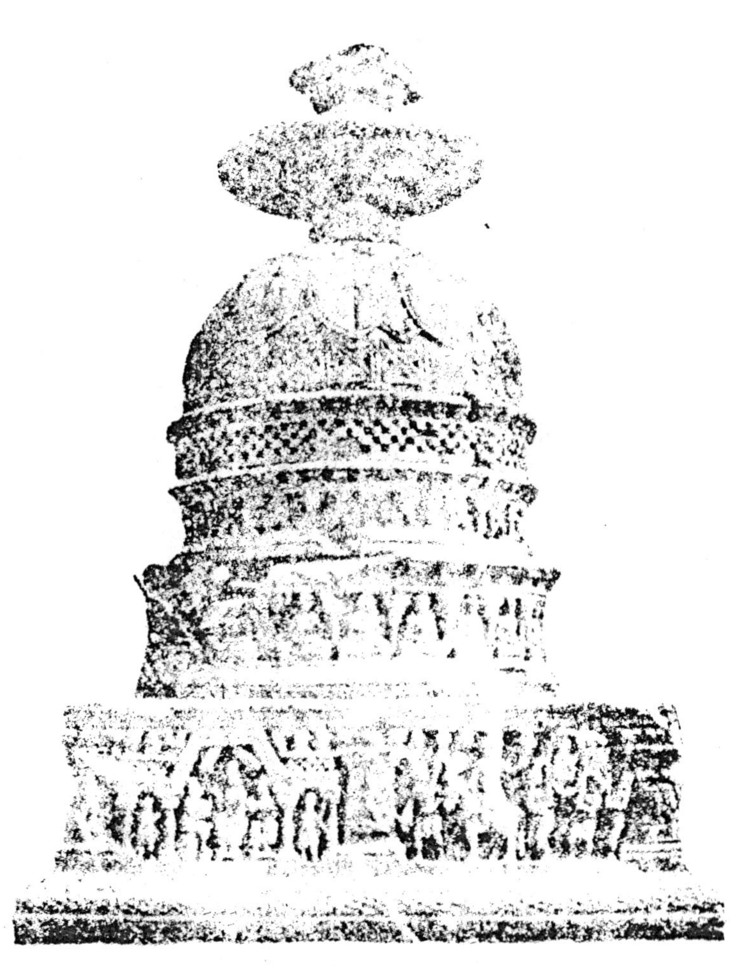

106. MINIATURE STÛPA FROM LORIYÂN TANGAI.
Imperfect restoration. (Calcutta).

Small model stûpas were found in large abundance at Buddha-Gayâ; and in the Swât valley several of a structural sort have been found, more or less disintegrated, but which might probably, with

[1] Cunningham, *Arch. Rep.* vol. V, pp. 49 and 196; Fergusson, *Ind. and East. Arch.* p. 174.

proper care, have been carefully pieced together on the spot, by some one who saw the position in which the different portions were found and knew how to combine them. As it is, in the Calcutta Museum, two restorations have been attempted with pieces, perhaps originally belonging to different examples, though all from beside the Loriyân Tangai stûpa.

One of these (fig. 106) is perhaps fairly correct, except that the piece on the top does not belong to it. The height to the top of the dome is 2 feet 6 inches, and the square base is in one piece, very carefully carved. On the side shewn are two compartments: that on the spectator's right is the return in state of the infant Gautama with his mother Mâyâdevî from the Lumbinî garden.[1] That to the left may be a representation of the interview of the *Ri*shi Asita Devala with *S*uddhodana respecting the future of the child. Another side of this base represents (1) Mâyâ on her couch and the descent of the white elephant, with four Devas looking down from two balconies; and (2) the Brâhma*n*a interpreting the dream to *S*uddhodana, which may be compared with another similar sculpture (ill. 7). The third side represents (1) on the right end the great renunciation in a sculpture differing but little from the one given before (fig. 53); and (2) the giving back of Ka*nth*aka to Chhanda, in which the horse is represented as on its knees in adoration of Gautama: *S*akra, as usual, stands with his *vajra* just behind him, and other five or six Devas appear on the scene. Of the fourth side only fragments have been preserved: it represented the birth and the miraculous bathing of the child.

The tier forming the lowest one of the drum of the stûpa contains a series of seated Buddhas. Above this, the second and third tiers have perhaps been transposed in position: the one has a chequer pattern surmounted by a modillion cornice, and the other an alternation of trees and small Atlantes supporting a second cornice of the same pattern. Over all is the dome carved with large leaves as a covering, and crowned by a square box-shaped capital (*gal*â), which was doubtless originally surmounted by an umbrella (*chhatra*).

The other stûpa (ill. 107) is much less satisfactorily put together from various pieces which could hardly have all belonged to the same structure. It is scarcely probable that, till very recent times, so small a *garbha* or dome would have been placed over so large a double pedestal; more likely the lower base belonged to another and larger chaitya, and the first tier above the dome is out of all proportion to the latter, while the one below it is as evidently out of place. The sculptured facets or shields attached to the dome, of which one is left, form a peculiarity not met with elsewhere, and seem to indicate the origin of the practice in Nepâl, of placing one of the Buddhas on each of the four faces of their great chaityas.[2]

[1] Compare this with the scene represented in Arnold's *Light of Asia*, ill. ed. p. 159. I owe the information respecting the other faces to Dr. Th. Bloch of the Calcutta Museum.

[2] *Notes on Ajanta Rock-Temples*, &c., p. 99; Wright's *Hist. of Nepâl*, pl. xi, p. 174.

The lions or Si*m*has at the corners and centre of each face, too, have not been remarked except in the Swât stûpas. The excavated Loriyân Tangai stûpa itself was a hemispherical dome with scarcely any basement, but with figures projecting at regular intervals round the lower courses of the dome.—J.B.

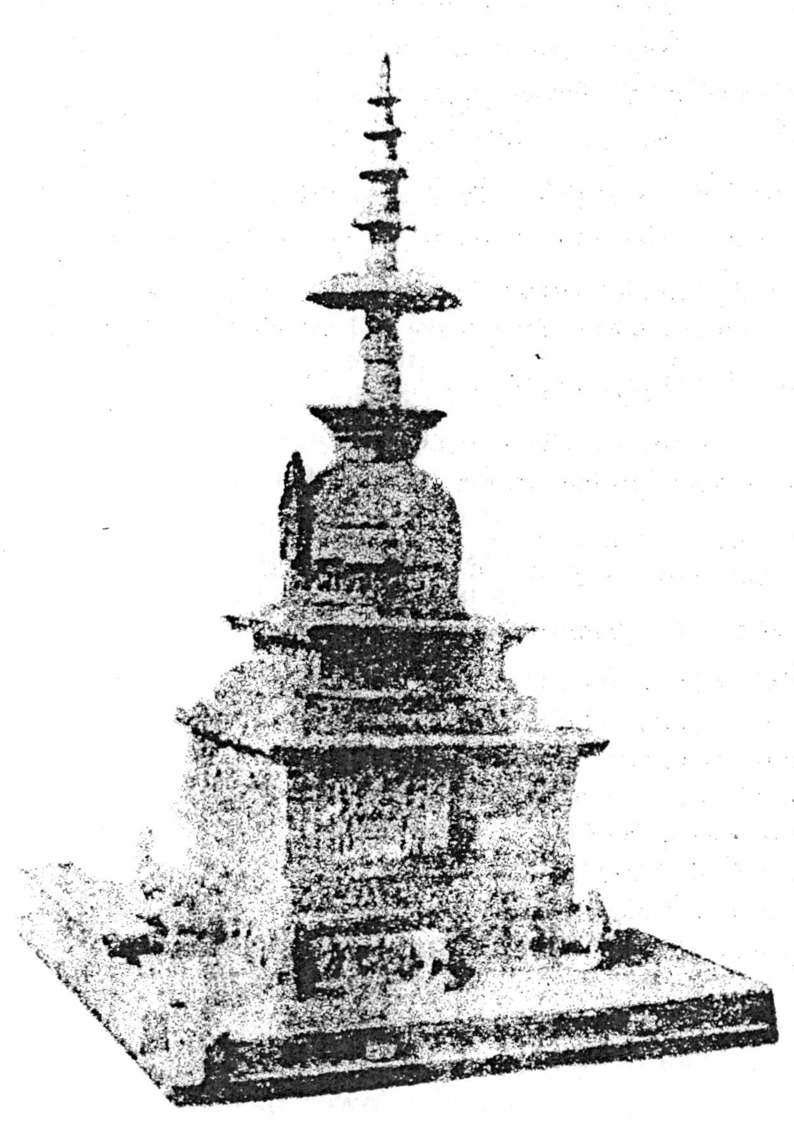

107. Model Stûpa from Loriyân Tangai.
Tentative restoration from various pieces. (Calcutta).

The influence of the Gândhâra school is very perceptible in later Indian art. The types which were described in Chapter I are, however, less altered than the composition. This appears most clearly in the case of the reliefs of the "rail" at Amarâvatî. A formal translation of compositions that have become typical certainly does not occur—though perhaps the birth-scene is an exception—as has happened in the case of the modern art of the northern schools of Tibet. China, and Japan; but the construction of the relief itself differs from those of Barâhat and Sâñchî. This is occasioned primarily by the introduction into the composition of the figure of the founder of Buddhism. This figure—distinguished, however, by the Bhâma*nd*ala—naturally appeared in the centre of the compositions, the other figures being arranged according to their importance, starting from the centre. The old plan of crowding together several scenes on the same slab holds good, so far as I can see. The external form of the reliefs of the Amarâvatî rail (conf. ill. 8) is also noteworthy. After the Roman fashion. they are inserted almost entirely in rosettes (flat *nelumbia*, blue lotus), which adorn the pillars of the enclosure—for example, the middle parts of the rail-bars. The single figures are refined, mostly over-refined developments of the older Indian art: the affected and strained attitudes of the feebly treated bodies are particularly striking; the treatment of the garments, so far as the arrangement of the draperies is concerned, shows the influences of the Gândhâra sculptures, although perhaps only by an indirect transition. The austere type of the faces in Barâhat—also noticeable here and there in Sâñchî—has likewise disappeared: in the full, effeminate, and very pleasing faces of the sculptures of Amarâvatî the Greek influence is also very apparent. Notwithstanding, the Indian element decidedly preponderates: the foreign elements are overpowered by the Indian style, and serve only here and there as means to an end. What was said above about the character of the Indian lyric—especially as regards its strongly marked erotic features—may be repeated to a large extent about Amarâvatî. The compositions are loaded with a crowd of voluptuous and grotesque figures: here and there appears a figure of great beauty, which, however, is smothered by the others. In spite of this, it may be said that the best reliefs of Amarâvatî are also the best Indian sculptures.

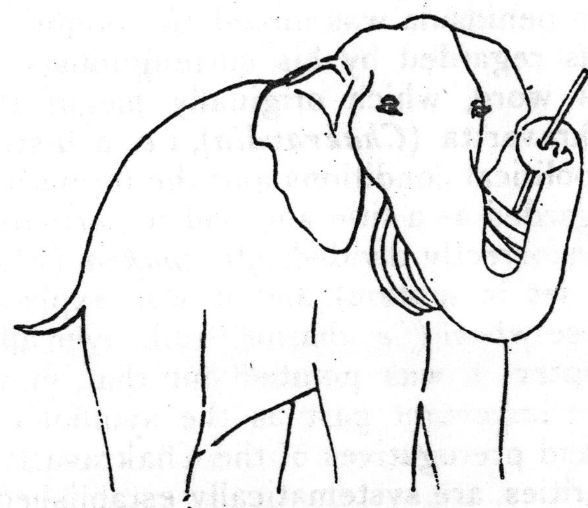

108. CHADDANTA ELEPHANT.
From the Ajantâ wall-paintings.
Beal, *Si-yu-ki*, vol. II, p. 49.

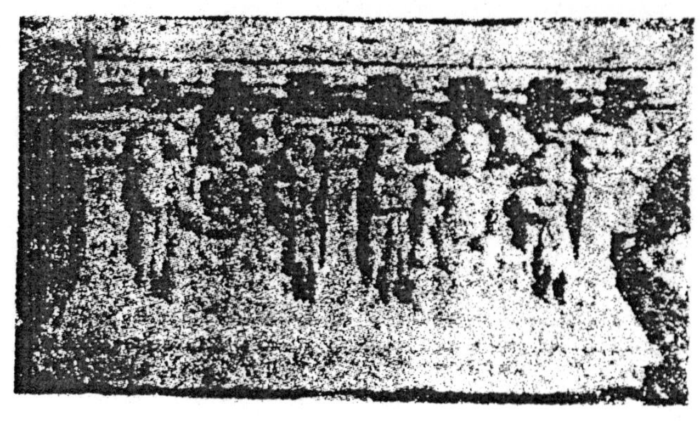

109. GÂNDHÂRA PEDESTAL WITH BUDDHA AND BODHISATTVA.

CHAPTER IV.

REPRESENTATION OF BUDDHA AND BODHISATTVA.

The appearance of Alexander the Great in India, at the head of a powerful army gathered together from different nationalities, presented for the first time to the Indian Aryans the spectacle of a universal monarch. The idea of a universal empire, first conceived by the Achæmenides, led up to by Cyrus and organised by Darius, had become the inheritance of the Macedonian: no wonder that it found an echo in India, which, since the days of the Achæmenides, had always been intimately connected with Irân. As has been mentioned above, even in Buddha's time, the kingdom of Magadha had become the dominant power in India. This power further increased under the Maurya (Pâli, Mora) dynasty, which Chandragupta had founded. The third king of the Maurya line, Asoka, afterward the patron of Buddhism, to whose influence the whole Indian peninsula was forced to submit, must have been the first who was regarded by his co-religionists as a Chakravarttî.[1] This word, which originally meant the possessor or ruler of a Chakravartta (*Chakravâla*), *i.e.* a district, was at that time, owing to political conditions and the formation of a religious terminology, regarded as a title and had a particular signification. The word was incorrectly divided into *chakra* (wheel) and *vartagati* (to turn, to set in motion), and it was explained as meaning "The king, whose wheel (*i.e.* chariot)[2] rolls over all the world." In a previous chapter it was pointed out that, in Vedic times, the wheel played an important part as the symbol of occult power. The attributes and prerogatives of the Chakravarttî, as well as his physical peculiarities, are systematically established—canonised, so

[1] Conf. Rhys Davids, *Buddhism*, pp. 219-20.

[2] The original meaning, however, was simply 'Ruler of a district.'

to speak In the first place, he possesses the seven jewels (Skt. *sapta ratnâni*; Pâli, *satta ratanâni*), *i.e.* the best specimens of each kind that appear during the reign: the jewel of the wheel, of the elephant, of the war-horse, of woman, of the pearl, of the general, of the minister. The order of succession is, as Fergusson says, strange but characteristic. We cannot enter upon a detailed examination of this remarkable emblem here, but it is interesting to notice that the wheel of the Chakravarttî has become, we know not when, a mystic weapon, swung and thrown by the hand: the Hindû religion bestows it on Vish*n*u as his attribute, &c. Moreover, the iron "quoits" of the faqîrs of the Sikh religion are well known.

The physical qualities of the Chakravarttî are those of the so-called "great Being" (Skt. *Mahâpurusha*; Pâli, *Mahâpurisa*). They consist of the thirty two greater and eighty lesser physical characteristics or marks. But these beauty-marks the Chakravarttî has in common with Buddha. Indeed, in contradistinction to the emperor, who ruled over the whole world, whose attribute of majesty is theoretically developed by the church, there appears the figure of a ruler of a supernatural world. This is Buddha, who, according to the legends, was born of royal race, and would have become a Chakravarttî if he had not preferred to reveal to man the true doctrines. In the old Bauddha legends (*Avidûrenidâna*) the contrast is most clearly expressed in the finely-sketched scene where Gautama leaves his home, and an angel opens to him the locked and guarded gate. Then Mâra Vasavartî, the god of passion, approaches and advises him not to leave his home and not to become a monk. "In seven days will the world with all its lands and their two thousand islands be thine." The wheel of the Chakravarttî is the symbol of Indian power: the wheel of Buddha is that of religion (Skt. *Dharmachakra*; Pâli, *Dhammachakka*

These apotheoses of king and of Buddha attained actual completion in opposite ways; Buddha and his doctrine became, as we may say, recognised by the state,—an expression which is hardly appropriate, inasmuch as the intolerently exclusive tendency of west Asiatic religions is not thereby indicated—and the grateful church gave the monarch a corresponding position in her system. That the whole theory was a gradual development is undoubted; the fact that representations of the so-called seven jewels appear first at Amarâvatî is a proof of this.[1] But, in any case, it was Aśoka who gave rise to this view.

The specialising of the physical characteristics of the "great man" rested on the ancient art of explaining signs, and—as will appear from what follows—formed the basis of the artistic efforts.

[1] For example see the reliefs in Fergusson, *Tr. and Serp. Wor.* pl. xli, 3, xlv, 3; on the plinth of a Siṁhanâda Lokesvara, *J. R. As. Soc.* (1894), p. 54, and pl. i, etc.; Pozdneev, *Zap. geogr. Obshch.* XVI, pp. 87f.; conf. also K. Kasawara, *Dharmasangraha* in *Anecd. Ox. Ar. ser.* vol. I, pt. v, p. 60.

It has been mentioned that, even in the time of the Chinese pilgrims, there were attempts to establish authentic representations of Buddha. It may be said that the desire to have a picture of the conqueror made claims upon the Hindû artists, which were utterly at variance with their methods of conception. The rich ornament, which so often prevents us seeing that the body represented is wretchedly formed, disappeared in consequence of the legend. Instead of the figure of a king in rich turban, with garlands of flowers, rich ear, breast, and loin ornaments, the narrow upper garment distinct in all its parts, and the comfortably-fitting covering of the lower limbs,—the artist had to represent the figure of a monk unadorned, with shaven skull, in a cowl-like garment,—but so to idealise it that it should be worthy to rank as a sacred representation. The attitudes which had to be given to the figure likewise sprang from the legends: he had to be represented meditating, teaching, consoling, and entering Nirvâ*n*a, *i.e.* dying. At any rate, these were, and remained, the fundamental types, though the canon devised a particular pose for almost every scene in Buddha's life. Thus there originated a figure sitting—Indian fashion—with crossed legs, and hands laid flat on one another in the lap,—meditating; the right hand falling to the ground,—calling upon the earth as witness; the right hand raised and held palm forward, while the left hangs flat by the side, or holds the folds of the garment.

It is natural that an art, like the old Indian, which had not become independent—as it was not in a position to give the necessary dignity to such unornamented figures—should bestow a supernatural character upon them by means of all sorts of accessories of an extraordinary nature. To a perfected art, which had at its disposal all the types of systematically developed schools,—perhaps the Greek of the Roman period, or, in the domain of painting, the Spanish of the seventeenth century,—this subject, the creation of an ideal portrait of an ascetic or philosopher, might have afforded material for masterpieces. But the actual capacity was childishly weak, and the ritualistic interest was the chief thing considered. An idealising response to this conception now showed itself: the great Teacher, who had entered Nirvâ*n*a, became more and more god-like to his followers: the flowery epithets of the legends were interpreted literally; he thus became possessed of supernatural gifts. A further impulse to idealisation was given by the fact that the executive art restricted itself to youthful types. Even on the most ancient Buddhist monuments a series of popular signs have been canonised by Buddhism: we find the foot-marks with the sign of the wheel, or the well-known Svastika as symbol of Buddha (conf. above, p. 72). Now the physical perfections of the great being[1] form a series of exactly similar distinctive marks. They vary somewhat in their order: indeed, some of the "smaller beauty marks" are specified among the larger, and so on.

[1] Conf. K. Kasawara. *l. cit.* pp. 53ff.

The customary order of the *mahâpurusha Lakshanas* or superior marks (*Lalitavistara, Mahâpadhânasutta, Dharmapradîpikâ*) is: 1, the head shows a protuberance (*ushnîsha*) on the skull; 2, the hair is glossy black (blue) like the tail of a peacock, or like pulverised eye-salve, it is arranged in short curls and each curl goes off from left to right; 3, the brow is broad and smooth; 4, between the eyebrows is a little ball (*ûrnâ*, Pâli: *unna*—tuft of hair) shining like silver or snow; 5, the eyelashes are like those of a bull; 6, the eyes are brilliant black; 7, he has forty teeth of perfectly equal size; 8, they lie close to one another: 9, and are dazzling white; 10, his voice resembles Brahmâ's; 11, he has an exquisite sense of taste (?); 12, the tongue is large and long; 13, the jaws are those of a lion; 14, the shoulders and arms are perfectly round; 15, the seven parts of the body are quite rounded and full (the palms of the hands, soles of the feet, etc.); 16, the space between the shoulders is filled out; 17, the skin has a tinge of gold colour; 18, the arms are so long that when he stands upright, the hands reach down to the knees; 19, the upper part of the body is that of a lion; 20, his figure is like that of the banian tree (*ficus religiosa*); 21, only one little hair grows from each pore; 22, these little hairs curl from above towards the right; 23, nature has concealed the marks of sex; 24, the thighs are well rounded; 25, the legs are like those of the gazelle; 26, the fingers and nails are long; 27, the heel is elongated; 28, the instep is high; 29, his feet and hands are delicate and slender; 30, his fingers and toes have a web between; 31, under the soles of the feet appear two shining wheels with a thousand spokes; 32, the feet are flat and stand firm.[1]

The eighty smaller marks (*anuvyanjana-lakshana*) are: 1-3, his nails are round, copper-coloured, smooth; 4-6, the fingers round, beautiful (?), long; 7-8, neither veins nor bones are seen; 9, the sinews are firm; 10, the feet are alike; 11, the heel is large; 12, the lines of the hand are soft (?); 13-16, regular, deep, not twisted and elongated; 17, his lips are red like the fruit of the Bimba; 18, his voice is not rough; 19, he has a thin, long and copper-coloured tongue; 20, his agreeable and melodious voice resembles the sound made by an elephant or thunder; 21, he is of full strength; 22, he has long arms; 23, his limbs shine; 24-29, they are delicate and large, powerful, regular, well-knit and well-proportioned; 30, the knee-pan is broad, big and full; 31-33, his limbs are rounded, graceful and symmetrical; 34-35, the navel lies deep and is regular; 36-37, his behaviour is noble, causing joy everywhere; 38, he sheds abroad an unearthly light that dispels all darkness; 39, he walks slowly, like an elephant; 40-42, he strides like a lion, like an ox, like a *hansa*; 43, in walking he turns to the right; 44-46, his sides are muscular, shining, straight; 47, his belly is like a bow; 41, his

[1] The Sanskrit names of the Lakshanas are given in B. H. Hodgson's *Illustrations of the Lit. and Rel. of Budh.* (1837), p. 129, or *Essays* (Lond. 1874), p. 90. Conf. Burnouf, *Lotus*, pp. 616-17; Alabaster, *Wheel of the Law*, pp. 113ff. and 312f. Sp. Hardy, *Man. Budh.* pp. 382f.; *Lalita Vistara*, pp. 93f.—J.B.

body is free of all dark spots that could disfigure it; 49-51, the eye-teeth are round, pointed and regular; 52, the nose is prominent; 53-63, the eyes are brilliant, they are clear, with a friendly expression, long and large, they are like a flower—the leaf of the blue lotus (*nymphæa*), have beautiful even brows, which meet, are clearly marked and black; 64-67, the cheeks are full and smooth, without disfigurement, without trace of hate and anger; 68-69, his passions are perfectly bridled and have attained perfection; 70, his face and forehead express perfect harmony; 71, his head is perfectly beautiful; 72-79, the hair of the head is black, of the same length, well arranged, perfumed, not disordered, not dishevelled, neat, in coils; 80, the hair forms the figures *S*rîvatsa, Svastika, Nandyâvarta and Vardhamâna.

Although many of these smaller beauty-marks are very difficult to describe and still more difficult to explain, it seemed necessary to specify them all, as they furnish a remarkable proof of the systematizing method of the Buddhists.[1] In the main—so much is clear—the basis is formed on a youthful figure with the peculiarities of the Hindûs, just as they are described even in Brâhmanical works: it is the type of the Indian hero. The long arms are specially strange. With the Hindûs as with the Persians, this is an old mark of noble birth. In old Persian names and cognomens, with which the Indian may be compared, this peculiarity is manifested; I need only recall 'Longimanus,' which corresponds to an O. Persian Darghabâzu, O. Indian Dîrghabahu, and to the Persian name translated by the Greeks—Megabazos (O. Indian Mahâbâhu), etc. With these appear characteristics of a supernatural, and—according to our ideas—uncouth nature, which militate against an ideal conception. Thus the tuft (*ûrnâ*) between the brows must have had its origin in the superstition that men whose brows run into each other are specially gifted. The representations of Buddha give the *úrṇâ* in the form of a small round protuberance over the root of the nose, which in older and more modern figures is frequently replaced by a pearl, and so on. The protuberance on the skull (*ushnîsha*) is likewise an abnormal physical peculiarity, which was thought to be extraordinary and supernatural.

The chief difference between ancient art and the art of the Gândhâra period is that the figure of Buddha is evolved from foreign models. As has been pointed out, the hairsplitting philosophy of the Buddhist sects led to a highly developed detail of the characteristics of a Buddha. The p e r s o n o f G a u t a m a t a k e s t h e f o r m o f a b e l i e f, which is commented upon in all directions. The idea of Buddha is the chief matter. The introduction of the image of Buddha makes the ancient p h i l o s o p h y more of a r e l i g i o n.[2]

If we return to the sculptures, we see before us, among the

[1] The greater *lakshanas* are 32=4X(2X2X2); the lesser 80=(1+2+3+4)X(2X2X2); and the *mangalas* on each foot are 108=4X(3X3X3). Is this accidental?—J.B.

[2] See above p. 67, note 2.

Gândhâra remains, the complete ideal Buddha, produced under Hellenic influence. And here we may give attention to the introduction of a retrograde movement and see how the type has become changed and deteriorated in different lands.

The attitudes required by tradition,—the most important of the physical characteristics established by superstition,—though they

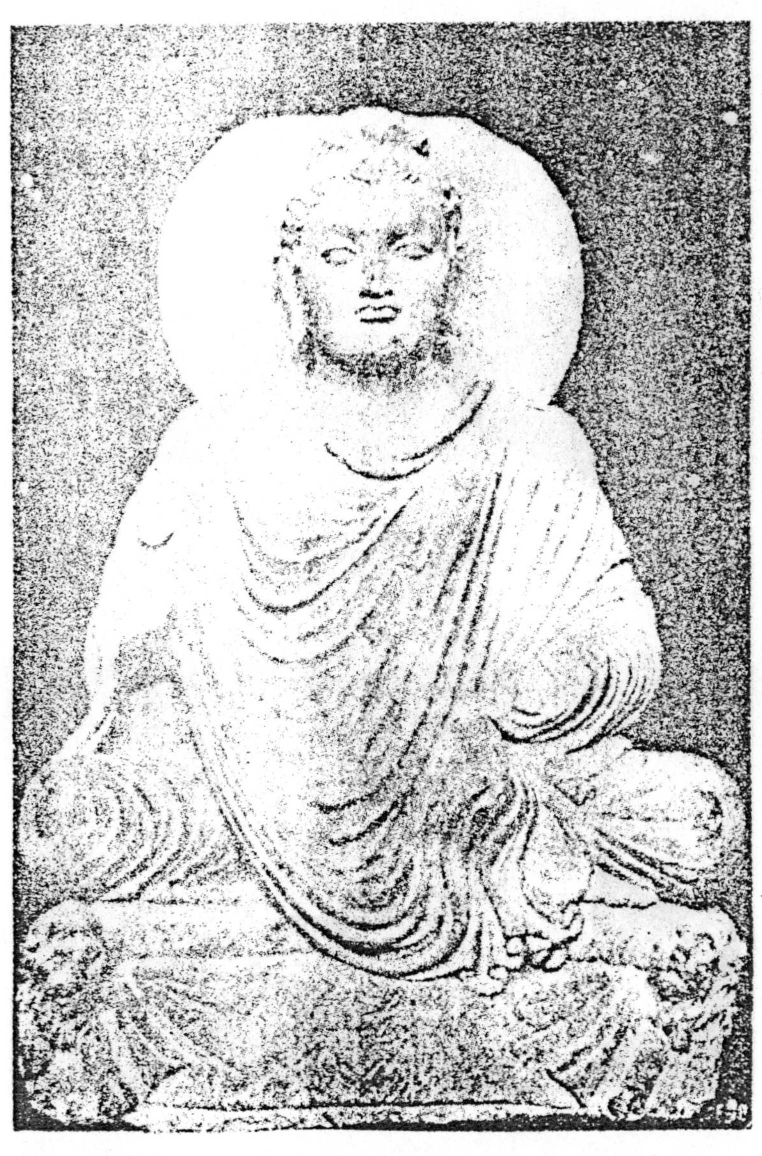

110. GAUTAMA BUDDHA FROM TAKHT-Î-BÂHÎ.
Height 20 in. Original in Berlin Museum.

remain latent, are faithfully retained in the sculptures of Gandhâra. In true Greek style, the disfigurement of the bump of intelligence (*ushnîsha*) upon the skull, is concealed by a cluster of locks of hair; in many cases the closely-cut hair, which the figure should have, is replaced, incorrectly, and in contradiction to the tradition, by an abundance of locks. The Apollo type of the Alexandrine period, which was used as a basis for the Buddha-head, gives an idealization, which is in entire opposition to the possibility of the portrait of Gautama. Nowhere do we see the head shaved bare: thus the idea

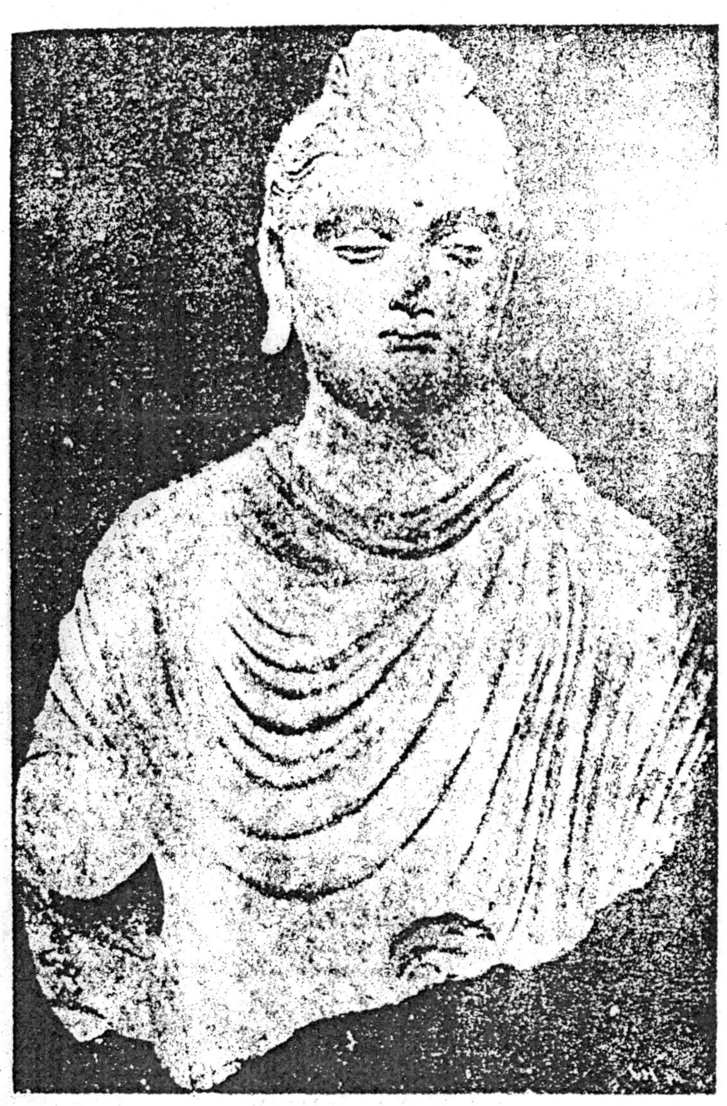

111. Buddha Torso from Takht-i-Bâhi.
Height 15¼ in. Original in Berlin Museum.

strikes us, that the short curls turning from left to right are only an attempt of a stage of art no longer able to represent the free falling waved hair. In translating the Apollo-ideal, two things may have influenced the Hellenists, or whoever effected this first translation. First of all, the character of the Greek god, not only as leader of the muses, but also as a nature god (Helios): in both phases he found his counterpart. In conformity with the old Indian nature-worship Buddha's epithets had become chiefly those of a light or sun-god; so much so, indeed, that in Europe it has been attempted to

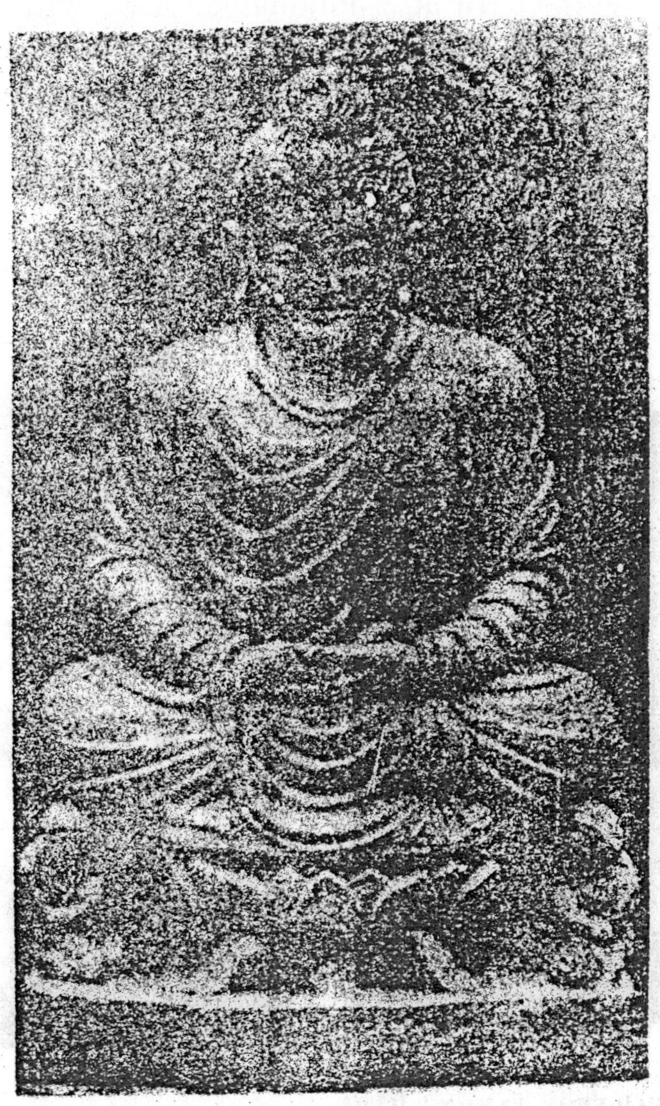

112. Gautama on the Padmâsana.
From Loriyân Tangai.

deny his historic existence, and to make of him an old sun-god! His appearance as teacher, physician of souls and healer, justified the other side. It must not be forgotten, either, that the district in which the translation took place, before the introduction of Buddhism, belonged to the fire-worship of Zarathushtra, which must have become the state religion, and which united the Indian provinces with the Baktrian kingdom. It is known, and has already been mentioned, that wherever the Greeks came upon the light and sun-gods of the barbarians, Apollo types were there evoked.

The sculptures of the Gândhâra convents have had a lengthy development, which cannot, indeed, as yet be exactly determined. But this is very apparent in the Buddha types, that along with an idealistic tendency which is certainly the older, as it preserves the Greek types, is found a realistic and clearly more modern one. But in both cases there are, if we may use the expression, Indian degeneracies. To the idealistic tendency belong Buddha-heads with youthful, Apollonic features, with gently smiling mouth, half-shut eyes with soft, full, fleshy parts, finely moulded nose, and sharply defined, luxuriant and elegantly arranged hair (conf. ill. 111). One, the finest, which the Berlin Museum possesses (ill. 110), even shows the coquettish locks before the ear, that were the fashion at Athens in the time of the Diadochs—successors of Alexander, and which, if I am not mistaken, are to be found on

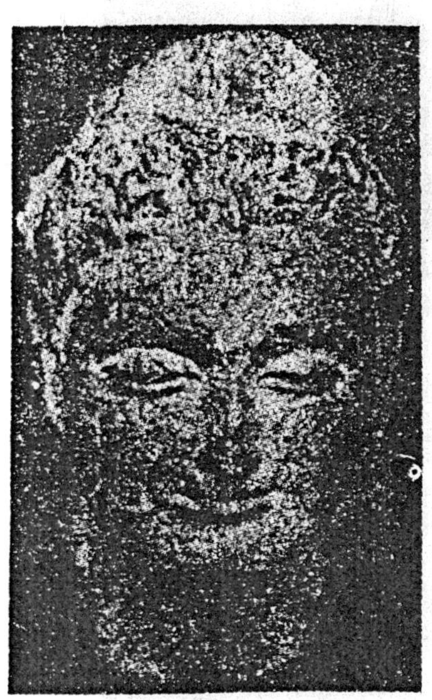

113. BUDDHA HEAD FROM TAKHT-I-BÂHI. Original in Berlin Museum.

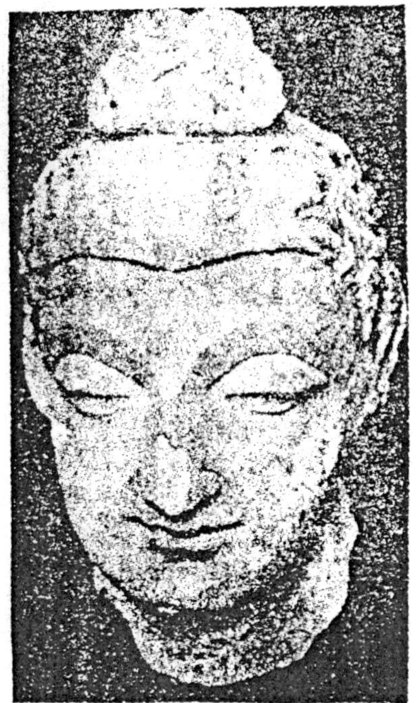

114. BUDDHA HEAD FROM TAKHT-I-BÂHI. Indian type. Original in Berlin Museum.

the Apollo Musagetes. With these examples we may also compare ill. 112,[1] a fine relief from Swât. It represents the Buddha, with a youthful face, the eyes half closed, a slight smile about the mouth, the *ûrnâ* unmarked, and the hair wavy and dressed in the style of the other Gândhâra reliefs with the robe over both shoulders. The

[1] *Jour. Ind. Art and Indust.* vol. VIII, p. 83.

sculpture represents the Jina upon the *padmâsana* or lotus-seat, supported, as usual, by two small worshipping figures.

Along with the idealistic type of purely Hellenic formation, are found heads of Indian race, executed in the way prescribed. On the one shown in ill. 114 the Indian element is distinct: the hair rough and treated in the orthodox way. A little later there follows the type of the Buddha-head shown in the relief represented in ill. 82. In the main it preserves the old idealistic forms, but they are preserved, as it were, artificially, and are deprived of all individuality and independence: a picture of still beauty absorbed in itself, which has an effeminate and unmanly effect.[1] The northern school has preserved this type well: it is shown in astonishing purity in the Buddha-heads of Bôrô Bu*d*ur (conf. ill. 115). The hair

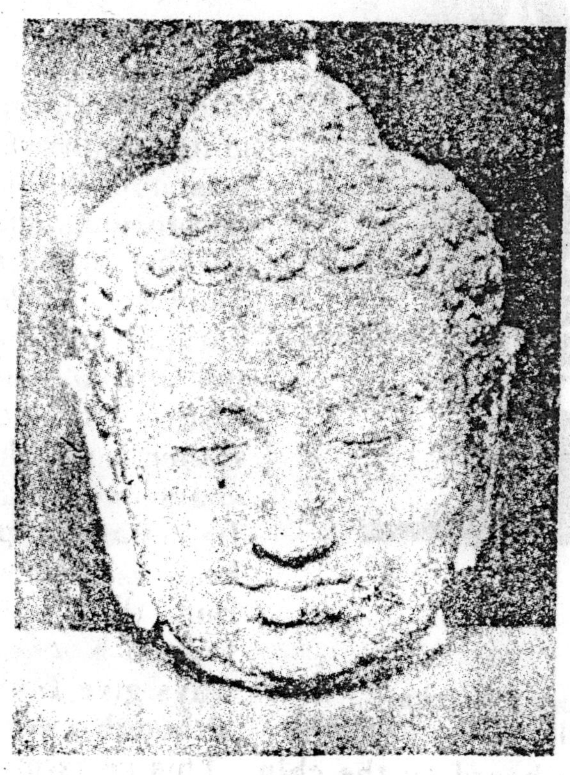

115. Head of a Buddha from Bôrô Budur.
Original in Berlin Museum.

is luxuriant as in ill. 82, and arranged in small locks as the canon requires. But the elongated ear-lobes are never missing, not even in the best heads. It appears that even this peculiarity, which shows so decidedly the laying aside of the royal ornaments, also arises from attempts made by Hindû artists in connection with the

[1] "The statue of Buddha should measure from the top of the *ushnisha* to the sole 125 fingers," so also the length of the outstretched arms "measures 125 fingers."—A.G.

Buddha type, before the Gâṇdhâra sculptors idealized it. For comparison another example (fig. 116) may also be here introduced. It was found among some ancient remains on the west bank of the Indus, just outside the Hazârâ district, and thus to the east of the other find-spots of such sculptures. Unfortunately it has been much injured by hewing off the arms and legs, and what remains is only about 2 feet in height. The hands are in an unusual position for a standing figure of the Buddha, but the face is particularly striking and of excellent workmanship.[1]

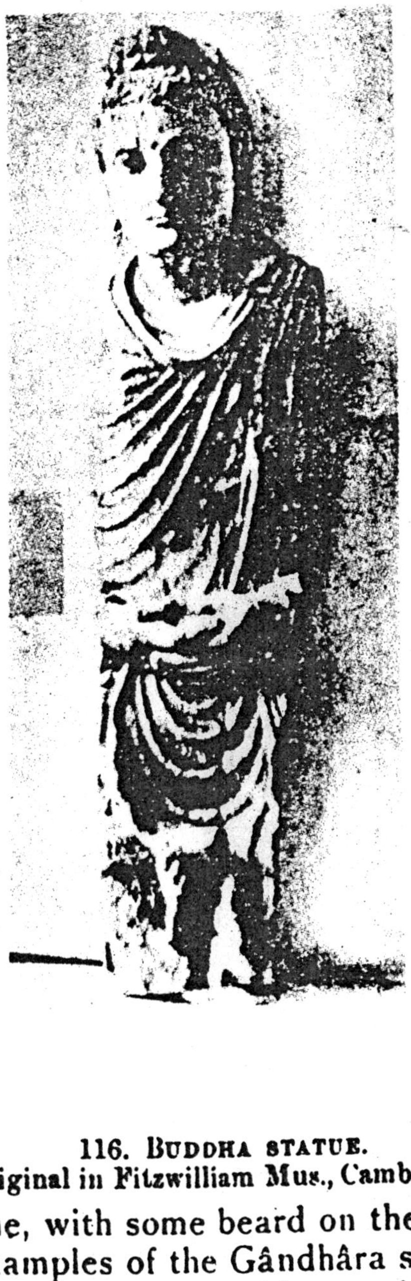

116. BUDDHA STATUE.
Original in Fitzwilliam Mus., Cambridge.

On the sculptures of the southern school, monumental as well as miniature, the treatment of the hair and of the ears degenerates into the unnatural inconsequence of its prolific reproduction, which was considered as a specially meritorious act.

The naturalistic tendency, likewise, working with purely antique materials, evidently did not appeal much to the Indian taste. It shows an austere, rather cold, Hindû face with coarse moustache (conf. ill. 117). In Indian sculpture no Buddha-head is seen with a moustache. But the old Chinese (and Japano-Korean) sculptures always give Buddha a moustache, although a very artificial-looking one, with some beard on the chin. This certainly corresponds with examples of the Gândhâra school, but how it comes about we do not know. A positive testimony is, however, at our command in Chinese sources. This is due to communications for which we have to thank Hirth,[2] relative to the artist Weï-chï-I-söng of Khotan, who flourished at the Imperial court of Chang-an-fu (7th century),

[1] *Jour. Ind. Art, &c.*, vol. VIII, p. 85.

[2] *Ueber fremde Einflüsse die chines. Kunst*, Ss. 46f. "But as to how that character, foreign to Chinese, but, according to Gonse, resembling Indian taste, came into ancient Korean art, I can give no better explanation than that afforded by an allusion to the origin of the artist who served as an example to the Buddhist painters, the Central Asian Weï-chï-I-söng. The Indian traits that we notice between the 7th and 12th

and upon whose influence the Indo-Baktrian elements of the eastern Asiatic art must be based. One of the principles which are to be kept in mind in the further examination of Buddhist iconography is—that the common forms of the different countries must be tabulated with reference to the prototypes in Gandhâra. The moustache appears in Gandhâra at times in the idealistic type. The Buddha figure from Swât district, represented in ill. 119, shows in the face powerful and full outlines, with fine features and smooth hair: the moustache is only indicated by some lightly-marked lines behind the corners of the mouth.

The treatment of drapery in the Buddha figures of the Gândhâra monasteries is almost entirely Grecian. The robe, in upright figures, is so laid round the body that it reaches to the ankles, covering both shoulders and the body. In the finer ancient pieces and good replicas (conf. ill. 117, 122) the robe is so disposed as to show the contour of the body, the folds following the lines of the limbs in a natural and unconstrained way. The robe is laid round the neck, and the folds marked by lines that are usually hollowed out (conf. ill. 122).

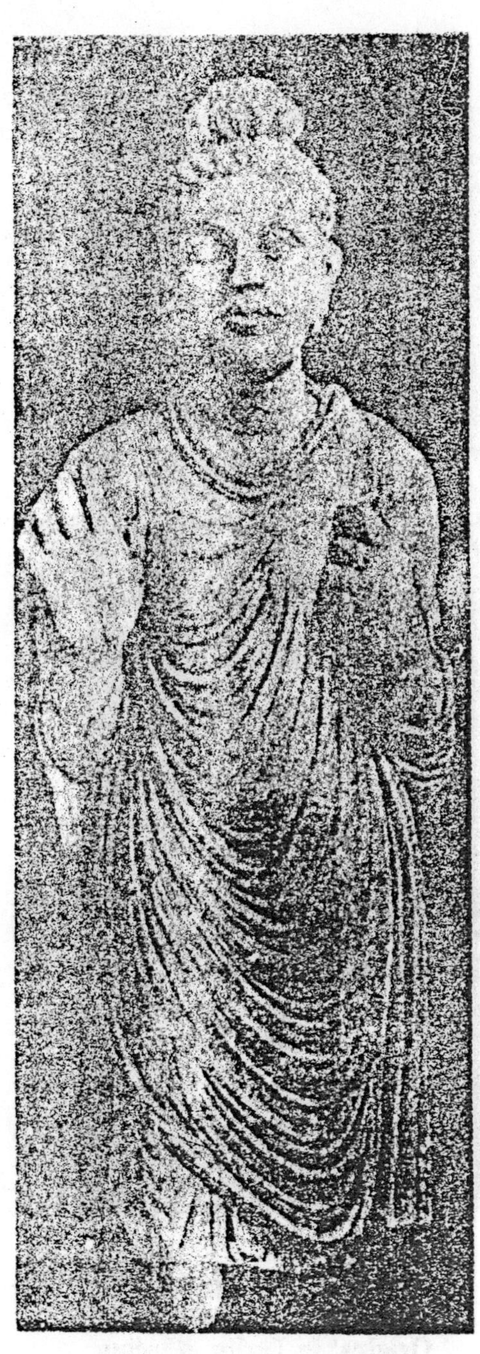

117. Gautama Buddha. Naturalistic type, with moustaches; from Swât. Height 44½ in. Original in Berlin Museum.

centuries must have been introduced by way of India and Khotan, the home of I-söng, with its art-loving princely court, and from thence by Chang-an-fu, the imperial city of the 7th century, and Korea and Japan."

The arrangement of the drapery appears to be flatter in the later reliefs,—those which represent Buddha with moustaches. In the northern school, and even in China and Japan, this way of arranging the drapery seems to have been preserved with wonderful tenacity. The ancient Chinese and Japanese Buddha-figures have preserved the 'draping' of the Gândhâra figures in a peculiar way. Ill. 120 shows a small modern miniature of a Buddha from Japan, painted on silk. The statue of the sitting Buddha from Takht-î-Bâhî, in ill. 110, may be compared with this. The miniature makes no attempt at shading, but the arrangement of the folds is rendered clearly enough by the black outlines drawn in. The old drapery is still better preserved in the standing figures. Modern paintings also show it distinctly, as in ill. 124, from Japan—from a large picture which represents the Paradise (Sukhâvatî) of Amitâbha.[1] It has been mentioned above, that in the earlier Gândhâra works the folds of the drapery are sharp and angular, sometimes even projecting at the edges. The Chinese wooden figure of a Buddha in ill. 125 shows a remarkable degeneracy from this thoroughly Greek idea. This wooden figure is, however, more interesting in respect that it is certainly a replica of a copy, which has been preserved in China and is traced back, according to the Chinese tradition, to Udayana's sandalwood figure of the Master.[2] The first Indian kings who are

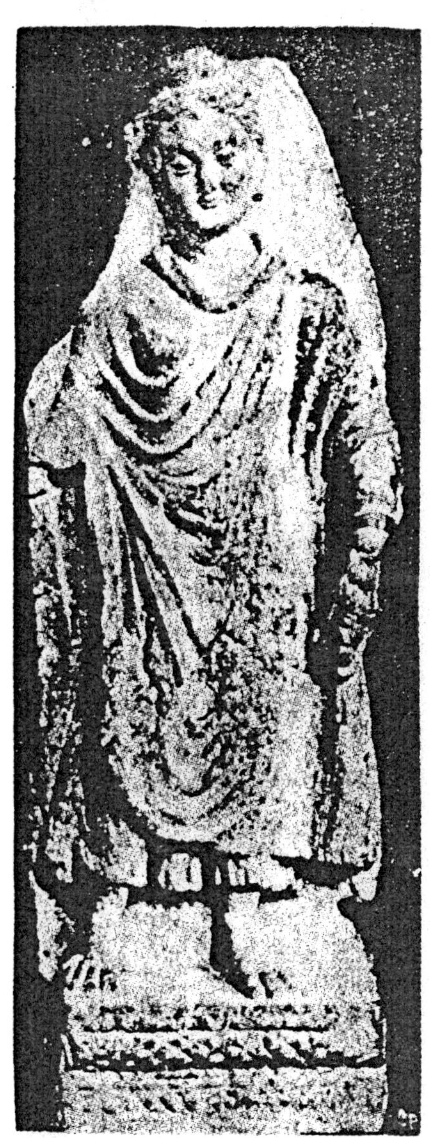

118. Gautama Buddha.
Takht-î-Bâhî. Height 31 in.
Original in Berlin Museum.

[1] Compare with this picture the beautiful legend in Schott's *Ueber den Buddhismus in China und Hochasien*, Berl. Acad. 1846, Ss. 55ff. Also Yule, *The Book of Sir Marco Polo*, vol. I, pp. 406ff.

[2] Conf. S. Beal, *Travels of Fah-hian*, p. 210 (front of cover), and Hofmann, *Buddha-pantheon von Nippon*, S. 150, fig. 559, pl. xxxviii*b*, and as illustration,—*Führer des Kgl*

mentioned as having possessed statues of Gautama were: Prasenajit of Kosala, who had seen the Master, and Udayana of Kausambi, at whose command the famous sandalwood figure was prepared by a master who had been sent to heaven,—which figure doubtless is

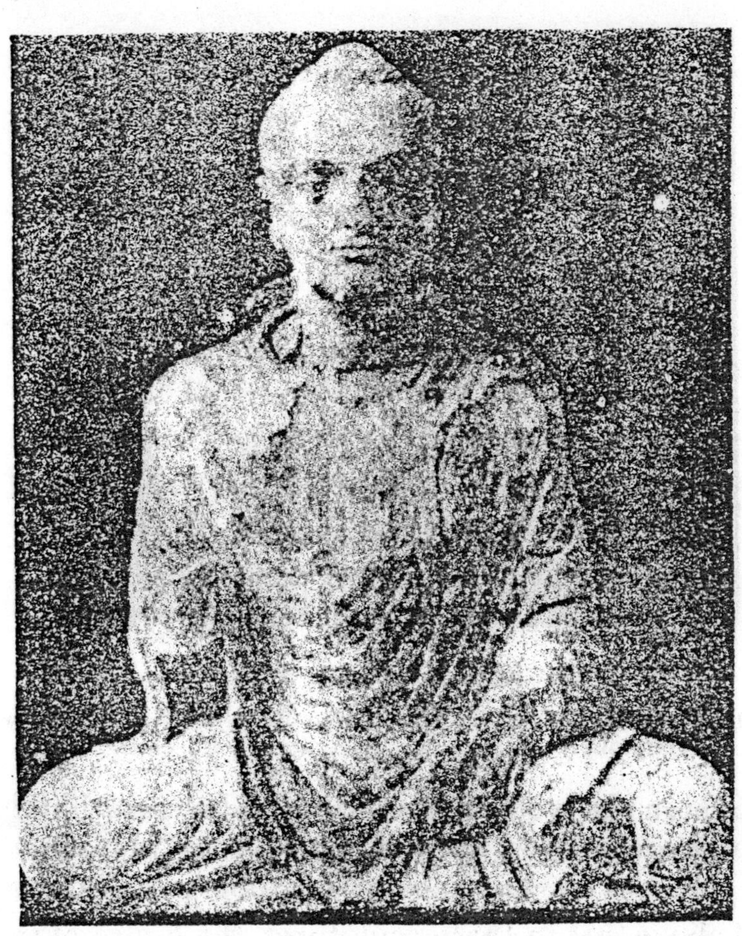

119. SEATED GAUTAMA BUDDHA WITH MOUSTACHES.
From Swât; height 28½ inches. The great aureole that was behind the head is almost entirely broken off. Original in Berlin Museum.

connected with the Gândhâra sculptures. We are indebted to Fâh-hian for the account of Prasenajit: to Hiuen Thsang for that of Udayana. Whether by the picture, which Prasenajit is said to have possessed, another type of the Buddhist ideal is intended is naturally beyond our knowledge. On the Buddha figure, shown in ill. 125, which goes back to Udayana's type of Buddha, the edges of the folds stand out in imitation of the ancient forms. the raised lines do not merge into one another, and they are modelled into grotesque ornaments at the sides, while the edges of the drapery,

Museums f. Völkerkunde, 7 Aufl. (1898), S.192. The reflection in the water: G. Huth, *Geschichte des Buddhismus in der Mongolei*, Bd. II (trans.) S. 409.

falling from the arms, have received a quite antique arrangement.

How strangely the Asiatics touched upon this representation is proved by the explanatory legends which a Tibetan historian quotes regarding the Buddha figure of Udayana. He relates how Buddha—

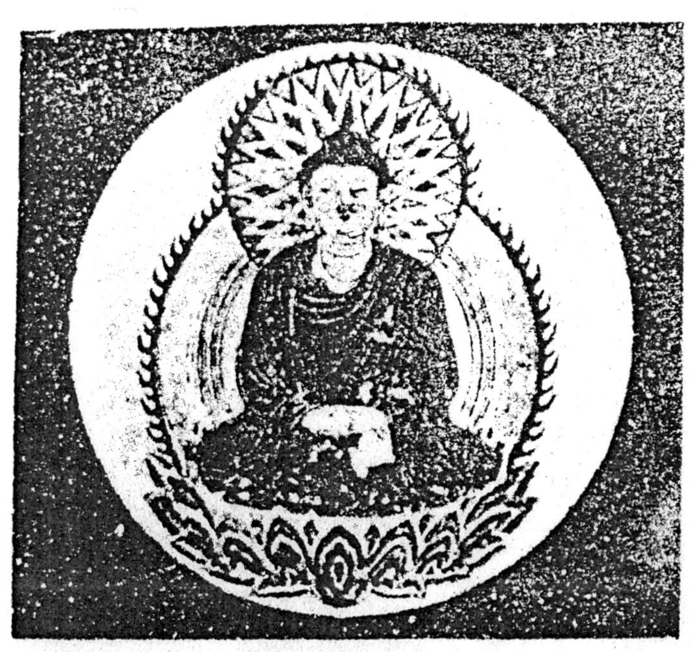

120. Figure of a Buddha.
From a modern Japanese representation, prevalent in the Chinese religions. Painted on silk. Berlin Museum.

in order to lighten the work of the artists, who were blinded by his glory—was mirrored in the water. The artists reproduced this reflection and thus the waving lines of the robe are accounted for.

It is noted above that in these sculptures, the figure of the Buddha is draped in two ways,—with the right shoulder and arm bare, or with the robe drawn closely round the neck and over both shoulders. When he is represented as seated either on the *padmâsana*—the lotus throne (as in ill. 121, and *Jour. Ind. Art, &c.*, vol. VIII, pl. 7, fig. 1, and pl. 8, figs. 1, 2),[1] or on the *vajrâsana* in the *bhûmisparsa-mudrâ*, as in ill. 49, the first mode seems to be the more usual; this is also frequent in the case of standing figures (see ill. 95), and even in some representations of the *nirvâna* (ill. 75, 76). But it occurs in nearly all groups of Buddhist sculptures and paintings in other parts of India.[2] The vesture fitting closely round the neck, on the

[1] *Arch. Sur. S. Ind.—Amarâvati*, p. 12.

[2] See *Ind. Monts.* pll. 98, and 102, fig. 1; *Amarâvati*, u.s., pll. xxvi, 1; xxxii, 4; xxxiv, 1; xxxv, 1; xxxvi, 3; xxxvii. 1, 2; xxxviii, 5; xxxix, 2; xli, 6; xliii, 5 and 9; lii, 1 and 2; and lv, 5; *Cave Temples*, pll. xxxi; xxxv, 1; li, and lvi; *Arch. Sur. W. Ind.* vol. III, pl. xlii; vol. IV, pll. xxvii, xxx, and xli, 1; vol. V, pl. xviii, 4; Griffiths, *Ajanta Paintings*, pll. 15, 24, 38, 39, 43, 51, 54, 61, 89, 91 and 151; &c.

other hand, is distinctly the more prevalent among the Gândhâra sculptures and is frequently copied elsewhere. Whether the rise of Buddhist iconography in the colder climate of Gandhâra and

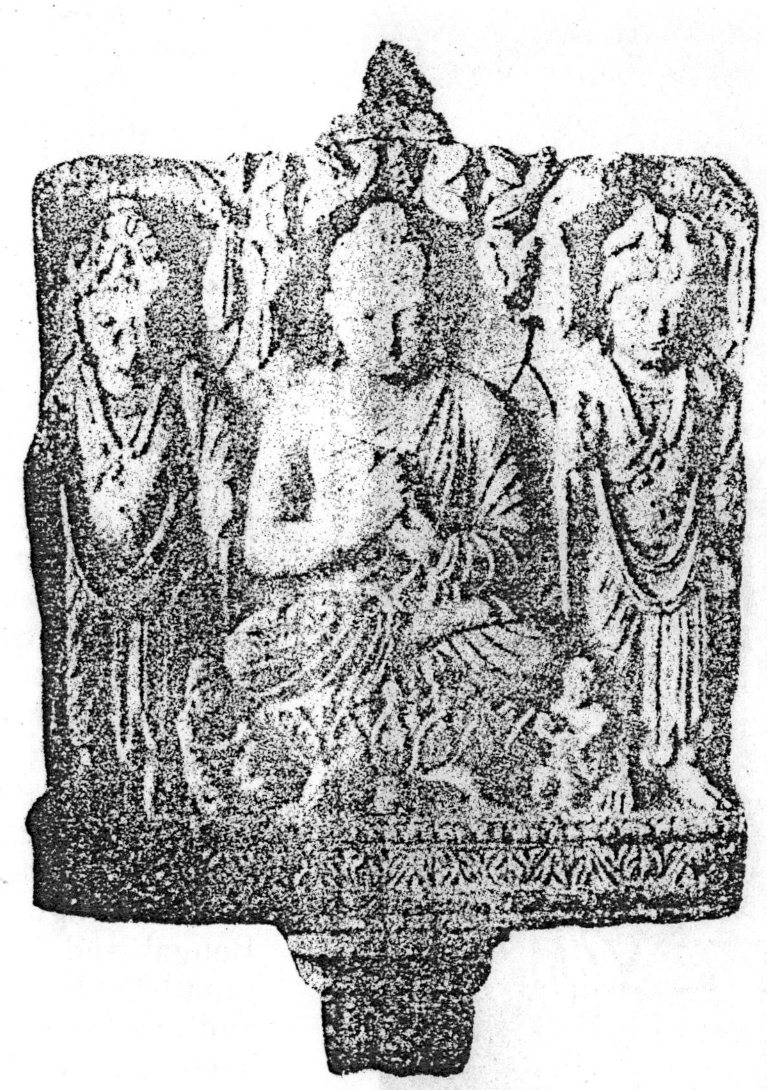

121. Buddha and Bodhisattvas.
15 inches broad. From Loriyân Tangai Calcutta Museum.

under foreign influence favoured the more warmly draped forms, may deserve consideration; but the instances of both styles of dress are numerous.[1]

The Buddha representations found in the stone enclosure of

[1] Dr. Th. Bloch, *J. As. S. Beng.*, vol. LVII. pt. i, p. 283, states that, "wherever we find a Buddhist statue which has the right shoulder bare, this is to be taken as a sign that the statue represents, not a Buddha, but a Bodhisattva." In presence of the examples cited, and the remarks which follow, this conclusion cannot be supported.—J. B.

Amarâvatî, are the principal Indian sculptures that follow the Gândhâra style (conf. ill. 123). Some Buddha statues found at Mathurâ have also the robe laid over both shoulders, and the folds executed on the dress point to the Gândhâra sculptures as models.

The Buddha image in the middle of the relief from Muhammad Nâri in ill. 82 is particularly remarkable, as in more than one respect presenting highly interesting features. As before mentioned, the head, especially in the treatment of the hair, is Indian; but in respect of the drapery the uncovered shoulder is striking. These two particulars belong exclusively to the Buddha-images of the southern school. The same character, however, is also found in the more recent Buddha figures from Bengal and Nepâl (Târanâthâ's Nepâl school) and in that of modern Tibet, which is dependent upon it. Evidently it is the old orthodox type[1] which becomes apparent here. The figures at Amarâvatî (ill. 123) and Mathurâ, which were influenced by the Gândhâra sculptures, seem therefore to have been supplanted by a national Indian type which

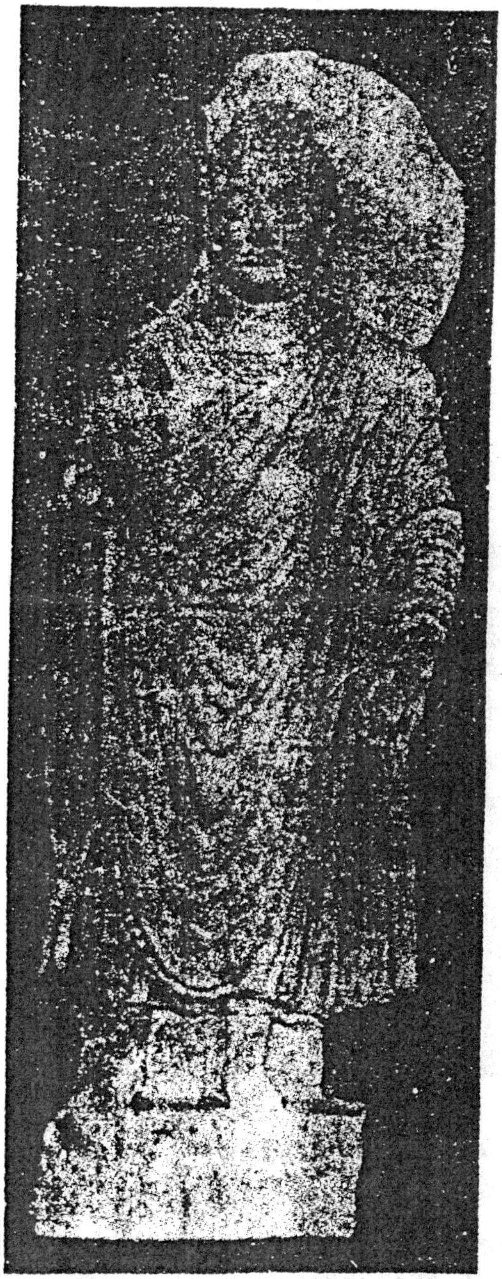

122. Gautama Buddha from Takht-i-Bâhi. Height 33½ inches. Original in Berlin Museum.

[1] The Borosan Buddha figures have also both shoulders covered. Conf. S. v. Oldenburg, *Vostochnaja Zametki* pl. 11 (no number) 1, 2, 3; Sven Hedin, *Through the Deserts of Asia*, vol. II, p. 70; a very fine old Indian bronze of the same type, *J.A.S.B.* ol. LXIV (1895), pt. i, p. 159, and pl. viii.

was afterwards preserved in the southern church and also in Nepâl and Tibet. Indeed, a Chinese source gives us the important information that the Buddha image depicted at Nâlanda was represented with bared right shoulder.[1] Ill. 126 presents an ancient Nepâl type; that shown by the great bronze dating from the 12th or 13th century, which is represented in ill. 127, is ancient Siamese; it is, however, extraordinarily like the ancient Burmese.

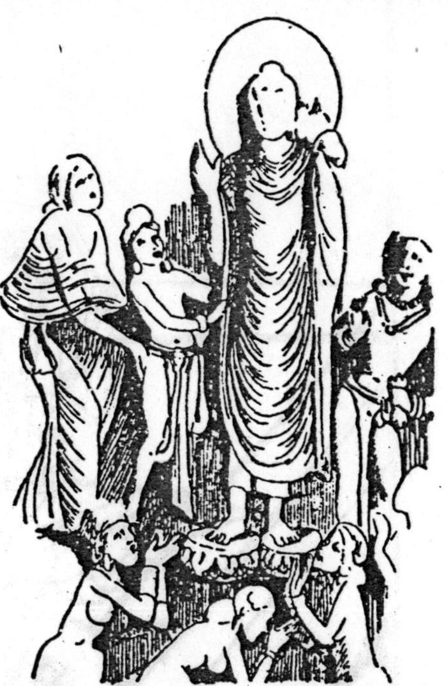

123. GAUTAMA AND HIS SON RAHULA.
With Buddha the vajra-bearer. Amarâvatî relief.[2]

Stress must here be laid upon the fact that, with our present knowledge of the subject, it is quite impossible to give a detailed description of the individual tendencies. The different types, therefore, can only be sketched so far as they are at present known; placed in relation to ancient pieces; and, only in very special cases of contact can any connexion be established. Above all, there are blanks in the accessible material—both in respect of the history of the religion and the monuments preserved. It eems as if the different types beonged to different schools. Thus it nappens that in China, Lamaism, *i.e.* Tibetan Buddhism, preserves the Indian type of Buddha with the bare right shoulder, which it got from Nepâl; while the ancient Chinese Buddhism, the so-called Foism, possesses the type, which in its draping, etc., points indirectly back to the Gândhâra sculptures. That, notwithstanding, it appears in Lamaist sculptures also, is not denied.

Besides we must take into consideration the fact that the southern school, at this time completely cut off from the northern one, by the revival of the Brahmanical cult, and, later still more radically, by Islâm, was not by any means entirely separated in the Middle Ages. In fact, the northern school, more than once, exerted an influence in dogmatic, but still more in artistic departments in certain countries belonging to the southern school.[3] The Buddhist statues of old Kamboja, and further, partly of old Siam, old Burma, modern Shân, and Lâos—which always appear in royal attire and crown—have a peculiar—perhaps local character, which is only a variety of the old Indian. Some further points, that strike us in the Buddha type, which appears for the first time in Gandhâra, are—the aureole, the sitting attitude, and the position of

[1] Conf. Hirth, *Ueber fremde Einflüsse auf die Chines. Kunst*, S. 51.
[2] From Fergusson, *Tree and Serp. Wor.* pl. lix, p. 189.
[3] Conf. in this connection B. Laufer's pertinent remarks in *Globus*, Bd. LXXIII, 2 S. 31, fig. 6.

the hands. All that is necessary has already been said on the aureole (p. 86).

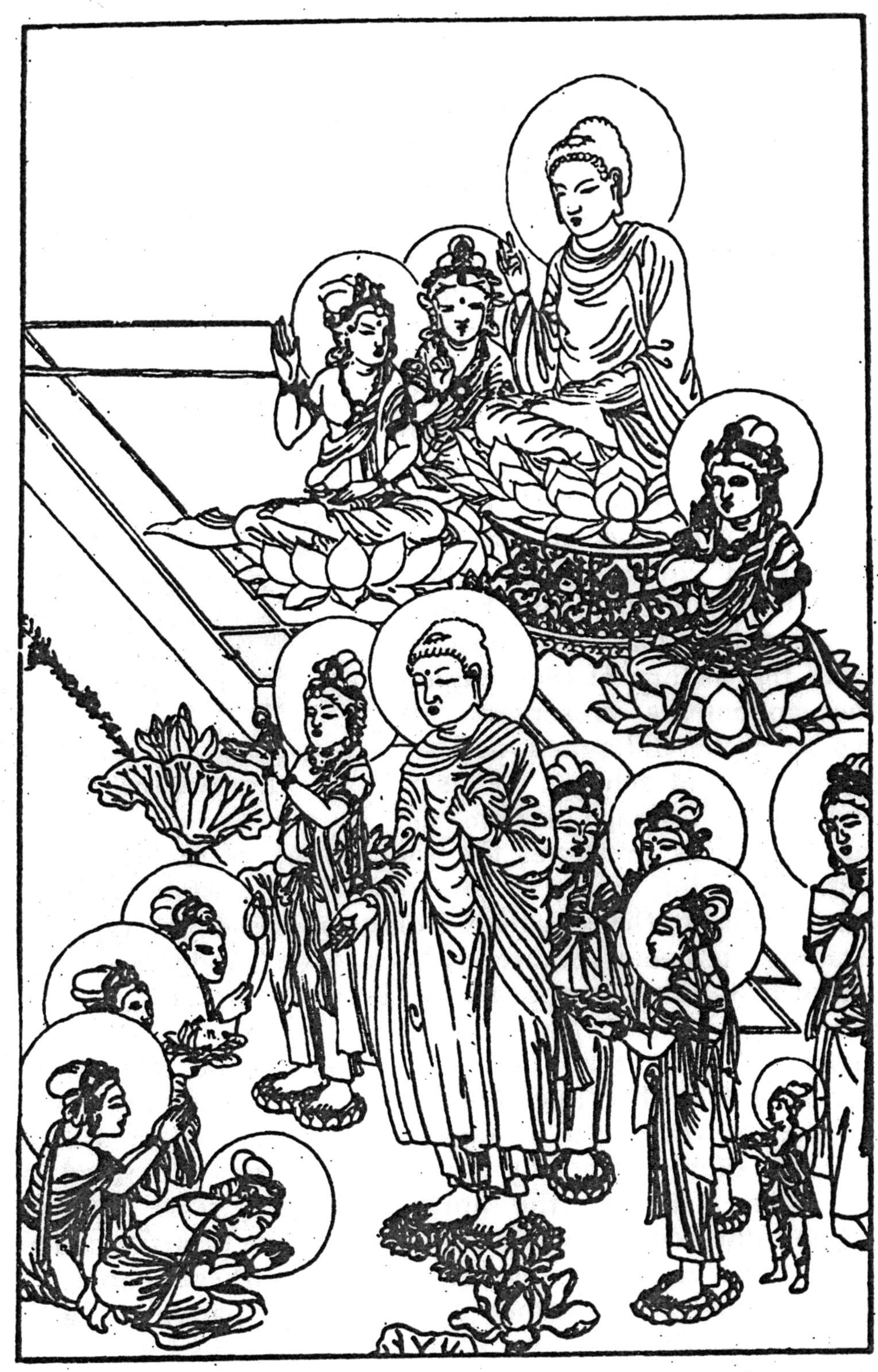

124. Buddha figures attended by Bodhisattvas.
From a modern Japanese picture representing Amitâbha's Paradise. Original in Berlin Museum.

The change of position in the limbs gives to art the opportunity of characterising the action it desires to give to the figure. As to the feet, as the Buddha-figure is debarred every movement, there only remains the sitting posture in which, as has been pointed out, the ascetics must give the standard; the upright position and a slight variation of it—the slowly stepping. In the reliefs—which we should imagine have been arranged in the workshop from model figures—the last type is the favourite one, and, as has been pointed out, with a leaning to the ancient idea of the sacrificing general.

The artist has more freedom in the question of the hands.[1] If we hold by the purely technical origin of our relief, let us watch how the sculptor changes his model figures, according to the legend which he is to represent. Thus gradually, certain hand-postures attached themselves to particular legends, and the position of the hands in the chief figure becomes an indication of the legend.

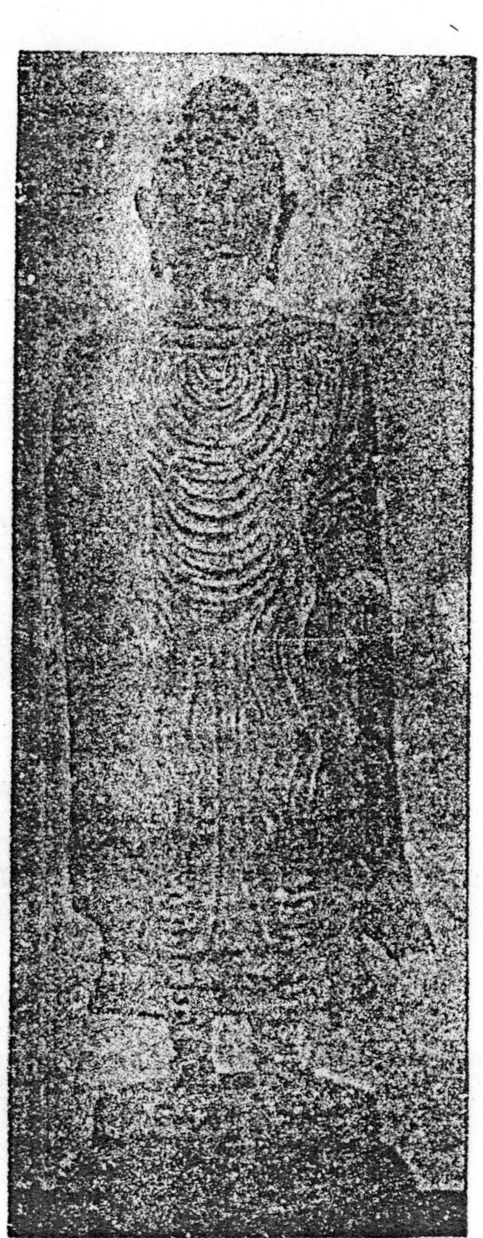

125. CHINESE BUDDHA FIGURE.
Carved in wood and gold lacquered.
Original in Berlin Museum.

If we leave the theoretical side of the *mudrâ*, we can gather so much for the practical art, that the whole life of Buddha, in its different incidents, required a series of modifications of hand postures, which were allotted for purposes of distinction to one and the same figure, and naturally we oftenest meet with those postures which illustrate favourite scenes.

What has been said is important on the following considerations: It has been above pointed out that, under the influence of art, the Buddha type broke free from the person; the idolatry, however, lay deeper and was older.

[1] On the *mudrâs*, see *Ar. Sur. W. Ind.* miscel. publ. No. 9, p. 99; *Ind. Ant.* vol. XXVI, p. 24; Waddell, *Lamaism*, p. 335f.; Grünwedel, *Mythol. d. Buddhismus in Tibet*, S. 200, n. 22; Schlagintweit, *Buddhism in Tibet*, pp. 56, 206; Foucher. *Etude sur l'Iconographie Bouddhique*, pp. 68f.—J.B.

Even while Buddha was still alive, the rudiments of a formal cult for him seem to have here and there appeared; various episodes, related in the *Jâtakas* and the literature allied to them, indicate

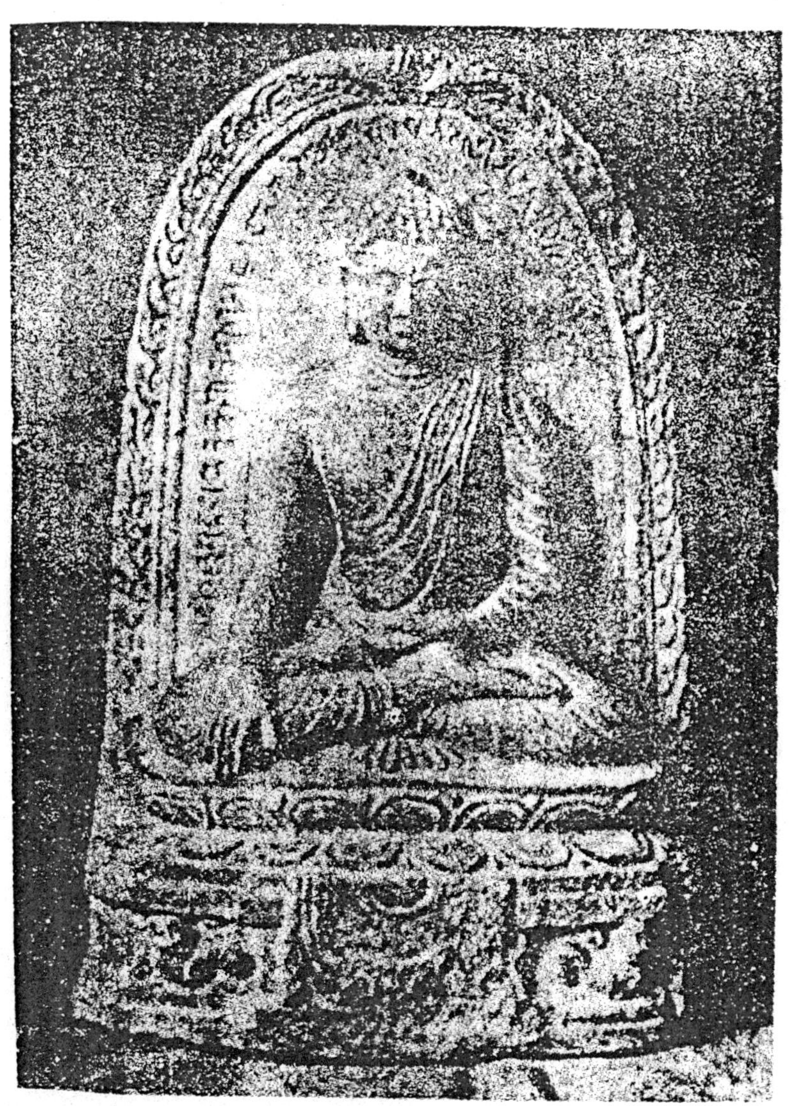

126. Old Nepâl stone figure of Gautama Buddha: Seated on the lion throne with the formula: Ye dharmâ hetuprabhavâh.[1] Original in Berlin Museum.

this. We learn how Buddha again and again seeks to make his position clear even to his most devoted followers, and yet how it fared with him as with all religious teachers at all times: they themselves become the objects of worship—the gods of their sects. Even the latest Indian reformer, the Bengâlî Chandra-sêna, of the

[1] On the formula conf. *Arch. Sur. W. Ind.* vol. V, p. 13, note 3.

Brahmâ-Samâj, in the present century has had to defend himself against this. The apotheosis is still easier after death. It is characteristic of the biography of every reformer that it is idealized and remodelled, and so gradually becomes legendary.[1] The description of the life of Buddha, the sources of the individual versions of which

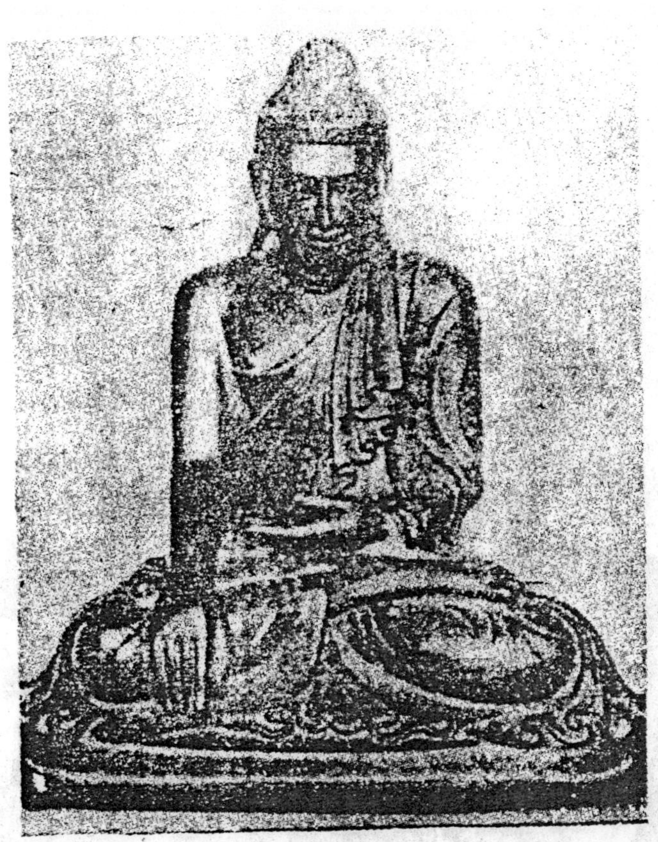

127. OLD SIAMESE BRONZE: GAUTAMA BUDDHA (P'ra Kodom) from the ruins of Kampeng Pet, 12th-13th cent. Size 12¼ inches. Original in Berlin Museum.

(the *Avidûrenidâna*, *Lalita Vistara*, etc.) have not been investigated, and between which no parallel has been made,—are imposing poems of considerable extent. The more the figure of the man, from whom a religious school has sprung, is deified, the more insistent becomes the question, whether he may ever come again. In India this development seemed a very natural one on account of the doctrine of the metempsychosis. The view of the Buddhist was not that Gautama, who had trodden the immortal path (*amata*m *pada*m), might come again, but rather that there were other beings who become Buddhas One word, which Gautama seemingly used

[1] Conf. *e.g.* the case of Nârâyana Svâmi, Heber's *Narrative* (ed. 1829), vol. III, pp. 29f., 34-42; *Ind. Ant.* vol. I, pp. 331-36; Briggs, *Cities of Gujarâshtra*, pp. 235ff and app. xiii-xxiv.—J.B.

for himself, and which is among the most difficult of his terms, is the word *Tathâgata*, "the one, who came thus." Originally, no doubt, it simply meant, "he who came like all other men." But

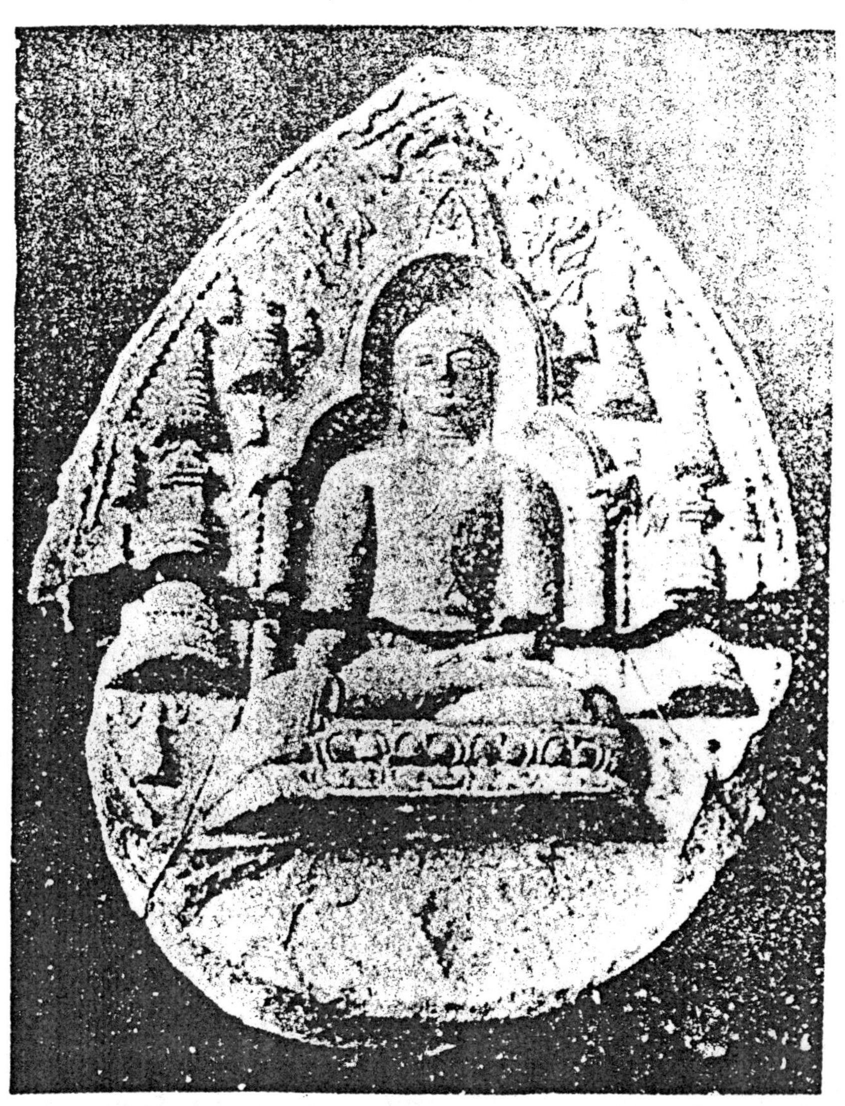

128. OLD INDIAN CLAY SEAL FROM BUDDHA GAYÂ.
Gautama Buddha surrounded by small stûpas; behind him the branches of the Bodhi tree and—as it appears—the spire of the temple at Gayâ.
Original in Berlin Museum.

soon an emphatic reference to the supernatural was seen in the term. So the circle of representation expanded till it was received as, "he who has come as his predecessors." In connexion with this is the idea that there have been, not one, but several Buddhas; and that each being, who wishes to become a Buddha, must in a former existence have met a Buddha and expressed to him his wish to become the enlightener. These teachers of mankind appear upon the earth at long intervals and the doctrine (*Dharma*) which they all teach is the same. With each there is a period in which the doctrine flourishes, then a gradual decline, then it is overborne by the barbarians and completely overthrown,[1] till a new deliverer appears and once more establishes the lost truths in all their purity. Gautama Buddha's predecessors are: Vipasyî (Pâli, Vipassî); Sikhî (Pâli, Sikhî); Visvabhû (Pâli, Vessabhû); Krakuchchanda (Pâli, Kakusandha); Kanakamuni (Pâli, Konâgamana); and Kâsyapa (Pâli, Kassapa). Both the northern and southern schools recognise these direct predecessors of Gautama (a complete list would give more); the details related about them in both traditions and the names of the trees, under which they obtained enlightenment, agree and point to one source.[2] But the representations of them given in the southern and northern church no longer agree. Of this, more hereafter.

The last Buddha of this age of the world, after Gautama, will be Maitreya (Pâli, Metteya; Tib. Jamba, written Byams-pa), "the loving one." The northern school fully recognises him and puts revelations into his mouth; indeed, he is venerated everywhere, almost more than Gautama. In the southern canon, so far as I can see, he does not appear; though he is mentioned in the Singhalese chronicle, the *Mahâvansa*. Maitreya is the Bodhisattva of the present age.

Mention has been made (p. 59) of the *Jâtakas*, which describe the previous forms of existence of a Buddha, that is a Bodhisattva—a being whose characteristic (*satva*; Pâli, *satta*) is enlightenment (*bodhi*), who while doing a pious action, in the presence of a Buddha, expresses his desire, in a later incarnation, to become a Buddha. According to the theory, Gautama also expressed this wish before former Buddhas (Pâli, *panidhim kar*). The sum total of his good actions (Pâli, *kamma*) allows him at each reincarnation to be born as a superior being in a constantly ascending scale of goodness, till, in the Tusita heaven, he resolves to accept another human existance, that he may show to bewildered man the way of salvation, and then to enter Nirvâna himself.

According to theory, the Bodhisattvas are innumerable; and it

[1] The "period of the first law" lasts 200 or some say 500 years from Sâkya Muni's death. The second era is called Saddharma pratirûpaka—"the law of figures or images," and lasts 1000 years; and the third epoch, the "last law" or period of declining religion, should last 3000 years, after which Maitreya renews the process.—Des Guignes, *Mém. de l'Acad. des Inscrip.* tom. xl. p. 201; Beal's *Romantic Legend*, p. 9.—J.B.

[2] Ante p. 74. The trees thus sacred to the seven Buddhas are respectively: Pâtali (*Bignonia suaveolens*), Pundarika (a kind of mango), Sâla (*Shorea robusta*), Sirîsa (*Acacia sir.*), Udumbara (*Ficus glomerata*), Nyagrodha (*Ficus indica*), and Pippala (*Ficus religiosa*). A remarkable correspondence exists here between the twenty-four past Buddhas and the Jaina Tîrthamkaras. See *Ind. Ant.* vol. XIII, p. 276; *Jour. As. S. Beng.* vol. V, pp. 321f.; Sp. Hardy, *Man. Budh.* p. 89.—J.B.

is the object of the religions of the Mahâyâna school,—which undoubtedly must be brought into connexion with our Gândhâra sculptures,—to aspire to the transmigration as Bodhisattva—"the great career," as opposed to the Hînayâna (the old school), the monks of which were only interested in their own salvation.

The Bodhisattva representation of later art is that of a royally attired young man, developed from the legend of the historic Buddha, who was, as we learn, a prince (ill. 129). Thus we may claim these youthful figures in rich attire, so frequent among Gândhâra sculptures, as Bodhisattvas.

They wear crowns or richly ornamented turbans, or curly hair; they are decked with bracelets, necklets and breast-chains. In common with the unornamented representations of Buddha, they have the mark above the nose, called the *ûrnâ*, and the nimbus.

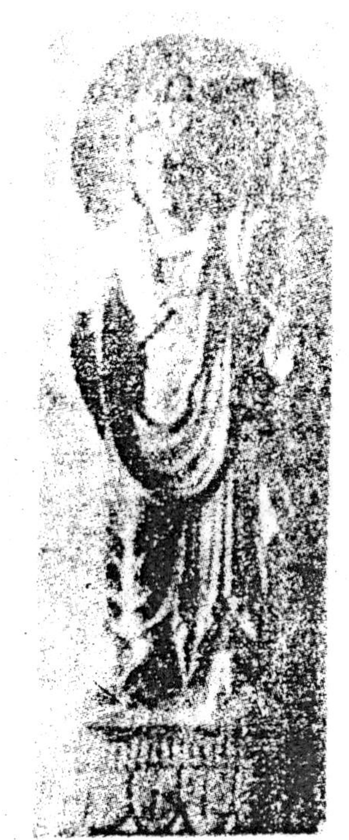

129. **Bodhisattva.** From Swât. Calcutta Mus.

The Bodhisattvas, as has already been remarked, belong only to the northern or Mahâyâna schools. Except Maitreya, they are unknown in Ceylon, Siam, and Burma. In Ceylon and Siam the usual attendants or supporters of Buddha in the temple shrines are *S*âriputtra and Maudgalyâyana,—the "disciples of the right and left hand," with Ânanda, Kâ*s*yapa, etc., standing by; in China, Ânanda and Kâ*s*yapa, frequently occupy the like positions, or with *S*âriputtra and Maudgalyâyana, Mañju*s*rî and Samantabhadra, form a group of six beside the Buddha. And in many of the Indian cave sculptures we find the attendant figures, as it were, in a state of transition, holding *chauris* as servants, and also with some of the insignia of the later divinities.

As Buddhism spread, the converts naturally carried into their new religion much of their reverence for the old Hindû gods, and they found that the traditions offered them already embraced Indra, Brahmâ, and others of their former divinities. Among the Hînayâna sects in the south, little change was made: Vish*n*u, Brahmâ, Nârâya*n*a, etc., were simply accepted under their Hindû names.

But with the Mahâyâna schools, whilst these gods were received, they were made to fit into an elaborate system of nomenclature and myth by which each was assigned a place in the illimitable æons of their cosmogony: Indra or *S*akra became *S*atamanyu and Vajrapâ*n*i, and his heaven of Swarga was named Trayastri*ms*a-loka; Brahmâ, so well known in Bauddha legend, had his chief attributes transferred to Mañjusrî—the "lamp of wisdom" and of supernatural power; and still Sarasvatî continued to be one of his wives, the other being Lakshmî; Avalokitesvara or Padmapâni, again, has some analogy to the attributes of Vishnu or Padmanâbha;[1] Virûpâksha, one of the "four kings," bears one of *S*iva's well-known names; the Sapta Tathâgatas take the place of the Brâhman Seven *Ri*shis; and even Ganesa has been taken over both as Vinâyaka and as the demon Vinataka (Jap. Binayakia).

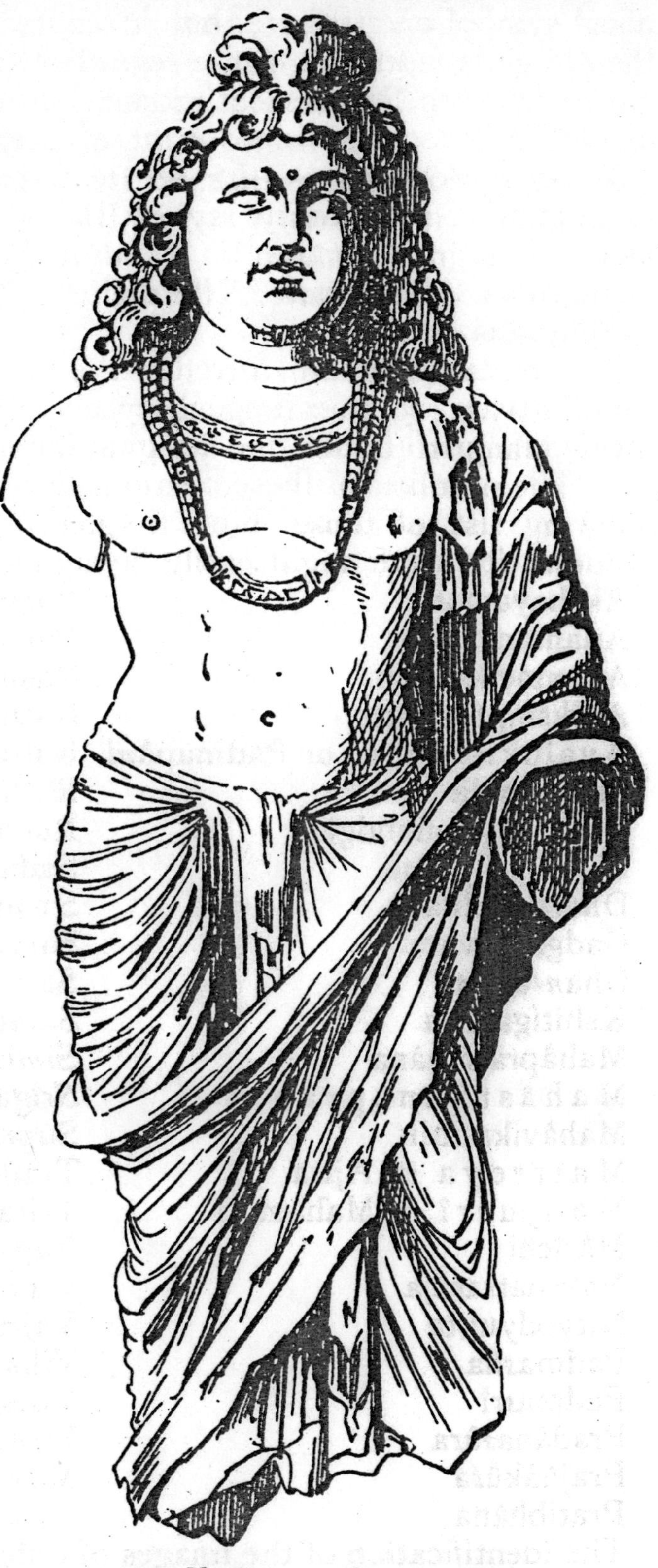

130. Youthful Bodhisattva.
Lahor Museum. From a photograph.

Then Maudgalyâyana, the *arhat*, became Mahâsthâma or Mahâsthânaprâpta Bodhisattva, and still kept his place at Buddha Amitâbha's left hand in a popular triad analogous to the *S*aiva Trimurti. But in the easy-going way of such a religion, Ajita or Maitreya—the Buddha of the future—was also given the same place, and with *S*âkyamuni and Avalokitesvara forms an alternative Triratna or triad.

This, then, seems to be as rational a theory as we can form of the genesis of these rather superfluous creations of the northern schools of Buddhism. In the later developments of Nepalese and Tibetan sectaries their rôle is enlarged and varied.

[1] See *Arch. Sur. W. Ind.* vol. V. pp. 14, 17.

When first adopted by the Mahâyâna sects, the Bodhisattvas were probably best known by names denoting some easily recognised symbol or attribute, but in course of time, as the forms of the old gods faded out of the regards of the later religionists, these gave way to the hierarchical nomenclature. And the new members of the Pantheon were in no want of designations: one of them—Vikau*t*uka Bodhisattva—has no less than 108 names: Mañju*s*rî, for example, is variously styled Balavrata, Mahâmati, Jñânadarpana, Kha*d*gin, Kumârarâja, Da*n*din, Mañjubhadra, Sthirachakra, Vajradhara, *S*ikhâdhara, Nîlotpalin, *S*ârdûlavâhana, Si*m*hakela, Vibhûshana, etc.

Different schools, too, introduced or specially favoured particular Bodhisattvas, *e.g.*, the Yogâchâryas exalt Samantabhadra, Vajrasattva, Mañju*s*rî (under the designation of Vajrapâ*n*i), Ratnapâ*n*i, etc. The number of these creations has thus become legion: the following list of those more frequently mentioned by name in Bauddha literature might easily be augmented:—

Akshayamati
Anantachâritra
Anantavikrâmin
Anikshiptadhura
Avalokite*s*vara or Padmapâ*n*i
Bhadrapâla
Bhaishajyasamudgata
Buddha*s*rîjñâna
Dhara*n*îndhara
Gadgade*s*vara
Gha*nt*âpâ*n*i
Kshitigarbha
Mahâpratibhâna
Mahâsthânaprâpta
Mahâvikrâmin
Maitreya or Ajita
Mañju*s*rî or Mahâmati
Mârîchi
Nakshatrarâja
Nityodyukta
Padma*s*îla
Padma*s*rî
Pradâna*s*ûra
Prajñâkû*t*a
Pratibhâna
Pûr*n*achandra
Pûr*n*amaitrâya*n*iputtra
Râsh*t*rapâla
Ratnachandra
Ratnapâ*n*i
Ratnaprabha
Ruchiraketu
Sadâparibhûta
Samantabhadra
Sarvasattvapriyadar*s*ana
Sarvârthanâman
Satatasamitâbhiyukta
Si*m*ha
*S*rîgarbha
Supratish*th*itachâritra
Trailokavikrâmin
Triratnârya
Vajragandha
Vajrapâ*n*i or Vajradhara
Vajrasattva
Vikau*t*uka
Vi*s*ish*t*achâritra
Vi*s*uddhachâritra
Vi*s*vapâ*n*i or Âkâ*s*agarbha
&c., &c.

The identification of the images of different Bodhisattvas is only possible in special instances: they mostly bear a very close resemblance to one another. But some of the more prominent of them have emblems by which they may be recognised: Avalokite*s*vara or Padmapâ*n*i has a white lotus in one hand, and on the front of his crown or *mukuta* is a small figure of a seated Buddha.

Vajrapâ*n*i has a *dâgaba* or *chaitya* as a cognizance (*chihna*) on his forehead and the *vajra* in his hand: but Mahâsthânaprâpta also appears with the same *chaitya* and with a diamond *vajra* supported on a flower. Mañju*s*rî has a book, either in his hand or on a flower, and a sword; and Âkâ*s*agarbha or Visvapâ*n*i is recognised by the same weapon placed on a flower; and so on.—J.B.

The fact that, in the scenes of the reliefs, which represent incidents before Gautama attained supreme knowledge, he is invariably depicted in the same way (conf. ill. 50, 81),[1] proves clearly that the figures described can only represent Bodhisattvas.

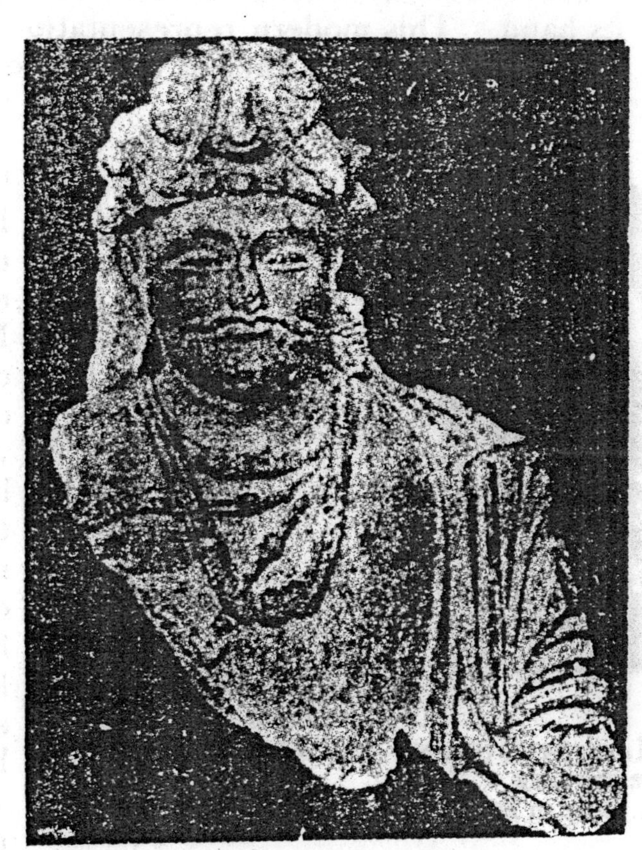

131. Torso of a Bodhisattva from Takht-i-Bâhi. Original in Berlin Museum. 12 inches in height.

Now later art, in a purely theoretic way, gives to individual Bodhisattvas the rank of Buddhas though not yet attained by them, and depicts them in the Buddha-type, though with strict adherence to a fixed posture of the hands; thus the Maitreya from Tibet (copied on page 134, fig. 85) is just a Buddha with the *Dharmachakra-mudrâ*—a position which, in Lamaism, always denotes Maitreya, but may also be used for other Buddhas.

Now arises the difficult question whether these positions are established in the Gândhâra sculptures, and whether, in the other attributes of the Bodhisattvas represented as princes, there may be a fixed and distinctive arrangement of the limbs.

Beginning with the last question, one attribute among the Gândhâra figures strikes us: it is a small bottle with a pointed bottom.

[1] Conf. Bowring's *Siam*, vol. I (1857), pl. at p. 316 (middle figure); Alabaster, *Wheel of the Law*, pp. 164, 208.

The modern representation of Maitreya (Tibetan, Jampa, written Byams-pa; Mongol, Maidari) in the pantheon of the northern school, as it has been developed in Tibet, shows the Bodhisattva in the ornaments and dress of a Hindû god or ancient Indian king,—generally of very youthful appearance. As a rule he is represented standing, but occasionally seated on a chair in European fashion. In the case of standing figures of Maitreya, the *dhotî* (under garment) is often caught up so high that the left leg remains bare to above the knee (conf. ill. 135). The modern attributes are the water flask or bottle (Tib. *bum-pa*; Skt. *mañgalakalâsa*)—the most important requisite, and the rosary.[1] Frequently both attributes rest upon the conventionally executed lotus flowers, which the figure holds in its hand. This modern representation is important, since it seeks to combine the more ancient types above referred to with the new attributes.

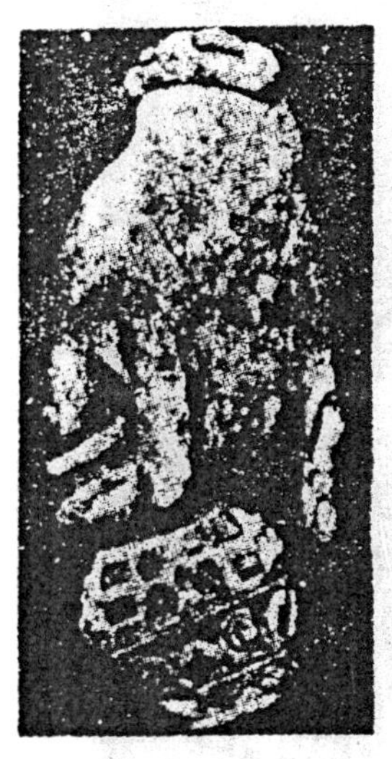

132. Hand with Greek ointment flask. Swât district. Orig. in Ber. Mus.

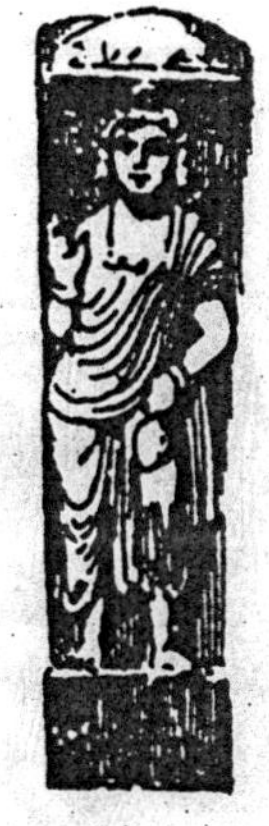

133. Small Bodhisattva Statue (Maitreya?) on a small relief fragment, from the lower monastery at Natthu, near Sanghâo. From Cole, pl. 20.

The old Indian bronze figure from Pekin, represented in ill. 134, now in the royal Ethnological Museum at Berlin, is clad in a short loin-cloth, the right hand without attribute, the left holding between the fingers something resembling the bud of a flower. On the lower side of the hand are traces of something having been broken off.

One of the oldest objects in the Berlin Museum is a bronze (of which, unfortunately, nothing is known for certain), which affords an interesting parallel. The figure represented in ill. 135 shows the same position of the hand as the Pekin Maitreya (ill. 134). It is executed, however, infinitely more carefully: the garments, the lips, are inlaid with copper; the crown ornaments, edges and pattern on the robe, and even the whites of the eyes are inlaid with silver. The style is that of Nepâl. The right hand holds the rosary; the left, in the same position as the

[1] Conf. *Veröffentl. aus dem Kgl. Mus. für Völkerk. Berl.* XI, 2/3 (1890) Ss. 47, 77. A Lamaist Maitreya standing with two lotus flowers (r. and l. hd.) conf. Uchtomskij, *Beschreibung der Or. Reise, s. k. H. d. Grossf.-Thronfolgers* (Russian ed., the German wants some of the plates) V, xxiv; also Grünwedel, *Mythol. Buddh. in Tibet*, p. 123). The Japanese Maitreya (Miroku) has his hands in his lap and a flask resting upon them, Hofmann, *Buddhapantheon von Nippon*, S. 145, fig. 176 (pl. xx), and S. 541 (pl. xxxvi).

Pekin bronze, holds a small bottle with pointed bottom. It appears that this flask also existed in the case of that bronze, but is now broken away; the flower-like knob in the hand is the mouth of the bottle. On the latter, the representation of a stûpa appears on the crown, in the distinctive manner of the Nepâl style. This last attribute, with the rosary, suggests that though the type of the figure—as well as the symbol in the left hand—is identical in both, we are hardly justified in calling this latter figure also a Maitreya. If, meanwhile, we leave this figure out of account, the further data tend to the determination of the Maitreya-type.

There is in the Royal Berlin Museum also a Tibetan miniature on silk which depicts Maitreya (described on a label as Byams-pa) in exactly the same attitude as in the two bronzes, though without attributes and with rich curly hair. Instead of a crown, the figure wears a fillet.

The truthfulness of the Tibetan tradition is shown by a comparison of the illustrations Nos. 82 and 85. The latter picture (from the collection of the brothers Schlagintweit) represents Maitreya as Buddha, *i.e.* in the form in which Lamaism depicts him as a perfected Buddha. His characteristic feature is the hands in front of the breast with the fingers arranged in a mystic position (*mudrâ*)—the so-called *dharmachakramudrâ*, which Gautama also receives especially in the representations of the sermon at Banâras. This picture is named and has already been published by Schlagintweit (*Buddh. in Tibet*, p. 88). Beside

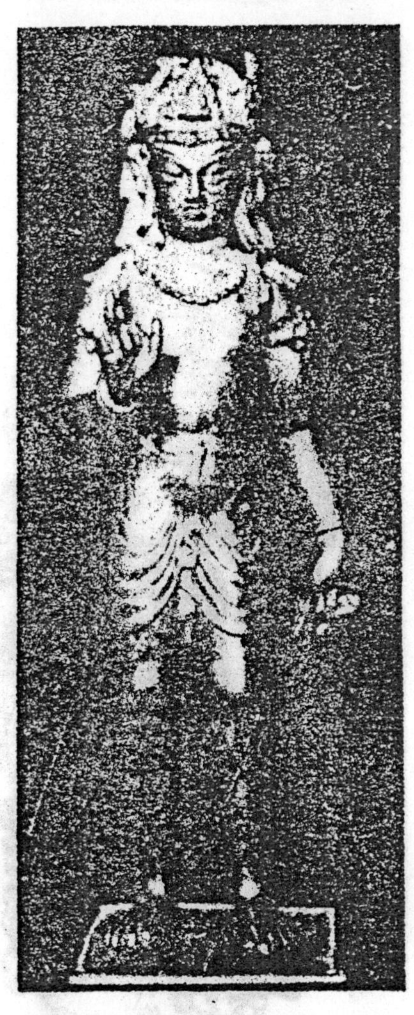

134. Old Indian Bronze of Jamba (Byams-pa): Maitreya from a monastery at Pekin. Height 8¾ inches. Original in Berlin Museum.[1]

[1] The title of "Byams-pa" the figure received in Pekin, and it is entered so in the MS. catalogue of the Pander collection. That catalogue was written in Tibetan letters in Pekin. If S. von Oldenburg (*Vostochn. Zam.* 363; *Globus*, 3 Feb, 1900, S. 73) says he is unwilling to speak about the figure as it is difficult to give a decision, I can only emphasize the accuracy of the title.

the chief figure, divinities rather smaller in size are represented as servants, and above are eight small Buddha pictures; the last of these is the same as the middle figure and must therefore be again Maitreya; the preceding one is undoubtedly Gautama. The other six must then be Gautama's predecessors: Vipasyî, Sikhî, Visvabhû, Krakuchchhanda, Kanaka-muni, Kâsyapa.[1] On the relief from Muhammad Nari, in ill. 82, eight Buddha statues are shown under the middle figure in splendidly composed types. The last of these, which, on the right of the sculpture, is turned towards the human worshippers (perhaps the donors of the relief?) does not wear the robe but has the customary lower garment, curled hair, and a small flask in the left hand: it is Maitreya. The preceding figure is the usual one of Gautama; the others are his six predecessors, as above. This shows that the royal figures of the Gândhâra monasteries with the flask may represent the Bodhisattva Maitreya, and that the Muhammad Nâri relief actually does so.

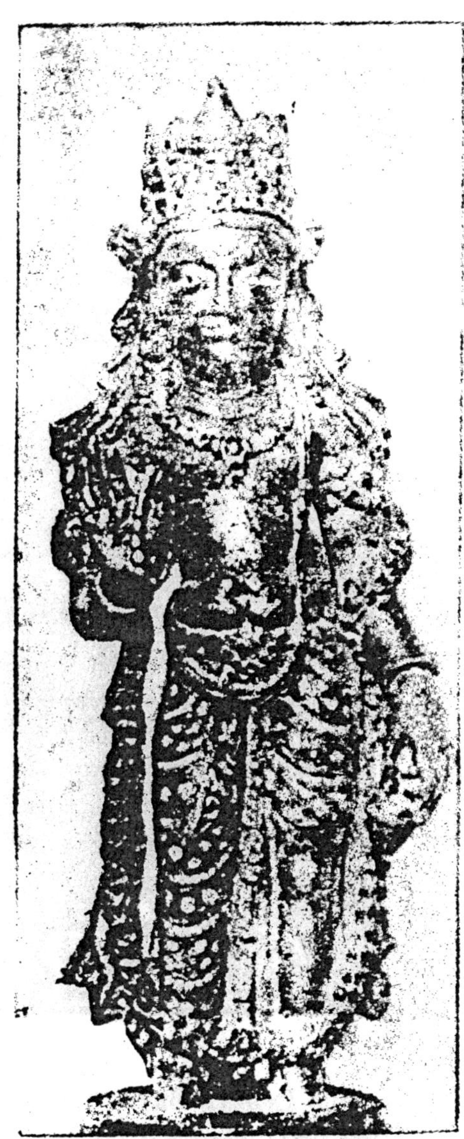

135. **Image of a Boddhisattva.**
Indian bronze inlaid with silver and copper.
Height 7½ inches. Original in Berlin Mus..

But this sculpture (ill. 82) proves still more: comparison with the Tibet picture shows that the central figure is the same: we may call it Maitreya represented as the Buddha.[2] Conf. p. 194.

[1] We find the same eight figures painted over the door of Cave XVII and on the wall of the shrine in Cave XXII at Ajantâ; in the latter, the names of the Buddhas are given below each, and of their respective Bodhi-trees above them; *Notes on Ajanta Paintings*, pp. 63 and 81; and *Inscriptions from Cave Temples* (Bombay, 1881), p. 88; also Griffiths' *Paintings from Ajanta*, vol. I, pll. lxi and xci, and pp. 36, 40.—J. B.

[2] Emphatically, we have to do with a Buddha figure with the *dharmachakramudrâ*.

Another result of this examination appears,—that even in the Gândhâra school had arisen the scheme of distinguishing their saints by the different positions of the hand and fingers. Single types in the life of Buddha become, as it were, permanent attributes for certain figures; thus, the position of the hands before the breast in the so-called *dharmachakramudrâ* is really that of the Buddha who 'turns the wheel of the law' (conf. p. 177). But even in the Gândhâra school, we find Maitreya in this pose as the Buddha of the future who will yet turn the wheel of the doctrine.

The representation of Kâsyapa-Buddha,[1] the predecessor of Sâkyamuni, is of interest. The attitude has not been noticed elsewhere, and was perhaps of no lengthened duration in the Buddhist sculpture of later times. The Berlin Museum possesses a small figure, somewhat chipped, which has doubtless formed part of a relief now destroyed, but which may be related to the figure shown on ill. 82. Kâsyapa's robe fits close to the body, and his right hand wrapped in it clasps it on his breast, while the left holds the falling garment. The other six Buddhas are thrown into the shade by this characteristic type, which in some ways reminds us of the statue of Sophocles in the Lateran.

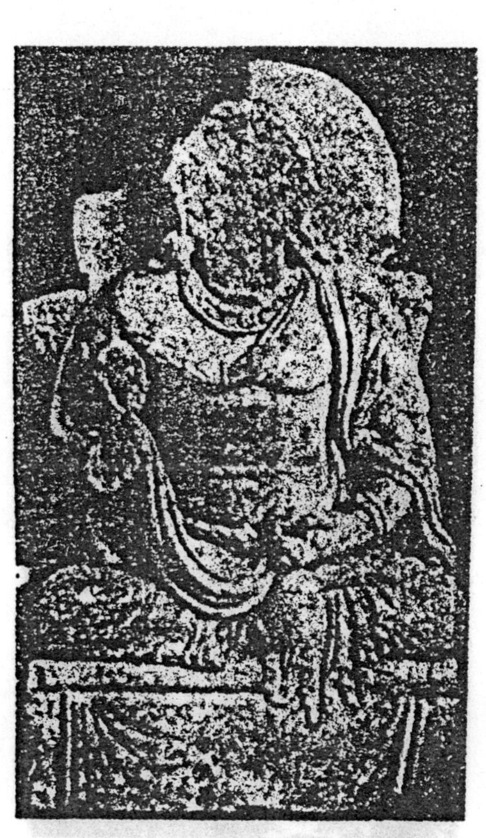

136. A BODHISATTVA FROM SWÂT: the head to be completed as in ill. 130. Original in Berlin Museum.

A systematic examination of all the types belonging to this group, along with the few representations to hand of the southern church, cannot be undertaken yet, from the want of available material. Suffice it to say, that even among the sculptures of the

This is the most common form in the shrines at Ajantâ. In Lamaism Maitreya has always this *mudrâ* when he is placed in comparison with Sâkyamuni. Conf. Schiefner, *Buddhistische Triglotti*, S. 1.

[1] Not to be confounded with the Brâhmaṇa of the same name mentioned at pp. 62f. For the awakening of Kâsyapa, conf. Schiefner, *Mél. As. Ac. St. Pétersbourg*, tom. VII (1874), pp. 417f.; S. Beal, *Ind. Ant.* vol. XII, p. 328. What is said above only points out that Kâsyapa is found in the above pose, but not that every image so represented must be Kâsyapa; conf. fig. 140 (p. 192), right side attendant.

Gândhâra period, alongside Gautama, Maitreya and Kâsyapa in particular play a prominent part. It may be pointed out that, in the eschatology of northern Buddhism, a highly interesting connexion is established between the two last named. Kâsyapa lies uncorrupted in his stûpa: when Maitreya shall appear on earth, he will rise, work miracles, and disappear in flames,—a legend which strongly reminds us of a Persian (and a Muhammadan) tale.

But here, too, we are perhaps justified in pointing out the striking similarity of the representation of the coming Maitreya with Saoshyant (Sosiosh), the deliverer in the Pârsî religion. Even though we do not know when the legend of Saoshyant received the development it now presents, still the dominant position of Maitreya in the northern school must have been influenced by it.

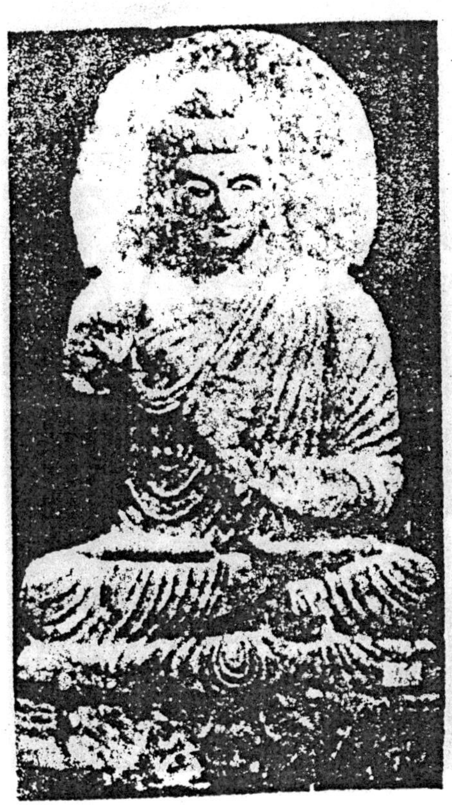

137. Buddha Figure in Dharma-chakramudrâ. From Kadam-kaki Khel in Swât. Original in Berlin Mus.

The worship of Maitreya must have been fully developed even in the fifth century, for the Chinese pilgrims know a set form of prayer to the Bodhisattva. The Gândhâra sculptures, corresponding in this with the report of Fah-hian, show the worship at its height.

Tradition connects Maitreya directly with the origin of the Mahâyâna school in representing the Tantras as received from Maitreya by the monk Asañga, who is regarded as the founder of the whole later pantheon.[1] The Mahâyâna school—the so-called "greater vehicle," no longer seeks after the deliverance of the individual, but for rebirth as a Bodhisattva. These aspirations were developed by the learned character of the monks in the northern system, who regarded the followers of the

[1] On Asanga, see Rhys Davids. *Buddhism*, pp. 208f.; Beal; *Si-yu-ki*, vol. I, p. 226; Eitel, s.v.; Schiefner, *Lebensbeschr. des Buddha Sâkyamuni*, S. 80; Vassilief, *Le Bouddhisme*, pp. 267ff. How far Maitreya is connected with the Mahâyâna school, is witnessed by the following independent proof. Ho-shang, the follower of the Mahâyâna, passes as an incarnation of this Bodhisattva and is always associated with the Lokapâlas, which agrees with our remarks, p. 130, &c *Veröffentl. aus d. Kgl. Mus. für Völkerk* Bd. 1, 2/3, S. 89.

old doctrine with disdain as representatives of the "lesser vehicle" (Hînayâna). Among the sculptures from the Gândhâra monasteries, we find such a multitude of figures bearing the Bodhisattva character, that it would be impossible to regard them all as figures of Maitreya, even if we believed that at that period the cult of this Bodhisattva was at its height.

Besides the symbol of the flask (compare the relief, ill. 136, and the hand, ill. 132) we find represented as a favourite attribute in the hands of the Bodhisattva large single blossoms of the lotus flower[1]

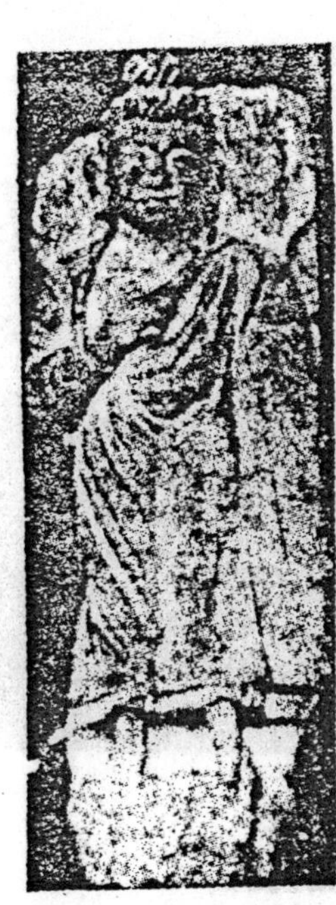

138. Small figure of a Buddha, broken from a relief which has been like that in ill. 82. From Kadam Kuki Khel in Swât. Original in Berlin Museum.

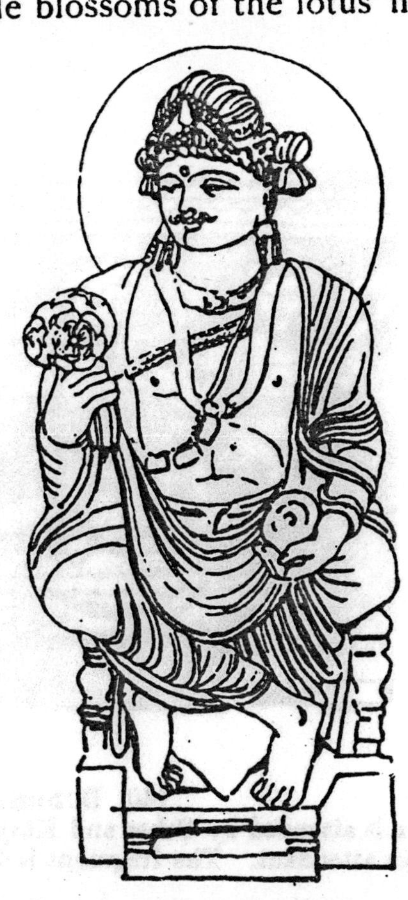

139. Figure of a Bodhisattva, with a bunch of lotus flowers in his right, and a vessel in his left hand. Plaster cast in Königl. Mus. f. Völkerk. Berlin.

or whole bunches of such: an attribute that is readily explained by the religious custom (flower offerings). Among Indian sculptures Maitreya is distinguishable by the lotus flower in his hand; I need only refer to the Bauddha figures found at Supârâ, which series closes with a Bodhisattva holding only a perfect lotus flower and no vessel. The two attributes—the flowers and flask—are well known from Sâñchî; in the Gândhâra school, indeed, the antique flask with the pointed bottom takes the place of the round Indian

[1] The lotus flower as Maitreya's emblem is noticed above p. 186, note 1. This is also shown in older art: Bhagvânlâl Indraji, *Supârâ and Padana*, in *Jour. Bom. Br. R.A. Soc.* vol. XV, p. 298, and pl. v. where the whole series proves that Maitreya (and not Padmapâni) is meant.

lôtâ. As has been already noted, modern art in Tibet assigns to Maitreya both symbols, but for the vessel the long-beaked ritual jar (*mañgalakalâsa*).

We may here notice a broken relief from Kâfirko*t* in Swât, now in the British Museum (ill. 140). The style of art is less educated or cruder than usual. To the left is a Bodhisattva seated on an *âsana*, holding a flask in his left hand, and the right raised in the *abhayapâni mudrâ*: this we take to be Maitreya. His breast and

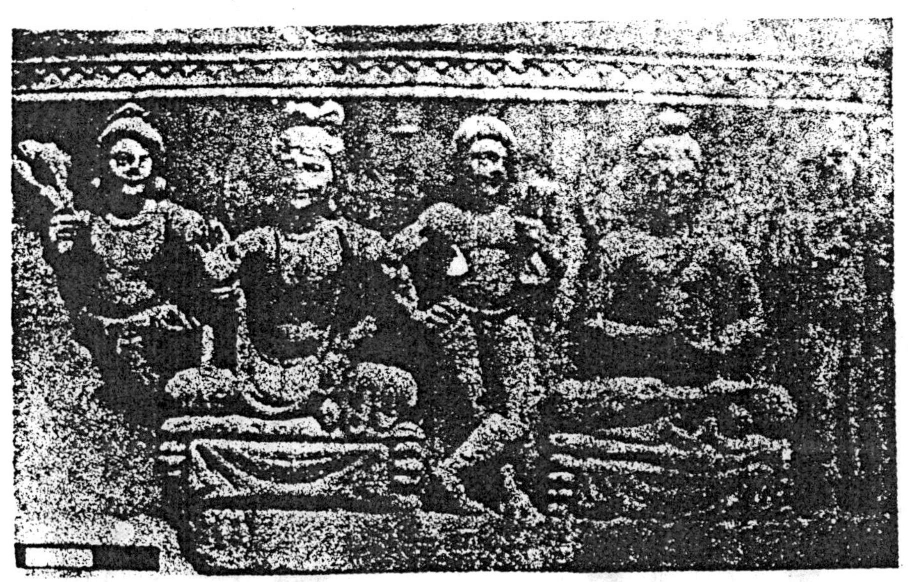

140. BUDDHA AND BODHISATTVA.

Buddha is attended by Ṣakra and Kâsyapa (?); the Bodhisattva is probably Maitreya with an attendant. The fragment is 7½ in. high and about 13½ in. long. Brit. Mus.

right shoulder are bare, but he wears bracelets, necklace, ear-rings, &c., and is attended by a figure with a large bunch of flowers. The rest of the slab is occupied by *S*âkyamuni, attended on the left by a monk whose right shoulder and arm are covered by his robe, in the style ascribed above to Kâ*s*yapa. On his right is *S*akra, in this case naked, except for a very scanty loin-cloth; and it is to be noted that, even now, in Nepâl, the Vajra-bearer wears no necklace or other ornaments.

Returning then to the bronze in ill. 135, we see that it represents the same type as the Maitreya in ill. 134. S. von Oldenburg claims ill. 135 for a Padmapâ*n*i, and he furnishes proof that it is so, and that, advancing from this, the name of Padmapâ*n*i might be applied to some of the Gândhâra sculptures.[1] But the name Padmapâ*n*i is

[1] *Vostochnya Zametki*, pp. 362-3. Oldenburg's doubts about the stûpa in the crown are unfounded: he conjectures ill. 134 to bear an incorrectly copied figure of Amitâbha; it undoubtedly represents a stûpa. This is an attribute of Padmapâ*n*i.' *Notes on Ajanta Paintings, &c.*, pl. xxv, 1, where the stûpa stands on the shorn head of Buddha. But Maitreya also has a stûpa in his hair; he is thus represented in the unpublished

unfortunately not a proper name, but an adjective in substantive form : "he with the lotus flower in the hand," a round-about name that may be associated with Vajrapâ*n*i. This Bodhisattva has always produced new representations, so that to-day it presents the most important figure in the pantheon of Tibet : he is incarnate in the Dalai-Lama.

Still, we must beware of generalizing too hastily ; the flask in the hand of a Bodhisattva figure, as S. von Oldenburg has pointed out, does not necessarily indicate Maitreya. The proper *chihna* must decide as to the individual Bodhisattva ; and the Am*r*ita flask appears in modern representations as an attribute of Avalokite*s*vara or Padmapâ*n*i. We find this in the 11th century in Nepâl ;[1] also at Bôrô Bu*d*ur,[2] where the existence of a small figure of a seated Buddha Amitâbha on the forehead points distinctly to Avalokite*s*vara ; at Aja*n*tâ,[3] we find Avalokite*s*vara with a jug or flask in his left hand and a deer-skin over his left shoulder ; and again holding the palm of his right hand forward (in the *vara mudrâ*), and clasping a flask with oval body and narrow neck in the left. In the caves of Bâgh in Mâlwâ (ill. 141) also the representation of the same little figure in the head-dress precludes doubt that the representation is that of Avalokite*s*vara.[4] Almost as certainly the

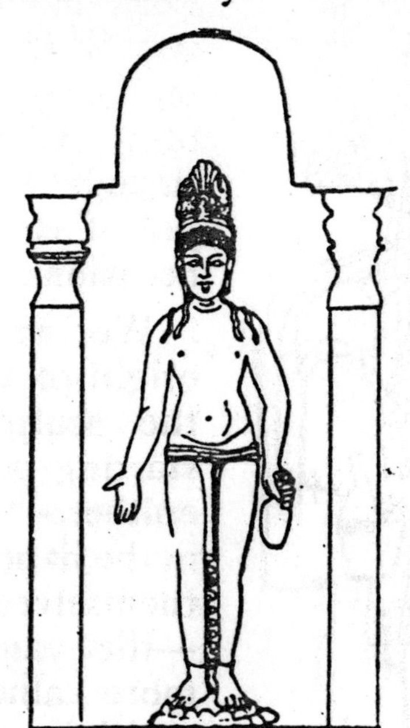

141. AVALOKITEŚVARA. From Bâgh Caves.

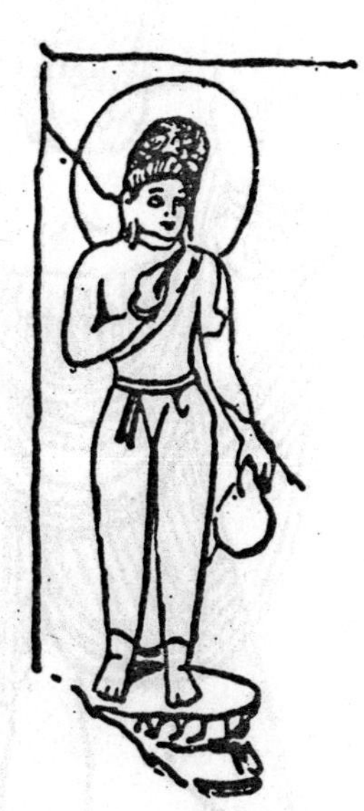

142. A BODHISATTVA. From Aurangâbâd Cave Temples.

Narthang print of the "five hundred gods," fol. 85, 1. A magnificent large gilded bronze Maitreya in the Berlin Museum, with the lotus flower, the wheel and a little jar upon it, and with the hands in the *dharmachakra mudrâ*, has likewise a stûpa in the crown. But Mahâsthânaprâpta has it also,—this Bodhisattva occurring very frequently in pictures representing Amitâbha's paradise (Japan) as a companion to Padmapâ*n*i (with Amitâbha on the crown)—as in the picture from which ill. 124 is taken. Individual Bodhisattva figures are seldom to be distinguished as to their names with absolute certainty. One must start from well-marked groups (triads, &c.) and so seek guidance. It appears as if tradition itself, by the arrangement of Bodhisattva figures in wrong succession, had become uncertain, and so named the individuals incorrectly. The same is the case in the representations of the Arhats—and here the Japanese tradition seems to be the best. Conf. on this J. Burgess, *Ar. Sur. W. Ind.* vol. V, pl. xx, 1, and xix, 6 ; *Jour. Ind. Art*, &c., vol. VIII, pp. 38, 63.

[1] A. Foucher, in *Rev. de l'hist. des Religions*, tom. xxx, p. 353ff.

[2] *Bôrô-Boedoer*, Atlas, pl. cclxxxi.

[3] Burgess, *Notes on the Bauddha Rock-temples of Ajanta*, pp. 35, 62,

[4] Burgess, *Arch. Sur. W. Ind.—Report on Elura Cave-Temples, &c*, pl. xx, fig. 2.

Bodhisattva from the Aurangâbâd caves[1] represented in ill. 142, is the same.

If now we compare fig. 135 above, with the Gândhâra statue represented in ill. 143, Prof. von Oldenburg calls attention to the resemblance,—only the rosary in the left hand is wanting, in its place a lotus blossom appears in the palm: it has a nimbus, but is without a crown.[2] Ill. 121 is an example of Buddha on the *padmâsana* between two Bodhisattvas, and possibly that on his right held a flask now broken off. It would then appear that, though Maitreya has the flask or jug, it is also an attribute, at least occasionally, of Padmapâ*n*i.

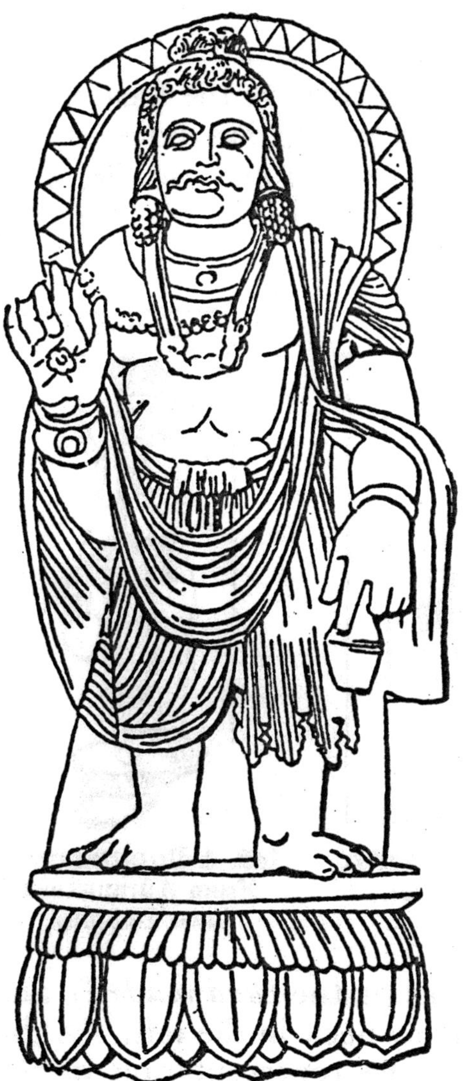

143. A Bodhisattva,—Padmapâ*n*i? Cole, *Græco-Buddh. Sculp.* pl. 25.

We may here also consider the origin of the system at least from the sculptor's side, taking as a starting point a merely descriptive epithet—"he with the lotus flower in the hand." Here the personalities themselves vanish under the touch,—the vaguer the beginnings the more abundantly the attributes multiply in the sequel, and new epithets[3] arise, from which again, under certain circumstances, new personages may evolve.

If we accept it as a fact that Padmapâ*n*i had become established in Gândhâra sculpture, it may be asked whether his spiritual father, Amitâbha, appears or not. Where later art represents him, he has either the garb and tonsure of a Buddha with the *dhyâna-mudrâ* (the hands clasped in the lap), or the garb of a Bodhisattva with the same posture of the hands holding in them a vessel with Am*ri*ta. Such Buddha figures actually appear in these sculptures (conf. ill. 82, the Buddhas sitting in the frieze), and Bodhisattvas

[1] Burgess, *Arch. Sur. W. Ind. Rep.* vol. III, pl. lv, 1. The scale of drawing deprives us of perfect clearness as to the *chihna*; but compare also woodcut 9, p. 80.

[2] *Globus*, 3 Feb. 1900, S. 73-75.

[3] For the common epithets and names of Padmapâ*n*i or Avalokite*s*vara, as Loke*s*vara, Trailoke*s*vara, Padma, Abhaya*m*dada, Âryapâla, Chintâchakra, Halâhala, Mahâka*r*u*n*a, Si*m*hanâda, &c., see *J. R. As. Soc.* (1894) pp. 76ff.; *Notes on Ajanta Paintings, &c.*, p. 100f. and pll. xxiv-xxvii. Avalokite*s*vara and Mahâsthâmaprâpta are both mentioned in the *Sukhâvati-vyûha*, §§ 31 and 34, which dates from as early as A.D. 100; conf. *S. B. E.* vol. XLIX, pt. ii, pp. xxiii, 48, 52, and 176.—J. B.

also occur, with both hands in the lap, holding the same little bottle or flask mentioned above. Yet it cannot be asserted with certainty that Amitâbha must be meant by these, though it is not improbable. Indeed, if we follow the Japanese tradition, even the middle figure in ill. 82 might be Amitâbha in Sukhâvatî; the side figures would then be Padmapâ*n*i and Mahâsthânaprâpta!

We would then have before us here the beginning of the theory of the Dhyâni or meditative Buddhas, which forms the basis of the Mahâyâna doctrine.

Even the southern school recognises four stages of mystic contemplation (Skt. *dhyâna*; Pâli, *jhâna*), which the northern school subsequently increased to five. These five Dhyânas correspond, in the cosmogony, to the series of heavens in five terraces,—the so-called Brahmalokas, which rise above the inferior heavens of the gods, Devalokas (conf. pp. 60, 61). The theory then arose that each Buddha dwelling on the earth had his mystic counterpart (*Dhyâni-buddha*) in one of the Dhyâni-heavens, and that each of them again had his Bodhisattva or successor. Thus, with the five human Buddhas of the present period of the world's existence (*kalpa*), are associated five mystic antitypes in the corresponding Dhyâni degrees with their five successors (*Dhyâni-bodhisattvas*). We have thus the following correspondences:—

Human Buddhas (Mânushi-buddhas)	*Dhyâni Buddhas.*[1]	*Dhyâni Bodhisattvas.*
1. Krakuchchanda	Vairochana	Samantabhadra
2. Kanakamuni	Akshobhya	Vajrapâ*n*i
3. Kâsyapa	Ratnasambhava	Ratnapâ*n*i
4. Gautama	Amitâbha	Padmapâ*n*i
5. Maitreya	Amoghasiddha	Visvapâ*n*i

After the advent of Maitreya as Buddha the present world will be destroyed.

Prof. Rhys Davids has called attention to the fact that the whole theory, according to which every human Buddha emanates from his *spiritus rector* (Dhyâni-buddha), bears a resemblance to the æons and emanations of the Gnostics, and he regards it as not impossible that these beings owe their existence to Persian influence. Noteworthy in this connexion is the name "Immeasurable light" given to Amitâbha—from whom Gautama is said to have emanated: it points distinctly to contact with the old Persian light worship.

The whole doctrine of the Dhyânibuddhas and Dhyânibodhisattvas appears to rest on the Zoroastrian theory of the Fravashis (Fervers). According to the Masdayasnian conception, every being, whether dead, living, or unborn, has his Fravashi, which joins itself to the body at birth, and after death intercedes for it. We have thus Irânian influence distinctly before us, which accords with the local surroundings of the Gândhâra school. It was

[1] See *Notes on Ajanta Paintings*, p. 99f., for the *mudrâs*, *chihnas*, colours and symbols of these Matântara-pañcha-Buddhâmnâya; there are also other arrangements in Nepâl of six, seven and nine.—J. B.

necessary to touch upon these crude materials, since only in this way can we comprehend the never-ending repetition of Buddha figures in the buildings of later Buddhism.

The Buddhas and Bodhisattvas from the rock-temples at Elurâ, represented in ill. 144 and 145, are of this sort. In ill. 144 we have the Buddha type repeated five times, perhaps for the five Dhyâni-

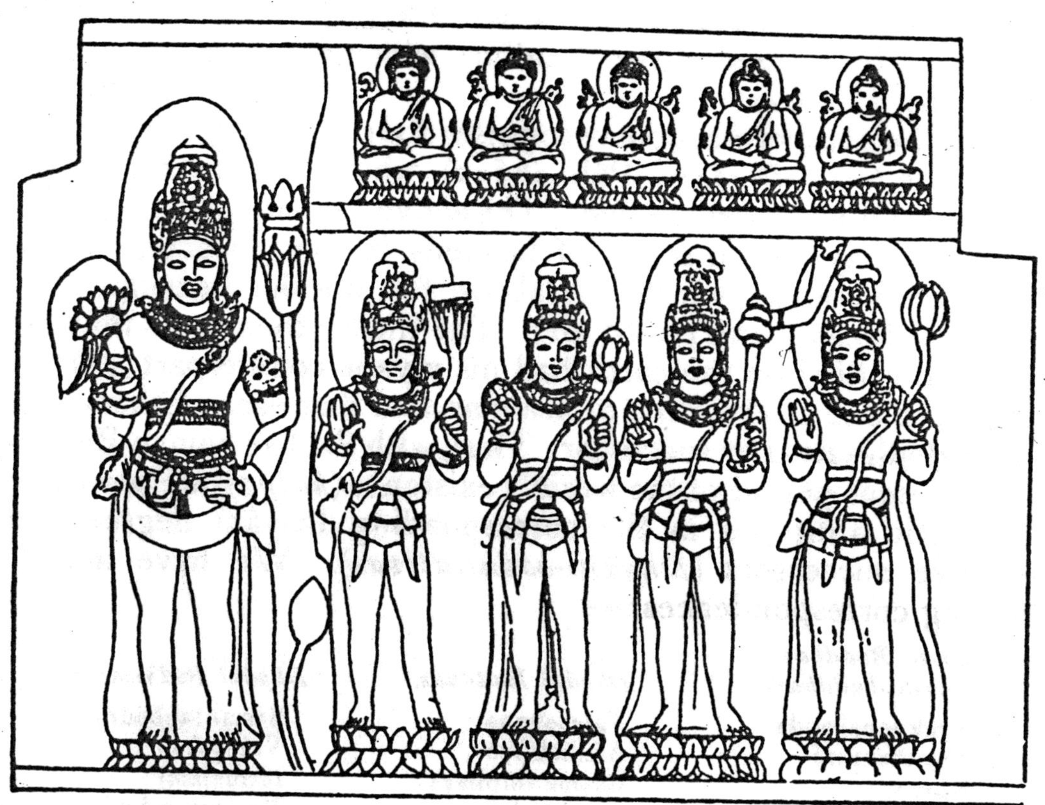

144. Bodhisattvas on the right side of the sanctum in Tîn Thâl. Burgess, *Rep. on Elura Cave Temp., Ar. Sur. W. Ind.* vol. V, pl. xx, 1.

buddhas—all having here the *dhyânamudrâ* (the hands laid one upon another in the lap); though if they represent Dhyânibuddhas other *mudrâs* are usually assigned to each, except Amitâbha. Beneath we see five Bodhisattvas in the usual royal garb as in Gandhâra—only more markedly Hindu; they bear lotus flowers, some with special symbols over them, and one has a small flag. Further, the outmost is represented larger than the others and with a *vajra* over the flower he holds: whether he represents Vajrapâ*n*i or Mahâsthânaprâpta has perhaps yet to be decided. So in the case of ill. 145, in which eight Bodhisattvas are grouped seated round the Buddha,[1] we might naturally suppose that Padmapâ*n*i with the lotus flower, and the little Amitâbha figure in the hair, is the one

[1] *Ar. Sur. W. Ind.* vol. V, pp. 16f. Bunyiu Nanjio was of opinion that the eight here figured are the Hachi-dai-chaku-shi or "eight great principal sons" [of Buddha], and reading from left to right he made the upper row Durgatipariśodhana, Âkâśagarbha, and Kshitigarbha; the lower three—Maitreya, Avalokiteśvara, and Mañjuśrî; with Samantabhadra on the left and Mahâsthânaprâpta to the right of the central figure. With these figures and others at Elura, compare those represented in Groneman, *Tjandi Parambânan op Midden-Java*, pll. xlix-lviii.—J.B.

on the left, and Vajrapâ*n*i is he with the lotus flower and thunderbolt over it.

This is the beginning of a purely formal distinction between figures which are always the same and all based on the same fundamental type—the seated figures gradually predominating very largely. With the varied arrangements of the fingers,—along with the colour of the body and of the garments changed by painting—other names always appear; and in this way an endless and altogether monotonous pantheon arises, with vague, merely allegorical names, and constant change of attributes. Now, as it was considered a salutary act of the best kind to represent as many Buddha figures as possible, all artistic activity naturally decayed, and after a time there were only reproductions of the established type that were more or less good, and more or less influenced by the native style. Rows of Buddha figures were employed in the decoration of temple façades, whole rocks were turned into terrace-reliefs filled with Buddhas, and caves filled with thousands of Buddha statues of all sizes.[1]

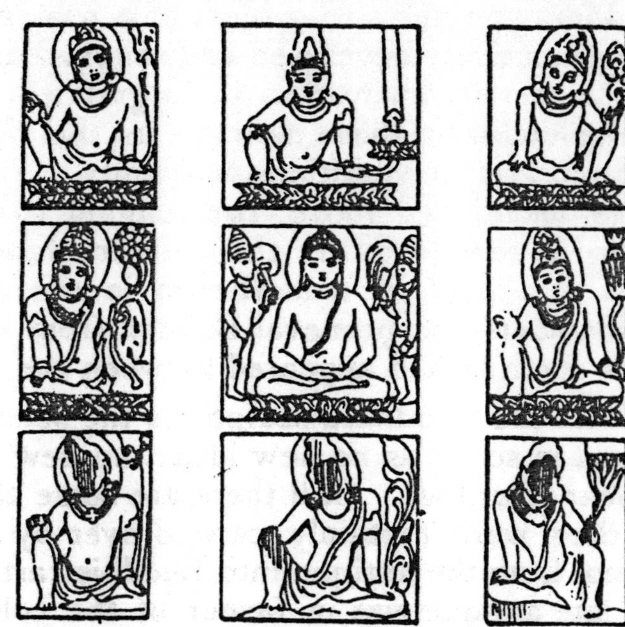

145. **Wall-sculpture** in the Tin Thâl (Elurâ). Burgess, *Report on the Elurâ Cave Temples, Ar. Sur. W. Ind.* vol. V, pl. xix, 6.

We now return to what was said in the first chapter. The Hindu idea of the world recognises man, that is the individual, only as a link in a chain of incarnations. These incarnations are phases of metempsychosis (*Sansâra*). They are completed in world ages which originate, flourish, deteriorate, and vanish; upon which new ones arise to be annihilated in their turn. For every period there are Buddhas; they appear as emanations from countless Buddhas of the meditative spheres—Dhyânibuddhas. In contrast to this is the western idea of constant progress, of constant improvement, which leaves the powers of the individual free to act, while the sum of the energy of the individualities forms an effective

[1] I would refer to the Pegu Caves,—R. C. Temple's *Notes on Antiquities in Ramaññadesa* (in *Ind. Ant.* vol. XXII, pp. 327ff.), pll. iv-vii. From these caves the Royal Museum, Berlin, possesses more than a hundred figures of Buddha. "In Wu-t'ai-shan, in the province of Shan-hsi in North China, the Yung-kang-ssu temple contains 10,000 small tablets with representations of Maitreya. In Ch'an-fo-ssu near Pekin, I have seen 1,000 beautifully carved reliefs of Amitâyus the god of longevity."—Pander in *Zeitschr. f. Ethnologie*, Bd. XXI (1889), S. 49.

counterpoise to occasional retrogression and relapses into barbarism. It is quite in keeping with the character of the Indian idea of the world that the image, the picture of the founder of the religion is reduplicated to infinity and so loses its individuality. The Buddha-type, the sole subject of a somewhat statuary kind, which was tentatively developed and canonised, is treated decoratively in the facade ornamentation of magnificent temples. In relation to the splendour of these monuments, this figure of the one great man is again lost in repetitions to infinity.

As mentioned above, the religion had struggled through this phase in another form: the counterbalancing element was the return to a kind of monotheism in the shape of the doctrine of Âdibuddha—the primeval Buddha, from which all others emanated. This doctrine had appeared between the 12th and 13th centuries.

With the Gândhâra sculptures the second period of Buddhist art closed in so far as no new ideas, no new principles of composition appear after that. Still there are some things we may point out, as they were certainly carried over by means of the Gândhâra school from the antique into Buddhist art. It is well known that the late antique was in favour of the colossal; Buddhist art likewise has the colossal, and, indeed, such are the favourite figures: Buddhas in teaching, standing, recumbent form (passing into Nirvâ*n*a), and also the statue of Maitreya. It is only necessary to recall the colossal statues at Bâmiyân, made famous by Ritter, to indicate how this form of representation has been adopted in Buddhist art.[1]

Another artistic feature, which appears even in the more modern Gândhâra sculptures, must, at least, be briefly mentioned,—though it is difficult on the basis of the present materials to explain it fully. This is the lotus flower as a seat, or a kind of pedestal of two lotuses under the feet of the upright Buddha. This earlier form, which in the more ancient (Indian) art belonged only to the goddess Sirî, seems to have been further developed in the Gândhâra school on the basis of Indian influence. In the case of standing figures it was possibly an illustration of flowery poetical epithets, "lotus-footed," and such like; in the case of sitting figures, the representation perhaps had reference to the meditative attitude called

[1] Ritter, *Die Stûpas oder die Architektonischen Denkmale an der Indo-Baktr. Königstr. u. d. Colosse von Bamiyan*, pp. 24f. Hyde (1700) is perhaps the first European to call attention to these colossi, in *Hist. Relig. vet. Pers.* p.132. Conf. Kaye in *Proc. R. Geog. Soc.* vol. I (1879) pp. 248ff.; and my note in Beal's *Si-yu-ki*, vol. I, p. 51, n. 175. There is a large recumbent figure at Aja*n*ta, Cave XXVI,—*Cave Temples*, p. 344. The Jainas also erect colossal statues; conf. *Ind. Ant.* vol. II, pp. 129f., 353f., and vol. V, p. 36.—J.B.

Conf. also on Bâmiyân, M. G. Talbot in *J. R. As. Soc.*. N.S., vol. XVIII, pp. 323ff.; other notes from the Chinese pilgrim by Kern, *Buddhismus*, Bd. II, pp. 212ff. The Maitreya colossus at Yung-ho-kung—*Veröffentl. Mus. Völk. Berlin*, Bd. I, 2/3, S. 77; in Lhasa, Waddell, *Buddh. of Tibet*, pp. 320f., 355; Graham Sandberg, *Handbk. of Colloquial Tibetan* (Calc. 1894), p.197; to these belong the Miryek (*i.e.* Maitreya) figures of Korea,—*J. R. As. Soc.* N.S. vol. XIX, pp. 555-7; the recumbent Buddha colossus, *Ind. Ant.* vol. XXII, pp. 127ff., pll. xvii, &c.

"lotus-seat" (*padmâsana*). At any rate, the Buddha standing on lotus flowers appears even at Amarâvatî (conf. p. 175) and in the ecclesiastical art of the present day it has become quite a common feature (conf. ill. 82, 85, 123, 124, 140, 141).

Two Bodhisattvas of the later pantheon have a distinctly individual character and thus have afforded material for some fine works which may be mentioned as showing, on the one hand, what was the chief ideal after which Buddhist art strove, and on the other, as clearly evidencing the extraordinary persistency of the Hellenic ideal of Buddha. They are the Bodhisattvas Mañjusrî and Padmapâni already mentioned, and which at a later date were so extraordinarily richly developed.

Mañjusrî, whose name means something like "having a lovely brilliance," may possibly have been a real personage, namely, the founder of civilization in Nepâl. In the system of the northern school he appears as the representative of that transcendental wisdom which is the aim of the Mahâyâna school.

His attributes are the sword "of knowledge," which he wields with his right hand to cleave the clouds of mental darkness (*andhakâra*), and in the left hand he has a book, which usually rests upon a lotus flower.

The relief in the Berlin Museum of a Mañjusrî from Java, according to the inscription on it, was made by Âdityavarmâ in the year 1265 *S*aka (*i.e.* A.D. 1343) and is a fine specimen of modern Buddhist sculpture (ill. 146).[1]

The Bodhisattva is sitting on a great lotus flower and leaning against a broad cushion; his legs are drawn up and crossed in the Indian fashion; and he is in rich dress. He wears a highly ornamented crown; ear-rings with pendent chains (conf. the ear-ornaments of the Bodhisattva figure from Gandhâra in ill. 131); neck and breast chains, chain girdle, upper and lower bracelets, finger and toe rings. From behind the crown hang twisted locks of hair. The upper garment lies in a narrow band about the breast, from the left shoulder to the right side. The under garment clings close and smoothly to the legs, and is richly adorned with very interesting figures (conf. ill. 33), the body is well shaped, full, delicate; the breast and ribs are rounded and unmarked by bones or muscles. The feet unused to walking, the soles are soft-like and pressed down to an almost impossible degree. The body in the main is full of charming, almost womanly beauty, and has a look of unnatural development, which does not arise from the physical energy of the being represented. The raised arm only holds the sword aloft, but does not strike—it only serves to hold the attribute. The whole style of the face shows in great purity the Buddha-type mentioned before (p. 160ff.); in it the forms of the Gândhâra school are quite recognisable. The appearance of meditative re-

[1] For the curious history of this sculpture, see *Zeitsch. d. Deutsch. Morgenl.* Bd. XVIII (1864), Ss. 494-505.

pose is secured by the nearly-closed eyes, the head pressed back on the nape of the neck, so that the very artificially formed, fleshy neck stands out prominently. The mouth is large but not broad, the under lip full, the upper puckered up at the corners almost to

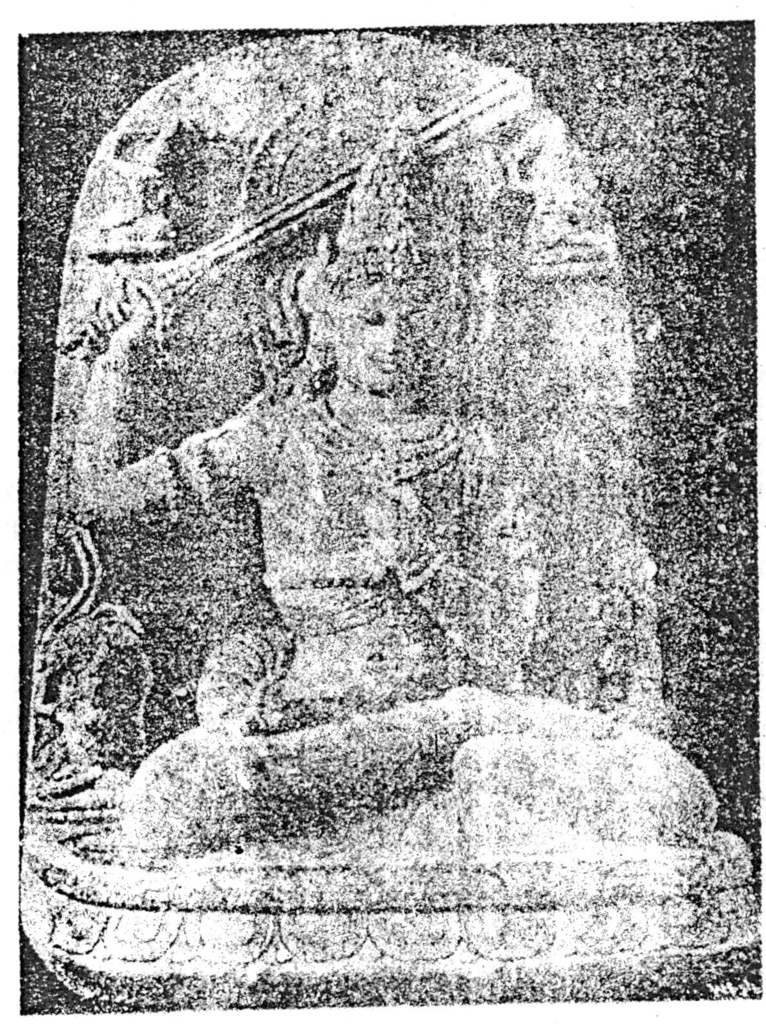

146. OLD JAVANESE RELIEF OF MAÑJUŚRÎ BODHISATTVA.
Inscribed with the date 1265 Śaka : 1343 A.D. Original in Berlin Mus.

a smile : but the smile seems to be overcome and perfect rest to be attained.

The head is best characterised by the distinctive marks of the fourth and highest degree of meditation (*dhyâna*). According to the ideas of the southern church, the different Dhyânas are as follows :—

1. The first Dhyâna is a state of joy and happiness which have arisen from a life of solitude, yet full of contemplation and enquiry, after the ascetic is freed from all sensuality and fault.

2. The second Dhyâna-degree is a state of joy and happiness, which have arisen from deep peace of mind without contemplation and investigation, both of which are overcome: it is the bringing to rest of thought—the mastery of contemplation.

3. The third Dhyâna-degree is the state in which he becomes patient through joy and the uprooting of every passion,—glad and conscious of the joy which announces "the worthy one," the arhat: patient, remembering, happy.

4. The fourth degree of Dhyâna is perfect equanimity and remembrance, without care and without joy, after the previous joy and care have ceased through the putting aside of that which gives joy, and after the putting aside of that which brings care.[1]

The lotus flowers upon which (in modern Tibetan representations) the book usually rests are employed for the decoration of the background. The tasteful arrangement of the leaves and buds, which are represented artistically and with great understanding of Nature, indicates the ancient Indian manner (conf p. 19f.): The book, in the usual form of palm-leaf manuscripts, tied round with a string, is held in the left hand. Four smaller figures of Mañjusrî, very much resembling the principal one, surround it,—above and below, right and left. From analogy with Tibetan pictures, these appear to be intended for other forms of the Bodhisattva. In this way that sort of arrangement is obtained which we have already noted in the Gândhâra reliefs (conf. pp. 130f.) and which is preserved in the paintings of the northern school. On a Tibetan picture the accessory figures would vary—in respect of the five sacred colours—with the character of the principal subject; and as Mañjusrî is mostly represented as red, they remain white, yellow, green and blue.[2] With the modern Tibetan painters these colours must bear a certain proportion to each other on the pictures: above all, the blue (wrathful) forms of the deities must not predominate.

Mañjusrî, as we have seen, may be regarded, to a certain extent, as the personification of meditation.

P a d m a p â *n* i,—"the all-pitying one,"—is an emanation of Amitâbha: having appeared on earth from a lotus flower for the deliverance of mankind, he labours to do away with all suffering and all sorrow in all the domain of creation, so that hell is emptied.[3] Then he returns to his throne, but soon again he sees misery and hell being filled once more. Out of grief his head bursts, &c.

Through the co-ordination of this personage with Kuan-yin, the Chinese goddess of pity, an interesting type has been formed. I do not refer to the purely Chinese (female) representations of this Bodhisattva, nor of the widespread eleven-headed ones, but of a

[1] But see also Childers, *Pâli Dictionary*, s.v. "jhânam"; Alabaster, *Wheel of the Law*, pp. 192-5; Sp. Hardy, *Legends and Theories*, pp. 178-180.—J. B.

[2] *Veröffentl. aus dem. Kgl. Mus. f. Völkerk. Berlin.* Bd. I, H. 2/3, S, 75, 145.

[3] See the interesting parallel between the early chapters of the *Kâranda-Vyûha* and the apocryphal *Gospel of Nicodemus*, by Prof. Cowell, *Jour. Philol.* vol. VI (1876), pp. 222-31, *Ind. Ant.* vol. VIII, pp. 249-53.—J.B.

type which, though derived from Indian forms, is entirely strange to the canon. So represented, the Bodhisattva sits with the right foot drawn up; his right hand rests with the elbow on the right

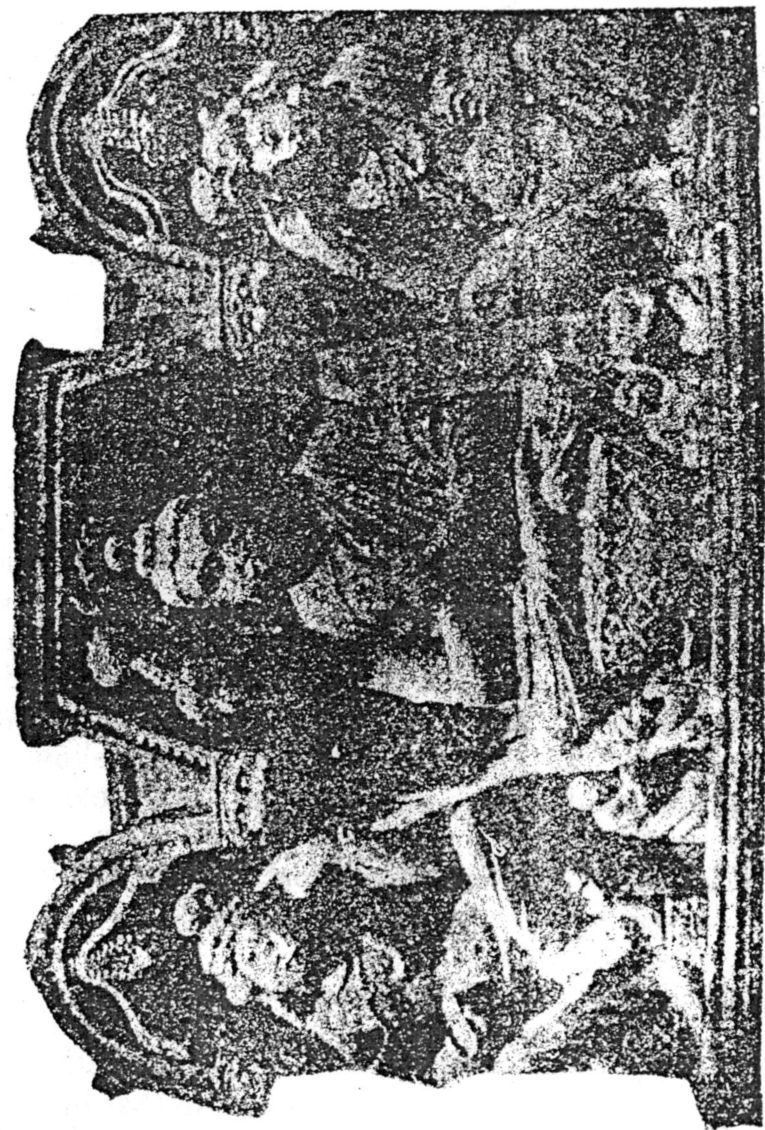

147. BUDDHA ON THE LOTUS-THRONE, WITH ATTENDANT BODHISATTVAS. From Loriyân Tangai. In Calcutta Museum.

knee, and the head is sunk sorrowfully on the hand, the left hand rests carelessly on the left leg which hangs down. The ornaments and costume, type of the head, &c., continued Indian.[1]

Among the Loriyân Tangai sculptures at Calcutta there is a relief that suggests comparison with such a figure. It is on a slab measuring 22 inches in length and 16 inches high (ill. 147). Buddha,

[1] Conf. Grünwedel, *Myth. d. Buddh. in Tibet*, &c., S. 27, Abb. 22.

with features of a somewhat uncommon type, is seated in the centre, on a *padmâsana* or lotus throne, in the attitude of teaching; a flowering plant overshadows him; and above is a canopy of three compartments, of which the two side ones have pointed arches; the joinings and ends of the three roofs are finished with tiger heads; and in each arch, over the head of its occupant, hangs a bunch of pearls or gems. The lotus on which Buddha sits is supported by two small figures rising out of the earth; in the one on the proper right we might be tempted to recognise Vajrapâ*n*i, but the turban, the covered breast, and roundish or conch-shaped object in his right hand is not in favour of this. A roundish object also lies on the seat in front of Buddha's left knee. The corresponding figure on the other side—with moustache, round object in one hand, and mace (?) in the other—is not identified. Behind the first a shaven-headed monk kneels in adoration; behind the other, the figure appears to be a female.

At each side of the central figure sits a Bodhisattva; that on the proper right probably Mañjuśrî (he "of glorious beauty") holding in his hand the book of Buddha's teaching; and the other attendant is Avalokiteśvara, or Padmapâ*n*i, with a flower in his left hand. Both these figures are very much in the pose of the Japanese figure just referred to.

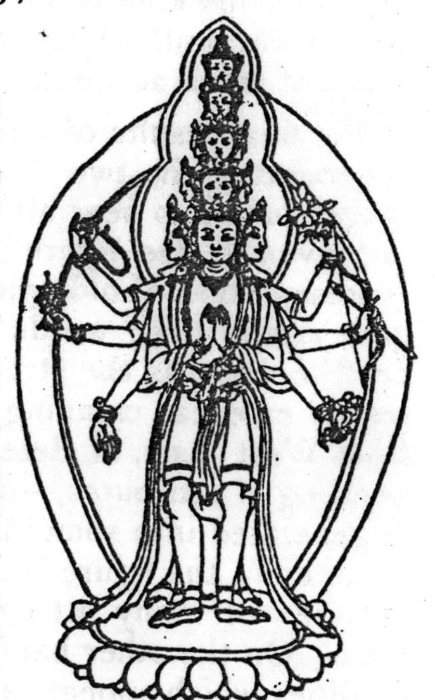

148. Avalokiteśvara.
A form of Padmapâ*n*i; from a Nepalese drawing.

The eleven-headed standing form of Avalokiteśvara is very frequent in Nepâl, Tibet, and Japan, and it occurs at an early date in the Ka*n*heri Buddhist cave temples, as well as among the ruins of Nakon Thom in Kambodia. In this form, as in others, he is represented with four or more arms,—with the upper right hand he holds up a rosary, and with the left a long-stemmed lotus flower (ill. 148). The uppermost head is regarded as that of Amitâbha, who is represented as his spiritual origin; the others are arranged above one another, in threes, as in the Hindû Trimurti, and either the lowest head is single, or the tenth counting upwards.[1] In representations with only one head, the figure of Amitâbha is placed as a crest on the *mukuta* or crown.

A favourite relief is what may be called the Litany of Avalokiteśvara or Padmapâ*n*i. It appears in the Bauddha caves at Elura, at Aurangâbâd, at Ka*n*heri, and both in sculpture and painting at Aja*n*tâ. In these scenes the Bodhisattva is represented standing on a lotus and holding the rosary in his right hand and a lotus stem

[1] *Cave Temples*, p. 357, and pl. lv; *Notes on Ajanta*, &c., p. 100 and pl. xxiv. 11; *Histoire de l'Art du Japon* (Paris, 1900), pll. xvii, xli, p. 911, &c.

in the left; at each side of the panel are representations of suppliants in danger from enraged elephants, from lions, snakes, fire and shipwreck, from murder, captivity, death, &c.,—from which Padmapâ*n*i delivers them. These scenes, taken in connexion with the late Mr. Beal's translation from Chinese of the "Confessional service of the great compassionate Kuan-yin," are of much interest, and show that at a date before the eighth century the character of this Bodhisattva must have been fully defined.[1] In other Ka*n*heri sculptures he is attended by a female or Târâ at each side; whether this is connected with the worship of these goddesses as female counterparts of Avalokite*s*vara, has not been investigated.

The figures of Mañju*s*rî and Padmapâ*n*î have been dwelt upon as showing how nearly northern Buddhist art approached mere personification. The purely spiritual element so entirely predominates that the human figure has become a mere form. But in the case of these two Bodhisattvas there remains at least a trace of personality, which in other representations--about which something must be said—is completely extinguished. The oldest personification of this kind is the goddess of transcendental knowledge—Prajñâ Pâramitâ (Tib. Sher-p'yin-ma), which, in style, as in worship, is not of much account.[2]

The final results of this multiplication of forms show a notable degeneration in two directions. On the one hand the limbs no longer suffice to bear all the attributes; several arms, several heads are given to the figure: it is reduplicated in itself. The literal representation of old epithets of strength and splendour probably gave rise to this: words like *Sahasrabâhu*, "the thousand-armed," *i.e.* "he who has the strength of thousands," and so on, received a purely external meaning. The ancient Indian method, borrowed from West Asia, of determining simple human forms by the appending of attributes,—in itself an altogether inartistic method,—degenerated into something repellant. Therewith real art comes to an end: the figure becomes a mere hieroglyph, the decking out with few or many attributes gives it the name of some religious idea. On the other hand, the chief figures are relieved of certain qualities which appear as particular Bodhisattvas—male and female. One of these goddesses of the latest Buddhism is "the victorious goddess of the skull-protuberance"—Ush*n*îshavijayâ[3]—"having the intelligence of the most splendid perfect one."

[1] See *Ar. Sur. W. Ind.* vol. III, pp. 75, 76, and pl. liii; vol. IV, p. 51, and pl. xxxiii, 3; *Cave Temples*, p. 357 and pl. lv. 1; *Notes on Ajanta*, &c., p. 42; and, for the "Confessional Service," *J. R. A. S.* N.S. vol. II (1866), pp. 403-25; Grünwedel, *Mythol. des Buddh. in Tibet u. Mongol.* S. 65; Waddell, *Lamaism*, pp. 15, 357.—J. B.

[2] Other mere personifications of early date are Dharma (Buddha's teaching) and Saṅgha (the assembly of monks, the "church"), the goddess of the six syllables (*om ma*n*i padme hû*m**), &c. Conf. also the beautiful figure of an old Javanese Prajñâpâramitâ in *Bijdragen tot de Taal-Land-en Volkenkunde van Nederl. Indië.* 6e Volgr. Dl. VIII (C. M. Pleyte, *Bijd. tot de kennis van het Mahâyâna op Java*), fig. 1.

[3] Tib. *g*Tsug-tor-*r*nam-par-*r*gyal-ma. See above p. 162. Also Grünwedel, *Mythol. des Buddh. in Tibet*, &c., Ss. 138, 148, 151.

As we have seen, the deities, Bodhisattvas, and Buddhas were represented in Gandhâra in groups of threes, fives, eights,—and it seems as though this arrangement had some influence on their attributes: analogies of composition certainly exist.

The illustration No. 121 from Loriyân Tangai, in the Calcutta Museum, is an example of a triad group. The relief is 15 inches broad and presents Buddha upon the *padmâsana* or lotus-seat with a standing Bodhisattva on each side. These can hardly, however, be directly related to the philosophical doctrine of the Ratnatraya as represented by Dharma, Buddha, and Sa*m*gha,—for these figures are not very prevalent in Nepâl, Tibet, &c. But they are closely connected with the popular worship of the three statues of "the past, present, and future Buddhas" represented by *S*âkyamuni with Avalokite*s*vara and Maitreya, and with the other triad of Amitâbha or Amitâyus with Avalokite*s*vara on his left hand and Mahâsthâma on his right. This latter, at least, is an early Mahâyâna arrangement since it is represented in the *Amitâyur-dhyâna Sûtra*.[1]

The pantheon of the northern school of Buddhism in Tibet, China, and Japan, is the most gigantic in the world, but it is infinitely monotonous. Hardly a single figure shows real life. It is interesting to note how this endless system of models, originated in Tibet, China, and Japan, which, with slight variations of hand-postures, attributes, and colours, is always increasing. It arose from the representation of the monk in China and Japan; in Tibet from the portrait of the hierarch. In the former, the representations of monks, which doubtless began with an ideal portrait of the chief disciples (Sthaviras) and of the ancient magicians, degenerated into caricatures; but in Tibet the real portrait has been developed from the ideal. The Bodhisattvas are always incarnated in the hierarchs of Tibet: Padmapâ*n*i is reborn in the Dalai Lama, &c.; but the Bodhisattvas are eternally the same. The different stages of incarnation of the saints, however, present variations in their individuality. The portrait of the grand Lama presents an interesting reaction from the artificial rendering of the regions of the gods. The divine in earthly form, in many cases, breaks through in an exquisite way: the figure remains artificial and does not depart from the canon; but the heads of these hierarchs, on the bronzes and miniatures of the ecclesiastical art, are mostly of real artistic value.

Of the many good examples of this class which the Berlin Royal Museum possesses is the richly-gilt bronze of the spiritual Prince of Tra-shi-lhum-bo (*b*Kra-shis-*l*hun-po) Pal-dän-ye-she (*d*Pal-*l*dan-ye-shes), who died in China in 1779 (conf. ill. 149). The portrait of this interesting man is remarkably fresh and faithful. In

[1] See *Sac. B. E.* vol. XLIX, pt. ii, pp. 176, 180ff. A quite similar relief is represented in *Amarâvati and Jaggayyapeta Stûpas*, p. 12. Mahâsthâma is, not improbably, a Mahâyâna deification or analogue of Maudgalyâyana, the right hand disciple of Gautama. Amitâyus is the *Sambhogakâya* or reflex spirituality of Amitâbha, the corresponding *Manushi Buddha* being *S*âkyamuni; his Bodhisattva is Padmapâ*n*i.—J.B.

the coarsely executed but beautifully arranged garment the last offshoots of the Gândhâra school are noticeable. It is in keeping with the political power of the Tibetan hierarchy that the representations of the Grand Lamas should take the first place among the objects to

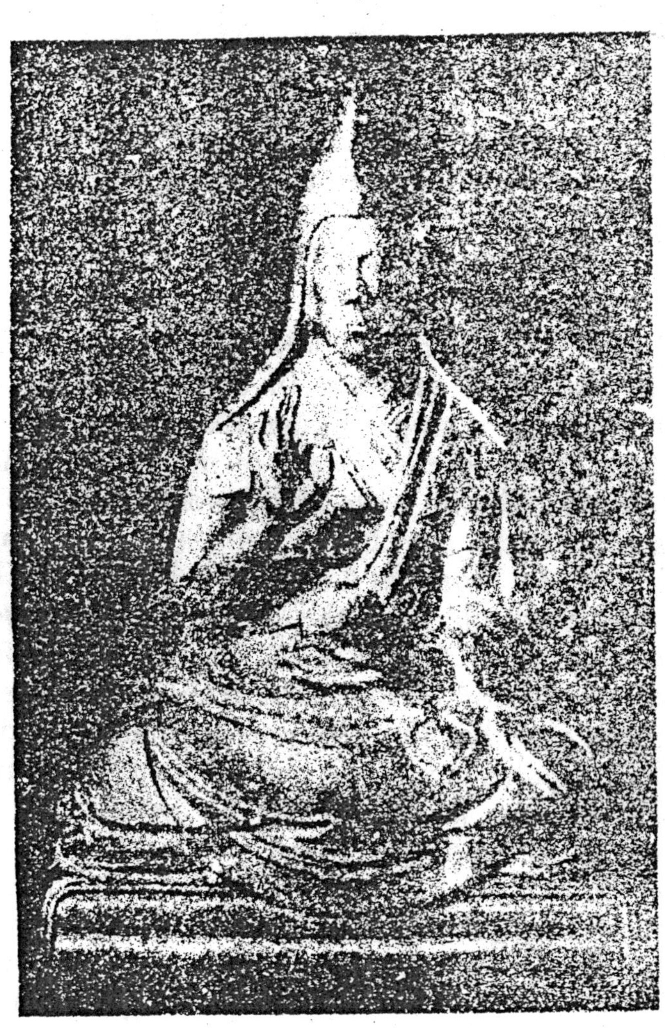

149. THE GRAND LAMA OF TRA-SHI-LHUM-BO PAL-DAN-YE-SHE (*b*Pal-*l*danoye-shes) 1737-1779). Gilt bronze from Tibet. The alms-bowl in the left hand is of lapis lazuli. Height 5½ inches. Original in Berlin Museum.

be venerated: the rudeness and persistent religiousness of the people has preserved this from the fate which befell it in China and Japan, forming a brilliant epoch—the caricatures of monks.

The individual element appearing in the portraits of the Lamas surpasses Indian art conditions: it points to the attainments in culture of the people of high Asia. And if we may correctly recognise the Issidones[1] of Herodotos as the people of Tibet, then the modern

[1] Tomaschek, *Aristeas von Proikonnesos*, in *Ab. d. k. k. Ak, der Wissensch. in Wien*, h. phil. Cl., Bd. CVI (1888), pp. 715f., 718f.

Buddhist cult supplies a true chart of the progress of culture among these high-Asian people, whose lot was connected in so remarkable a way with the Hindûs from the time when the Greeks obtained correct information about India. On the Lamaist altars, beside the relics of a barbarian stage—trumpets of human thigh bones, votive bowls of skulls, tambours of children's skulls—appear Buddha pictures in which traces of late antique artistic elements, still strongly inspiring, have a mystic existence; but beside these are the ideal portraits of the old Indian pa*n*d*its and their successors the Lamas, with their intelligent—or, if we might rather say,—crafty faces. It we bear in mind, however, that they were the representatives of culture in those barbaric lands, that they were able to subdue and tame for ever the Mongols, the fiercest conquerors and warriors in the world, and that too without a religious war,—we can only rejoice that these valuable portraits, in modified antique forms, have been handed down.

The application and conversion of old sacred types to caricatures has appropriated even old compositions. Among these, as an instance, is the representation of the Nirvâ*n*a scene. The sketch

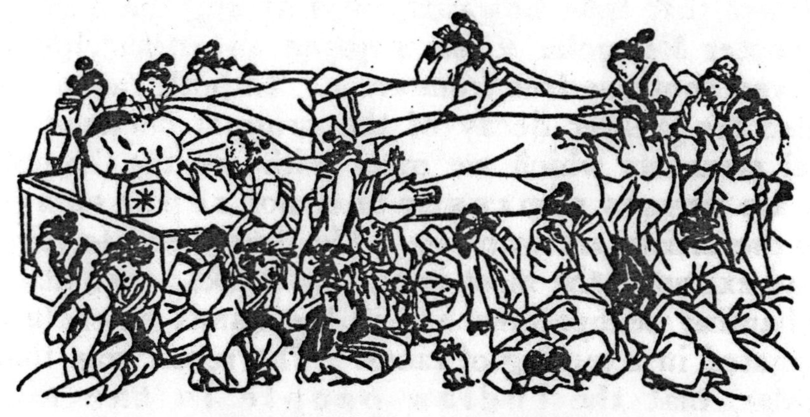

150. **Death of a worldling.**
From a Japanese coloured print; conf. Nos. 70-74.
Original in Berlin Museum.

(ill. 150), from a Japanese picture, represents the death of a worldling in this manner. His numerous lady friends, and even a small lapdog, give free expression to their grief over the death of the "gentleman," who, larger than them all, lies before them.

It may be asked what is the use of all the æsthetic debate about "Japanese colour printing" so long as the chief facts are unknown to us, so long as we are not in a position to understand the wit—which here, fortunately, we do.

With reference to the formally conserved antique elements, outside India,—as was already noted in connexion with Indian ornaments,—a noteworthy phenomenon occurs: In India, foreign forms get merged in national ones; metamorphosed in all sorts of ways, they have held a long and highly varied existence, carried down into the Brahmanic art of the Middle Ages; while in lands outside India, the canon developed from the Gândhâra sculptures is more closely conserved. We need only note the markedly antique elements still visible in the Javanese Buddha and Bodhisattva heads (ill. 115 and 146) compared with the Gândhâra types (ill. 110, 111), or the Chino-Japanese arrangement of the garments (ill. 120, 125). The whole phenomenon is connected with language which, I believe, gave rise to the learned and hierarchical character of the northern monastic system. The southern school adhered to the Pâli language, because the current Prâk*ri*ta dialects of India proper were mutually intelligible enough, and the development of culture was common to all. Transitions between the Prâk*ri*ts existed just as certainly as between the modern idioms of Aryan origin in northern India. But the people of the Panjâb had not followed the Brahmanic development (conf. above p.7), and even if in some lands under the Indo-Skythian rule, Aryan dialects were spoken, they undoubtedly became widely different. To them came the entirely allophylian tribes of the Indo-Skythian kingdom—Hellenes, Yueh-chis, the tribes of Dardistân, Kashmîr, Persians, Turks from the east, etc. For this reason, Sanskrit, the language of the learned in the north, was chosen at Jâlandhara for the language of the sacred texts. From that time onwards, even among the Lamas of Tibet and of remoter Mongolia, it has enjoyed an artistic life, which did not, however, continue free from error. In both cases the classical form veiled the greater decay of the original doctrine. The only individual elements which we meet with are the Lama portraits. But they are persons represented, not representers. The names of the artists are wanting. The forms are foreign: foreign people had executed the most important works; even at the present day mechanical occupations are in the hands of exclusive castes that originated in a mixing of races. The result was that art was not popular, that the Indian people in the mass continued indifferent to such matters. The peasant class, the core of Hinduism, continued in its primitive condition. Among primitive peoples, he who can carve a figure is by virtue of that fact a magician. What must have been the effect when the foreign artist covered buildings of quite a novel sort with decoration in a fixed style,—of hybrid creatures, etc., or found means to bring the image of the universally venerated Emancipator down from heaven! This explains why the Tibetan historian Târanâtha speaks of the ancient buildings as having been erected by Yakshas (fairies) and Nâgas (snake-demons). These names conceal those of the foreign artists. A similar state of things, founded on analogous facts, arose in the German middle ages. The builders of the first cathedrals were, for the most part, foreigners; the people regarded them as superhuman—as in league with the Evil One. More than one architectural or plastic monument of the early middle ages has received a traditional explanation which, apart from the humorous element, reminds us of the Jâtaka fable related above. The fact that Greek architectural anecdotes were also directly received, belongs to literary history.

An Indian element which soon appears is, as we have noted, the r e p e t i t i o n o f t h e s a m e f o r m s ; it is parallel with the like phenomenon in the texts; the mystic magical power of the ritual text with its repetitions,—always regarded as of great importance in India,—led to the general disintegration in later Buddhist literature. The repetitions of the motifs brought about the dissolution also of Buddhist art.

Naturally, it was not possible to shake off fixed, influential attributes and to express the character of a mythological being by a corresponding representation of the body, such as Athens attained to when at the height of its glory. Still attempts at it are not wanting; India was not so distant from it in its warm appreciation of Nature. If we consider the representations of the Nâgas, and especially the Nâgas as the reliefs at Amarâvatî (ill. 8) and the paintings of Ajan*t*â (conf. Griffith, *Ajantâ*, vol. I, pl. 12) show them to us, we cannot fail to see in the excessively twisted bodies attempts to impart to them the characteristic of the body of the snake. In spite of this, the old attribute—a snake's hood on the neck—was naturally not to be omitted.

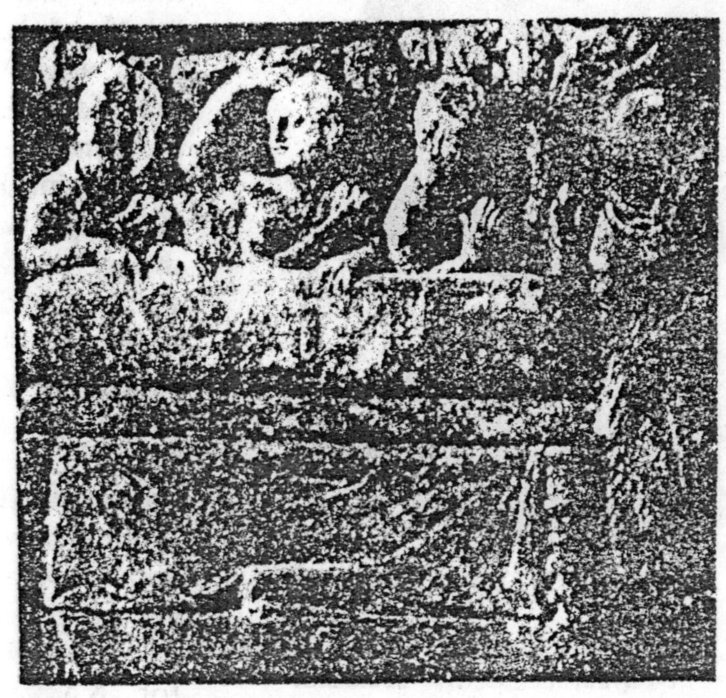

151. The Coffin of Gautama.
From a stûpa at Nalâ near Sanghâo, excavated by Major Cole, 1883.
From a photograph.

In conclusion, we may append two or three further illustrations which differ somewhat from those already given.

Notice has already been directed (pp. 113, 119, 122) to a figure which appears at the feet of the dying sage in most of the representations (ill. 70–77). Since these pages were printed off, I have come upon a photograph of a relief (ill. 151) from a stûpa at Nalâ near Sanghâo.[1] It measures 13 inches in length by 11½ high, and is quite a unique representation. The trees behind and the figure on the right with the bed on which it rests, identify the box, with three monks beyond it, as the coffin of Buddha. And, the figure at the foot, being saluted by one of the monks, as if he had just arrived, seems to support the conjecture already made, that this may be Mahâ-Kâ*s*yapa, before whose arrival it was found impossible to remove the corpse for cremation.[2] This Kâ*s*yapa was a Brâhma*n*a of Magadha or Bihâr, and the chief survivor of the eighty principal disciples or *Sthaviras*. On his arrival at Ku*s*inârâ, where Gautama died, having bared his right shoulder,—it is said the corpse put the feet out from the wrappings for Kâ*s*yapa to worship; other versions say he changed the garments that enshrouded the body for others from his own store, and having replaced the cover of the coffin, the fire burst forth from the pile and consumed the

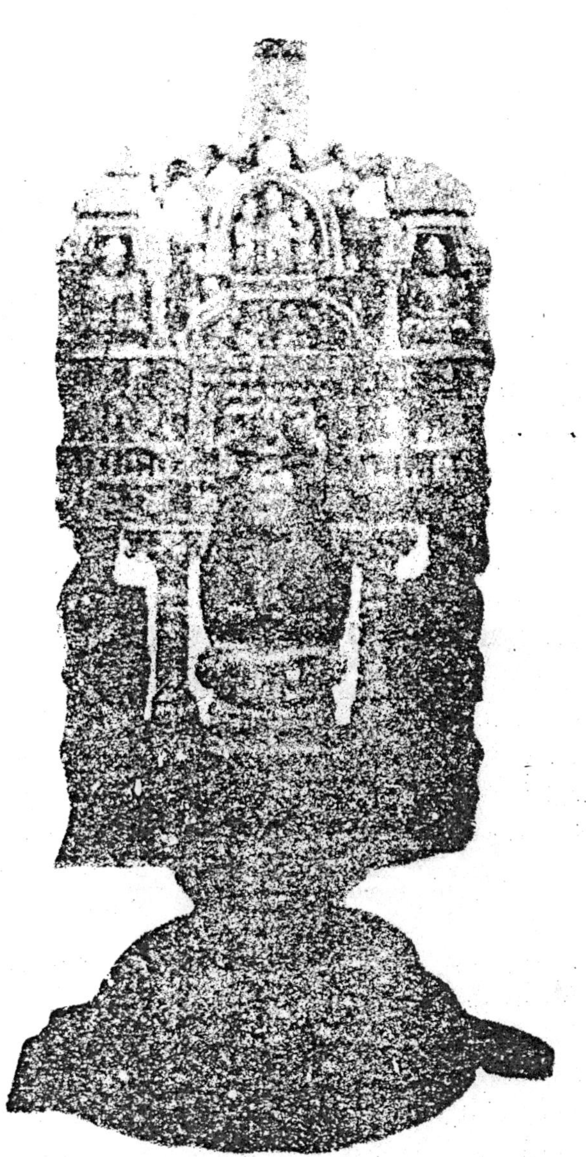

152. MODEL SHRINE from Loriyân Tangai, in Swât district. Original in Calcutta Museum.

[1] "Sent to Lahor Museum, Dec. 1883,—No. 31-10 in Major Cole's Catalogue." This is all the information I have found respecting this sculpture.

[2] Conf. S. Hardy, *Man. Budh.* p. 360f.

body.[1] After this, Kâsyapa convened the first Buddhist council for the settlement of the canon; and is reckoned as the first Patriarch. Sâriputra and Maudgalyâyana—the right and left hand *Sthaviras*, —had died before Gautama.

In the museum at Bombay are two representations of the Nirvâna scene from Marjan stûpa near Miyân Khân. The best preserved is on a slab measuring 22 inches by 15, having a broad pilaster at each end. This personage there appears placing his hand against the foot of the figure of Gautama and inclining his head, as if reverencing the dead. This seems to support the probability that Kâsyapa is intended. Vajrapâni stands behind him, holding the *vajra* between his wrist and armpit; the seated figure and tripod appear in front of the bed; and those behind it are Devas with naked busts.

The sculpture represented in ill. 152, came from Loriyân Tangai in the Swât district, and is in the Calcutta Museum. It measures 2 feet 9 inches in height and 15 inches across. As will be noted, it is cut quite through the slab round the central figure. It is a remarkably fine piece of sculpture, and must have been regarded as a sort of altar. The central figure is, of course, the Buddha on the *padmâsana*, in the teaching attitude; his right shoulder and arm are bare, and the robe is very carefully traced out. Over his head is a sort of canopy from which hangs a garland of flowers in a double loop, descending to touch the *ushnîsha*, resembling a *krobylos*, on his head. On each side, supporting the canopy, is a Persepolitan pillar with humped bullocks on their capitals; the base and shaft are only a slightly enriched copy of the pillars we find at Nâsik in the second century A.D. On the architrave above them are animal heads and the Buddhist rail or lattice pattern. Outside the pillars sit two Bodhisattvas—probably the same as in preceding examples. From above the architrave people (or Devas) look down, and over these is a cornice, supporting a small model of a temple at each end, in which sit two Buddhas. The central space is in two tiers,—the lower having two small figures of seated Buddhas and worshippers; the upper, an arched panel, contains a standing Buddha and two companions. Below the main figures is a cornice over a frieze ornamented by little figures carrying a great flower roll, such as is so common at Amarâvatî, with a worshipping figure at each end. The stone fits into a socket in a base covered with a leaf-pattern.[2]

Lastly, from among the many detached pieces of sculpture from the Swât districts, of some of which we have only photographs by Mr. Caddy, while the originals do not seem to have reached the Indian Museum, two more are represented (fig. 153). The measurements are, of course, unknown, but the head of Buddha appears to be of some size, and is a strikingly good piece of workmanship, showing the Gândhâra style of art at about its best. The face is distinctly

[1] Rockhill, *Life of Buddha*, pp. 144, 145.
[2] *Jour. Ind. Art and Industry*, vol. VIII, p. 83.

less Indian than usual, but dignified and calm; the *ushnisha* is again manipulated into a sort of Greek *krobylos*; and the ear-lobes, so

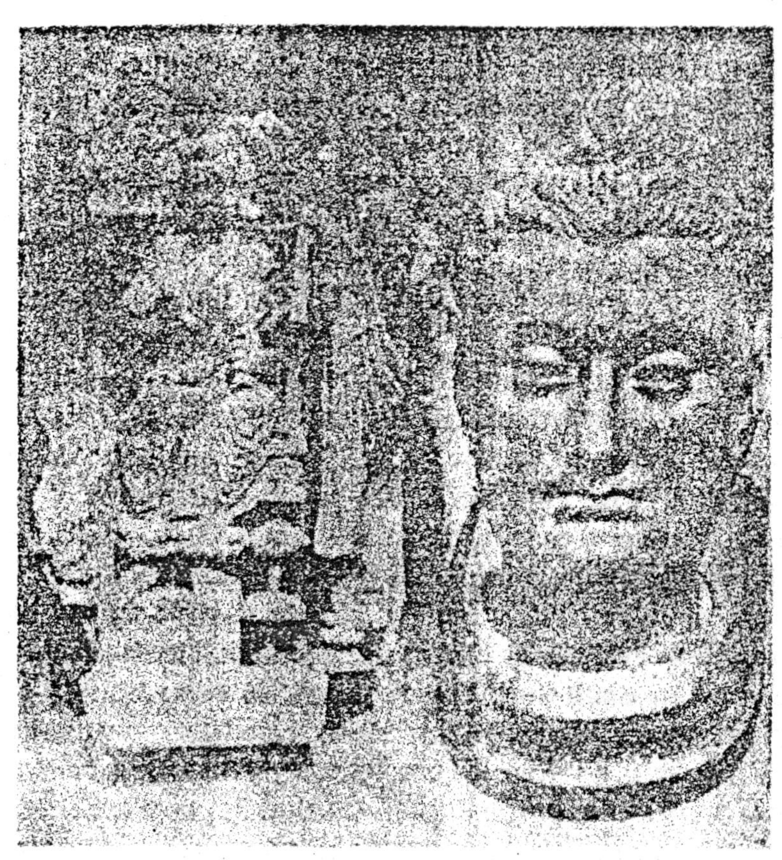

153. Head of Buddha and fragment of sculpture, from Swât. From a photograph.

far as the photograph indicates, are not lengthened downwards in the usual way.[1] It may be compared with the illustrations Nos. 110-119, 121, 122, and 131.—J.B.

The foregoing sketch of the Gândhâra school has been carried as far as is possible with the scanty materials to hand: it is a programme which demands long and continuous work. The last word has not yet been said, for the treatment in detail can only be carried out in India,—and especially in the museums of Lahor, Calcutta, and Peshâwar.

The results of the above investigations may be summed up somewhat as follows:—

1. Talent in sculptural art exists only in a limited degree among the Indian Aryans. The capacity for plastically developing perfect figures is wanting, as is also the feeling for well-proportioned composition. On the other hand a powerful poetic tendency is

[1] *Jour. Ind. Art and Industry*, vol. VIII, p. 87.

evidenced, which, under the influences of tropical nature, readily borrows images from natural life, and, to the detriment of the composition, executes these broadly, idyllically, but with a fine emphasizing of the characteristic features. The gift of observation, sharpened by speculative training, leads to the humourous depicting of situations which very happily show the marked differences between the various classes of the people, and even ventures upon religious representations; but, notwithstanding this, the whole world of ideas remains subject to the religio-philosophic conception. The character of the people wavers between sensuality and pessimism.

2. The Greek influences shown by the art of the A*s*oka period follow in the track of older and very energetic Persian influences. This rôle of intermediary on the part of the Persian kingdom is, in a general way, characterized by Herodotos and Ktesias.

3. West Asian forms—the attribute of the thunderbolt, the so-called orientalizing of animals—afford types for Hindû gods and other mythological beings of the older school. The fabulous Indian animals mentioned by Herodotos, Ktesias, etc., belong to this category (conf. p. 42ff.). The wings of the hybrid animals sometimes appear in action (see pp. 48, 53); sometimes as flames.

4. The Gândhâra school represents a long development which begins with antique (heathen) forms and seems to end with Christian ones. The reliefs preserved are, indeed, for the most part, replicas of old models which are entirely based on Grecian composition laws, as, for example, the Bodhisattva at the gate (p. 98). In respect of style, the Gândhâra school is influenced by the more ancient one; as, for example, in the Nâch girl (p. 111), and Persian pillars (p. 151f.).

5. Hellenic deities in the character of the times of Alexander (*i.e.* local divinities) are traceable in Gandhâra: the god of the gate (p. 95), the earth goddess (p. 98), the gods that look down and which perhaps imply a date (p. 129f.). The following Greek divinities exist latent,—Zeus (p. 91), Gê (p. 100), Paignia (p. 148), Nikê (?) (p. 113). Athenê Promachos is directly represented as a Greek goddess. Apollo served as a pattern for Buddha (p. 164).

6. These Grecian representations have exercised a distinct influence on the texts of the northern school; for example, Vajrapâ*n*i (p. 91f.), and the Mahâpathavî (p. 100). Certain texts (such as the *Lalita Vistara*) are, so to speak, descriptions of reliefs or pictures.

7. The Buddha type, which, in China, passes as that of the king Udayana, reverts indirectly to the Gândhâra type (p. 170).

8. The types of the Gândhâra school (as well as the Grecian mode of composition) are still traceable in the Buddhist ecclesiastical art, as well as in the Buddhist schools of Tibet, China, and Japan.[1]

[1] Palaeologue, *L'art Chinois*, is certainly right as to Chinese art and its so-called mythology, which offers merely schemes without a history and gives no new interpretation to Buddhist elements. The prince in gala costume, stiff and motionless, with the little tablet; the officer (wrestler); the two-sword juggler; and the long-bearded old man in dressing-gown,—represent nearly all the national Chinese types, which always recur.

The iconographical texts of the canonical literature of Tibet, as also the materials accumulated in illustrated Chinese encyclopædias, and certain portions of the Tantra (Sanskrit) literature, will require to be worked, by the aid of the monuments, into a history of types:—in the preceding, only a sketch has been attempted.

9. In many sculptures of the Gândhâra school, the pictorial element is so strongly in evidence that one might imagine that an early school of painting had existed in Gandhâra, whose extreme offshoot is represented to some extent in the Tibetan ecclesiastical paintings; for example, the nimbus (p.86), and the reliefs of "the flight of the Bodhisattva," "the birth of Gautama" (pp.112f., 135). Conf. in this connexion, F. W. C. Müller, *Japanisches aus Java, Feestbundel aan Dr. P. J. Veth aangeboden*, S. 223, and Julien, *Hiouen Thsang*, tom. I, p. 110.

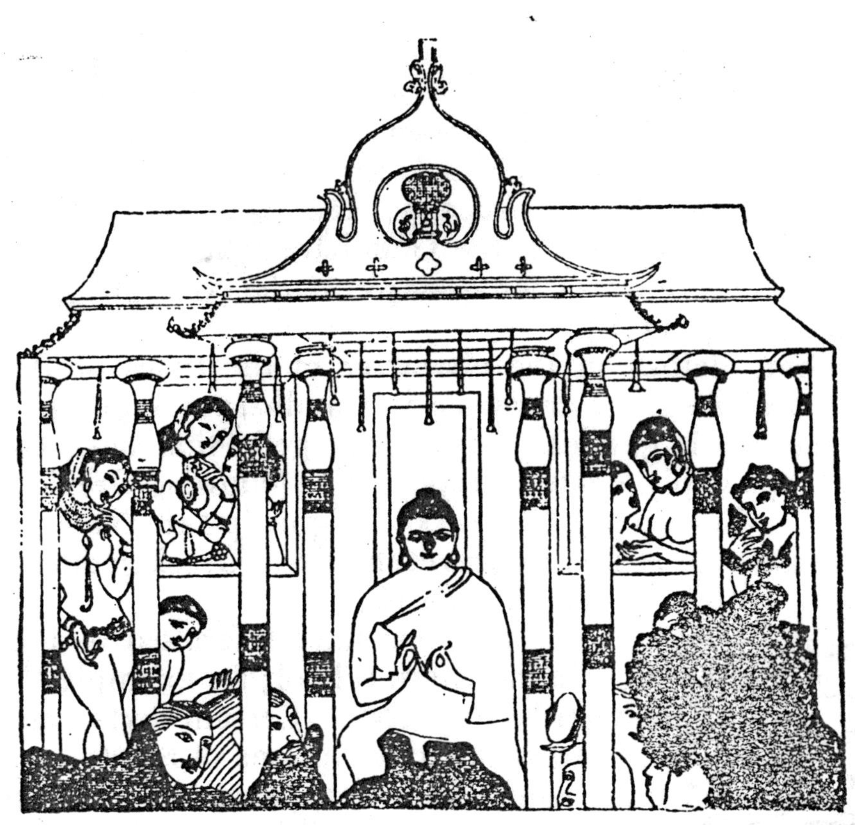

Buddha teaching in a Vihâra.
From a wall-painting in Cave XVI at Ajantâ.
See *Cave-Temples*, p. 308.

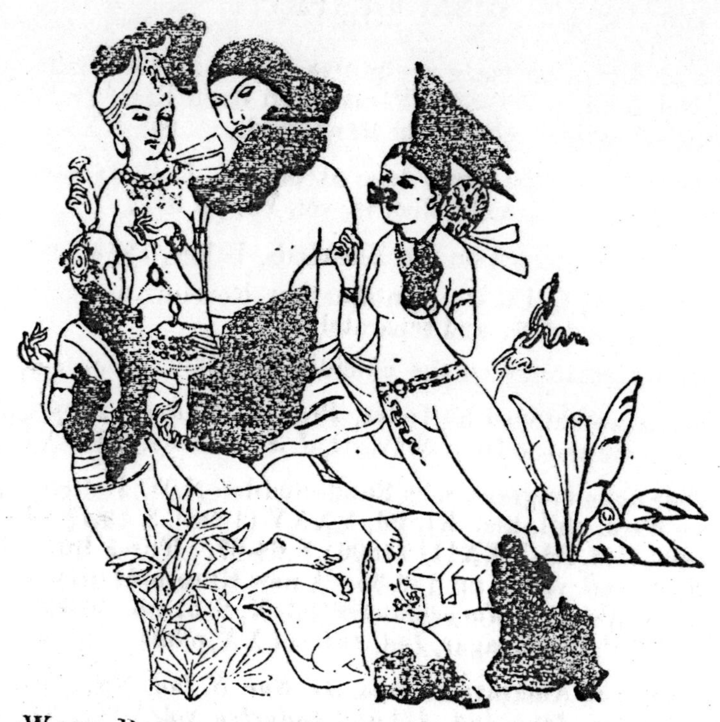

WALL PAINTING FROM CAVE XVIII AT AJANTÂ.
Perhaps Apsarâs flying through the air.
(*Cave Temples*, p. 310f., Mrs. Speir's *Life in Anct. India*, p. 370).

BIBLIOGRAPHY.

Archæological Survey of India,—Gen. Cunningham's Reports.

Archæological Survey of Western India, vols. I—V. Burgess.

Archæol. Survey of Southern India: Burgess, Report on Amarâvatî Stûpa, &c.

Archäologische Zeitung.

Epigraphia Indica, vols. I and II.

Indian Antiquary.

Journal of the American Oriental Society.

Journal Asiatique.

Journal of the Asiatic Society of Bengal.

Journal of the Bombay Branch of the Royal Asiatic Society.

Journal of the Royal Asiatic Society of Great Britain and Ireland.

Journal of Indian Art and Industry,—vol. VIII (1899).

Journal of the Royal Institute of British Architects (1894).

Veröffentlichungen aus dem Kgl. Museum für Völkerkunde, Berlin.

Wiener Zeitschrift für die Kunde des Morgenlandes.

Zapiski Vostochnago otdelenija Imperatorskago Russkago archeologicheskago obshchestva.

Zeitschrift der Deutschen Morgenländischen Gesellschaft.

J. Abbot, Note on a small Indo-Greek sculpture; *J. A. S. Ben.* vol. XXVII, p.262. Indo-Grecian sculptures from the N.W. Frontier, *ib.* vol. XXIII, p. 394. On a sculpture from the site of Bucephala, *ib.* vol. XVI, p. 664f.

John Anderson, Catalogue and Handbook of the Archæological Collections in the India Museum; 2 parts; Calcutta, 1883.

Baden-Powell, Memorandum on the sculptures fonnd in the Lahor Museum (not seen).

E. Clive Bayley: Notes on some sculptures found in the district of Peshâwar, *J. A. S. Ben.* vol. XXI, p. 606-621. Remarks on Babu Râjendralâla Mitra's article on some Baktro-Buddhist relics from Râwalpindi, *ib.* vol. XXXI, p. 184.

S. Beal: Some remarks on the great tope at Sâñchî, *J. R. As. Soc.* N.S. vol. V, pp. 164f. Legend of Dîpañkara Buddha, *ib.* vol. VI, pp. 377f.

H. W. Bellew: General Report on the Yusufzais, Lahor, 1864, pp. 109-151.

Bhagwânlâl Indrajî, Ph.D.: Antiquarian Remains at Sopârâ and Padana, *J. Bom. B. R. As. Soc.* 1882; and separately.

J. Bird: Historical Researches on the Bauddha and Jaina Religions, 1847.

Th. Bloch: Buddha worshipped by Indra, *Proc. A. S. Beng.* 1898, pp. 186-89. An inscribed Buddhistic statue from *Srâvastî*, *J. As. S. Beng.* vol. LXVII, pp. 174-205.

G. Bühler: Ueber neue epigraphische Funde aus den N.W. Indien, *Anzeiger d. k. k. Ac. d. Wiss. zu Wien*, phil.-hist. Kl. Bd. XXXV (1898), S. 12-17. Ueber ein græco-buddh. Piedestal, *ibid*, Bd. XXXIII (1896), S. 64-67. Three Buddhist inscriptions from Swât, *Epig. Ind.* vol. I, pp. 133-35. A new Karosh*thî* inscription from Swât, *Wien. Zeitsch. f. d. Kunde d. Morgenlandes*, Bd. X, S. 51-58. The date of the Græco-buddhist pedestal of Hashtnagar, *Ind. Ant.* vol. XX, p. 394; conf. vol. XXI, pp. 166f.

Jas. Burgess: Notes on Amarâvati Stûpa, *Ar. Sur. S. Ind.* No. 3, Madras, 1882. The Gândhâra Sculptures, *Jour. Ind. Art and Industry*, vol. VIII, Nos. 62, 63, and 69. Notes on the Bauddha Rock-Temples of Aja*ntâ*, their paintings and sculptures, and on the paintings of the Bâgh caves, modern Bauddha mythology, &c. (Bombay, 1879); *Arch. Sur. W. Ind.* No. 9.

Report on the Buddhist Cave Temples and their inscriptions; Lond. 1883.

Report on the Elura Cave-Temples, and the Brahmanical and Jaina Temples in Western India; Lond. 1883. Report on the Amarâvatî and Jaggayyapeta Buddhist Stûpas; Lond. 1887. Report on the Antiquities of Bidar and Aurangâbâd districts; Lond. 1878.

The Ancient Monuments, Temples and Sculptures of India, Part I. (Lond. W. Griggs, 1897), plates 5-151. *Jour. R. Inst. Br. Arch.* 1894, pp. 112f., 144.

Henry H. Cole: Memorandum on Ancient Monuments in Eusufzai; Simla, 1883; repr. in Second Report, pp. cxiv-cxxxviii. Preservation of National Monuments, India: Græco-Buddhist Sculptures from Yusufzai, 1885; and Great Buddhist Tope at Sanchi, 1885.

Alexander Cunningham: The Stûpa of Bharhut; Lond. 1879. The Bhilsa Topes; Lond. 1854. Mahâbodhi, or the Great Buddhist Temple at Buddhagayâ; Lond. 1892. Reports of the Archæological Survey of India,—especially vol. I (1871): Gayâ, pp. 1-13 (conf. vol. III, pp. 79ff); vol. II, Peshâwar, &c.; vol. V, Yusufzai district; and vol. XIV (1882), Panjâb.

Ernst Curtius: Die grieschische Kunst in Indien, *Archaeol. Zeit.* N.F. Bd. VIII, S. 90ff. (1876), and in *Gesammelte Abhandl.* Bd. II, S. 235-243.

Harold A. Deane: Note on Udayâna and Gandhâra, *J. R. As. Soc.* 1896, pp. 655-675, and 1898, p. 460.

James Fergusson: History of Indian and Eastern Architecture, Lond. 1876. Tree and Serpent Worship, 2d ed. 1873; conf. *Ind. Ant.* vol. III, p. 59. Archæology in India, Lond. 1884. Age of Indian Caves and Temples, *Ind. Ant.* vol. I, p. 257f.

On the Rock-Temples of India, *J. R. As. Soc.* vol. VIII (1846), pp. 30-92. On the Identification of the portrait of Khosroes among the paintings in the Ajanta Caves, *J. R. As. Soc.* vol. XI (1879), pp. 156-68; conf. *Ar. Sur. W. Ind.* No. 9. Description of the Amarâvatî Tope at Gantur; *J. R. As. Soc.* vol. III (1868).

James Fergusson and Jas. Burgess: The Cave-Temples of India, Lond. 1880.

Alfred Foucher: L'art bouddhique dans l'Inde d'après un livre récent, *Rev. de l'hist. des rélig.* tome XXX, pp. 319-371. Étude sur Iconographie bouddhique de l'Inde, Paris, 1900.

Catalogue des peintures népâl. et tibét. de la collection B.-H. Hodgson, Paris, *Ac. des Ins.* 1897. Les scènes figurées, de la légende du Bouddha, *J. As.* 9 sér. t. V, pp. 523ff. Études de critique et d'histoire, Sér. II, pp. 101-118.

R. Friedrich: Ueber zwei Inschriften auf einem Bilde des Mañdjuçrî jetzt im Neuen Museum zu Berlin, *Zeitsch. d. Deut. Morgenl.* Bd. XVIII (1864).

A. Führer: Indoskythic Architecture and Sculpture of the Mathura School, *Jour. Ind. Art and Ind.* vol.V, p. 58. Monograph on Buddha *S*akyamuni's Birthplace, Allahabad, 1897.

Percy Gardner: Greek and Skythic Kings of Baktria and India: Catalogue of Indian Coins in the British Museum, Lond. 1886.

Goblet d'Alviella: Des influences classiques dans l'art de l'Inde; Bruxelles, 1897. Les Grecs dans l'Inde, *ib.* Ce que l'Inde doit à la Grèce; Paris, 1897.

G. A. Grierson: On a stone image of the Buddha found at Rajâg*r*iha, *J. As. Soc. Ben.* vol. LXIII, pt. i, pp. 35-38.

John Griffiths: The Paintings in the Buddhist Cave-Temples of Ajantâ, 2 vols., Lond 1896.

On the Aja*n*tâ frescoes, conf. *Ind. Ant.* vol. I (1872). p. 354; vol. II. pp. 152-153; vol. III, pp. 25-28, 269ff; vol. IV, pp. 252, 339; *J.R.As.Soc.* vol. XI (1879), pp. 156-168; *Ar. Sur.W.Ind.* No. 9; *J. A. S. Ben.* vol.V, pp. 557-61f.

Lepel Griffin: Famous Monuments of Central India, London, 1886.

F. S. Growse: Supposed Greek Sculpture at Mathurâ, *J. As. S. Beng.* vol. XLIV, pp. 212f.; or Mathurâ, a District Memoir, p. 156f.

Albert Grünwedel: Mythologie des Buddhismus in Tibet und der Mongolei, Leipzig, 1900,

F. Hirth: Ueber fremde Einflüsse in der chinesischen Kunst, München, 1896; or *Jahresber. d. geogr. Gesellsch.* 1896, S. 223-288.

J. Lockwood Kipling: The classical influence in the architecture of the Indus region and Afghanistan, *J. R. Inst. Br. Arch.* vol. I (1894), pp 34ff.

G. Kizerickij: Chotanseija drevnosti iz sobranija N.F. Petrovskago, *Zap.* IX, 167ff.

D. Klementz, W. Radloff: Nachrichten uber die von der Kaiserl. Acad. der Wissensch. zu St. Petersburg in Jahre 1898 aus gerustete Expedition nach Turfan, Hft. I., St. Petersburg, 1899.

Dr. Leitner: Græco-Buddhist Sculpture, *As. Quart. Rev.* 2d ed. vol. VII (1894), pp. 186-89. Alt- und Neu-indische Kunstgegenstände aus Prof. Leitner's jungster Sammlung. K. K. österr. Mus. fur Kunste und Industrie; Wien, 1883. Dr. Leitner's Græco-Buddhist Sculptures, *Ind. Ant.* vol. II, p. 242ff.

Sylvain Levi: Notes sur les Indo-Scythes. *Jour. As.* 9 sér. t.VIII (1896), pp. 444-84, and t. IX, pp. 5-42.

Rev. W. Löwenthal: Account of some of the Sculptures in the Peshawar Museum, *J. As. S. Ben.* vol. XXXI (1862), p. 411.

F. C. Maisey: Sânchî and its remains, Lond. 1892.

I. P. Minayeff: Recherches sur le Bouddhisme (Ann. du Mus. Guimet), Paris, 1894.

Sergius von Oldenburg: Zametki o buddijskom iskusstve, Vostochnyja Zametki; St. Petersburg, 1895. See *Jour. Amer. Or. Soc.* vol. XVIII, pp. 183-201. Scena iz legendy carja Aśokí, *Zap.* IX.

Tavernor Perry: The classical influence in Indian Architecture, *J. R. Inst. Br. Ar.* vol. I (1894), p. 147ff.

Bâbu Râjendralâla Mitra: Buddhagayâ, the hermitage of *S*âkyamuni (Calc. 1878. The so-called Dâsyus at Sânchi, *Ind. Ant.* vol. I, pp. 36-40.

Alex. Rea: South Indian Buddhist Antiquities: including the Stûpas of Bhattiprôlu, Gudivâdâ and Ghantasâla, and other ancient sites in the K*r*ishnâ District; Madras 1894.

Ritter: Die Stupas (Topes) oder die architektonischen Denkmale an der indobaktrischen Königstrasse und die Kolosse von Bamiyan, Berlin, 1838.

Émile Senart: Notes d'Épigraphie Indienne, *Jo. As.*—especially 3, De quelques monuments indo-bactriennes, *J. As.* 8me sér. t. XV, pp. 113-163; and 7, Deux épigraphes du Svât, 9me sér. t. XIII, pp. 526-37, 555.

R. Sewell: Report on the Amarâvatî tope, 1877. See *Ind. Ant.* vol.X, p.56. Early Buddhist symbolism, *J. R. As. Soc.* N.S. vol. XVIII, p. 364ff. Some Buddhist bronzes and relics, *J.R.A.S.* 1895, pp. 617-62.

William Simpson: Buddhist Architecture—Jellalâbâd, *Tr. R. Inst. Br. Arch.*, 1879-80, pp. 37-64; Indian Architecture, *ib.* 1861-2, pp. 165-178. Classical Influence in the Architecture of the Indus region and Afghanistan, *Jo. R. I. B. A.* (1894), pp. 93-112, 191ff. The Buddhist Caves of Afghanistan, *J. R. As. S.* N.S. vol. XIV, pp. 319-331. Some suggestions of origin in Indian architecture, *ib.* vol. XX, pp. 49-71. The Buddhist Praying-Wheel (Lond. 1896).

Wm. F. Sinclair: Architecture in India, *J.R.As.S.* N.S. vol. XX, pp. 272-76.

Vincent A. Smith: Græco-Roman influence on the civilization of ancient India, *J. As. S. Ben.* vol. LVIII, pt. i, pp. 107-198; vol. LXI, pp. 50-76; vol. LXII, pp. 84-87. The date of the Græco-Buddhist Pedestal from Hashtnagar, *Ind. Ant.* vol. XXI, p. 166f.; conf. Bühler, *ib.* vol. XX, p. 394.

V. A. Smith and W. Hoey: Ancient Buddhist statuettes, &c., *J. As. S. Ben.* vol. LXIV, pt. i, pp. 155-62.

R. Phené Spiers: Classical influence in Indian architecture, *J. R. Inst. Br. Arch.* 1894, p. 150ff.

M. Aurel Stein: Zoroastrian deities on Indo-Scythian coins, *Ind. Ant.* vol. XVII, pp. 89-97. Detailed Report of an Archæological Tour with the Buner Field-Force, Lahor 1898; conf. *Ind. Ant.* vol. XXVIII.

M. G. Talbot: The Rock-caves and Statues of Bâmîan, *J. R. As. S.* N.S. vol. XVIII, pp. 323ff.

N. W. Thomas: On a pictorial representation of the Wheel of Life from Japan,—*Mind*, Jan. 1901.

Dr. L. A. Waddell: Græco-Buddhist Sculptures in Swât, *Imp. As. Quart. Rev.* Jan. 1896; conf. *Actes Or. Cong. Paris*, sec. i, pp. 245-7. The Indian Buddhist cult of Avalokita and his consort Târâ, *J. R. A. S.* 1894, pp. 51ff. Buddha's Secret from a 6th century pictorial commentary and Tibetan tradition, *ib.* pp. 367ff. The Buddhism of Tibet, Lond. 1895.

S. J. Warren: Two bas-reliefs of the Stûpa of Bharhut, Leiden 1890.

H. H. Wilson: Ariana Antiqua, London 1841.

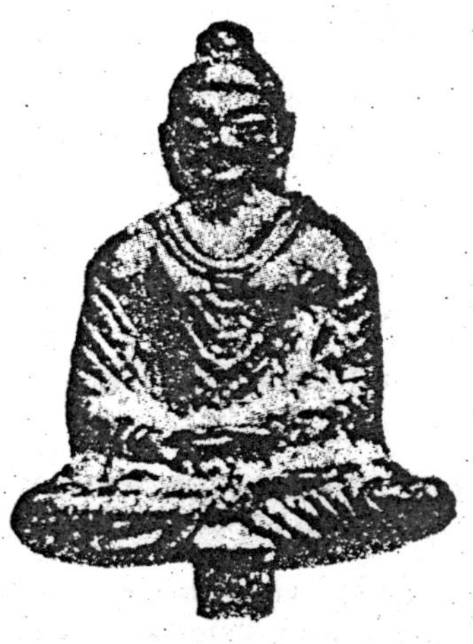

Bronze figure from Khotan, in the collection of N. F. Petrovskiy. (*Globus*, 3 Feb. 1900).

INDEX.

A.

C.

D.

R.

S.

T.